The Third SUSPECT

**DAVID STAPLES
AND
GREG OWENS**

Red Deer College Press

The Publishers
Red Deer College Press
56 Avenue & 32 Street Box 5005
Red Deer Alberta Canada T4N 5H5

Acknowledgments
Edited for the Press by Bob Weber
Cover photograph courtesy of the *Edmonton Journal*
Cover design by Kunz + Associates
Text design by Dennis Johnson
Printed and bound in Canada by Webcom Ltd. for Red Deer College Press

Financial support provided by the Alberta Foundation for the Arts, a beneficiary of the Lottery Fund of the Government of Alberta, and by the Canada Council, the Department of Canadian Heritage, and Red Deer College.

COMMITTED TO THE DEVELOPMENT OF CULTURE AND THE ARTS

Canadian Cataloguing in Publication Data

Staples, David, 1962–
The third suspect
ISBN 0-88995-131-4
1. Giant Mine Strike, Yellowknife, N.W.T., 1992. 2. Murder—Northwest Territories—Yellowknife. 3. Strikes and lockouts—Gold mining—Northwest Territories—Yellowknife.
I. Owens, Greg, 1962– II. Title.
FC4173.9.G52S72 1995 971.9'303 C94-910902-9
FII00.Y44S72 1995

Contents

Acknowledgments

Thanks to all our sources, who need not be named here for they are named in the pages of the book. I hope our story does justice to what they went through. I hesitate to single out anyone, but I'm compelled to mention Terry and Claudia Legge and the other men and women from the Canadian Association of Smelter and Allied Workers (CASAW) Local 4 who talked to us. To professor Bob Rupert of the Carleton School of Journalism for giving me my first break. To the Yellowknife scrum, Drew Wilson of CJCD Yellowknife, Joclyn Cozac of CBC Yellowknife, Kevin Ward of Canadian Press and Liza Sardi of the *yellowknifer*, for their friendship and assistance. To my Devon friend Dan Woodruff and the Kings of All Campers: Jeff Nisi, Scott Bolton, Al Stewart, Larry Cosh, Ian Lakhram and Brian Collins. To Peter Adler for his sage advice. To John Grigsby Geiger for showing me the way. To our bosses at Red Deer College Press, Dennis Johnson and Carolyn Dearden, and at the *Edmonton Journal*, Murdoch Davis, Allan Mayer, Linda Hughes, Michael Cooke, Sheila Pratt, Steve Makris, for their strong commitment to our journalism. To Greg Southam, Marina Jiminez, Gail Echlin and Rick Pape, who all contributed mightily at the *Journal*. I would like to thank our editor, Bob Weber, in particular, because he gave as much to this project as we did.

—DAVID STAPLES

It's difficult to thank everyone, but here goes. I wish to thank all the RCMP officers who helped us in so many ways. You know who you are. To my father, Jack, thank-you for spending many a day and night helping to transcribe (for free) numerous hours of taped interviews—a thankless job for any journalist or writer. Thanks to Faith Farthing, who also spent endless hours transcribing tapes (at a very modest fee). Of course, Dennis Johnson deserves a lot of credit for taking on two enthusiastic future authors and making a dream happen. Thanks to Drew Wilson, who made two strangers in a sometimes hostile environment feel at home and who provided invaluable assistance with gathering the research material for the book. A special thanks to our managers, fellow journalists, desk editors, librarians and others at the *Edmonton Journal* whose support meant so much. Thanks always to Greg Southam, whose photos appear in this book. Bob Weber, our book editor, who suffered through with the rest of us, can't be thanked enough. And to the rest of my friends and family, especially my mother, Joyce, whose support throughout the years, the last three in particular, made it possible for me to take the leap and follow through.

—GREG OWENS

To my wife, Gillian,
and my parents,
Marjorie and Brian Staples.
—DAVID STAPLES

To my loving wife, Jo,
with whom all things are possible.
—GREG OWENS

This book was researched through direct interviews with the main players, except Roger Warren, who spoke at length both in court and in taped interviews with the RCMP. Documents, testimony and witnesses' accounts have been reproduced exactly as written or stated, except where the sense of a statement was unclear. In such cases, minor changes to grammar and punctuation have been made in order to avoid confusion. All references to currency are in Canadian funds unless otherwise indicated.

Chapter 1

AN ENDANGERED SPECIES

THE DULL SETTING SUN skirted the tips of the evergreens, then faded behind the hardrock hills. Soon it would be this way even in the middle of the frozen day. The dark of the Arctic winter would be good for the hunter, Chris Neill thought, but he knew it would also be good for him, the hunted.

Neill walked around his house, turning off lights, opening window blinds. When the house was dark, he sat down on the couch in the front living room. He stared out into the black. It was mid-September now, and the midnight sun of summer no longer shone. He could no longer see far down the street, but he could see the sidewalk directly in front of his house while remaining unseen himself. He would be able to spot any attackers before they spotted him.

Neill had struggled to learn the laws of predator and prey since the day in early August when he had taken his final step in defiance of his union. On that day, six weeks ago, he had returned to his job at Yellowknife's Giant gold mine, crossing the union's picket line, crossing the front line of a war zone. He had since turned his home into a fortress. Electronic security devices cloaked the property, but even so, Neill was uneasy. Every clank, crack and bump fired up his adrenaline. Restless nights and the constant jolts had left him exhausted.

An endangered species, his enemies were calling him. Well, that's how he felt.

Neill got up from the couch and continued preparing for the night. His measures had become increasingly elaborate. At first he had set up a video camera in the downstairs living room, the one with the big screen TV, the mining certificates on the wall, the big black leather couch, the black leather chairs. The camera had looked out on to the backyard, but after he set up motion sensor lights and built a fence out back, he was confident the back was covered. The master bedroom overlooked the backyard, so if anyone triggered the motion sensors, he would wake up. Neill had moved the video camera and set it up with a second camera in the upstairs living room, the one with the pink couch, the lace curtains and the floral-pattern carpet. Neill pointed the cameras in either direction so he could record a complete sweep of the street. He hooked up both cameras to video cassette recorders set for long play so he could record eight hours.

Neill had been able get his hands on only the two cameras, so to make it look as if every angle of the house was under video surveillance, he gathered up as many other appliances and gadgets as he could find that had small red power-on lights, such as his electric razor and his beeper. He put the decoys in windows on each side of the house and on each floor.

Neill didn't want to leave his vehicles on the street, so he expanded the garage by ripping out the boot room. Earlier that night, his wife, Tracey, had parked her '89 Cadillac inside next to his 4 x 4 Blazer. Until things settled down, he was hiding his other vehicle, a red '82 Camaro, at a friend's house.

Before heading up to bed, Neill checked to see if all the doors were locked. He turned on the spotlight that illuminated the front yard and driveway. He activated the motion sensor lights. The web was complete. If anyone came to paint the word *scab* on his garage door or bust in and slash the tires of his vehicles or scrape them with a car key, they stood a good chance of being videotaped, then arrested. But it wasn't the vandalism that Chris Neill most feared. Already arson and bombings were common occurrences at the mine site just outside of town. Neill wondered how long it would be before the strikers started using such tactics in town, too. Yes, it was just a strike, it was just a job, but Neill felt certain the striking miners were angry enough to take things one step further.

He had already taken one videotape to the Royal Canadian Mounted Police (RCMP). It showed strikers Al Shearing and Tim Bettger, two of the most feared union men, driving by his house. Shearing had stuck his head out the window as if to get a good look at the Neills' place.

If Shearing, Bettger or any other vigilante strikers wanted to get at him or his property, Neill knew they could. There was no stopping them, but he hoped that maybe the cameras and lights would discourage them.

When Neill had crossed the picket line, he'd understood he was crossing a border separating two groups of people who looked the same, did the same work, held the same hopes, but at the moment wanted nothing so much as to annihilate each other. He hadn't crossed because he was anti-union. He was pro-Chris Neill more than he was against anything. He was a gregarious, friendly man, a big talker, a big spender. He loved his beautiful young wife, loved his expensive toys, his big paycheck, his new $220,000 home with its three bedrooms, three bathrooms and lots of space for the couple's expected family.

To Chris Neill, the union wasn't a religion or a brotherhood—it was a business. It should benefit him. If it didn't, if his union brothers were so pig-headed as to turn down a reasonable offer from the company, then the union wasn't worth having, though Neill did accept that the union had helped make the mine safe.

Mining was always a balance between safety and production. Both the miners and the mining companies were willing to set aside niggling safety precautions if it meant more production. Money came first. Why else would a man spend his life in a hole in the ground? It was the union that reminded everyone that safety should never be set aside, though Neill himself didn't need much convincing. His father, Carmen, had died in a nonunion potash mine in Saskatchewan when someone kicked a bucket of molten metal over on him. Carmen died from his burns. He had been twenty-nine, the same age Chris was now. Chris wondered if his dad might still be alive if there had been a union to protect him.

Carmen Neill had been a founder of the Oshawa, Ontario, chapter of the Satan's Choice motorcycle gang, and Chris Neill had inherited some of his father's flamboyance and aggression. But Chris had also learned responsibility. He helped his mom care for the house and the three other kids, but he didn't get along with his stepdad. In his teens, he moved out to live with some family friends, Alice and Ron Rivers. Ron was a gold miner in Timmins, Ontario. After high school, Neill followed him underground. He was content there until he heard the mines in Yellowknife were hiring and paying big.

Somba K'e, the Money Place, the Dogrib tribe called the city. Yellowknife owed its life to gold. It was built on the gold-rich hardrock of the ancient Precambrian shield. In Yellowknife, the saying went, the gold was paved with streets.

The promise of adventure and profit lured Chris Neill just as it had thousands of others in the town's short history. In 1933, the advent of the bush plane allowed the Eldorado Radium and Uranium Mine to open on Great Bear Lake. Next came a series of gold finds around Yellowknife Bay on Great Slave, the tenth largest lake in the world. Through the thirties and forties, a handful of mines opened in the area: Con Mine, Negus, Thompson-Lundmark, Sunset Yellowknife, Ptarmigan, Conwest, Giant and Gorskie Mine, a one-man operation run by Louis Gorskie, who stored his gold in a beer bottle so he could show it off to friends. By 1946, Yellowknife had become a magic word, said the *Saturday Evening Post,* a place of bearded prospectors with dreams of another Klondike, college-trained geologists talking of gold-studded ore and agile promoters elbowing one another to be first at the counter with a new stock offering.

The Money Place was a jumble of shacks then, a graceless boomtown. Slowly, though, it grew, first getting a restaurant, then a bank, then a school, then a hospital, then a road to Edmonton, then a mayor, then a shopping center. In 1967, Yellowknife, with a population of twenty-five hundred, was named capital of the Northwest Territories. Yellowknife boomed again in the seventies as mineral prices shot up, bringing every amenity of the larger centers of the South.

While Yellowknife was a capital, it didn't feel like a stodgy government town. It was full of young men and women in their twenties and thirties, all of them looking to make money and spend it. Few of the young people had family in town, so they pulled together. After a few years most of them moved back south, but a few fell in love with the city and the North, and they settled. Chris Neill hoped this might be his happy fate.

Three years back Neill had got a job at Giant, the area's largest gold mine. He was a hardrock miner, meaning he drilled the rock face with a 130-pound hydraulic jackleg drill, then loaded the holes with explosives and rigged them to blow. It was dangerous, difficult and dirty. Even if a man was up to it, the work eventually broke down his back and hands. Most miners had only fifteen to twenty years to make big money, but in those peak years the pay was outstanding. In salary and bonus, Neill made more than $100,000 each year.

Neill earned a bonus for every foot of tunnel that he blasted. Every day at Giant he had the same goal, to snap out a round, as the miners called it, to advance his eight-foot by eight-foot tunnel another eight feet. Every day he hoped that when his explosives blew, every single inch of rock he had drilled would crumble. If he made a mistake, a few feet of rock, known as bootleg, would be left standing. This had to be reblasted, which slowed him down and cut into his bonus. But if everything blasted perfectly, the rock broke right down to the buttons, the small indentations left by the tip of the drill in the rock. Neill liked to boast he blasted to the buttons every day. Some of the old-timers chuckled about the kid's claim. They nicknamed him Buttons.

Buttons Neill thought he was God's gift to breaking rock, but while he was strong and ambitious, he wasn't as good as some. Instead of finessing the jackleg, Neill used his strength to get the job done. He would go through twice as many drill bits as the other miners. He lacked the craftiness of the old-time hardrock warriors of Giant, the Joe Pandevs and the Roger Warrens, the men who looked as if they had been snapping out rounds forever.

In Yellowknife, Chris Neill became a regular at Checkers, the hot singles bar. He got a reputation as something of a playboy. For a time he dated Miss Yellowknife. He didn't seem at all the type for Tracey Quintal. She was hardworking, serious and ambitious, but she was also a beautiful young woman with blonde hair, blue eyes and the looks of a model, though at 5'2", not the height. Tracey, too, had come to Yellowknife for the opportunity. She worked as a legal secretary, then as an administrative assistant at the federal Department of Justice, earning $50,000 a year. She lived with her aunt and uncle and didn't like going out to bars. The one time she was persuaded to attend a friend's birthday party at Checkers, Chris Neill saw her and began to pursue her. He was no six footer, just 5'8" tall, but he was muscular from working out at the gym. His hair and eyes were dark, and his features were handsome.

With his boyish face and eager, friendly manner, people couldn't help but like him, especially women. The couple's first date was at the March 1989 Caribou Carnival. Neill ditched a previous date to go out with Tracey.

That summer they moved in together. Neill proposed. He hit it off with Tracey's dad, Ron Quintal, an oil-patch worker. When Chris and Tracey visited the Quintal's home in the small town of Onoway, Alberta, Ron and Chris slaughtered a cow, then ate the liver as a father-son bonding ritual. On December 28, 1990, Chris and Tracey were married in Hawaii. Tracey's brother Darcy was Chris's best man. A dozen members of her family showed, but no one from Neill's family came.

Chris and Tracey were unlike many of the old-time mining couples. No hockey jackets, no cigarettes, no beer drinking. They looked as much like young lawyers as anything. They liked to spend money, and to bring home more, Neill took on apprentice miners. It slowed him down to train another man, but whatever rock the two of them broke, he got to keep the entire bonus.

Neill never wanted to be a lifelong miner. The work was too arduous. But while he was at it, he was obsessed. He talked mining nonstop with his buddies Spanky Riggs, David Vodnoski and Jim O'Neil. At dinner parties, the wives forbade shoptalk. Otherwise that would be all they heard.

Neill saw himself becoming a mine inspector one day, or maybe, if he could stand the drop in pay, joining the Yellowknife fire department. He was already a mainstay volunteer. He bought himself a nifty safety suit from California. He spent two evenings a week at the firehall and slept at the station every second Friday. He and Tracey couldn't drive by the hall without going in to talk to the guys. She was constantly cooking for the fire department gang.

The men at Giant were tightly knit, especially the underground workers. They were bound by a code that grew out of the peril of the underground. Along with the threat of dismemberment and death from a blast came the basic fears that go with working in tunnels: fear of the dark, fear of small, enclosed spaces, fear of suffocation, fear of poison gas and fire. Few men could stand up alone to the strain. They needed each other. The essential part of the miner's code was unity. Each miner understood that even if he hated the man working next to him, he had no choice—he had to check up on him, help him, even risk his own well-being to save him if he was in trouble. Only if every miner lived by the code could a man absolutely count on getting help if he was ever in need.

Most admired at Giant were men skilled at mine safety, men a fellow could really count on in a dangerous spot. Neill organized his own mine rescue team and became the captain. He rarely looked at a book, but in his bathroom he had manuals on mine rescue and fire fighting.

Every year, territorial, provincial and national mine rescue competitions were held. Neill's team trained for two years. Then in April 1992, only a month before the strike started, it won the mine rescue competition at Giant. For Neill, it was a moment of triumph. Every man in the underground had praised him.

But now all that was forgotten. The same men cursed him to his face. Neill believed they would beat him senseless if they had a chance. Some of the others who had crossed the picket line tried to ignore the hatred, but Neill wasn't like that. He was a fighter. He could barely stand to take the put-downs every day on the picket line. He was damn sure he wasn't going to take any guff at home. His biggest fear was that the strikers would do something to Tracey.

"You know, someone could just put a stick of dynamite in here," he often told her, pointing at the front door. "They could just walk up to the front of the house and put it in our living room. You could be coming down the stairs and you'd be dead."

Tracey thought he was becoming paranoid. A few times when she came home late and saw that the security system was already up, the red lights shining from the windows, she laughed. This was Canada, 1992, after all, not the Dark Ages, not some lawless Third World country. As Tracey saw it, the striking miners had a right to picket, but the company had a right to bring in replacement workers and to welcome any union man who wanted to cross the line and reclaim his old job.

"These people aren't going to kill people here," she told her husband. "This is getting crazy. We're talking about Yellowknife, this innocent city."

But Neill knew his wife didn't understand what was going on at the picket line. He hadn't allowed her out there since the beginning of the strike. She hadn't seen the Road of Shame, the lineup of antiscab signs set up by the strikers for the line crossers to read each day. She didn't know about the sign that said "Chris Neill Is An Endangered Species."

Neill had overheard talk on the scanner about strikers hunting for union line crossers and out-of-town replacement workers at the local bars. He'd also overheard the sick jokes about strikers raping scab wives, sinister voices on the scanner saying that the women were nothing but scab breeders anyway. Such talk was just angry, drunken babble meant only to intimidate. Neill knew that, but he was also worried. Some of the trash talk had come true. There had been plenty of rumors about the strikers breaking into the mine and trashing the place. Then it had happened. There had been rumors about the strikers wanting to shut down the mine, and soon enough the bombs started going off. No one had died, but the blasts were more destructive each time.

His security system now armed, Chris Neill walked upstairs to the bedroom and lay down beside Tracey. A loaded rifle lay on the floor beside him.

Tracey fell asleep, peaceful, untouched by it all. God, he had to keep it that way. He shut his eyes and dozed off only to awaken with a start.

No light in the clock radio; no light in the backyard. The power was out. His cameras were down. His place was wide open. Neill shot out of bed.

"Come on! Power's off!"

Barely awake, Tracey had to get up and go. She wasn't allowed to get a drink of water or go to the bathroom. She had to move.

Neill grabbed the rifle, then hurried out to the garage. He had to pull open the garage door because the electric opener didn't work with the power out. He got in his truck and drove down the street. He parked facing his house. He shut off all the lights, then watched, ready to flip on the high beams and swoop.

Tracey headed to the downstairs living room. She knew her job was to keep an eye on the backyard, just as it had been all summer. The strikers had made a habit of taking down power poles, shutting down the mine for a few hours, but also turning off the lights in town. Tracey had no idea what she would do if a couple of union men actually crawled over the fence, but she sat up, fighting off sleep, and waited. Minutes passed—ten, twenty, thirty, an hour. She had to pee, but she knew if she did, just then Chris might come in and be angry with her for abandoning her post.

In his truck Neill fingered his rifle. He believed the strikers were sophisticated enough to coordinate things, have one team take down a remote power pole while other teams in Yellowknife were positioned to attack. They'd come in their camouflage gear with slingshots, hunting knives, spray-paint cans, maybe a homemade bomb, cocky now because his video cameras were down. He told himself he would use his rifle. He had made that decision weeks ago.

Someone would have to die before this thing ended, he knew that now. The strike wasn't like a hundred others in Canada, where only tempers got out of control. This strike was packed with dynamite and ready to blow.

Neill sat in his truck, watching for his enemies, but also searching for some way out. Nothing came to him. Nothing ever did. He couldn't pack up and leave. He wouldn't quit his job. He refused to let the union win. But, God, he was tired. His thoughts spiraled with the latest rumors. He relived the latest picket-line confrontations. He tried to think about how everything had started, but the events ran together. The hatred of the past year spun out of control inside him, but he could neither fight nor escape.

Chapter 2

THE AMERICAN DREAM

GIANT MINE was a scar on the hardrock hills. It was a conglomeration of stark, mustard-yellow buildings, massive open pits, ponds of refuse water and a foreboding smokestack.

Yellowknifers knew Giant well. It was only ten minutes from town. A much-used public highway, the Ingraham Trail, cut right through Giant's property. But the ugliness of the mine raised no protest from most Yellowknifers. It was accepted. The Giant and Con gold mines had been the main private enterprise employers in Yellowknife for fifty years. The money flowing from Giant made up fifteen to twenty percent of the local economy.

There was none of the romance of the Gold Rush at the mine. No pickaxes, no donkeys, no bearded prospectors and no nuggets were found there. It was industrial mining, a sprawling factory where the product was muck, the ore-rich rock blasted from Precambrian hardrock 2.7 billion years old.

Rape and pillage, the miners called the method used to harvest the muck. The highest ore grades had been taken out soon after Giant opened in 1948. The miners of Ventures Inc. got .800 ounces of gold out of every ton of ore during Giant's golden childhood in the 1950s.

Gold prices shot up from $35 (U.S.) an ounce in 1970 to an average of $612 (U.S.) an ounce in 1980. Even though Giant's ore grade dropped from .607 to .196 ounces per ton, Ventures, then Falconbridge Inc., made a profit in thirty-five of the thirty-seven years the two companies owned and operated the mine. The companies cleared more than $87 million.

The mining cycle was continuous. Geologists determined the richest pockets. Tunnels branched out in that direction. The miners went to work. As the ore pocket was depleted, geologists explored for new ore bodies. That process had turned Giant into a labyrinth, a web of one hundred miles of tunnels. Horizontal tunnels were called drifts, vertical tunnels were shafts and angled tunnels were raises or manways. Both the shafts and the raises had ladders along the walls so men could climb up and down, moving from drift to drift.

If a stranger to the mine were plunked down in the middle of it and abandoned, he might well wander the drifts and climb the manways for days. Even an experienced miner could get turned around in the dark and be hopelessly lost in a second.

The mine was dangerous. Pipes and boards hung from the low ceilings. Pockmarks and craters pitted the slippery floor. Throughout the day, the tunnels howled with the mechanical screams and groans of diesel machinery. The aftershocks of blasts that blew down the tunnels were so powerful they could pick up a man like a feather. Industrial accidents had killed, on average, one man every three years at Giant.

More than seventeen million tons of ore had been taken from the ground, but hardrock miners such as Chris Neill rarely saw the gold they mined. It was uncommon to see a vein of dull, dark-looking gold, or V.G. as the miners called it, visible gold. The powdery gold had to be purified at the mine mill. The muck was drilled, blasted, crushed, then crushed again, screened, binned, crushed yet again, classified, floated, thickened with chemicals, roasted, agitated, thickened again, agitated again, thickened yet again, clarified, filtered and melted. At last the purified metal was poured into a gold bar and shipped off to the Royal Canadian Mint in Ottawa.

In the early 1990s, gold prices had leveled off at under $400 (U.S.) an ounce. The lower price made many past techniques for extracting gold uneconomical. Labor contracts negotiated during the $600 (U.S.)-an-ounce days had also become uneconomical. At Giant, the drop in prices pushed the mine owner, Pamour of Australia, into bankruptcy.

Pamour had bought Giant for $200 million from Falconbridge in 1985. Peggy Witte, the part-owner and president of Royal Oak Mines Inc., bought Giant from the banks for $33 million in November of 1990.

Witte rarely met anyone who equaled her drive and intelligence, but if her intelligence was keen, it was also cold. She was headed for a divorce and she had no children. She had been pretty in her youth, but now she was middle-aged, overweight and had the unhealthy pallor of someone who worked too hard and ate too much restaurant food. She spent her life in airplanes, hotels, boardrooms and grubby mine build-ings, but she reveled in it. Her work created jobs and wealth for her, her employees and her shareholders. She was born to a ranching family in Nevada and educated as an engineer at Nevada's MacKay School of Mines. She got her first big job at a copper mine in Tucson, Arizona. She worked as a shift boss, assistant mill foreman and metallurgist. She had never drilled or blasted, but she had made her mark developing an innovative technique for milling muck. The technique brought her to Canada, where she worked as a consultant for the Ontario government. Just as gold prices peaked, she and her husband, Bill, started their own consulting firm, Wittech. Five years later, she started her own mining company, Neptune Resources. In the next three years, she raised tens of millions to develop Colomac Gold Mine, one hundred miles north of Yellowknife, the biggest plan for an open-pit mine in Canada. She lost control of Colomac when costs got too high. A senior partner forced her out. She got $2 million, which she invested in her new company, Royal Oak.

With Royal Oak, Witte was no longer interested in developing new mines. Instead, she saw that an empire could be built by taking over underperforming and undervalued properties. Again, she went to work raising millions, this time to purchase Pamour Mine in Ontario, Hope Brook in Newfoundland and Giant in the Northwest Territories.

Witte raised money by selling a company that was smart and tough. At Giant, she laid it out for her shareholders in basic dollar terms: it had cost $415 (U.S.) to produce an ounce of gold at Giant in 1989, the year before she took over. The cost was cut to $395 (U.S.) in 1990. After a full year of Royal Oak management, it was down to $327 (U.S.). Her plan was to cut it to $300 (U.S.) in 1992, with a further cut to $280 (U.S.) the following year. Witte's logic was straightforward: the mine was failing because labor costs and mining practices were out of line with the current price of gold. If things didn't change, the mine would shut down just as dozens had across Canada.

If an employee was easy to do without, Royal Oak got rid of him. If it was possible to do the job with less, that's how it was done. If the current managers and employees balked, well, they had better open their fucking eyes, as Witte sometimes told her senior managers. She could speak the language of the underground as well as any hardrock miner. She was fond of saying she wasn't in business to be screwed over.

By 1991 Royal Oak had become the sixth largest gold producer in Canada. The *Northern Miner* named Witte the Mining Man of the Year. But Witte's drive also made enemies.

One of the most important forums for debate in Yellowknife was the "Letters" page of the local newspaper, the *yellowknifer*. After Witte's recognition, Jim Evoy, president of the Northwest Territories Federation of Labour, wrote a letter decrying the selection: "The excessive individualism personified by Ms. Witte will be the ruination of Canada if it goes unchecked."

Evoy's view was shared by many of the 230 men of the Giant Mine union, the Canadian Association of Smelter and Allied Workers (CASAW) Local 4. CASAW Local 4 was an isolated crew on the fringe of the Canadian labor movement, a hard-headed group of men unwilling to give up one penny of compensation or one speck of control.

CASAW had taken over the union in the seventies, and the leadership was proud that the mine was no longer a peaceful place, that the men were no longer subservient. Under CASAW no miner had to take crap. Supervisors could no longer transfer around men they didn't like. They could no longer get away with favoring a certain few with overtime hours. The CASAW hardcore suspected that every management dictum was either propaganda or a power game. Most bosses were seen as sycophants who spent their time bootlicking and yakking with other bosses. All the company cared about was profit. Without the union there would be no concern for safety. Without the union the men certainly wouldn't be making an average salary, including bonuses and benefits, of $77,000 a year.

Many CASAW men instinctively disliked Witte because she was a woman and an American. Witte soon gave them more tangible reasons to hate her, chief among them her STEP disciplinary program. Royal

Oak started to rate the men in seven categories. If a man erred in any category—if he was late for work or broke a safety rule or was insubordinate—he took a "step." After seven steps he could be fired.

Some of the mine managers were enthusiastic about the new owner and the new discipline. Giant had been a slack, laid-back place for a long time. Sloppy work habits had built up. Some men had openly flouted the rules. No one had been fired for years at Giant. But Royal Oak canned thirteen men in its first year, including several members of the CASAW executive. At once, the union filed grievances to get the men back, and almost all of them won their cases.

Harry Seeton, a dedicated union leader, was treated with particular contempt by the new management. Seeton was yelled at and put down. When he refused to work in an area he believed unsafe, he was threatened with dismissal. The company tried to lay him off, but his seniority meant he bumped a more junior man out of a job.

Witte's methods infuriated not just slackers and CASAW executive members, but also some of the company's best workers, including Terry Legge. Legge was no rabid trade unionist, but he was a leader of the mine's Newfoundland contingent, a group of fifty to sixty men, a quarter of the unionized staff. Legge was an open, gregarious man, but his mood was as changeable as the weather over St. John's, suddenly darkening with thunder, rain and lightning. He had dark eyes, short, dark hair and a black temper. Whatever came into his mind, he let fly, and to hell with what anyone else thought.

Legge and his wife, Claudia, were from Goose Bay, Labrador, where he had worked as an airplane mechanic. He had always loved to take things apart and reassemble them. He could fix any engine. There was no room for error in the work, and he had become a perfectionist, his dedication absolute. He lost part of his hearing by listening too closely to the loud engines to judge if they were running as they should. He had never heard of workers' rights. But eventually his boss asked too much and Legge exploded, telling the man to fuck off, that after seven years he'd had enough.

Legge had come to Yellowknife after that, fifteen years back. A buddy from Goose Bay told him about the big money in the gold mines. Not only that, the fishing and hunting were great. Legge came up and was hired on at Giant. They liked the look of the strong, twenty-five-year-old Newf, 5'11", two hundred pounds. Legge became a heavy duty mechanic, traveling around the mine to fix the diesel mining equipment. In Goose Bay, he had earned $1,100 every month. At Giant he made that much in two weeks.

Claudia, too, was excited about the change, hoping to see a bit more of the world than Labrador. Her first thought was that Yellowknife was beautiful, a wonderland of snow, ptarmigans and Inukshuks, the traditional stacked stone marking posts of the Inuit.

In Labrador, Legge would have shoveled shit against the wind if that's what he was asked to do. He had never known he had the right to refuse unsafe work. He thought a man put up with abuse from his boss or he quit. At Giant he saw how the union allowed the men to keep their self-respect.

In 1980, as the price of gold and Falconbridge's profitability peaked, Legge went on strike with his CASAW mates. He thought it was fun, a summer vacation mostly. There was fighting at the picket line. The RCMP riot squad had to clear out strikers who tried to block fuel trucks from coming in, but Falconbridge finally caved. Legge got a big raise and a $500 signing bonus for returning to work.

In Legge's mind, Falconbridge had class, as did Pamour when it took over. Men who had worked at the mine for ten years were presented with a beautiful $400 silver tray with their name engraved on it. At the long-service dinner, the company went all out, nothing but the best—seafood, steak—and for once the miners wore shirts and ties.

The Legges decided to stay in Yellowknife. They bought a trailer home, then a share in a cabin at secluded Lake Chedabutco. Claudia got a job as a secretary at the local hospital. The couple added two more sons to their firstborn son who had come with them to Yellowknife.

Legge got close to the men in the machine shop. When one of the millwrights finally retired, it was arranged that Legge would get the job. It was the best work he'd ever had. He would take apart pieces of equipment that looked like they should be in the dump, then put them back together so they worked another four or five years. All the equipment at Giant was junk, but it was good junk, German-made, a pleasure to work with in Legge's opinion. Legge never read anything more than a newspaper or a magazine, but give him a broken tool and a schematic diagram, and he'd have it figured out in no time. Such was his expertise that if there was a big problem and the manufacturer had to be called, Legge would often be asked by the boss to get on the phone and explain things. This pleased him more than anything: Terry Legge, troubleshooter. He made good money, as much as $70,000 a year, not bad for a boy from the Rock with a grade eleven education, but it was the respect he craved.

After the Royal Oak takeover, Legge wanted to give the new company a look-see. A new broom sweeps well, he told his friends in the shop. A few days into the regime, Mike Werner, the new mine manager, came on a tour of Legge's work area. The place was covered with cut-out pictures of pinup girls in bikinis.

Werner pointed at the pictures. "You responsible for these?"

"Some of them, maybe," Legge said. "But most of them, no. They've been up for years."

"Well, it doesn't matter. I want 'em down."

"Well, hey, what's the problem?" Legge asked, trying to sound conciliatory.

"There is no problem. They're our walls. Take them down."

Legge hadn't heard that tone of voice from a boss since his days in Labrador. He looked at Werner, a short man, and thought: You little fuck, givin' me fuckin' orders. Legge couldn't comprehend what Werner had against the pictures. No one had ever complained about them. None of them showed nude women, Legge thought, all of them were quite tasteful and lovely. Better than looking at dirty, greasy old walls. He left the pictures up and went back to work.

Later that day mine superintendent Terry Byberg came to see Legge. Byberg explained that Peggy Witte herself had come down and had said the pictures had to go. Byberg then told Legge something about some black judge in the United States who was in trouble for making sexual advances on a woman. Witte didn't want the same kind of stuff happening in her mine in this country.

"What do you mean?" Legge asked. "What does that have to with some black judge in the fuckin' States? What's wrong with these pictures? Forget 'em."

"You might not have a problem with them, I might not have a problem with them," Byberg said, "but if I'm told to wear blue shoes tomorrow, I wear blue shoes. If for no other reason, you take them down because these are her walls."

At home that night, Legge complained to his wife about the situation. Claudia knew Terry well enough to know it meant trouble. He was not one to be pushed around. Still, Claudia tended to agree with Royal Oak's new bosses. She figured it was just like with their kids—if it's your home, you make the rules.

"A bunch of pictures coming off the wall!" Claudia told him. "Is that something to bitch about? You know, Terry, it's a new company and they may have better ideas. Don't be so hard against change."

Claudia had made him think. He was almost forty now. Maybe he was getting set in his ways. Then again, maybe not. Didn't this have to do with rights? With respect?

The next day, Legge took down the pictures, but did it in quiet rage. He thought, I've got friends that fuckin' died in here! Lots of them! Danny Mino, he was blinded. Vince Corcoran was fuckin' killed. Other guys crippled up. They didn't do that for themselves. They done it for the company. Now this company comes along and says you can't do this and you can't do that because we do it this way in the States. Well, fuck off back to the States! This is my fuckin' home more than it's her fuckin' home.

From then on, whenever Legge saw Peggy Witte, he was pleasant—that was the only manly way to be—but he felt like he had a belly full of broken glass.

In December 1990, one month after the takeover, management announced it was canceling the children's Christmas party and getting rid of the long-service party. No more silver trays, no more dressing up and going out. The men were also told they couldn't read at their work sites unless they were reading work material. Legge could have a newspaper or magazine in the lunchroom, but he wasn't allowed to leave it for anyone else to read. The company didn't want union handouts left around.

Next, Royal Oak started to search workers as they went home. It was another innovation from the United States, the bosses said. Anyone could be pulled in for a spot check. Legge knew some guys might take a wrench or toilet paper, but he also knew if any big ticket items went out, it was just as likely some manager who did the taking.

The CASAW men refused to sign releases that would permit the company to search them. They believed the whole thing was designed to intimidate. Two CASAW members were suspended for refusing to be searched.

Peggy Witte wanted Royal Oak stamped on each man's forehead, Terry Legge thought. She was a woman in a man's business. It was as if she had to say to every man she met: "You fuck with me and I'll bust your balls. You do as I say, you don't do as I do. This is mine."

When times had been good, Legge had never had much to say to Claudia about work, but now his frustration with Royal Oak spilled out daily. He was astounded to find that on most issues she sided with Peggy Witte, or Miss Witte as she called her. He called her Miss Piggy.

"If you got nothing to hide, then you got nothing to worry about," Claudia said of the searches.

"Well, I don't have anything!" he shot back. "But how about my fuckin' rights? Somebody saying, 'I'm gonna search you'? Come on!"

Claudia wondered if Royal Oak wasn't going about things the wrong way. Terry had always been angry when drunk, but that side of him was disappearing since he had stopped drinking. Now, though, Miss Witte seemed to tap right into his vein of anger. If she wanted to bring in change, why be so abrasive about it?

But Claudia also wondered if Terry and his buddies would be so angry if a man was telling them the same things. It was a bad mix: a woman who wanted to show these men who was boss and men who resented it.

Terry Legge had never been a big union man. Sometimes the executive officers held meetings and were the only ones there. They got upset because the men weren't paying enough attention, but Legge shrugged it off. He thought Harry Seeton and his gang were too much against the company having any authority. Now, with Royal Oak in charge, Seeton's thinking started to make sense. Legge came to believe a strike was inevitable. He heard that the issue in the first new contract talks wasn't how much Royal Oak was going to give, but how much it was going to take back.

The contract between CASAW and the company was up on March 31, 1992. Witte made it clear to the union's bargaining committee that her shareholders weren't interested in supporting high union wages at an unprofitable mine. Witte claimed the Yellowknife operation was a loser, its future in doubt. Gold was trading at a twelve-year low, $336.50 (U.S.), about $20 (U.S.) per ounce less than what she said it cost Giant to produce it. The union would have to accept a number of concessions, management said, including a six percent cut in pay.

Witte prepared for the possibility of failed talks. If the union went out she planned to bring in strikebreakers. Witte told herself she had no alternative. The mine cost $600,000 a month in maintenance costs. Without men to produce gold, Giant would shut down, and there would be no jobs for the union men when the strike ended. Under federal law Witte had the legal right to bring in strikebreakers, but it would be a blow to the union. Not one strikebreaker had worked in a Canadian mine for more than fifty years, not since the cruel 1930s when management refused to accept that unions had a place in the business. Nevertheless, Witte had her managers prepare a secret feasibility study.

The contract expired and the two sides kept meeting, but every day a strike seemed more probable. And then, in the last week of April 1992, against all expectation, Witte and CASAW's bargaining committee worked out an agreement.

The CASAW men got to keep almost every benefit gained in previous contracts. Some of the problems in the disciplinary system were worked out. There would be no improvement in the pension plan, but there was good news on salaries. The men's pay would be hitched to the price of gold. If gold prices went up, so would paychecks. In its report to the membership, the bargaining committee wrote: "We feel this tentative agreement represents about the best we can expect at this time. Your committee feels it has upheld the no-concession order of the membership and created an excellent possibility for major wage increases. Your committee also feels that no potential gain exists in striking the company in these times.

"This has been a long, stressful, sometimes agonizing time for this committee of yours. Our sole concern has been the welfare of the members and particularly your families. Since the outcome affects them just as much as it does the worker, these thoughts have been foremost in our minds the entire time, and we never let them stray. We feel we have accomplished the mission to the very best of our ability, and hope our labors meet with your approval. The Local 4 bargaining committee strongly recommends acceptance of the tentative agreement."

The union men had complained for months that Royal Oak was out to break the union, but the tentative agreement proved them wrong. If Witte wanted to break CASAW and force a lockout, she could have found many reasons to pull away from the tentative agreement.

But she knew it was better to work out a compromise, gain enough to please the shareholders and keep the mine running.

To Chris Neill the agreement sounded great. Neill was dead against any wage rollback, but he hadn't expected any increase either. "Man, I can't go anywhere in Canada and get a job real quick," he told Tracey. "No one will pay me what I'm getting paid at Giant."

Neill had never been bothered by the STEP system. The management seemed to pamper him and the other big-bonus miners, letting them off for minor infractions when another man might have received a step. Indeed, Neill was one of Peggy Witte's biggest boosters in the mine. He identified with her ambition. He thought the union protected too many do-nothings. They not only slowed things down, but their sloppy work was dangerous. Neill went so far as to write the *yellowknifer* to attack a CASAW leader's behavior at a union meeting. "He made a very derogatory statement, this being that any employee who did receive a good evaluation was a suckhole. . . . We, the so-called suckholes, have demanded an immediate apology or his resignation from our union."

The Royal Oak negotiators had hoped the CASAW bargaining committee would build on the momentum of the tentative agreement by quickly holding a ratification vote. But days passed and nothing was done. More and more grumbling was heard. In the end it was ten days before the general membership met to vote.

At the meeting the bargaining committee was overwhelmed by the CASAW hardcore, men like mill worker Dale Johnston and Harry Seeton. The hardcore were a minority, but they knew it wasn't in their interest to accept the deal. Royal Oak was bent on firing them or moving them to such lousy jobs that they would be forced to quit.

Royal Oak had miscalculated the impact these men would have. The company had only wanted to get rid of what it considered the bottom rung of its workers, a few dozen men. But by going after them, the great mass of men in the middle, who were neither hated nor loved by management, became anxious. Every time a man was fired, the others were that much closer to the bottom of the heap. They feared their day would soon come. They were prepared to listen when Seeton and Johnston said the bargaining committee had failed to protect past gains in collective bargaining. The whim of the boss was again dictating how a man was treated, how much overtime he got and where he got to work.

Anyone who didn't get along with his shift boss could get screwed. What Royal Oak was proposing was nothing less than an all-out attack on every worker's dignity.

Terry Legge stood up to join in the attack. "I have no problem with the executive," he said. "I'm happy with the work they've done, but just because they're recommending we take it, that doesn't mean that we have to take it, guys. They have to recommend it because that's all they feel they can get. But I feel, fuck it, if that's what she wants, and she wants to push us out through the gate, then let's go through the gate."

In the end only twenty percent of the CASAW men voted to accept the deal. Most had become so emotional they were more interested in smiting Peggy Witte and Royal Oak than doing what their bargaining committee had told them was best for them and their families.

When Terry Legge got home, he found his logic didn't work as well on Claudia as it had on his buddies at the union hall. At her own secretarial job, Claudia had never backed her union. She thought her bosses treated her well. When her union's contract had come up, she was shocked to see her benefits package laid out. My God, she thought, she could have a massage and her benefits would pay for it! She thought the people who wanted more should grow up, and she thought the same about her husband and CASAW. But Terry thought Claudia was clueless, the type who would scab on her own union during a strike.

Night after night, Legge and his friends met at his trailer home and rattled on. Claudia listened in. She didn't pay attention to the details—all she heard was the anger, the frustration and the obsession. The CASAW men expected her and everyone in the world to drop everything and focus their attention on the evil of Peggy Witte.

Despite the union's vote, Witte worked to avert the strike. Royal Oak handed over its ledgers to the union so the men could see the company wasn't lying when it said the mine was a money loser. The strikers, with Harry Seeton assuming the role of leader, were unimpressed. "Do not fall prey to management scare tactics and games!" read one CASAW pamphlet. "Stand up for yourself and let it be known that we live in the North and our costs do not go down, so why should we give up anything that is going to affect your own and your family's well-being?"

On May 10, 1992, seventy-two percent of the union membership voted to go out. With the result in, Witte turned hardcore herself.

First, she threatened to shut the mine. Next, the CASAW men were informed that the company intended to bring in replacement workers. Many of the miners didn't take the threat seriously. It was too outrageous to be believed. If she tried, it would mean war. She'd be asking for violence. Yet even by making the suggestion, Witte had crossed a line. The strikers could no longer see her as a person, but only a crude stereotype—Miss Piggy, the fat, greedy, immoral American she-devil.

"We can't let Miss Piggy push us around!" the battle cry rang out. "We can bring her to her knees!"

At one union rally, miner Wayne Campbell came in with a crowbar, wearing a motorcycle helmet. "Well, I got the thing for the scabs," Campbell said, holding up the bar. "I'm gonna put this right up through their ass."

Any man thinking of breaking ranks with the union was sure to get a visit. Terry Legge dropped in on his good friend, miner Keith Murray, after he heard Murray was thinking of working during the strike.

Murray had just started back at Giant after being off two years. Away from the mine he saw how little most jobs paid. He also saw how hard it was to find work. When he got back, the money had never seemed better and the work conditions seemed the same as ever.

"Keith, clarify something for me," Legge said to his friend. "You know that the strike is going to be in a few days. The boys said you were gonna fuckin' be crossin' the line. Fuckin' tell me different."

"Well, Terry, you know, Keith takes care of Keith."

"Keith, come on! Quit fuckin' around with me! You're not going to go fuckin' scabbin' over the line. You wouldn't do that."

Murray just shrugged. Legge couldn't believe it, and neither could Murray's best friend at Giant, miner Roger Warren. Murray and Warren had mined in Manitoba together and then come up to Yellowknife.

"I can't believe that fuckin' Keith," Legge said to Warren.

"Yeah, you think you know people," Warren grumbled. "You think you fuckin' know people."

Peggy Witte hired a company called ProCon to recruit replacement workers in Ontario, the Maritimes and British Columbia. The plan was to fly them to the mine site in helicopters and have them live there. Their pay would be $16 an hour, not the $22 an hour the CASAW men made. Royal Oak made it clear to the union that there were plenty of men across Canada willing to work for that wage. Many miners were out of work. Many would consider crossing a picket line to be no more degrading than going on welfare. Royal Oak prepared for the men by setting up a makeshift bunkhouse in the C-dry, a large building where the miners changed into their gear.

CASAW men staked out the airport, looking for Royal Oak recruits as they arrived. The strikers also started to follow vehicles that left mine property.

Along with the crusade against the scabs, the union men started to say safety was the strike's key issue, that Royal Oak wanted to cut back on the number of days spent each month on safety inspection tours. But management said it only wanted to change the way safety tours were conducted. It said it didn't want to search the whole mine every month, but wanted to concentrate on one section and do a thorough job.

The CASAW men planned to go out at 12:00 A.M. on May 23, but Royal Oak locked out the strikers earlier in the day. Management sent the day shift home with their clothes, then sent home the night shift as soon as they arrived. The bosses wanted to head off any vandalism.

The strikers couldn't be contained at any gate at Giant because the Ingraham Trail ran through the property. Picket gates were set up on the various access roads to the mine. The strikers put up the names of any man who crossed the line on a Road of Shame. The Ingraham Trail was littered with anti-Royal Oak placards and graffiti:

"Werner, Byberg, Witte
A waste of human flesh
A disgrace to mankind
A freak of nature."

And:

"Little Mike Werner
Tucked in his corner
Eating American Pie
Along comes Peggy
Proud of her Witte
Charming each other with Baskets of Shit
And leave the lumps for the scabs beside."

And:

"Canadians Fighting Canadians: the American Dream."

Helicopters started to fly across the line, bringing in the strike-breakers. The airlift enraged the strikers. Legge told his buddies he wanted to take a gun and blow the choppers out of the sky. He hoped one of them would crash and all the passengers burn. He and the other union men crowded every gate, determined not to let one scab get into the mine by road.

The strikers had a big gas horn hooked up at the main gate. It bellowed every few minutes, making the men on the inside cringe. Few could sleep.

Legge didn't care to hear any sob stories from men who crossed the line. Any time in his life when he'd been unemployed, he'd just gone and got another job. Besides, when he looked across the line with binoculars he didn't see any men with their ribcages showing.

"You piece of shit!" he yelled at the unfamiliar faces. "How does it feel to steal another man's job? How does it feel to be in prison?"

Chris Neill remained convinced that the issues in the strike were either bogus or easily solved, but he was angry about the replacement workers. He hated the idea that someone was now doing his job, mining his heading, earning his bonus. On the strike's first night, the strikers knocked down a power pole to shut off electricity in the mine, burned down a shack, assaulted a security guard and pelted the mine buildings with rocks. Neill joined in, first getting drunk at a wedding in town, then heading out to the picket line to kick ass. The Cambrian security guards, brought in from Sudbury, looked like they needed a beating. Neill got into the middle of a wild melee.

The next morning, however, he felt ashamed. "It's crazy what's going on out there. Somebody's going to get killed," he told his buddy Jim O'Neil. "Man, I threw a couple of rocks at the bastards. It's easy to get caught up in the whole thing."

Neill also told O'Neil that he had run into mine superintendent Terry Byberg on the picket line. Byberg was an old friend of Neill's godfather, Ron Rivers, and had told him the whole strike was not necessary, that only a few small issues separated the two sides. He challenged Neill to do something before things got out of hand. Too many CASAW men were followers, Byberg said, not enough leaders. He promised to fax Neill the full text of the tentative agreement.

Jim O'Neil was eager to see the document when Chris Neill got it. O'Neil was a shaft mechanic at Giant, a sensitive and intelligent man who took the contract talks personally. He had never liked CASAW. He thought it was a renegade, unprofessional union. O'Neil had voted to accept the tentative agreement, but when he saw a strike was inevitable he realized solidarity was important. He volunteered to be a strike captain, even buying radio equipment to coordinate the activity at the various strike gates. But the violence of the first night left him shaken.

When Neill and O'Neil got the agreement from Byberg, they studied it for hours. They could see very little wrong with it, just picky little stuff. Later, they talked on the phone with Byberg and mine manager Mike Werner, who told them the company was willing to move on the outstanding issues.

Neill and O'Neil decided they should take their concerns to union leaders Harry Seeton and Bill Schram, the president. But Seeton and Schram rebuffed them; they thought Neill and O'Neil were being used by the company to divide and conquer. The rejection only made Neill and O'Neil more convinced the executive didn't want a settlement but was only interested in fighting the replacement workers and crusading for antiscab legislation.

"This is ridiculous," Neill said to his friend. "Somebody is going get killed here. We've got to let the membership know that there's room to move. That's their right to know that."

The two men decided to speak out at once by getting on local radio. First, they went to CJCD, a local radio station, where they met reporter Mark Dickey. They told Dickey their concerns about CASAW's leadership. Dickey aired an interview with the two men.

Ten minutes later Dickey got a call from CASAW's vice-president, Ken Cawley.

"It's ridiculous that these guys have gone on the air and done that," Cawley said. "These guys should watch their asses. There are people out there who want them."

Dickey taped Cawley's threat and aired it as well.

Next, Neill and O'Neil headed over to the Canadian Broadcasting Corporation (CBC), where they met reporter Joclyn Cozac. She wondered if the two strikers knew how much trouble they were causing for themselves by stepping into the negotiations.

Cozac sat down to read through the men's notes. Neill had his scanner on the desk. Just then, over the scanner came an angry voice: "I heard that Neill and O'Neil have cooked up some deal. They're going to the media talking about it."

"What are you talking about?" asked another. "I haven't heard anything."

"Apparently they got some deal they want to put to the members. They were over at CJCD and they're over at CBC right now."

"What are we going to do about it?"

"I don't know. Kill them, I guess."

O'Neil and Neill at once called the RCMP and their lawyer, gave a brief interview to Cozac, then went right home. Jim O'Neil loaded his rifle and waited. He fully expected the union gang to barge into his house. It didn't happen, but from then on he lived minute to minute, making sure he did nothing to put himself in a dangerous spot. He left town for a while. He decided he wanted nothing more to do with the strike and thought about quitting his job and the union. When he got back to Yellowknife, he called up Terry Legge to sell him the radio he had purchased for the strike-line communications.

Legge offered to take O'Neil down to the union hall to patch things up.

"No way," O'Neil said. "This is gonna be too long a strike. It's just a matter of time before somebody gets killed, and I don't want no part of this."

"For fuck sakes, Jim, knock off the bullshit. Wake up. We all got to pull together here. Everything is okay."

But O'Neil's mind was made up. Legge could only shake his head, believing that men like Jim O'Neil and Chris Neill were overreacting, that they had no faith in the union cause.

Chris Neill didn't leave town after the threat, but he was angry enough to return to work. He made a call and arranged to get a helicopter flight. Tracey dropped him off at a designated spot outside of town. From the moment he left her, Neill feared something was going to happen to Tracey. He talked about her all day at work and called a half-dozen times. He forbade her from going out of her office for lunch.

Neill found work in the mine disorienting. He recognized almost no one. He didn't know if he could trust the men working next to him. That night he stayed with a few other CASAW line crossers and shift bosses at a house at the old Giant Mine townsite. His direct boss, Don Moroz, could see how upset he was. Neill shouldn't be here, Moroz thought. He should be out driving cab or fishing, anything but this. "Chris, it's up to you what you got to do, but this isn't a very nice situation," Moroz told him.

Neill decided to get Tracey to pick him up the next day. Tracey had to head down a gravel road to the pickup site, an isolated gravel pit. She met up with a truck driven by a CASAW striker. She drove on, pretending that she was out in her Cadillac for a leisurely drive through the country. She saw the helicopter coming in to land. She kept driving, then pulled a U-turn. Suddenly, she heard Chris yell, "Pop the trunk!"

Neill jumped into the trunk and pulled the hatch down, locking himself in. Tracey headed back to town. Just as they came upon the parked CASAW vehicle, Neill yelled out, "Are we past them yet?"

Tracey jumped with fright, but no one had heard her husband. She kept driving, at last finding a secluded spot for him to jump out. Both were relieved that the striker hadn't seen him.

Six CASAW men had stayed at work right from the start, including Keith Murray. Terry Legge considered CASAW line crossers like Murray to be traitors and trash, even worse than the replacement workers. If this had been a war and Murray had left their troop, Legge would have had him charged with desertion and shot. Legge thought the line crossers were just greedy. They had their condos and homes and cabins, and they didn't want to give up any of it, even if it meant betraying the union. Legge saw one line crosser driving a new truck one day. He felt like going over and beating the vehicle with a hammer, then pulling the line crosser out and doing the same to him.

At first, CASAW line crossers were stuck on mine property with managers and replacement workers. It seemed to Keith Murray that he was in a Third World country with the natives about to attack from the bush. The strikers blocked the gates and had shut down traffic in and out. Initially, the RCMP refused to intervene. Royal Oak was told the police couldn't ensure the safety of its people coming in and out of the mine. The strike was a civil matter and unless there was an emergency, the police said they'd stay out.

Police officers stood by when the strikers threw rocks and pounded on vehicles, breaking windows, punching at the men inside. The Mounties didn't want to be seen as favoring the company. At the beginning most strikers had no trouble with them. One Mountie even came down with ice cream and a cake made by his wife.

Many of the Mounties and the strikers were good friends. They knew each other from the hockey rink, the swimming pool, the gym, the theater, the mall. The Mounties knew the CASAW men were only fighting for something they thought was right.

The company's twenty-two-man security force was overwhelmed. After four days the contractor decided he'd had enough and quit. Bill Tolmie, the security chief, told the *yellowknifer:* "The strikers basically can do whatever they want and terrorize the interior. My belief is that somebody is going to have to be killed or injured before action is taken."

Royal Oak next hired the more formidable Pinkerton security force, which brought in fifty-two guards. The Pinkertons were stationed at the entrances to the main access roads. They tried to intimidate the miners, but the miners weren't afraid of a fight. They stepped up their campaign of taking down power poles with chain saws and explosives so the mine would have no electricity. Putting out the lights, the union men called it.

Royal Oak tried to use the courts to tame the strike. The company wanted to disallow the union from picketing between midnight and 6:00 A.M. But CASAW's lawyer was able to persuade the judge that this would allow the company too much leeway to move in men and materials. Nevertheless, the number of picket gates was limited to six, and the union could have no more than five men at each gate.

The RCMP's fifty-man riot squad and twelve-man Emergency Response Team was brought in to try to regain control. Officers from across the Territories also came to do two-week stints patrolling the picket lines. The strikers thought the changes in the police presence were sinister. Suddenly, all the friendly local cops seemed to be gone, and the new cops always seemed to side with the Pinkertons. The strikers felt Witte had pulled strings and now had control of the Mounties.

On May 30, one week into the strike, the company tried to bring in replacement workers on a bus, but the strikers smashed the windows. The next day, mine managers and strikers hurled rocks at each other over the fence at the main gate. Even mine manager Mike Werner got in on the rock throwing. Legge saw Werner chucking rocks at a striker's tent at one of the picket gates. Werner took out the window of one striker's truck. To retaliate, Legge pulled out a slingshot and let fire.

When Claudia Legge first heard her husband and the other strikers talk about wanting to blow up the helicopter or about wanting to kill this scab or that one, she didn't know what to think. Are they serious? No, they're not serious. They're blowing off steam. When the talk didn't go away, though, when it only got angrier and angrier, Claudia decided to bring it up with her husband.

"That's really scary to hear you say stuff like that."

"Oh, you know we don't mean it."

"Well, don't say it. I'm tired of hearing it. You guys would have more support if there was no violence."

"That's easy to say! But you see somebody doing your job, and you tell me what you'd do."

Claudia tried to make her husband see the other side, that the replacement workers weren't scabs, they were just men. "The people that are in there are probably people who haven't had a job in years, who probably want the job and just want to do something good for their families. Like you, Terry, that's your thing, to bring home the bacon and provide for your family and you're really proud of that. The people that's in there probably had the same value, but have been out of work for three years and when somebody gives you an opportunity and promises you safety and promises you all kinds of things, I could see them going for it."

"You don't know what you're talking about!" Legge exploded. "I brought home the bacon but didn't have to take it from another man."

After two weeks, sixty replacement workers were working and living at the mine site. Spirits had picked up somewhat for both the workers and the managers. Many of the bosses were happy to get back to the basics of mining: drilling, blasting and operating scoop trams, the tractors used to shovel the muck from the headings. It had become a personal challenge to the men inside to defy the union, to get the mine up and producing. The strikers were so sure that Giant couldn't be run without them that it would be nice to prove them wrong. Production got back on track quickly. Within a few weeks, the mill fired up again, smoke billowing from the stack, a sign to the CASAW men that things weren't going their way.

In early June, negotiations between CASAW and Royal Oak ended. Bill Lewis, a federal mediator, was appointed only to find the two sides more militant and unreasonable than ever. The union now called for a huge increase in pay. Witte said that unless the union paid the company the $1.5 million it had already lost because of the strike, there would be no deal. Witte suggested that when the strikers came back they should agree to work Saturdays for free in order to make restitution. Witte's other new demand was that she be able to lay off as many as fifty men involved in picket-line violence.

Witte used the platform of the "Letters" page in the *yellowknifer* to point out that thirty-three mines had shut down in Canada in the last year and hundreds of miners were out of work. Since the replacement workers had come in, Giant's safety record had improved and productivity was up. "This whole strike seems so illogical to me," she wrote. "Do my hourly workers not realize what is happening to the mining industry throughout Canada?"

The CASAW men who had thought the strike would be a short vacation followed by Witte's quick capitulation now knew they had been wrong. Desperation crept into the tone of the strike-line rants.

"Does somebody have to die before we get rid of these fucking scabs?" one striker yelled at a CBC television cameraman.

"They do, they do," said striker Roger Warren in reply. "And we'd better soon get it done."

Terry Legge had a hard time turning off his rage. He would never hit Claudia, but he had to be careful because he was so angry when he came home from the picket line that he sometimes felt like punching her out. He wondered why she couldn't back him like other wives backed their men. Claudia did go to the union hall once. She saw the scab-hating posters everywhere on the walls and wanted to throw up. Claudia didn't want to be like the other wives; she thought they were addicted to the strike.

On the June 11 television news, Legge was inspired by a story at the Clearwater Lobster plant in Arichat, Nova Scotia. Replacement workers had been brought in there, as well as an RCMP riot squad. That day, five hundred strikers and union supporters had met for a rally in front of the fish plant. They got riled up and stormed the place. Fifty replacement workers and security guards had to be lifted from the roof of the processing plant by helicopter.

The attack seemed to pay off for the strikers. The provincial government at once announced an inquiry into the matter. The company said it would not bring in any more replacement workers for the time being.

At the union hall, Legge started to hear the same thing again and again: "We're going to take that fuckin' place over like the boys down in Newfoundland!"

"What boys in Newfoundland?" Legge said. "That was down in Nova Scotia, boy. Bunch of fuckin' Blue Nosers."

Legge hoped he and his union brothers could run the Pinkertons off the property, then take over the C-dry, barricade themselves in if necessary and wait for the strike to end. It was no grand strategy. It was more like: Let's kick some fuckin' ass and throw these guys out. When Claudia heard the talk, she told Terry, "Look, fine, you want to go and knock out the power, you go and knock out the power. But don't you ever lay a hand on anybody. If you ever lay a hand on anybody, if you do it intentionally to hurt somebody, then that's too far for me, Terry."

On the night of June 14, 150 strikers and CASAW supporters gathered at the main gate for a rally. They jeered the company and the replacement workers. A rock flew at them, and that was it: the union mob started yanking on the mesh fence. It came down. Just for a moment, the crowd hesitated, then fifty union men, some of them wearing masks and balaclavas, charged onto the property. They pushed back the Pinkerton guards, broke windows and tore apart the mess trailer. One striker, James Mager, clad in a balaclava, smashed a security guard's knee with a stick. Another striker, James Fournier, lifted a rock over his head, as if to crush the downed man, though later Fournier said he really just wanted to scare him. RCMP Inspector Dennis Massey saw Fournier with the rock and thought the guard's life was in danger. Massey took out his gun and aimed. He would have shot the striker, but just then, some other men got in his line of fire. Instead, Massey blasted off four warning shots.

Terry Legge thought about heading to the C-dry, as the strikers had talked about, but he kept getting distracted by other skirmishes. He came around the corner of a building to see three strikers standing over a Pinkerton. The security guard was holding his leg tight. One of the strikers nailed him with a stick, hit him so hard the guard's helmet rolled off his head. The other two strikers joined in smacking the downed man. Legge rushed over and stood over the guard. The Pinkerton was just a kid, twenty years old at most.

"You want to get your fuckin' ass over that hill as fast as you can go," Legge told the guard. "But don't fuckin' stop because if you do I'll fuckin' whale on you myself."

The Pinkerton got up and limped away. The strikers looked at Legge.

"Fuck him," Legge said. "Come on guys, let him fuckin' go. You already hurt him. You don't want to kill nobody."

The Pinkertons retreated over a hill. Strikers ran in every direction, scattering across the mine property. If there was a plan before, there wasn't one now. On top of the main administration building, Legge spotted a man with a video camera, taping all the action. Legge knew that could mean big trouble so he headed there, hoping to knock down the camera.

Just then, strikers shouted out that the RCMP riot squad had arrived. Legge knew it was over. He and the other men retreated, but they walked out proudly.

"Well, I guess we done it," Legge told his buddies. "We drove off the Pinkertons!"

As far as he was concerned, even if the RCMP charged him and threw away the key, it had been worth it. But Claudia told him the riot was pointless. She knew intimidation wouldn't work on Peggy Witte. Claudia had started to have a recurring dream where everyone in town went down to the picket line and yelled out, "That is enough!" She kept on at Terry that violence wasn't the answer, but he remained convinced that the only way to get Witte and the government's attention was to keep acting up.

Three days after the riot, Dennis Patterson, Justice Minister of the Territorial government, called on Federal Labor Minister Marcel Danis to draft binding arbitration legislation, forcing an end to the strike. "The risks to public safety will remain intolerable if urgent action is not taken now," Patterson said.

But Danis refused to act. This was a private dispute, after all. No essential service was involved. The world would get along just fine without a few more bars of gold. The two sides would have to work it out, although Danis said the federal government would continue to send mediators to help find a solution.

The official union position on the riot was that it had been orchestrated by the RCMP, or as they now called the force, the Royal Oak Mounted Police. The Mounties could easily have confronted the strikers at the gate and stopped the riot before it started, Harry Seeton believed. But the police wanted the strikers to venture onto mine property so they could later charge them and get them off the picket line.

In the end fifteen strikers were charged with various offenses as a result of the riot, and Royal Oak got a new injunction forbidding picketing by any striker who had been charged with an offense. After studying the riot videotape, Royal Oak also fired any striker deemed to have taken part. Thirty-eight CASAW men got termination notices, including Terry Legge.

Things quieted for a few weeks after the riot. Strikers who had been caught up in the violence saw how out of hand things could get. They were frightened by their own anger. They normally didn't do anything worse than drive fifty in a thirty-mile-an-hour zone. Yet during the riot, for a few minutes, they had believed that the old morality no longer applied, that they could do anything and it would be all right, do anything and get away with it. It had been both exhilarating and terrifying. Some strikers stopped going to the line. They never wanted to get that caught up again. Things had come too close to something really serious happening.

The new mood was again reflected in the letters in the *yellowknifer*. Said striker Steve Christensen: "It's making people crazy. Someone is going to get killed." Striker Conrad Lisoway urged the politicians and the townspeople to act to end the strike before it was too late: "Don't let me say I told you so. Do something before you have to! Nobody wants to see anybody die because if somebody dies their blood will be on everyone's hands." And Giselle Tremblett, a striker's wife, wrote: "Many of you know these men and know that they are very easygoing and quiet, but they have been backed into a corner that they can't seem to get out of, and when this happens the best of people fight back the only way they know how, and, unfortunately, in this case it has come to violence."

Some Yellowknifers, however, refused to accept excuses for the violent behavior. Sharon Kerr, the nurse at Giant Mine, wrote: "The issues of this dispute are important and seem all-consuming to all Giant employees. But none of these matters are worth a human life.

"I ask each individual to stop and carefully, rationally consider the implications. Ask yourself the following questions: Do I want to die? Am I willing to kill someone? Or to have someone I know kill someone?

"Acts of physical violence are not accidents. Someone must make a conscious decision of their will to do the act. . . . Therefore each of us must exercise our will and decide now that: I will not put myself in a situation to be killed. I will stay away from violent confrontations. I will not ever kill or injure another person. I refuse to accept that there is any justification for physical violence. I will not let people or circumstances dictate to me in this matter. I will actively refute this ideology in other people—remember, what you allow, you approve.

"Not one of us is expendable. A place in labor history as either company or union breakers, a new law: can we possibly entertain the thought that these are worth a life? Each person involved here is a real person with the right to live. Let us, as rational human beings, put an end to this type of talk and action. May we go down in history as a group of men and women who faced an extremely difficult situation and solved it with dignity."

Chapter 3

SOMEONE MUST DIE

THE MOST RADICAL of the CASAW men called themselves the Cambodian Cowboys. They believed they were the union's elite strike force. They wore camouflage gear to the strike line and called each other nicknames over the radio to confuse the Pinkerton security guards, or the Pinkies, as the Cowboys called them.

Al Shearing led the Cambodian Cowboys. Shearing had been fired on the last day of work, an act that had further radicalized the CASAW men. Shearing was a mine mechanic in the underground. He worked on most of the mine's diesel equipment. He was forty-five years old, thin-faced, with unkempt hair and a droopy mustache. He stood only 5'6" and weighed just 140 pounds, but he had a reputation for utter fearlessness. He'd work over an open shaft without safety gear, just to show the others he could do it. A beam stuck out over the top of the mine's headframe, the metal superstructure for the shaft elevators. Shearing used to sit out on that beam, with no safety rope, and eat his lunch. In the winter, he was the one who volunteered to climb up into the headframe and clear away the hanging ice.

He was a dedicated worker. He was often called in the middle of the night to come to the mine and fix something that no one else could. Even after fifteen years at Giant, no job was too small or too dirty for him. He was most respected, however, for his work as a mine rescue captain. If a man at the mine ever got hurt, was ever lying in pain and suffering in the dark, the man he would most like to look up and see was Al Shearing.

Shearing was also a strong union man. He had grown up in Newfoundland foster homes, and it was no stretch to say that in the union he had finally found a family. He had been a shop steward and a union trustee. Royal Oak management would never have harassed him because he was a good worker, but he could not tolerate attacks on the brotherhood. One week before the strike, he had been suspended for insubordination because he refused to work the weekend. Later, he told another mine employee that he planned to shoot ball bearings across the strike line. The employee told her boss, who told mine manager Mike Werner. Werner called Shearing to his office. Shearing asked Harry Seeton to lend him support at the meeting. When Werner saw Seeton, he told Shearing the meeting was confidential and Seeton would have to leave. Shearing then wondered why mine superintendent Terry Byberg was present. When Seeton got up to go, Shearing went with him. Werner threatened he'd fire Shearing if he left, but Shearing kept walking. Despite his exemplary work record, Royal Oak canned him that day. If any union man still doubted the company was rotten, that firing persuaded him otherwise.

It made Shearing into a martyr and he reveled in the role. When he returned to the picket line late that first night of the strike, he was in his camouflage jacket and pants, and he wore them through the summer of 1992. Shearing wasn't great with words and he wasn't a thinker. He'd never be union president or lead the bargaining committee, but if an electrical power pole had to come down he was the man to do it. He called himself the Night Crawler.

Shearing fell in with a scoop mechanic named Tim Bettger, a massive, menacing man, six feet tall and three hundred pounds. Bettger had fierce dark eyes, a black beard and a hunger to show himself as a man of action. He was known as the Bear. Bettger's contentiousness quickly got him on the wrong side of many Mounties, though a few respected him. Some strikers thought nothing of jabbing at a cop from behind, but Bettger wasn't one to bushwhack an officer. Some nights when things got ugly and the strikers refused to let any vehicles in or out of the mine, Bettger prevailed on the men to calm down and let the police do their job of guiding the traffic.

The Night Crawler and the Bear became inseparable at the union hall, around town and at the strike line. Royal Oak managers referred to them as St. Bernard and Chihuahua. The two men made their intentions clear to the security guards. Bettger shouted to them that the strikers knew the mine inside out, that they knew where explosives were and that they could use them. Shearing bragged that there were twenty-six different entrances to the underground and he knew every one of them.

The mine was impossible to guard. Only the main buildings were enclosed by a fence. The property could be approached from the bush and just as easily from the Ingraham Trail. There were thirteen main entrances to the underground and numerous smaller ones.

Pinkerton used roving patrols and guard dogs to try to maintain order. Some of the Pinkies were calm, responsible and professional, but others looked like they'd been dragged from the bars to fight strikers. Many could only speak French, which didn't help strike-line communication.

The Pinkies and the Cambodian Cowboys threw rocks at each other and shone bright lights on each other. Sometimes the Pinkies drove their trucks up to the doors of a picket shack, blocking the exit, then turned on their brightest headlights. Sometimes they'd sneak up in the middle of the night, then pound on the shack's walls or knock over the barbecue.

With the Pinkies acting up, most of the CASAW men were glad to have men like the Night Crawler and the Bear around to get some measure of revenge. A number of other men, including Terry Legge, joined with the original two Cambodian Cowboys to create havoc. Legge never wore battle fatigues, but he had his slingshot to sting the Pinkie dogs, and he was up for plans to take out the electricity. The Cowboys got so good at the task that they once felled three power poles in one swoop.

The union newsletter, *Fool's Gold*, applauded their efforts: "Those pesky damned night ravens screwed up the power again last night. It's tough to run a mine without power so these mysterious birdies are actually our allies in this fight. . . . Curiously enough, it (the bird) only drinks Molson's Canadian or Labatt's Blue. Funny kind of bird, ain't it?"

The power often went out in Yellowknife as well as at the mine. At the union hall strikers started getting angry calls from citizens and businesses like Gramma Lee's and the Golden Harvest Bakery. The bakery would have an oven full of goods that would go to waste when the power died.

After the June 14 riot, the Cambodian Cowboys decided more decisive action was needed. Striker Gord Kendall, a chain-smoking, hard-drinking, big-talking miner, came up with a plan to break into the mine and terrorize the replacement workers with threatening graffiti. Kendall bought a disposable camera and rounded up miner's lamps and a bolt cutter. Shearing and Bettger immediately volunteered for the job. Kendall picked a miner named Art St. Ammand to go along because St. Ammand was an old-timer who knew the route and would also be a stabilizing influence. Striker Luc Normandin agreed to drive the three-some to the mine.

On June 29, five weeks after the strike had started and two weeks after the riot, Bettger, Shearing and St. Ammand broke into the head-frame shack of the Akaitcho shaft, an isolated ventilation shaft in the northwest corner of the mine property. Shearing looked down into the shaft to see someone had removed the first few sets of ladders. To get down to the first landing, he had to slide down a wire cable. He found the ladders there and set them up for the other two men.

They started down. Wooden ladders ran along Akaitcho's rock walls. The ladders didn't go straight down, but angled back and forth, with a landing every ten feet. The eight-foot by eight-foot shaft had no lighting. The ladders weren't terribly slippery, but they were damp. The shaft descended 425 feet. Then the three men had to find two more ladder systems to get down the rest of the way to the 750-drift, a main transportation railway corridor 750 feet below surface. St. Ammand had fashioned a billy club out of a pool cue, but he decided he wouldn't need it and left it hanging on a pipe at the bottom of Akaitcho.

The mine's main C-shaft elevator was one and a half miles away. Once they were on the 750, the Cambodian Cowboys walked straight down the line toward the elevator. At an underground garage known as the 712-scoop shop, they went to work with red and white spray paint, putting graffiti all over the walls: "Beware, we'll be back, fucking stubble jumper" and "The Molly Macguires were here." The latter was a reference to the secret organization of coal miners that committed acts of terrorism in West Virginia and Pennsylvania from 1862–1876. On a scoop tram, they wrote "Scab Mobile." They opened up a toolbox and painted inside it as well. Bettger took pictures.

The three stole blasting caps, fuses and fourteen sticks of powder. Their escape retraced their steps. The mission took them about six hours. Afterward, they gave their camera to Kendall, who arranged to develop the film.

Three weeks later, on July 22, the Cambodian Cowboys struck again. This time Bettger set a bomb on the mine's satellite dish. The dish was located on the side of a large hill overlooking the old company housing units where many of the replacement workers now lived. Bettger loosened the bolts on the bottom of the dish, hoping that the blast would send it tumbling down the hill in a grand gesture. Instead, the explosion only blew a hole in the dish, knocking it out of commission, but not knocking it over.

The following day CASAW's daily bulletin claimed Royal Oak was dying a death of a thousand cuts. "Every single problem we create for them has to be dealt with by someone out there, diluting their manpower, raising the costs and inflicting mental strain. All members should keep an active and devious mind-set. Confusion to the enemy!"

In the same newsletter, the union offered to organize a protest at any bank that caused a striker trouble on his mortgage. Strikers would also pull all their business from the bank. A more whimsical item concerned rumors about a new mine manager as Mike Werner had left for another job. "The possible candidates mentioned have Attila the Hun on the inside track with the Marquis de Sade as the dark horse."

As the violence escalated, the RCMP created a special four-officer task force led by Constable Randy McBride, with Constable Nancy Defer, Constable Ken Morrison and Corporal Ken Murray. Their first task was to investigate the June 14 riot and lay charges. Next, the Mounties looked into the fires and explosions at the mine. They concentrated on the satellite dish blast, which appeared to be the most serious; if the dish had tumbled down the hill, it could have killed someone.

Forming a task force was unusual for the Yellowknife police, but Yellowknife had never seen anything like the Giant Mine dispute. McBride, Defer, Murray and Morrison spent the summer investigating more than 350 strike-related complaints. To McBride, the strike had all but ruined the town. Before, people had been willing to help out if someone needed a hand. But it all went by the wayside in only a few short weeks. People were afraid to talk about the strike because they never knew who was listening. McBride and his fellow officers weren't liked by either side. Both factions accused them of favoritism. The police found it almost impossible to take a statement from most CASAW men, even if a striker was the complainant. The strikers were even less helpful if they were being charged. The thought that they were justified in breaking the law made it easy for them to keep quiet. McBride saw the build-up of violence, but felt helpless to do anything about it. A terrible feeling grew in him, just as it was growing in many people, that somebody was going to have to die before things would come to an end.

After the satellite dish bombing, the Mounties decided to visit a handful of key union men, asking them to help solve any crime that involved explosives. The police went to men who weren't the real bad guys, but who were in the know. Constable Morrison visited Terry Legge.

"I need information," he told the striker. "I'm not going to tell you I can offer you $500, $400 or $300, but I'm talking to you now, person to person, and I'm saying that these people out there are going to hurt somebody if we don't stop them. I don't care if we charge these people, but give me enough information so that I can go at them and put enough pressure on them to make them stop."

Legge and the other strikers weren't hostile toward Morrison. They understood he had a job to do, but as for information, they had nothing for him. None of them wanted to be a snitch. The word on the line, whispered often and loud enough so eventually even the RCMP heard it, was: If you're going to do something, do it alone and don't tell anyone. If you see something, turn the other way. You don't want to know.

By early July, ten CASAW men had crossed the line, but dozens more were thinking about it, including Chris Neill. In July Neill worked at the Ptarmigan Mine outside of town. To get there, he had to drive down the Ingraham Trail through Giant every day. As he passed, some of the strikers would get in their cars and follow him, making sure he didn't pull into Giant Mine property. In their windows, the strikers had signs reading "CASAW Cops."

Neill was making okay money at Ptarmigan, but he and Tracey weren't saving anything. Neill didn't want to just get by either. His plan was to buy an airplane with his friend Jim O'Neil, then train for his pilot's license.

At the end of the month, Neill came home from work one day and told Tracey, "I'm done at Ptarmigan on Friday."

"Oh, how come?"

"I quit. I'm going back to do the job that I love, that I never wanted to quit in the first place. And no one's going to tell me what to do."

"Are you sure?"

Chris Neill nodded. "You know, if I'm not on the company side, doing the job that I love, the job I didn't want to leave, then I'm obviously on the other side. And if I'm other on the side, I'm with a bunch of terrorists. I don't want to have anything to do with that."

"Well," Tracey said, "I think it's the right move."

"It is right," Chris insisted. "This is a free country. You can't have people tell you what to do."

The first time Neill had gone back to work, he'd taken a helicopter in and come out in the trunk of his wife's car. This time, he told Tracey, he would drive in the front gate and come home every night. No way was he going to leave her alone.

Before going in, Neill wanted to talk over his decision with Noel O'Sullivan, who was in charge of Giant's underground. Through the summer, O'Sullivan had received similar overtures from many men. Though he was a Royal Oak manager, O'Sullivan refused to encourage any of them to come back to work. He felt in his gut that crossing the line was no answer, even if men had big mortgages to pay and feared they would never work again at Giant. O'Sullivan was originally from Ireland, and in the old country he had seen what happened to men who crossed picket lines. Their houses were burned to the ground, or they were beaten up, their legs broken. He expected the same would happen in Yellowknife. He didn't want to live with that on his conscience.

"Should I come to work?" Neill asked him over the telephone.

"Chris, I can't make that decision for you," O'Sullivan said. "I really don't know what went on that is causing you people to have a certain amount of hatred towards your union. Anything I know or that I think I know is all hearsay. But Chris, if it's going to have the same effect on you as it did the last time, then it's best that you don't come in. You're going to have an accident. You're not going to be thinking straight, and you're going to drill a bootleg or something else. You've got to be focused when you're underground. You can't be walking around blind."

Neill also talked to mine superintendent Terry Byberg, who assured him he could have his old job back. Neill next got together with Jim O'Neil and a group of other CASAW men who were thinking about crossing.

Jim and Jane O'Neil had $70,000 in savings to draw on, but like Chris and Tracey, they had a new house and O'Neil wasn't making any kind of money using his airplane to haul Arctic char from Cambridge Bay to Yellowknife. When O'Neil called Byberg, he was told thirty CASAW men had crossed. The nonsense and the violence had gone on long enough, Byberg said. It was time to end the strike and get back to work.

O'Neil, Neill and the other CASAW men started to think that if a large group of them crossed together, it might be a devastating blow and start the strike crumbling. CASAW would be discredited and a new union could take its place. O'Neil believed that it would soon be over, that after the riot the union was toast, that things might have worked out at the Nova Scotia lobster plant where the strike was now over, but they had gone terribly wrong at Giant. O'Neil had even asked Byberg for his advice on a good labor lawyer to help the miners sort things out after the disintegration of CASAW.

The men decided to cross the day after the August long weekend. That morning, Tracey picked everyone up in her husband's 4 x 4 Blazer, then dropped them off at Tim Horton's, where a van from the mine picked them up. Along with Chris Neill and Jim O'Neil were two more friends who had decided to cross, David Vodnoski and Shane "Spanky" Riggs.

The van headed out of town, past the vast open pits and murky lakes of refuse water. Neill was laughing and joking and was by far the most relaxed in the van. He was the leader, the one who had called up everyone to go, and he seemed most certain it was the right thing to do. Past the Road of Shame the van headed, past the placards with the names of the men who had already done what these four were about to do. The CASAW strikers sat in shacks and around fires at the main gate's picket station. The van came up to the gate and drove through. It passed by the astonished faces of the strikers. The union men couldn't believe that so many new men were crossing at once.

The line crossers all signed contracts saying they would accept the gold escalation pay scale and work a seven-day schedule. Neill hadn't been looking forward to meeting the replacement worker who had taken his job, but now that he met with a few ProCon men, his attitude changed. "You know, I can completely understand these guys," he told Tracey when he got home that night. "They have families, two or three kids. They've used up all their unemployment, they're on welfare now, they've lost their homes, they have nothing. I can't blame them for wanting to come to work for a decent mine."

Retribution came fast. O'Neil woke up the next morning to find the tires on his camper flattened. In big red letters, the word *scab* had been spray painted on the garage door of his new home. O'Neil made a half-hearted attempt to scrub the paint off. The truth was, he didn't mind it that much. It was almost a badge of pride. It showed the community what was happening to the line crossers. But Chris Neill couldn't stand to see the graffiti. He kept bugging his friend to clean it up. At last Neill got a can of white spray paint and did it himself.

"That's a pretty messy job," Tracey said when she saw his handiwork.

"I don't care. It covered it up."

Both O'Neil and Neill went to work setting up their video surveillance and lighting systems. O'Neil set up a video camera in his garage, focused on the street. He put up two big lights on top of the garage in front and back. He, too, kept a loaded rifle by his bed.

One day a militant striker named Conrad Lisoway drove by the Neill's house when Chris Neill happened to be outside. Neill had enough time to hide behind a fence. Lisoway slowed down in front of the house and looked in. Just then, Neill jumped out and pounded on the hood of Lisoway's vehicle, scaring the hell out of the striker.

Around town both the line crossers and the strikers lived by the same credo: If a rumor hasn't started by noon, we'll start one. Gossip was malicious and unstoppable, and the names Neill and O'Neil were often in the middle of it. Neill especially hated the talk about him crossing to support his lavish lifestyle. He believed the union men had long been jealous of his big salary, his pretty wife, his cars and his property.

Both Neill and O'Neil became increasingly tense. The two men visited each other almost every night and were constantly on the telephone. Tracey and Jim's wife, Jane, didn't think the relationship was completely healthy. The two seemed to fuel each other's paranoia. Whenever O'Neil visited the Neills, he made sure the door was locked after he entered.

"Your windows aren't closed," he told Tracey.

"Jim, this is a big house, no one's going to hear."

Still, O'Neil went around and shut all the windows, then checked the back door and the garage door to make sure they were locked as well.

On the job things were chaotic despite Witte's claims that the mine was running at full capacity. Neill was mining and training his friend David Vodnoski. Neill had few problems, but O'Neil saw that other areas were breaking down. He was put in charge of cleaning up the room where drill bits were stored. Bits had been piled everywhere. O'Neil reorganized the bits and resharpened them, then set up a checkout system.

At first O'Neil and Neill drove to work together, but when O'Neil got the job in the bit room, his shift changed, starting and ending one hour later each day. When Neill got home at night he was restless until he was sure that his friend had also made it back safely. Neill invariably called up Jane ten minutes before Jim was scheduled to arrive home. The two talked until he walked through the door. Neill always promised Jane that if anything happened, he would protect Jim. He told her to stay calm, though she was far calmer than either man.

Tracey and Chris Neill were still relative newlyweds, so new in marriage and their relationship that they had never argued. If anything, the strike pulled them closer together. They were rarely apart, except when he was at work. Tracey never left the house without him, except to go to work herself. When he was at the fire department, she went with him. One day the Neills were out shopping when a CASAW striker accosted them.

"You're going down!" the striker shouted at Chris from his checkout aisle. "You fuckin' scab. You're goin' down big time."

Tracey was appalled that the man would be foulmouthed with kids around. An older woman in front of the striker was also upset by him. "Look," she said, "you're a big piece of shit. My husband works at the power company, and he has been called out again and again because of you assholes cutting the power lines out there."

The striker cursed the woman before turning his attention back to Chris. This time Tracey cut him off. "Shut up, you big fat pig!"

The striker called Tracey a slut, then left. Afterward, Tracey was so angry she told her husband they should follow the striker home. "Let's just drive by his house to see if he feels intimidated."

"No way," Chris said. "We're not going to go anywhere near him."

After three or four weeks it seemed to get easier to cross the line. The new battleground was the "Letters" page of the *yellowknifer*, where both sides indulged in name-calling and reputation smearing. The campaign started after the O'Neils' house was vandalized and union strike coordinator Dale Johnston was quoted as saying it was no big deal. "They were members that voted against the strike. And they've made their decision to go back so they'll be treated accordingly."

Johnston also said that Jim O'Neil and Chris Neill were the same two who had tried to cut a deal with Byberg and Werner earlier in the strike, though they had no mandate. It was just as well they had crossed. "Once a scab, always a scab. It's good to keep all the scabs in one place."

Jane O'Neil fired back a letter in response: "We refuse to be bullied by you and will not tolerate any further actions of this nature. Your union executive are sacrificing the entire membership in their vendetta with Royal Oak. Change your tactics before you lose what little dignity you have left."

Striker Edmund Savage replied: "As for the tension that exists on our legal picket line, it has been diagnosed as being the scab disease (scabs are not human, they are a disease) and the only vaccine that exists needs to be legislated."

And striker Jim Fournier wrote: "Miners owe their comfortable lifestyles to vigilant unions and hard, valiant strikes. . . . This strike is going to be a significant memory for everyone involved for the rest of our lives. I, for one, could never forget turning my back on my friends and co-workers because of a skewed priority list. And make no mistake, they won't either. These defections have hurt the union, but we will rise above it. Many ties have been severed, never to be joined. When we raise our arms in victory, where will these men be?"

Jim O'Neil replied: "Mr. Fournier was very right. Union battles have advanced the worker's lifestyle through workplace safety and better job and employee benefits. But what about this particular strike? If you asked ten men, 'Why are you on strike?' you would probably receive ten different answers.

"It is a case where personal animosity took control over fair and just representation. This personal vendetta against Royal Oak has led many men and their families into a situation where answers are getting harder to find."

The next attacks were personal, directed right at O'Neil, saying the union had saved his job on at least one occasion, and he couldn't comprehend the safety issues because he worked only around the shaft, not throughout the mine. Wrote striker Mark Eveson: "I hear you on the radio saying when this is over, we will have to restructure our union. I have news for you, ex-friend, whichever way this ends, you will not be part of any union. So why talk about something that, for you, no longer exists? In closing, Jim, I say to you, 'Wake up and smell the kaka [*sic*] because you are standing in it right up to your neck!'"

O'Neil returned the volley: "All I see now are people that claim they are concerned about safety: yet property is being vandalized and blown up and people are being threatened."

Chris Neill applauded his friend for standing up to the strikers in such a public way. Neill wrote no more letters himself, but he thought he did his part. If the CASAW men yelled at him when he crossed the line, Neill was likely to give them the finger.

A few of the line crossers also waved their paychecks at strikers. When Terry Legge saw that, he wished he had a gun. One night, Legge was outside the picket shack when a line crosser cursed at him, then drove off in his truck. Legge wanted to chase the truck and kick in the man's head, but he was calmed by striker Roger Warren.

"Come in and sit down before you hurt yourself out there," Warren said. "Don't fuckin' worry about those pieces of garbage."

Legge was spending a lot of time with Warren, who cautioned against fighting and joining in any clandestine action. Still, Warren was as angry as anyone about the scabs. He told Legge he suspected Peggy Witte was backed by bigger companies, and though Legge wasn't so sure, he didn't disagree. He had learned not to argue politics with Roger Warren; Warren was too well informed and too fierce in debate.

Warren got especially angry one day when he saw a miner cross the picket line on a bicycle. He told Legge that until the government stepped in or something major happened, nothing was going to end the strike. "We're going to be here until fuckin' hell freezes over."

Legge had to agree. There were no negotiations and none forthcoming. But Legge could not accept that the line crossers and replacement workers would keep working, not if he couldn't work. Around the union hall and his supper table, Legge's rhetoric was desperate. "We'll shut the fuckin' place down," he told his union brothers. "We will flatten it. There will not be one fuckin' piece of stick left standing. Why walk away and give it to the fuckin' scabs? Come on!"

Claudia heard this latest talk and told Terry he had to stay away from the line. At last he agreed with her. He had been fired, but he still expected to get his old job back. Still, he didn't need more trouble. He decided to put in his time working the radio at the union hall. He also spent a few weeks alone at his cabin at Lake Chedabutco. He knew he needed a break, that he was getting too angry. He saw the anger in the other men as well, and it made him think something ugly was likely to happen soon. Again and again he told Claudia, "This is not going to end without a death. Peggy Witte is going to keep going forever with the scabs."

Legge guessed it likely would be a CASAW man who would die, killed in a brawl at the main gate, and only then would the government change its laws to outlaw scab labor. Legge thought he was prepared to die for the cause. When it came down to it, he now believed in his union as much as any religion.

In late August, three months into the strike, Legge was approached by the Cambodian Cowboys to see if he'd help out in their latest plan. After the failure of the satellite dish bombing, Shearing and Bettger had decided they needed more knowledge and more materials to construct a more sophisticated explosive device. In late July they had headed out of Yellowknife for a week-long shopping spree in Vancouver. They ran up $754.23 on Bettger's VISA card. At places as suspicious as West-Lynn Military Surplus in New Westminster and as mundane as the K-Mart in Langley, they shopped for their paraphernalia.

At a meeting at Al Shearing's apartment, Bettger showed off his new bomb, complete with a timing device. Along with Shearing, Legge and Lisoway, Bettger worked out a plan to set the bomb at the building housing the four air compressors for the mine's main ventilation shaft, the B-shaft. The vent shaft station pumped 7,000 cubic yards of air into the mine every minute so the miners could breathe and the diesel equipment could operate. The bomb would go off near the air compressors, but not on them. The message would be clear—this time it's a little bang, but next time we could knock out the compressors. No air for the miners to breathe, no gold for Peggy Witte. The Cowboys wanted to prove to Witte they could shut her down anytime.

On the evening of August 31, the Cowboys headed out, and Legge tingled with anxiety. He certainly didn't want to kill anyone with a bomb. He was satisfied, though, that the vent shaft station would be empty. The bomb would be set to detonate shortly after the four men left. No unsuspecting victim would wander in and get killed.

The vent shaft station was wide open, no barbed wire or motion sensor lights. It was located right next to the Ingraham Trail, but the Cambodian Cowboys decided to approach it from the back, driving part of the way cross-country toward Vee Lake, then hiking through the bush the rest of the way.

Legge and Lisoway wore black. The Night Crawler and the Bear had on their camouflage outfits. The bomb, stored in Bettger's jacket, was made of twelve sticks of powder, a battery, a detonating cap and a timing mechanism. Bettger and Shearing went into the station to plant the bomb. Legge and Lisoway stayed on the hill as lookouts. Only one vehicle passed, the Pinkies taking some workers to a mine entrance. Legge worried they'd hear him because of his chattering teeth. He felt weak in his legs.

Bettger and Shearing were at the station for only half an hour, but it seemed like forever to Legge. This wasn't berry picking. He had never been in any more trouble than a fist fight.

The bomb rigged at last, the Cambodian Cowboys hustled off. They waited in the dark for the pop of the explosion. Minutes passed. No pop. Legge thought his heart was going to burst. Still no pop. Bettger searched his mind for what might have gone wrong. At last he hit upon something—maybe he hadn't had the right amperage in his batteries to ignite the blast. The men were too frazzled and it was too late to go back that night. They all agreed to return the following night to fix the bomb.

When he got home Legge couldn't sleep. He was consumed by visions of the bomb suddenly going off the next day and killing someone. It came to him that he wasn't really needed on the return mission. He decided to back out. While Bettger, Shearing and Lisoway returned the next night to reset the bomb, he monitored the radio in the union hall. Just after midnight, news of an explosion at Giant Mine came across the scanner.

Chris Neill was in bed when his scanner picked it up. At once Neill called up the mine. He got hold of manager Bob Steinke, who said an explosion had gone off at the vent shaft station.

"Is anyone dead?" Neill asked. "Do I have to come out there?"

"No. Everything's okay."

After hanging up, Neill sat on the edge of the bed, tears in his eyes. "You know, Tracey, if that would have been successful they would have killed every man underground. I don't want to bring bodies out from underground, I don't want to do it, but it's going to happen. Somebody is going to die."

It could easily have happened with this vent shaft bomb, Neill thought. The compressors were powered by propane. If a fire had started, they could have blown. Since the twenty-odd auxiliary fans inside the shaft would have kept running, a down draft might have been created, pulling in the smoke. Deep in the mine, men might have been asphyxiated.

After the blast, the gossip around Yellowknife was that the vent shaft explosion was a bungled job, a couple of assholes from the union who didn't know what they were doing. Harry Seeton, who had taken over from Bill Schram as union president, told the *yellowknifer* that the union leadership condemned this kind of thing. "It's completely against our way of operating." Other union men said the bomb had been set to discredit the union. They suspected the Pinkertons were the culprits.

Chris Neill decided to take a leave of absence from the fire department. He feared that if someone was killed at the mine, the strikers might hold up the fire truck at the picket line because he was on it. He'd heard about union guys saying they would be only too glad to rip him right off the moving truck.

Neill was becoming pale and losing weight. When he drove around town he always checked his mirrors, searching for a CASAW cop. In his truck, Neill brought a scanner, a baseball bat and a video camera to take pictures in case he was attacked. At work he talked endlessly about the latest threats and disputes. His shift boss, Don Moroz, tried not to bring it up with him or any of the other line crossers because they'd get carried away. Moroz wanted them to focus on the job.

Neill was sure the CASAW men had gone berserk. More and more he dwelled on what awful things might happen to Tracey and his property. Tracey couldn't go to the corner store without him warning her to take great care.

"You're overreacting all the time," she told him.

"You don't know these people. You don't know what they're capable of."

Tracey got worried enough that she called up the police and talked to Constable McBride. She asked McBride what they could do to be safe. The safest thing would be to leave town, McBride knew, but he couldn't say that. This was Canada. No one should have to leave town. Yet he didn't know what else to say.

When Tracey's mom, Roseanne Quintal, came to Yellowknife to visit in mid-September, the couple tried to act normal, but Roseanne could see the strain on her son-in-law. At last she asked him about it.

"By the time this strike is over I'm either going to have a nervous breakdown or an ulcer," he told her.

On September 17 Roseanne flew home to Edmonton. When she met her husband, Ron, at the airport, she broke down crying, stricken by what she had seen in Yellowknife.

Chapter 4

SEPTEMBER 18, 1992

A T 7:00 A.M. on September 18, 1992, Tracey Neill stood at the dresser in her bedroom and put on her jewelry, preparing to go to work. As Chris did every morning, he got out of bed to hug and kiss her good-bye. Tracey headed downstairs, and Chris called after her, reminding her to come home right after work because the cement truck was coming at 4:30.

For once Neill had slept well, tired after working in his yard until 11:00 P.M. He had been shoveling gravel, preparing a spot of even ground for the cement mixer to pour a pad for the couple's new satellite dish. Neill wanted to get the job done before winter set in.

He got up to feed the couple's dog, Koni, then let it outside. Neill didn't take a shower before going to work. Why get clean just to go underground and get covered in grime? He went around the house, shutting down video cameras and turning off lights, then got in his 4 x 4 and headed to work. He pulled in around 7:45 A.M. and parked in his usual spot near the C-dry.

Neill and the other miners of the 712 work crew were held back that morning to watch a safety video. Most of Neill's shift were CASAW line crossers, not replacement workers. One of them, Joe Pandev, had arguably been the most respected and well-liked miner at

Giant. Pandev was fifty-five years old and had been a hardrock miner for thirty years. Any man still going after that many years of drilling and blasting had to be a marvel. The bonus with Joe Pandev, though, was that he was a great guy, a friendly, even-tempered man. "What do you say about a guy who has mined for thirty years and has got the disposition he's got?" shift boss Don Moroz wrote in Pandev's evaluation report.

Other men bitched at Moroz, but Pandev would take any job and say, "No problem." Like many miners, Pandev was a small, thick man, 5'4", 150 pounds. A big man might try to bull the drill into the rock, but Pandev had learned that if you fight the drill all the time, the drill will wear you down. He used the weight and thrust of the hydraulic jackleg to do the work for him. Of the two types of mining—drift (carving out the transportation corridors) and stope (blasting out the gold-rich ore itself)—Pandev preferred stoping. He read the rock face as if he had it memorized. If the cuttings spraying out from his drill were milky white, Pandev knew there was little gold in the ore. But if the cuttings were black as oil and had a rotten egg smell it meant the rock was rich. Pandev would sometimes disagree with the geologists and engineers about where the ore vein was heading. Most often he was right.

Pandev had been married to his second wife, Judit, for eight years. Both she and Joe were immigrants, she from Hungary, he from Yugoslavia, and both still had heavy accents. Joe's first wife had died in 1983. Judit's first husband was killed in a mining accident at Giant. Both had three kids. Joe's kids were now in their twenties; Judit's were still teenagers. The couple already had five grandchildren, with another one expected. Joe was just over a year from retirement when the strike started. He and Judit looked forward to his leaving Giant in July 1993. They planned to move to the Okanagan with Pandev's old partner, Martin Kolenko, who was now a manager at Giant Mine. Kolenko and Pandev hoped to do a lot of fishing and gold-panning.

Pandev had voted against the strike. He knew there were a hundred unemployed men who would crawl over each other to take his job. He also feared he would lose his pension. Still, Pandev told Judit he would not cross the picket line. His feelings changed, however, as the violence escalated. A few of his own union brothers seemed like bullies and madmen. He stopped going to the picket line. In early August a CASAW strike captain visited Pandev's house and told him that in the future strikers who did not picket would not have a vote at union meetings. For once, Pandev erupted. He had been in Yugoslavia during World War II. He knew strong-arm tactics when he saw them.

"Is that so?" he told the striker. "Okay, I never needed the union before. I'm going back to work. I'm working my ten months, and I'm getting the hell out of here."

It was a big day for the rest of the CASAW line crossers when Joe Pandev crossed the line. Kolenko was happy he was there, though he hated it that many of the strikers went after his old friend. They took videos and photographs of him as he drove through the picket line, just like they did to every other line crosser. Pandev's name was added to the Road of Shame.

CASAW strike coordinator Dale Johnston visited Pandev at home.

"I heard you went back to work," Johnston said.

"Yes."

"I'm really sorry you did that, Joe. I'm really sorry."

Pandev shrugged and said nothing. Judit told Joe that if the strikers ever tried to block his way into the mine, he should just step on the gas. He told her she was nuts, that it was best to turn the other cheek. But every day when he got in his van to go to work, he took off his hat, bowed his head and prayed.

In late August, Royal Oak hired Pandev's son Joey to work at the mill, which raised Pandev's spirits. That morning of September 18, he and Joey came to work in the same van. They talked about the strike on the way, how dead in the water the strikers were, how the strikers should get smart and realize it was time to come back to work.

At the mine Joey headed to the mill while Pandev went to get dressed in the C-dry. He put on coveralls, a yellow plastic miner's hardhat, insulated gloves and rugged boots with steel-reinforced toes. He got safety glasses and a safety belt, which had an attached emergency oxygen mask. The belt also had a battery for his light. The light had three feet of cable. He could either carry the light or attach it to the peak of his helmet.

Pandev found his blue plastic name tag on the C-dry bulletin board. He carried the tag and hooked it on the board of his shift boss Don Moroz. This was a standard safety precaution. If the mine had to be evacuated in an emergency, each man out would return his name tag from the shift boss's board to the main board in the C-dry. If a tag wasn't returned, it meant that the man was still underground and might be in trouble.

Pandev, Chris Neill and the other miners watched the safety video, then talked for a moment before heading over to the C-shaft, the mine's main corridor to the underground.

"Have a good shift," Moroz told his men, then smiled. "Get some work done down there today. Don't just sit around and bullshit."

Two elevators ran up and down the C-shaft. The skip elevators could each haul three tons of ore while the man-cage could take eighteen men at a time. The miners piled into the man-cage, a Spartan contraption like an old service elevator. They dropped swiftly into complete darkness. The only sound was water pouring from the drifts down into the shaft.

The man-cage stopped at the 575-drift. Two men got off, miner Fritz Ramm and Noel O'Sullivan, the mine's general foreman. O'Sullivan had agreed to show Ramm what he would be doing that day.

The man-cage dropped to the 750-drift. Eight miners from the 712 work crew got off. They had to wait for miner Malcolm Sawler, who had been late getting on the cage. When Sawler arrived, the nine men prepared to depart. They would be the first men to go down the rail line on the 750-drift that morning. The mine had been all but empty since the central blast at 3:10 A.M. After the last workers from the night shift had come up on the man-cage and returned their blue name tags to the C-dry bulletin board, the mine foreman had turned the blast key, igniting the dozens of charges left behind by the previous shift. Afterward, the mine was left vacant so the smoke could clear.

The miners of the 712 work crew boarded a man-car, a railway car used to transport men to and from their work sites. The man-car had a steel frame, plywood sides, a plywood roof and hinged steel doors at either end. This particular man-car was known as the Silver Bullet, named after a train in Newfoundland. It had been painted silver when the British Royal family had been scheduled to tour the mine. But the visit had been canceled. Years of use had worn off the Silver Bullet's glossy paint.

The man-car had two benches. Four men sat on each side of the car. A small electric locomotive, known as a loki, pushed the man-car. Trammer Arnold Russell drove the loki.

Old George Samardzija, who repaired track in the mine, saw them off. He had a smile for his good friend Pandev.

"Hi Joe, how are you?"

"Good morning, George. I'm okay."

The man-car headed down the 750-drift, leaving behind the light of the 750-elevator station. In complete darkness, save for the men's lamps, the Silver Bullet moved along at about twenty miles an hour. Water flowed back toward the C-shaft in a ditch on the right side of the track. A four-inch high pressure water pipe, a two-inch water pipe and a two-inch high pressure air pipe ran along the ceiling of the drift. The high pressure air and water powered the jackleg drills.

The men wore their lanterns around their necks, not on their hats as they would when they worked. This way they could face a friend and chat without blinding him. The man-car was always a good place to talk. It seemed funny for a group of big men to be crammed into such a little car. Above ground, the men were nervous and tense from the strike, but here, at last, they felt safe. It was the one place they could relax, away from the threats, the name-calling, the CASAW cops tailing them.

Six of the men were CASAW line crossers and three were ProCon replacement workers. Along with Chris Neill and Joe Pandev, the CASAW men were Norm Hourie, David Vodnoski, Shane Riggs and Vern Fullowka.

Norm Hourie and his brother Allan had started at Giant only six months before the strike. Another brother, Johnny, had signed on at the mine only a few weeks back. Norm, fifty-three years old, was known as a packsack miner, a man who moved from contract to contract, taking short-term jobs across the country. He had four children, two from his first marriage and two from his wife Doreen's previous marriage. Hourie was quiet, but respected for his experience and knowledge. He had no time for the vitriol of the union and stayed on the mine property when the other men had gone out on May 23.

David Vodnoski was twenty-five years old and a newlywed. He and his wife, Doreen, had married in June. He became stepdad to her two children. Vodnoski grew up in the small towns of Carrot River and Choiceland, Saskatchewan, where his father ran sawmills. He had started at Giant four years back, working as a trammer and scoop operator. He was now Chris Neill's trainee. Vodnoski was a happy, sociable fellow. He had never agreed with the strike and set his own deadline of two months for the union to settle before he decided to cross.

Shane Riggs was a twenty-seven-year-old scoop-tram operator and the only bachelor in the group. All the men knew him as Spanky. He was good friends with Neill and Vodnoski. All three had the same energy and drive. The managers loved their enthusiasm. Riggs was the same height as Joe Pandev, but with thirty extra pounds of muscle from weight training. He came from a strong union family in Lake Cowichan, British Columbia. He didn't vote to strike, but he had been as antiscab as anyone. He had joined up with the CASAW vigilantes on a few escapades. His mom, Carol, cooked food for the men on the strike line. But after Riggs got charged for some minor strike-line shenanigans, he quit going to the line. He feared he would lose his job. It broke him up that his good life in Yellowknife might be over. He and his sister Linda had just bought a new trailer home, but to make the last mortgage payment he'd had to roll up his quarters. He had crossed with Vodnoski, Chris Neill and Jim O'Neil. He was quiet at first, but after a week he got back to being his old bubbly, it's-great-to-be-alive self. He helped get his brother Peter a job as a mechanic. A few days back Riggs had been asked to start training as a miner; he was thrilled about the prospect.

The last of the six CASAW men was Vern Fullowka, a farm boy from Invermay, Saskatchewan. All four of his brothers had gone into mining as well. Fullowka was thirty-eight now, had a wife and two young children, and had been a miner for seventeen years, working in Manitoba, British Columbia and Ontario. At Giant he ran a mechanized jumbo, a drill that was operated from a tracked vehicle. He was a tall, thin man. He rarely drank and rarely spoke. He was a cautious, efficient miner.

During the first months of the strike, Fullowka had been a picket captain. But after a while money got tight for his family and he felt pressure to cross. When he made the move about three weeks back, many of his fellow strikers were astonished. A few were worried. A rumor went around that Fullowka had kept a diary of all the union's illegal activities. Fullowka didn't discourage the rumor. "They won't touch me because I have a lot on them," he told Chris Neill.

Another rumor, however, was that Fullowka was a CASAW plant, a spy. Some of the Royal Oak managers were suspicious of him at first, but Fullowka's good friend Rick Titterton, another line crosser, vouched for him.

Of the three ProCon men—Robert Rowsell, Malcolm Sawler and Arnold Russell—only Rowsell wasn't a career miner. For ten years, he had run his own truck. He had got into mining only a few years back, becoming a jackleg and jumbo drill operator. Rowsell was born and raised in Harrington Harbour, Quebec. Before coming up to Yellowknife with ProCon on September 7, he had been unemployed for five months. He was thirty-seven, had a wife and two kids, and although he first turned down the chance to work at Giant, his poor finances persuaded him to change his mind.

Malcolm Sawler had lost his job when a Thunder Bay nickel mine shut down. Sawler started at Giant in August. He was thirty-eight and another packsack miner. He had worked for almost twenty years in towns such as Sudbury, Ontario; Nanisivik, Northwest Territories; and Cluff Lake, Saskatchewan. He had three kids, two with his first wife, one with his second. On the job, he worked hard and fast.

Arnold Russell was a scoop-tram operator. Russell grew up in Bathurst, New Brunswick, then worked in tire sales before getting a series of mining contracts. He had been unemployed for eighteen months when ProCon sent him to Yellowknife in late June. He and his wife, Karen, had four children. Russell, a storyteller and joker, was popular with the other miners.

The Silver Bullet passed the roaring sound of the main ventilation shaft. The man-car was now on the best section of track in the mine. Three years earlier, Pandev's friend Samardzija had taken out the old track, graded the red silty soil, and put in new track, true and straight. There were no switches coming up, no reason for the men to look ahead down the tracks.

And then the man-car hit the bomb.

The left front wheel triggered the detonator. The explosion was like a bolt of lightning blasting down the shaft. The crack echoed like thunder. It created a fireball more than two thousand degrees Fahrenheit. It melted and tore apart the Silver Bullet. It blew open the high pressure water and air pipes. All eight men in the man-car were hurled against the hardrock ceiling, then smashed against the drift's right wall. The impact obliterated the men closest to it. Flesh, bone and shards from the man-car blasted up into every crack in the rock. There was little blood; the heat seared it in. Most of the men died instantly, all of them within a few moments. Arnold Russell, who had been driving the loki, was thrown backward and ended up in the drainage ditch. His body blocked the flow of water. Soon, the area was flooded. All was dark, the only sound the roaring hiss of spraying water and rushing air.

Two thousand feet down the drift at the electrical charging room for the lokis at the C-shaft elevator station, George Samardzija sat pouring coffees for himself and two replacement workers, Henry Puzon and Serge Duguay. When the blast erupted, all three hunched over, afraid. The door of the shop slammed shut. The concussion knocked over a garbage can.

Samardzija had no idea where the blast came from. He called up to the C-dry to ask the managers if there was supposed to be any blasting on 750 that day. No one knew.

Samardzija shrugged and went to work. Duguay and Puzon took a loki and a train of six ore cars down the 750-rail line. A few minutes later, they came back. They had a strange story for Samardzija, telling him they had come upon the loki and saw it was derailed. There was a lot of smoke and they didn't go any closer. The two men also reported that the doors to the main vent shaft had been blown off their hinges.

Samardzija again called up to surface to report this news, but with his heavy accent all the managers made out was that the vent shaft doors had been blasted. Samardzija next tried to call down to the 712-scoop shop, where Joe Pandev, Chris Neill and the seven other men of the 712 work crew should now be. He got no answer, but he did get through to two replacement workers, Norm Morneau and Serge Arsenault, who were one level below in the mine. Serge Duguay talked to Morneau since both spoke French.

"Is there anybody at work in 712 yet?" Duguay asked.

"No."

"I'm not sure, but I think someone blasted the man-car."

"Anybody hurt?"

"I don't know."

"Shit, you better go and check."

After hanging up, Duguay, Samardzija and Puzon headed down the tracks on the loki to inspect.

At the other end of the 750-drift, Noel O'Sullivan was also piecing together what had happened. O'Sullivan and Fritz Ramm had been walking along the 575-drift when they heard the blast. O'Sullivan checked his watch: 8:45 A.M.

Shock waves from the underground explosion reverberated and ric-ocheted. The origin was almost impossible to determine. But the blast didn't worry O'Sullivan. Yes, it was a bit early, but maybe a shift boss had found some debris blocking a stope and was getting rid of it.

O'Sullivan and Ramm continued to walk along the railway track of the 575-drift. O'Sullivan was fifty-two, but he set a pace that left younger men hustling to catch up. He never slowed down or went faster, just hammered along steadily. He wore the standard issue yellow plastic hard-hat, but he didn't attach his lantern to the peak of his hat; he carried it in his hand. If anything alerted him, he was ready to quickly shine the light to his side or above.

He was at home in the mine and he looked it. He had a strong jaw and nose, big shoulders, muscled arms. His graying red hair hung down in bangs, early Beatles style. At 5'11", 205 pounds, he was tremendously strong, but his real strength was his attitude. He had worked at Giant for twenty-five years, twenty of them as a supervisor. He had never lost his respect for the dangers of the underground, but he was never daunted either.

Now, as the roar of the deadly blast faded from the mine tunnels, O'Sullivan instructed Ramm on his job at 407-stope, then left to check out other stopes, his lantern cutting through the darkness, a long, ghostly finger pointing the way. He walked down the B-ramp, a wind-ing road cut through the hardrock into the mine. He stopped in at the 712-scoop shop to check up on the work crew. He was surprised to find no one. Joe Pandev, Chris Neill and the other men from the 712 work crew should have made it there long ago. He had said good-bye to them thirty minutes earlier. All they had to do was go down one more level, get off the C-shaft man-cage, wait for Malcolm Sawler to come down from the surface, then board a man-car. It should have taken them ten to fifteen minutes at most.

O'Sullivan noticed another odd thing: the air pressure valve read zero. Just then, the 712 shift boss, Don Moroz, pulled up in his Toyota truck.

"So nobody has been at their work site yet?" O'Sullivan asked.

"That's right," Moroz said. "And the cross shift didn't leave very good instructions about where they left the 50-scoop when they left. It should be here in the scoop shop, but someone left it at the 575-break-through area."

Moroz had taken the winding B-ramp down from the surface. He had spotted the scoop tram on his way down. He figured one of the replacement workers must have left it there instead of returning it to the 712-scoop shop. He knew Spanky Riggs was scheduled to use the 50-scoop tram that morning and he would be upset that it was out of place. Riggs was probably looking for it now, Moroz figured.

O'Sullivan and Moroz tried to call the surface, but for some reason the telephone line was dead. Just then, two replacement workers drove up in a scoop tram, Serge Arsenault and Norm Morneau, who had earlier talked with Serge Duguay.

"Things don't seem to be right this morning," O'Sullivan said. "Is there anything you can tell me about it?"

"We heard on the phone that a man-car had been blasted, but that's all we know," Arsenault said.

O'Sullivan was thinking the worst now. Still, he would not let it get the better of him until he had checked it out. He and Moroz decided they had better walk down the 750-drift toward C-shaft. Smoke filled the tunnel with the acrid smell of a blast. O'Sullivan and Moroz could see only a few feet ahead of them. After walking for five minutes, they noticed that the high pressure air and water lines running along the tunnel's ceiling had been ruptured. Water gushed on the floor, then flowed downhill toward the C-shaft. Air hissed, making it hard to talk. In a moment, they came upon the twisted metal and splintered wood of the Silver Bullet.

And then O'Sullivan and Moroz saw them.

One body lay in the water ditch at the side of the track. The others were hanging on a pile of rails next to the wall—a stack of arms, legs, hands, torsos, heads. A torso and a pair of legs seemed to grow out of the hardrock wall.

It's a prank, O'Sullivan said to himself, a bit of dark humor. Someone has loaded mannequins into a man-car, then blasted it to cause a scare. Maybe it's someone trying to send a message: This time it's a joke, but next time it will be the real thing.

O'Sullivan yelled into Moroz's ear to go back to the 712-scoop shop and shut off the air and water valves. Moroz took off running.

Just then, O'Sullivan felt something malleable under his foot. He looked down. Beneath his miner's boot was flesh and bone burned black. It was real.

"Does anybody need any help?" O'Sullivan shouted at once.

No answer.

The blowing air and water were so loud he knew no one could hear him. He also knew it was no use. Thank God for that, O'Sullivan thought. No one would want to survive this blast, that was obvious, even on first glance. It looked like enough explosives had been used in the small corridor to collapse a bridge. Any man who had lived would wish he were dead. He'd be maimed, blinded, totally dependent. For the sake of the men and their families, let them be dead, O'Sullivan prayed.

Still, he repeated his call: "Does anybody need any help?"

He moved forward, getting past the bodies and twisted man-car by walking along the other side of the drift. He stumbled. He looked down to see he had stepped into a large, shallow crater. He hadn't seen it because the area was flooded.

O'Sullivan got out of the crater to stand in the middle of the tracks. He looked around, trying to think. The crater hadn't been there before, he knew that. He could tell from the position of the dead men and the man-car that the blast had come from that side. That meant it came from outside the man-car, not inside. If the miners had broken regulations and were carrying explosives in the man-car, and if somehow those explosives had gone off in a derailment, the men would have been blasted in every direction. They wouldn't be stacked on top of one another.

Not that a derailment could cause an explosion anyway. O'Sullivan knew you could smoke around AMEX explosives, a mixture of fertilizer and diesel fuel, and they wouldn't go off. You could drive a truck over AMEX or drop it a hundred yards, and it wouldn't go off. It would just turn to mush.

It came to O'Sullivan in a flash that this blast had to have been caused by a bomb, planted at the side of the drift so the miners wouldn't see it.

It must have had some type of impact detonator, maybe a trip wire, O'Sullivan thought. It was murder. It had to be. But why?

Miners do not kill miners.

O'Sullivan could not conceive of anyone at Giant committing such an act even in the midst of this bitter strike. Maybe set a bomb underground, but not one rigged to kill. It went against everything O'Sullivan believed about his business. It mocked his code.

Miners do not kill miners!

It flashed through O'Sullivan's mind that maybe none of the CASAW men had done it. Maybe it was a hit man, some hired gun from the South brought in to do the dirty work.

The air and water lines shut down. It was quiet then, except for a few drips. No talk, no breathing, no moans, only the quiet and the dark. In a moment O'Sullivan saw the headlight of a loki coming from the direction of the C-shaft. It stopped on the edge of the blast site. Three men got off, George Samardzija and the two ProCon workers, Henry Puzon and Serge Duguay.

"Oh my God!" Samardzija wailed as soon as he saw the carnage. He started to cry. He backed away, bent over and vomited.

Duguay took off running, heading back down the mine toward the C-shaft elevator station. On his way he ran into three men, Jim O'Neil, Keith Murray and George Coombs.

O'Neil and Murray, both trained in mine rescue, had been dispatched from the C-dry after Samardzija reported that the doors of the vent shaft had been blasted. They picked up Coombs on their way. The three of them saw Duguay's light coming forward, bobbing in the darkness. Duguay ran right by, howling: "They're all dead! They're all dead!"

Murray told Coombs to go after Duguay and make sure he was safe.

"If you want to go back to the station, now is a good time," Murray told O'Neil. "This could be our friends killed back there."

"No, I'll keep going."

At the vent portal, the plywood doors were splintered and blown back into the shaft. The six-foot steel bars that had held the door frame in place were peeled out of the wall.

The two men continued on, the scent of the blast much stronger now. The first thing they saw was the battered loki sitting across the tracks. Next they saw Noel O'Sullivan and the piles of bodies.

"Have you checked for signs of life?" O'Neil asked him.

"No."

O'Neil and Murray kicked into rescue-team mode. Along with O'Sullivan, they climbed onto the mass of men and started digging through, hoping to find a pulse or some other sign of life. Most of the corpses were face down. Many of the heads had been obliterated. Some were flaps of skin. On the ground were severed hands still in their gloves. Wire and lunch buckets and hard-hats and clothing were tangled. It was hard to tell where one man started and another man ended. After a quick count, they thought there were seven bodies.

O'Neil bent down to check the dead man who was blocking the drainage ditch. Water flowed over his face. Only his mouth and nose were visible, his eyes below the surface. "I can't tell if I can feel a pulse here or not," O'Neil said. "We got to get him out of the water."

O'Neil, Murray, O'Sullivan and Moroz, now back at the scene, lifted the man and put him on the tracks. They checked his mouth to see if his airway was blocked. His face was burnt and unrecognizable. He had no pulse. O'Sullivan checked the man's pocket for identification. It was Arnold Russell.

The angry talk started at once. "Those CASAW fuckers, they should fuckin' die. They will die."

Keith Murray spat with anger. "How could they?" he kept asking. "How could they?"

"Forget it!" O'Sullivan cut in. "We got a job to do. I got to go up and report it, or else you guys go up and I'll stay here."

O'Neil, Moroz and Puzon volunteered to stay. Puzon guarded the south end, Moroz and O'Neil the north.

"Make sure you watch Don," Murray said to O'Neil, pointing at Moroz, who had been sickened after he inadvertently stepped on a body part. He was weeping and throwing up.

Murray, O'Sullivan and Samardzija left the scene, Murray getting on Samardzija's loki and starting to drive away. He went twenty feet but could go no farther. He was overcome with fear, thinking he might somehow trigger another bomb. He got off and started walking. On the ride up on the C-shaft man-cage, the three men said nothing.

By the time they got to surface, ninety minutes had passed since the blast. O'Sullivan went to report what had happened to mine superintendent Terry Byberg. Royal Oak's vice-president, John Smrke, happened to be at the mine that day and was in Byberg's office. He was on the phone, and O'Sullivan could tell he was talking with Peggy Witte. Smrke relayed to Witte everything that O'Sullivan said. Smrke looked stunned when O'Sullivan said the bomb was deliberately set.

"How can you say that?" he asked.

O'Sullivan explained how the crater was at the side of the tracks, and the men were blasted against the far wall.

"Do you have any idea how much explosive was used?" Smrke asked.

"Either two bags of AMEX and a detonator and a primer, or one on one, a bag of AMEX and a box of powder."

Royal Oak called in the RCMP. Constable Randy McBride, who had headed up the task force on the strike-line crimes, arrived with the first group of officers. McBride asked O'Sullivan to come into his car for a short interview. As they talked, tears dripped down O'Sullivan's face. He had to stop a few times to wipe his eyes and blow his nose.

Back at the blast site, Puzon, O'Neil and Moroz stood with their backs to the dead men.

"Who are these men?" O'Neil asked Moroz.

"It's my crew." Moroz pulled out a piece of paper. "I got to write down the names." He began listing them. "Joe Pandev, Chris Neill, Vern Fullowka, Spanky Riggs . . ."

O'Neil started to shake. Chris Neill! He could not believe he was hearing the name. Chris Neill! He could not believe the corpses he saw were these men, his best friends. Chris Neill! O'Neil and Moroz started to cry. For a moment, they hugged.

"This is no accident," O'Neil spat. "This is strike related. This is CASAW's doing. That fuckin' union. I'm not going take no more of their bullshit."

O'Neil could see no one else setting such a bomb, not here, not to kill. He had heard the rumors that CASAW strikers Al Shearing and Tim Bettger had set the satellite dish and vent shaft bombs and had been down into the mine in this area on their June 29 graffiti mission. The graffiti had warned they would be back. It looked like someone from CASAW had made good on that promise.

The next group at the site was a first aid worker, a Pinkerton security guard and a government mine inspector. A second group soon followed, O'Sullivan leading Terry Byberg, John Smrke, Dr. Ross Wheeler from Yellowknife's Stanton Hospital and two RCMP officers, Sergeant Wiley Grimm and Constable McBride.

Dr. Wheeler had volunteered to help out when he heard the emergency call. At the C-shaft headframe he was told by the RCMP that he would find no one alive. His job would be to pronounce the men dead so the police investigation could proceed. Shortly after 11:00 A.M., the group traveled down the man-cage.

Dr. Wheeler had lived in Yellowknife for twenty years, but he'd never been in the mine. Fear of the underground seized him. He worried that somehow he would end up buried alive. He found the journey along the 750-drift dreamlike. The mine walls looked phony, as if they had been made in Disneyland. The helmet lights danced; the place reminded Dr. Wheeler of a strange subterranean disco. After what seemed a very long walk, the group arrived at the blast site, coming face-to-face with Jim O'Neil. Dr. Wheeler looked in the miner's eyes. He had never seen anyone so completely shattered.

"Gentlemen," O'Neil said, "I hope you're ready for what you're about to see. It's the most disheartening, gross scene you'll ever see in your life."

O'Neil looked at Byberg. "They got Chris," he said, choking back a sob.

Byberg put his hand on O'Neil's shoulder.

Dr. Wheeler shut out the horror, shifting into his emergency room mode. He checked the bodies, making sure to count them, making sure there were no vital signs.

"Doc, what do you think?" Sergeant Grimm said. "You think they're all dead?"

"Yeah. I think they're all dead."

"Okay. You guys can leave now," Grimm said.

Only Constable McBride stayed behind to guard the blast site. McBride didn't go out of his way to examine the scene. The more people who ventured in, the more contaminated it would be for the investigators. He didn't want to damage any evidence. Besides, he was too distraught to do any kind of systematic work. The smell of the burnt flesh sickened him.

McBride had seen plane crashes, train crashes, bodies burned beyond recognition in fires, but he had never seen men so mutilated. It didn't look real to him. This is the way it must have been in Vietnam, he thought. One minute you're whole and healthy. The next minute you're dismembered.

McBride was shaking. He had been in hairy situations before and had always reacted coolly, but now he was terrified, overcome by a feeling of personal danger, a fear that the murderer might still be lurking in the mine. There were a million places to hide down here.

McBride focused on a light far down the drift in the direction of the 712-scoop shop. It seemed to be getting closer. He studied it, and, yes, it was coming at him. When he blinked, however, the light was back where it belonged, unmoving, far down the tracks. Surrounded by darkness and death, it was easy to let the mind get carried away.

At last McBride heard footsteps. He braced himself for an attack. He listened hard and could tell it was two people, not one. In a moment, O'Sullivan appeared with Sergeant Grimm, come to relieve him.

Thank God, McBride thought.

At the surface Jim O'Neil felt so disoriented he could hardly walk. He looked around the headframe area. It was the same place he had seen a thousand times, but he barely recognized it. Flashing lights, ambulances, police, fire engines, people milling about, all of them seeming to shake, all moving in slow motion. An RCMP officer asked O'Neil to come with him to the second floor of the C-dry, then asked what he had done and seen that morning. O'Neil choked up. He started to weep. No words came. "I just can't do this right now," he managed to gasp.

A moment later O'Neil saw his wife, Jane, who had rushed out to the mine as soon as she heard something had happened.

"Tracey is downstairs in the mine office," Jane said. "She wants to see you."

O'Neil knew he couldn't see Tracey. He wouldn't be able to hide the truth from her. He looked at Jane and told her, "They got Chris. They got him and Dave and Spanky. Until it's official, I don't want to talk to Tracey."

O'Neil put on his mine rescue gear and sat down, waiting for the call to come help remove the bodies. He had to do that one final thing for his best friend.

Stench gas had been released in the underground, alerting all the men to get out as quickly as they could. By 11:00 A.M., the mine was completely evacuated. Nine unclaimed identification tags hung on Moroz's bulletin board in the C-dry: Joe Pandev, Norm Hourie, Malcolm Sawler, David Vodnoski, Chris Neill, Shane Riggs, Arnold Russell, Robert Rowsell, Vern Fullowka.

Through the early afternoon, the mine offices at Giant filled with angry, distressed talk, much of it from miners who believed that only luck had taken them elsewhere in the mine that morning. Most were so tormented that they left for home. They didn't show up for work the next day either. Some would later go for counseling.

O'Sullivan realized it was his duty to remain calm. It helped that he had handled other deaths in the mine. He knew his job: don't go overboard assigning blame; release information about the deceased to the families only when the information is solid; cooperate with the people in charge of the investigation. He sat in his office and had a coffee. He tried to call his wife, Minnie, but the mine's one telephone line was busy. Minnie had also been trying to get through with no luck. She had heard about the blast on the radio. When she finally did connect, she was told her husband was underground. At last, O'Sullivan got through to home. Gerry Brown, a good friend from church, answered.

"Do I got the wrong number or is this O'Sullivan's?" Noel asked.

"Glory be to God," Brown said. "Yes, it is."

"Who is speaking?"

"This is Gerry Brown. Are you okay?"

"Of course I'm okay," O'Sullivan answered. "What would be wrong with me? Let me speak to Minnie."

"Just a minute. Hey, Minnie. It's Noel."

O'Sullivan could hear her crying in the background. "She's not able to come to the phone," Brown said in a moment. "She's feeling really bad. How bad is it out there?"

"It's bad."

"Are there people killed?"

"Yes."

"How many?"

"I can't tell you."

"Anyone we know?"

"Yes, but I can't tell you who they are or how many. But it is not good. I'll talk to you later."

It occurred to O'Sullivan that he could have been killed by the bomb. His plan had been to go to 750, and only a last-minute plan to help out Fritz Ramm took him to 575 instead. And if he had got off the man-cage at 750 he would have gone in ahead of the men in the man-car; they would have had to wait for Sawler. O'Sullivan would have been first down the tracks. Nevertheless, he tried not to take the attack personally. Such was O'Sullivan's confidence that he believed the bomb might not have got him. He thought there was a chance he would have spotted the tripping mechanism with his lantern.

His faith told him it was not right to think about equaling the score. He had to accept what had happened. Still, it was damn hard. The blast scene kept coming back to him. His heart beat with the hunger for vengeance. Already rumors were spreading that when news of the blast got to a bar called The Gallery, a bunch of CASAW men stood and cheered.

As if to convince himself that forgiveness was indeed the right course, O'Sullivan went about persuading other men to do the same. One by one, he grabbed hotheads and took them into his office.

"What can you do?" he asked them. "You can go downtown, and you're going to end up with your ass in the slammer. Or you may end up with your head kicked in. You're going to deal with guys who are just as angry. They will have very little time for your anger. Leave them alone. Everything will take care of itself in due course. Let the cops do their thing, and we will just assist them and see what happens from there."

As he left the mine, Don Moroz saw Tim Bettger, the Cambodian Cowboy kingpin. Moroz stopped his truck and shook his fist at the Bear.

"Fuck you, you prick," Bettger yelled out.

For a moment, Moroz thought about getting out of the truck, but he calmed down. That wasn't the answer, not for him either.

Along with other relatives of the dead men, Tracey Neill was drawn to the mine. During the morning coffee break at work, one of Tracey's friends saw fire trucks heading down the highway toward Giant. Tracey looked out the office window to see a St. John's Ambulance rushing toward Giant as well. She knew then something bad must have happened. St. John's was only called out for major emergencies.

Tracey got a call from the receptionist, who said CASAW's lawyer had just called the Department of Justice. The lawyer wanted to get an application in before lunchtime to allow CASAW's mine rescue team onto mine property to help out. Tracey didn't like the sound of that at all. She knew Al Shearing was one of CASAW's mine rescue men. If something had happened at the mine and Al Shearing was in on it, Tracey thought it would be crazy to allow him to visit the scene of the crime. Would he even do his rescue work properly if it came to saving the life of a replacement worker?

Tracey headed to the office where a group of senior administrators was discussing the CASAW application. They were leaning toward not allowing it, but Tracey piped up anyway, reminding the administrators about Shearing's strike-line record. The application was denied.

At lunch, Tracey and a friend, Susan Tettenborn, decided to head out to see what was going on. Susan's husband, Carl, worked in the mine mill, and the couple lived in the old company housing at the Giant Mine townsite. They took Susan's truck. On their way, a radio report said there might be as many as fourteen people dead in an accident at Giant. In a way, the high number of casualties relieved Tracey. She knew that Chris couldn't be one of the fourteen. He worked on his own with David Vodnoski. He was never with a large group of men underground.

Strikers, RCMP officers, security guards, reporters and townspeople milled around Giant's main gate. Tettenborn's truck was met by striker Bryan Wells.

"You can't go through," Wells said. "This is a picket line."

"Get out of my way!" Tettenborn barked. "I live out here."

Another union man, Rob Johnson, a friend of the Neills before the strike, waved the two women through. Tracey couldn't help but stare at Johnson. The stricken look on his face confirmed that something awful had happened.

Tettenborn parked her vehicle in front of Chris Neill's 4 x 4 near the C-dry. Tracey heard from one of the firefighters that the underground had been evacuated, but the mine rescue team was still down. Fire chief Mickey Beauchamp told her she shouldn't be in the area.

"I know, I know," Tracey said, but she decided to stay anyway. I'm being nosy, but maybe I can help, she thought. If there's a mine rescue I can maybe make sandwiches and serve coffee. I'm the wife of a guy who is on mine rescue, after all.

All around her were the wives of day-shift miners. Tracey saw the upset expression of one woman with a son and husband at the mine. Tracey tried to reassure the woman that everything was okay, but now Tracey, too, was crying and shaking.

Tettenborn told Tracey she'd just got a phone call from mine secretary Karen Duncan. Tracey was to go to the main office, Duncan had said. Tracey's cousins were already there. At the main office, Tracey was sent to a downstairs room, cold and bare, cement walls, no carpet, a fridge, a coffee maker, one long table, a few chairs, couches against the wall. She found her cousins Eric and Helen Malmsten, who had also come out to the mine when they heard something was wrong. Linda Riggs sat at the table with her fiancé, Dean. Linda had on her brother Spanky's Northwest Territories mine rescue jacket, with the black, yellow and white of Giant Mine's former corporate colors. Tracey had on a jacket, a mine rescue windbreaker, but her nose was still running from the cold.

The room slowly filled. The people kept to themselves, saying little. Judit Pandev was the first in the room to find out what had happened. She felt caged in the basement so she wandered out, hoping to spot Joe. She asked everyone she met if they knew what was happening. She had a terrible feeling inside, recalling the mining accident that had killed her first husband.

At one point Judit saw the ambulances leave. They were empty, no injured men, no dead men. She was joined by her son Timmy, her sister Helen and Helen's husband, Mike, a CASAW striker.

In a moment she spotted Fritz Ramm, one of Joe's co-workers on the 712 crew. Fritz was embracing his own wife and children.

Judit hurried over. "Fritz, what is going on? Where is Joe?"

"Judit, I am sorry. I wish there was something I could do for you."

"Nah, nah, nah, forget that," Judit spat. "Don't tell me that bullshit."

She turned away abruptly, only to run into George Samardzija. Judit could see how distraught he was. "George, you're here. Fritz is here. Where is Joe?"

"I'm sorry," Samardzija said. "He's gone."

"You're full of shit!"

"No, I'm sorry. I saw it."

"No, you're wrong,"

"I saw it," the old miner wept. "I'm sorry. I'm sorry."

"No! There is no way! To hell with you, too!"

Judit searched for Joe's best friend, Martin Kolenko. She knew Kolenko would tell her the truth. When at last she found him, she only had to look at him to know. She broke down crying. Kolenko hugged her close. "Jeez, but you were hard on your husband," he said. He didn't know what else to say. He and Joe had been such friends, talking about things they wouldn't tell their mother, their father, their brother. He knew everything about Joe and Judit. But he couldn't think of how to comfort her.

Judit went back down to the basement room and sat. "This can't happen to me twice," she wept.

Linda Riggs was also crying now. She darted about the room, speaking in a loud voice, angry, confused, profane. "That goddamn union!"

Tracey Neill looked on, not comprehending. What's going on? Why is everyone assuming the worst? "Come on, Linda," she said. "Both Chris and Shane are in mine rescue. They're probably just busy helping out."

Tracey didn't know why Linda was so quick to blame CASAW. She thought it could have been a small accident. It could have been anything. A mine is a dangerous place. But Tracey felt bad now; whoever was dead or injured, she almost certainly would know them or at least some of their friends and relatives.

Terry Byberg, Noel O'Sullivan and John Smrke walked into the room. They were still covered in dirt from their trip into the mine. Byberg had asked O'Sullivan to come with them because he would know most of the family members. The men wanted to know if all the relatives had arrived yet.

Byberg recognized Tracey, but he quickly turned away from her. One of the relatives asked him to explain what was happening.

"I can't," he said.

Judit Pandev hurried over to O'Sullivan, whom she had known for years.

"Is it Joe?"

"Judy, there's been a terrible explosion," O'Sullivan said. "I believe Joe is dead, but I can't swear to it. We don't know who they are."

O'Sullivan tried not to say another word. He knew if he started talking now he'd give the whole story away.

But Judit hammered at him. "It's Joe! I know it's him!"

"Listen, Judy, we just don't know. We know the name of only one of the dead men, but we can't reveal that name. It has to go to the next of kin first. But it's not Joe. Now, I can't say any more until we know for sure who is going to come up. The police are doing their checks right now."

"You're lying! You're not telling me the truth!"

Judit had never known such anger. If she had seen Peggy Witte then, she would have ripped into her. Hadn't Royal Oak promised it would do everything it could to protect them and the men? "Where are the promises of safety?" she raged at Byberg. "What the fuck were you guys doing if not protecting?"

Tracey Neill started to feel uneasy. She knew if Chris was involved in a mine rescue, Byberg would have told her that Chris was busy but would be in touch. Tracey wondered if she should go to the hospital; Chris might be there with an injury or smoke inhalation.

After O'Sullivan, Smrke and Byberg left, the next person in was miner Jerry Gallagher. Linda Riggs jumped at him. "What's happening? Tell me what's happening."

"Understand, I can't say anything. I can't."

"Who did this? I know the union did this."

Gallagher broke down then, hunching over, his face in his hands. He dropped to his knees and started to cry. "Fucking sabotage! Fucking sabotage!" He got up and ran from the room.

Again, Tracey didn't know what to think. Man, that is weird. That's Jerry. He doesn't cry. He's a tough guy. She considered taking some action, maybe getting all these women together to make some food for the rescue teams. Chris and the other men were definitely going to be hungry.

Another hour passed. It was now 2:00 P.M., more than five hours after the blast. At last Byberg and RCMP Inspector Dennis Clark walked in and shut the door. Clark laid a piece of paper on the table. Linda Riggs was sitting there and glanced at it. At once, she started to cry, putting her head in her hands and shaking.

Oh my God, Tracey thought, it's Shane. She started to cry, too.

Inspector Clark and Byberg went around the room, asking for each person's name. In the end, they asked only one teenage boy to leave. Tracey felt sorry for the boy, believing he was being taken away to be told that his father was dead.

But Inspector Clark returned to stand behind the table. "There was an explosion in the underground," he said. "We can't identify anyone for sure, but there is a ninety-nine percent chance that no could have lived through this blast. There are seven bodies at the site, but we have nine people missing. We've checked through the mine now, and we don't think anyone could have lived through this."

The RCMP officer picked up the sheet of paper. He began reading off names: "Josef Pandev. Vern Fullowka. Shane Riggs. Malcolm Sawler. David Vodnoski. Norman Hourie. Robert Rowsell. And Arnold Russell. . . ."

Tracey was crying now, but when she heard the officer say "and," she thought his list was over.

". . . And Chris Neill."

Without another word Clark left the room. Tracey did not hear Chris's name. She still thought he was alive. His name was spoken, but she did not hear it. There was too much noise in her head. Her cousin Eric offered to drive her to his house. They left the mine through a side gate. On their way out they drove past Chris's truck.

Tracey kept thinking about what the RCMP officer had said, that there was a ninety-nine percent chance the men were all dead. That's ninety-nine percent, not one hundred percent. And they found only seven bodies. Maybe Chris is buried somewhere. Maybe there is some sort of rescue going on right now in the mine. Chris carried a breathing apparatus so he could live for a while. He's really smart, so he wouldn't get into a situation where he was in too much trouble.

At Helen and Eric's place, Tracey phoned her parents in Edmonton. She told them something had happened to Chris, and they should get on the next plane to Yellowknife. Next she phoned Chris's sister Wendy in Peterborough, Ontario. "Look, I think Chris is dead, but I'm not sure," she said, then recounted the story, ending up with how the men were still unaccounted for.

A radio had been turned on to catch the news. Tracey heard a commercial for a cement company. She remembered the load of cement coming for the satellite dish and told her cousin Eric to call and cancel it. When he made the call, he found the order had already been canceled. Tracey took this as a good sign. No one else knew about the concrete. Chris must have done it. That meant he was alive. (Later, Tracey would find out that a friend who worked at the cement company and knew Chris was on mine rescue had stopped the order when he heard about the blast.)

At 6:00 P.M., Jim O'Neil found out that the bodies were going to stay down at 750 at least overnight. He decided to go see Tracey. He thought he had better be the one to tell her what had happened. She might not believe anybody else. O'Neil found out she was staying at her cousin's. He drove there, knocked and walked in.

Only then, seeing O'Neil's anguished face, did Tracey finally know for sure. He looked as if he had aged twenty years in one day. He was always so excited and moving about. Now he walked slowly, as if he were in chains. He sat beside Tracey on the couch.

"Tell me," she wept. "Tell me. Tell me."

"Yeah. They got Chris."

Judit Pandev ran out the door as soon as Inspector Clark read Joe's name. She gave the keys to Joe's van to Joey. She didn't want to see it ever again. She got in her own car with her sister Helen and her son Timmy. For a moment she thought about barreling over the strikers on the picket line. Instead, she stopped the vehicle, then rolled down her window. "Listen you guys, you did this, you watch your back! You take it from me, I'm coming after you!"

In town, Judit told Helen and Tim she was going to do something stupid, and she didn't want them to try to talk her out of it. She didn't want her mind straightened out. She drove to the sporting goods store owned by CASAW's strike coordinator Dale Johnston. Johnston's son Sean was serving customers. Judit went to the back of the store and looked around until the customers left, then went to the cash, where she found Dale Johnston.

"I want to buy a rifle and some ammo," she told him.

"Oh, you want to buy a gun."

"Yes, and you'll be my first target."

"Listen, I don't like to be threatened."

"I don't like to be made a widow."

"I'm going to call the cops."

"Go ahead. Call the cops. I don't give a shit who you're calling," Judit said, then as she stormed out she added, "You watch your kids. You'll be sorry."

At RCMP headquarters, dozens of officers moved in a hundred directions that day. The place was a giant roulette wheel with people shooting in, getting a new task, then getting shot out again.

When Constable Ken Morrison heard the news, he was shocked. All summer he had expected something, but not this. Morrison turned to another officer. "They fuckin' did it," he said. "Those bastards finally fuckin' did it."

To investigate the site, Yellowknife superintendent Brian Watt called up the RCMP's post-blast team in Ottawa, experts in piecing together what had gone on in explosions. The post-blast team's leader, Inspector Don Watson, implored Superintendent Watt to take every step to protect the blast site. "Leave everything as intact as possible."

Mounties flew in from across the Northwest Territories that day to help with the initial investigation and provide support for the expected night of trouble. When Corporal Dale McGowan of Hay River got the call, he was told to pack for five days, but wasn't told why. As he hurried to catch his plane, McGowan heard on the news a snippet about the explosion at Giant and the number of deaths.

McGowan was excited to be going. He had spent a career doing community policing in small northern and prairie communities. He was just newly promoted to plainclothes investigator for the general investigative section in Hay River. The biggest cases he had ever worked on were violent assaults. He was used to dealing with small-time thieves, drunks and bullies, not bombs going off. This trip was going to be something new.

Like many Mounties in the Territories, McGowan had earlier that summer been called in for a tour of duty on the Giant picket line. He had worked fourteen straight night shifts in August as a uniformed officer, traveling up and down the line in a police van. He had learned pretty fast what the strikers' beefs were, both with Royal Oak and the RCMP. They had constantly been on McGowan's case, and he hadn't liked it. He had felt like he was a bad guy, not because of who he was or how he acted, but merely because of his uniform.

Nevertheless, McGowan had identified with many of the CASAW strikers, the quiet ones who didn't say much, just stayed in the picket shack and let the big mouths do the shouting. They were working men, regular people who had got in a bad situation. Sometimes things got out of hand and they all got fired up. McGowan felt his job was to give them an ear so they could blow off.

Throughout his tour he was forever heading out to rock throwings. Just when he got it stopped, things flared up somewhere else. McGowan thought it was mostly a lot of chickenshit stuff where the Pinkertons and the CASAW men felt free to mouth off because there was a fence between them and Mounties around to referee. McGowan had a name for the name-calling: yeah-yeahing, as in, "Oh yeah!" "Yeah!" "Oh yeah!" "Yeah!"

On the night of September 18, however, the name-calling was a prelude to the real thing. Dozens of replacement workers headed out from the mine site into Yellowknife. They poured off the property with the rage of men who had been bottled up and beaten down too long. Before they got the next plane out, before they left this shithole of a place, the ProCon workers wanted to beat up any CASAW striker they could find.

Fist fights broke out through the evening. CASAW line crosser Craig Richardson threw a beer bottle through the union office's window. A replacement worker burst into the office, yelled "Murderers" and a fight broke out. "CASAW murderers," was spray painted on a store and at the union hall. Nine people were arrested, three for breaking windows. The bars shut at 9:00 P.M.

The Yellowknife RCMP detachment was overwhelmed. McGowan and every other officer on hand was sent out to patrol the streets. He was in plain clothes, a shirt and tie, his revolver in a holster, but no one paid attention to whether he was a cop or not. No one had any thought for him at all. They were absorbed with hatred and grief.

McGowan was a big man, 6'2", 215 pounds, with a square jaw and a heavyweight's build. He had spent a career breaking up bar fights. He knew that men liked to get into the rut now and then and butt heads, but the fighting this night was unlike anything he'd ever seen before. If someone didn't intervene, the two sides might beat each other to death. Emotions boiled over in a second.

At one point McGowan stepped in to stop a furious man, a big miner, who was ready to kill his opponent right out on the street in front of Yellowknife's famous Gold Range tavern.

"Calm down, guy," McGowan said. "This is not the way to deal with it. Don't get yourself in trouble."

As soon as McGowan grabbed hold of the miner in a bear hug, the man went limp. He started to weep on McGowan's shoulder.

"I worked with those guys," the miner cried. "I worked with them."

McGowan didn't know if the man was a replacement worker, a line crosser or a striker. But the miner was huge, full of muscles, a chiseled face, a man who earned his wage with his back and his hands. And now he was weeping. It was then that McGowan understood what had happened that day. All the threats, the violence and the rage had created this open, throbbing wound. It was the bloodiest crime in the history of the Canadian labor movement, and he was standing in the middle of it. There he would remain for thirteen of the most demanding, exhilarating and painful months that any police officer could ever know.

Chapter 5

MINERS DO NOT KILL MINERS

THE CASAW UNION HALL on the edge of downtown Yellowknife had no moat, parapets or cannon, but it was a fortress nonetheless. At home a striker might get hell for putting the battle with Peggy Witte ahead of the welfare of his own family, but at the union hall it was as simple as the poster on the wall: "We Will Last One Day Longer than Royal Oak."

No one could question that belief, not even the small voice in the back of many strikers' heads that said maybe the union should have accepted the tentative agreement. Each man would be thousands of dollars ahead by now. But at the union hall that small voice was drowned out. There was another poster on the wall, a child's drawing of a burning Miss Piggy rocket ship. The caption read: "Scabs landed on the sun for one sec. But then the ship melted and . . . Look, a pudel [*sic*] of slime."

The union hall was in a plain, one-story building. The main tenants were a bowling alley and the Polar Bowl bar, the union hangout. A thick wood door blocked the hall's entrance. It wasn't locked during the day, but it radiated a feeling that in order to enter a visitor had better be ready to stand up and be counted as a CASAW supporter.

The door opened to a bare room with a few tables and chairs, the walls covered in anti-Royal Oak, antiscab posters. There was an office for private meetings in the corner. The one window was covered over with cardboard. The place smelled like a smoker's car and rang with the echo of a million angry curses. It wasn't a place for men thinking about crossing the line or for the RCMP or for members of the media. Indeed, the real way in wasn't through the door at all—it was through action: joining in marches, attending rallies, knocking down power poles, hurling rocks, writing the newsletter, following scab vehicles, working a regular picket shift. But even the formidable door couldn't keep out the shock wave of the September 18 bomb. That morning CASAW strikers retreated to the union hall, not only to listen to the scanner and the radio, but to be among brothers. No man could stand up to something like this on his own.

When the news of the blast came over the scanner, Al Shearing, the leader of the Cambodian Cowboys, wept. He suggested the union organize a mine rescue team. Someone told him no union men would be welcome at the mine because of the various court orders.

"Fuck the injunctions!" Shearing said. "People may be hurt."

The union men got their lawyer working on it, then drove out to the mine. At the gate they were told they wouldn't be needed. There would be no rescue.

Terry Legge was torn by the news. He was shocked, but he thought if the men had not crossed the picket line, they would still be alive. Maybe that didn't justify what had happened, but it was the truth. They should never have fuckin' been there!

"Look at these people," striker Terry Regimbald said to him, gesturing at the others in the union hall. "Look at them."

"What?" Legge asked.

"Well, there's a lot of sad faces around here. What do you think?"

"I think we should set off another charge and get the rest of them," Legge said. "I hope to fuck there is fifty of them killed. I hope the whole fuckin' ground opened up and swallowed them up. Maybe it was God gettin' fuckin' vengeance."

But in the afternoon, when the names of the dead came out and the RCMP announced they were treating the matter as a criminal investigation, Legge was shattered. Sure, blow up a satellite dish or the vent shaft, but this? Nine men dead. Jesus Christ! Legge knew that he and his buddies had thrown rocks, shouted across the picket line, chopped the odd power pole, even set off bombs to make a little noise. But that was it. That was as low as it got. None of them was capable of this. Maybe the company was, but not the union. Joe Pandev, Chris Neill, Verne Fullowka, Shane Riggs—Legge couldn't believe he was hearing the names. All of them were friends, all of them good men. Yes, Legge had wanted to punch each of them in the face for crossing the line, but to see them dead? No way! No fuckin' way!

There was no time for Legge and the other CASAW strikers to mourn. Already the telephone at the hall was ringing with angry, accusatory voices at the other end. Legge took it as his job to face the abuse.

"Are you happy now? You murdering bastards!"

"CASAW murderers!"

"You fuckin' bastard. I'm going to kill you and your family."

Legge decided the last call was enough. He phoned the RCMP. "Terry Legge here," he told the officer. "I just got a death threat."

"You did? Well, what did they say?"

"Well, don't you fuckin' know? You got the phone bugged!"

"Well, what do you want me to do about it?"

"Nothing, guy," Legge said bitterly. "Nothing."

He hung up. He was scared now for himself and his family. But the attacks made Legge even more sure no CASAW man could have set the blast. It didn't make sense. Things had started to turn for the union, what with their Vancouver lawyers just filing an unfair labor practices complaint against Royal Oak for trying to bust the union.

Four months on the picket line had forged a skin of iron on Legge and every other striker, one that absorbed any blow and deflected it back. It was second nature by now to take any information and view it through a CASAW filter so that it looked bad for Royal Oak, not for them. The blast was no exception. As news dribbled in, Legge and the other strikers started to think things didn't add up. They had found out that the blast had happened around 8:40 A.M., yet the police and fire department weren't notified until 10:20 A.M. Why so long? What had happened in those one hundred minutes? And who was benefiting from this blast anyway? Royal Oak, that's who. There would be no quick end to the strike now. The unfair labor practices complaint was airtight in the minds of the strikers. But would the union get a fair hearing now? Not a chance.

A theory quickly took shape about what had really happened. The men in the mine had been killed in a blast, no doubt about it, but it was an accident. Instead of waiting for their explosives to be delivered to them that morning, they had taken a shortcut, taking the powder with them on the man-car. They might have even put bags of AMEX up on the man-car's flat roof. The man-car derailed—something that often happened in the mine. The AMEX and a blasting cap fell out. Something weird happened, maybe a wheel ran over the cap, and it ignited the AMEX. Kaboom!

Carrying powder in a man-car was against mine practice and government regulations, but CASAW's underground workers assured the men who worked in the mill that this happened all the time. Time was money, after all, so why follow the nitpicking rules? For the union, there was a pleasing irony to the theory—the scabs had crossed the line out of greed, and now they were dead out of greed, bending the rules to earn more bonus money. Not only that, but the CASAW men had always said they went out because the company was threatening the safety of the men. Didn't this prove it?

The theory went that when the Royal Oak bosses saw what had happened and realized they'd face charges, they made a plan. The Pinkies were sent down to the blast site to make it look like murder. In Legge's mind a Pinkie could have done something as simple as taken his watch off, crushed it and thrown it into the carnage to make it look like a bomb's timer.

Legge's conviction grew stronger through the day. Striker Marvin Tremblett came back from the picket line to report that right after the blast, a Royal Oak replacement worker had come to the front gate and yelled at the CASAW men: "They put a bomb on the tracks where the man-carrier went!"

Where did the scab get his information? How did he know a bomb was on the tracks? It was like he was reading from a script. If it was up to Legge, he'd have got that scab under the hot lights right then. Sounds like he had all the answers.

Another story spreading around the hall came from striker Darcy Taylor, who had been sitting at a restaurant that morning. At the table across from him was a local RCMP sergeant. Word came over the radio that seven men were unaccounted for at Giant.

"Jesus Christ," Taylor had said to the sergeant. "Did you hear that? There are seven men unaccounted for?"

Taylor said the sergeant had looked right back at him and said: "Not so. That's seven men murdered."

Here was more proof. All along, the RCMP had victimized them by taking Royal Oak's side. If the cops were saying it was murder, that it wasn't an accident, wasn't that more proof that it *was* an accident?

The CASAW men heard that some politicians down at the Territorial legislature had picked up on the RCMP's comments and were saying the blast was criminal in nature. It seemed everyone was joining in the CASAW-bashing.

As the union's conspiracy theory took shape, news came that a Royal Oak line crosser had told a striker something even more incriminating, that a major shipment of explosives had been delivered to 750 that morning and the nine men went down the line with it. With this latest tip, CASAW president Harry Seeton decided to issue a press release, headlined: "Striking Miners Support Victims' Families." After offering sympathy to the families of the dead men for the tragic fatal accident, the release said: "Replacement workers have reported to the CASAW office that mine workers were being transported with a load of explosives containing fifty bags of AMEX, ten boxes of stick powder and two boxes of B-line explosives. 'It is a cardinal rule that you never transport explosives along with workers no matter how much time or money it might save. The public can only hope that all the facts will be given due attention after the period of mourning,' said union president Harry Seeton. 'We are shocked at the despicable conduct of the Territorial Government Leader and Minister of Transport, who have already made allegations without basis within hours of the incident on this day,' said a grim-faced Seeton. 'Their rash comments indicate there may be more political connections than anyone could have imagined.'"

Throughout the strike, the CASAW men felt they'd had the moral upper hand. If everything else was against them, if the bank threatened to take their trailers and their wives threatened to leave, if the company fired them and the RCMP arrested them, they could still walk proud because they believed they were right. It was a legal strike. It was Witte who had locked them out, brought in the replacement workers, then made threats about breaking the union. And the RCMP, well, obviously they had been bought.

After the September 18 blast, however, the morality of the strike was turned upside down. The line crossers and strikebreakers, not the

CASAW strikers, were the objects of sympathy now, and the strikers couldn't tolerate that, not so quickly, not all at once. When the news reporters came down to the hall the day of the blast, they walked into the full force of the union's confusion, pain and denial.

"We need an inquiry, not to let these people get in the mine and cover it up," said the union's advisor Jim Evoy of the Northwest Territories Federation of Labour. "Royal Oak is calling the shots. Royal Oak is telling the RCMP what happened. This bullshit has to stop. We need an immediate investigation, and we don't need that investigation by the Royal Oak Mounted Police."

The union hall erupted in applause.

A moment later Terry Legge erupted on his own. "Everyone knows what happened but the fuckin' media and the public," he said to CBC reporter Eric Sorenson.

"The story is not all out yet," Sorenson said.

"You got that fuckin' right! What the media is doing is promoting violence."

The following day, Saturday, September 19, Royal Oak's John Smrke issued his own press release saying Seeton's press release was ridiculous, that the powder shipment went into the mine after the men went down, and in any case there was no way that many explosives and nine men could fit in a man-car. Smrke even organized a demonstration for the media, showing how eight miners filled a man-car.

Seeton and the union leadership shot back, saying the union would hold its own press conference on Sunday at noon. For now, the union said it wanted Chief Mine Inspector Dave Turner, who normally investigated mine accidents, to be involved in the RCMP's investigation. CASAW also called for union involvement in the investigation and an independent public inquiry, which would be free from any political interference. "CASAW unequivocally states that no strikers were involved in the mine accident, and CASAW welcomes an independent inquiry to refute all scurrilous accusations put forward to date," the release said.

The RCMP's media relations man, Sergeant Dave Grundy, had been out moose hunting and didn't hear about the blast until he got home late Saturday night. The following morning Grundy went into the office at 6:30 A.M. and heard a moment later that the post-blast team had studied the blast site and had determined the bomb was deliberately set.

Grundy wrote up a release reporting the new findings, saying the RCMP were treating the blast as a multiple homicide. Grundy got approval for the release, then faxed it out at 11:50 A.M., only ten minutes before CASAW's press conference was to begin, though Grundy didn't know that.

Newspaper, radio and TV reporters from across Canada gathered in the union hall to listen to CASAW's leaders. The hall was packed with strikers and reporters. At the front was Seeton, advisors Jim Evoy and Harold David. Slightly off to the side was a fourth man, old-time miner Roger Warren; Warren was to answer any technical questions the media might have about explosives.

Evoy, Seeton and David started in, David accusing Royal Oak of a cover-up. "What was going on from the time of the explosion to the time it was reported to the RCMP?"

As the union leaders spoke, the telephone kept ringing. Terry Legge answered each call, trying to listen to the press conference at the same time. More people called up with accusations. Legge had just read in the *Edmonton Journal* that the loki had pushed in the man-car, which wasn't against any law, but was frowned on since it could more easily cause a derailment. He was convinced now that a derailment had caused the blast.

A call came in from the CBC. Legge handed the phone to CBC radio producer Judy McLinton. McLinton was told about the RCMP press release from Grundy. She was so shocked she almost blurted out the news right then. McLinton said she'd pass on the information. Legge got the gist of the conversation and was alarmed, but there was nothing he could do about it. He watched as McLinton picked her way to the front row of reporters, finding CBC-TV reporter Eric Sorenson. "We just got a fax from the RCMP," she whispered. "They say it's murder. You ask about that."

Sorenson put his hand on her arm. "Are you absolutely sure? I don't want to ask this if it's wrong."

"Yeah."

Sorenson got up to ask his question. "I understand the police are saying it's a bomb. What do you say about that?"

Evoy asked to see the release. Sorenson told him it was on its way. There was a short break until it arrived and the CASAW leadership examined it.

"As usual the one-upmanship continues in this dispute," Evoy said at last. "This does not translate into the fact that strikers or their supporters perpetrated this crime. Please understand that, and understand that well. This does not translate into working people in the North murdering their fellow workers, and I hope that is very goddamn clear."

"It goes against everything that is holy," Harold David said. "Miners killing miners? It's just an obscenity."

"I've had it," Evoy said. "That's enough for me."

The press conference broke up in hostility and angry talk. Strikers milled about, complaining that the RCMP had timed the release to coincide with their press conference and the media were probably in on it as well.

Just then the telephone rang again. Legge picked it up.

"Hey you fuckin' CASAW murderer, keep your fuckin' head up."

"Fuck you!" Legge slammed the phone. He'd had enough. He grabbed the newspaper article about the man-car being pushed in by the loki and headed over to confront Sorenson.

"That was a derailment that set the explosion off!" Legge barked at the reporter. "The explosion came from the side of the drift because there was a derailment. I'll bet my life on it, okay?" Now that he was ripping, Legge only got louder and angrier. "It was a goddamn accident, and if people don't fuckin' get the truth out, I'm telling you there will be fuckin' deaths, but it won't be fuckin' accidental!"

Photographers madly gathered around Legge as he spoke. He turned to walk away, but another CASAW man told him to stop talking so much. Legge turned on his heel, lashing out his finger as if it were a saber: "You don't tell me to stop!" he said, his face red, veins bulging. "That's the fuckin' truth! If people don't start listening, somebody else is going to get hurt! We've been talking for four fucking months about safety here! Nobody is listening! There it is in front of your eyes!" He pointed at the newspaper article. "Fuckin' read it!"

The video recorded. The cameras clicked. Instant picture, instant sound bite, instant front-page, top-of-the-newscast story. That night, Legge was on television across Canada. The next day, his picture appeared across the country in newspapers. The photograph of his anger eventually ran in *Time* magazine. Legge's rage was now CASAW's symbol.

When Claudia saw her husband on television that night, she couldn't believe it. She wished Terry had been standing there making some kind of profound statement, yet there he was, emotional, lashing out, crashing like thunder and lightning. But then, that was Terry. That's the way he'd been since they met in high school back in Goose Bay.

She found out from Terry, though, that the quote that had been used—him saying if the media didn't get the truth out, there would be more deaths—was easy to misinterpret. He explained to her that when he said there would be more deaths, he was referring to the numerous death threats the strikers had been getting. If the media didn't report that the blast was an accident and take the heat off the union, Legge told Claudia, he really feared someone would make good on one of the threats.

Still, Legge felt ashamed. He realized he had lost control. His profanity made him cringe. His mother called him up from Labrador. "If I'd have been near you, I would have washed your mouth out with soap," she said, and both of them laughed.

For most of the summer, the Royal Oak managers, line crossers and replacement workers had taken CASAW's abuse silently, but now they went on the offensive. One day after the blast, shift boss Don Moroz was crossing the line in his truck when he noticed striker Sam Pollock giving him a cold stare, the same cold stare Moroz had put up with for months. But now Moroz rolled down his window. "Sam, you're not even worth pissin' on," Moroz said. "Compared to those boys who died inside, none of you boys are worth anything."

Around town CASAW strikers were shouted at on the streets and in the stores. Striker Marvin Tremblett got an anonymous letter saying every CASAW member should be dropped from a helicopter with balls and chains over Great Slave Lake. Tremblett, like many of the CASAW men, refused to accept the abuse, especially if it came from a line crosser.

"Hey, buddy, I can go home at night, and I can sit with my kids and my kids respect me!" he yelled back at one line crosser. "They're proud because I didn't cross the picket line! They know I didn't kill nobody! When they ask me if I killed anybody I can tell them the truth: no! If they ask you, 'Are you a scab?' you cannot tell them no. You got to tell them the truth: yes! You got to live with that the rest of your life. Not me."

The name-calling spread to the schools. Down at the union hall,

Tremblett fumed about an incident where a line crosser's kid had picked on his daughter. "I told the cops if anybody lays a hand on my kids, Dave Grundy will not have to go and investigate. I will walk in and say, 'Here, it's murder.' The person who lays his hands on my kids will pay the price."

Many of the strikers stopped going out to the picket line for a time. The ones that did huddled together, talking, drinking. They were afraid someone would come and blast the shack with a gun.

At a union meeting, one striker mentioned that it would be a good idea to bring in counselors to help the men deal with their grief. At once, striker Roger Warren stood up to protest. "We don't need counseling for dead scabs. You can take your counseling and shove it."

Legge took the brunt of the abuse, getting it on the street and at home. Yellowknife was a small enough town that to have an unlisted number seemed pretentious and rude; almost all the strikers were listed, Legge included. On the telephone, he paid for his TV outburst.

"Are you satisfied now that you've killed nine people?" said one caller.

"No, I'm not satisfied," Legge exploded. "We missed you, asshole!"

But Legge felt sick at heart. He was forty years old, fighting for his job, for his family, and to be called a murderer was too much. One part of him continued to feel terrible about the nine men, but there was no way for him to express it.

After Legge's TV appearance, a few of Claudia's friends came up to her at work.

"God, if there is anything we can do, just let us know," they said.

Claudia wondered why they were sympathizing with her. She hadn't lost her husband. But the hospital social worker also came to her. "Claudia," she said. "If you want to talk to me, I'm here. We can talk about anything."

"If anybody needs to talk, it's Terry, not me," Claudia said.

Claudia tried to fight back any doubts she had about her husband, but his anger only made her more worried that he was somehow involved. She knew that he would never go into the mine and plant such a deadly bomb, but maybe he and the other strikers were trying to blow up something else and it had gone haywire. Maybe it was poor timing. It had to be an accident. Even considering the union's hatred of the scabs, Claudia thought that no one from the union would kill.

Claudia wondered if Terry was going to be in trouble with the RCMP. Heck, if she was a cop she would have arrested Terry just because of how he looked on TV. Claudia reassured herself that he hadn't been down in the mine that night and early morning. She knew he had been at home.

When the RCMP contacted Legge for an interview, Claudia told him he'd better tell them everything he knew. "If you broke the law, tell them what law you broke. It's better than them coming after you for murder."

At home Legge sat and talked with friends or on the telephone, trying to sort through what might have happened. For years he had been telling Claudia about all the unsafe practices in the mine. Now maybe it had caught up to everyone, Claudia thought. She hoped it was an accident. She couldn't see why the RCMP would say what they did, that it was murder. Not even she was prepared to accept that just on the say-so of the Mounties.

Chapter 6

THE
FIRST
SUSPECT

T HE MURDERER left one crucial piece of hard evidence—a set of
footprints in and out of the mine. Constable Myles Mascotto
found the first of the footprints late on the day of the bomb
blast. Mascotto had been assigned to search all the remote entrances to
Giant Mine for signs of forced entry. The first four entrances he
inspected were either locked or covered over with rocks. Mascotto's
fifth stop was the Akaitcho shaft, the same shaft the Cambodian Cowboys had used on their graffiti sortie of June 29, three months back. No
mining had gone on in the Akaitcho area in fifteen years, but the shaft
hadn't been closed over. It was both an emergency escape route and a
ventilation shaft for the fumes of the central blast.

Akaitcho was far from any other building or shaft at the mine. It
was only half a mile from the Ingraham Trail, but it was tucked away
behind a hill. The shaft's black headframe wasn't visible from the road.
All that could be seen was the untouched landscape of ancient
hardrock hills covered with small pine trees, hardy grasses and lichens.
There, a man felt as if he were in the middle of the lonely Arctic, not
just a few miles outside the city.

Inside the headframe a shack had been built to cover the shaft.
Mascotto found the window on the shack open. On the ground outside

the window was a forty-gallon drum. When he inspected the top of the drum, Mascotto discovered a lone footprint in the grime. At once, he sealed off the area.

Corporal Dan Stevely, who had come up that day with Corporal Dale McGowan from Hay River, was sent to study the print. Stevely was an identification expert, an Ident man in RCMP-speak, a specialist in photographing and examining crime scenes, an experienced officer, balding, gray-haired and mustached, with the air of a high school chemistry teacher.

Stevely got to the Akaitcho headframe at 5:00 P.M., seven hours after the blast. A Royal Oak worker opened the locked shack so Stevely could inspect. The floor was sandy loam. The path from the door to a storage closet was well trod. Most footprints in the area had the V-mark of steel-reinforced Royal Oak mining boots. The only other footprints led from the window to the shaft. Clearly someone had climbed on the barrel and walked across the floor to the shaft. The intruder's footprints were more defined and fresher than the V-tracks of Royal Oak boots. The unique print wasn't made by a miner's boot at all; it had a bar-shaped tread, more like a hunting boot. Stevely measured the new footprints and found them to be thirteen inches long. He opened the hinged wood door over the shaft and stared into the darkness.

In the following days, Stevely and other RCMP officers went through the mine, hoping to find more examples of the distinctive Akaitcho footprints. The RCMP also put down a roll of brown wrapping paper at the door to the Yellowknife detachment. When suspects came in to be interviewed, they left behind their prints on the paper. None of them, however, made a perfect match with the Akaitcho print.

The first important tip in the investigation also came on the day of the blast. A longtime gold prospector named Robert Carroll came into the office with a story that he passed on to his old friend RCMP Sergeant Rob O'Brien.

Carroll was a character, a wizened, old-time prospector who hustled for a living on the fringe of the mining business. He told O'Brien that he had been at Nettie's coffee shop that morning, the place where most old-time Yellowknifers gathered for breakfast each day, a dingy but warm restaurant where men kept on their ball caps, old Inuit women drank coffee and smoked, and a sign on the wall read: "Stress:

The confusion created when one's mind overrides the body's basic desire to choke the living shit out of some asshole who desperately needs it."

At about 9:00 A.M., before news of the blast was out, Carroll said he was having coffee when into the restaurant walked an old acquaintance, CASAW striker Roger Warren. Warren scanned the room, hesitated, then walked over to sit at a secluded table. He sat and ate, then got up after a few minutes to pay, but he went to a till that wasn't operating. He stood there for twenty to twenty-five seconds until the waitress finally got his attention. Warren looked very fatigued and stressed. He clearly didn't want to talk to anyone.

After he heard about the blast, Carroll suspected it was sabotage and thought the police should know about Warren's odd behavior. Carroll suspected that Warren knew something was going to happen that morning.

Fear and rumor are the staples of any unsolved murder, but this was especially so with the mass murder at Giant Mine. Not only the CASAW strikers viewed the case through the fuzzy lens of strike-line politics. The Royal Oak men at once assumed the mass murder had been ordered by the union's executive and carried out by one of the Cambodian Cowboys, most likely Al Shearing, the Night Crawler.

From the start, Shearing was also the RCMP's prime suspect, with Tim Bettger, the Bear, at number two. The police had code names for the men, Target One and Target Two, so they could talk about Shearing and Bettger in public without giving anything away. The focus was on these two, but the RCMP officers investigated any person with the right credentials. The murderer had to know how to handle explosives. He had to know Giant's underground; even with a detailed map, it would have been too confusing for a stranger to make his way in and out of the mine. The murderer had to have either worked at Giant in the past or work there now. He was either a Royal Oak manager, a replacement worker, a CASAW line crosser, a former employee of Giant Mine or a member of the striking union. The only way for someone to be eliminated as a suspect was to have a good alibi and, if the Mounties still weren't sure about the man, to take and pass a polygraph test.

The police knew the chances of finding anything of importance at the blast site were small, but the attempt had to be made. The post-blast team arrived from Ottawa on Saturday morning, September 19.

The team was made up of two explosives experts, a forensic chemist, an Ident man and a computer specialist.

Inspector Don Watson and his team had trained for jobs just like this. They regularly blew up houses, cars and airplanes in blind tests to see if they could determine how much explosive and what kind of triggering mechanism had been used. The main problem was that the force and heat of the explosion usually destroyed the components of the bomb. Either they were blasted off into the distance and never found or they were reduced to powder.

Along with damaging the vent shaft doors six hundred feet away, the Giant blast had hurled the eighty-nine-pound steel door of the man-car thirty-four feet. The water that had run through the site had likely washed away some evidence and the chemical residue from the bomb.

Watson was pleased to find that the bacteria-free conditions of the underground kept the bodies fresh; there was no need to move them out too quickly. The team had the luxury of examining the scene without further disruption.

The investigators constructed a grid of three-foot by three-foot squares, branching out from the blast site both north and south, ending where debris could no longer be found. Every clump of dirt in each square was put through a sifter. Anything found was bagged and marked with a grid designation.

After studying the blasted man-car and the area immediately surrounding the blast site, Watson made his first report, noting that the blast came from the side of the tracks, not from within the man-car: "It is unlikely that the explosion occurred by explosives dropped from the top of the man-car. The only logical explanation is that the explosion was deliberately set."

There were no unmanned trains in Giant Mine. Both man-cars and ore cars were pulled and pushed by manned lokis. The murderer would have known the bomb would kill at least one person. The blast was almost certainly murder, not manslaughter, not an accidental killing.

The Yellowknife detachment lacked investigators with the expertise to deal with the case, so a call went out to the RCMP's homicide unit in Edmonton. The Edmonton team, led by Sergeant Al McIntyre, arrived shortly after the post-blast team. McIntyre was a seasoned homicide investigator, but he was a modern manager as well, a team player, a facilitator. He didn't bully or yell; he set an example of uncomplaining diligence and helped his people do their best work. He was forty and had spent his life preparing for this assignment. He had been a sober, serious-minded kid, mechanically inclined, hard working, his father's son. His dad, Don, was an electrician and a perfectionist; if a job called for two wraps of tape, Don McIntyre put three or four just to make sure nothing would go wrong. Al decided to join the RCMP while still in high school. He married his high school sweetheart, Sylvia, and spent the first years of his career in small Saskatchewan and Alberta towns. He was promoted to a plainclothes investigative unit in Calgary. Eleven years back, his first major murder investigation was to hunt for the man or men who had abducted, raped, beaten to death and burned the corpse of a young woman in a small Alberta town. When a likely suspect was picked up, Constable McIntyre and one other officer got the job of interviewing him. The suspect broke down and confessed.

McIntyre went on to be the primary investigator on more than eighty homicides. He was more of a technician than a passionate lawman, a calculating, efficient investigator. He had come to firmly believe in the death penalty, not out of vengeance, but because he saw too many killers who had either killed again or would kill again if they got the chance. They were like missiles with no guidance systems. They had to be knocked out of the air.

McIntyre didn't feel he had to be in on all the big interviews. He saw other men who were better at that than he was. He had come to understand that teamwork was crucial. He was also thorough. He always tried to send five or six investigators to a fresh crime scene, not one or two; if things weren't handled correctly at the start, the investigation would pay for it later.

He had trained as a sharpshooter and negotiator on the force's Emergency Response Team (ERT) for crises such as hostage takings. His role with the ERT had taken him to Yellowknife earlier in the strike. Along with the riot squad, his team had responded to the June 14 riot. When his team had arrested Jim Fournier and James Mager, the two strikers who had assaulted and injured the Pinkerton guard, strikers had pelted the Mounties with rocks.

McIntyre had been on the thirteenth hole of a golf course on September 18 when he got the call to come up to Yellowknife. He brought with him wiretap specialist Bill Farrell, crime analyst Dean Ravelli, assignment officer Dick Bent and investigators Dave Rodwell, John Turgeon and Rod Hamilton. As soon as the Edmonton men walked into the makeshift headquarters on the third floor of the Yellowknife detachment, dozens of officers stopped talking and studied them. Corporal Ravelli scanned the crowd and didn't recognize one face. The attention took him aback. He'd never felt so much pressure in his life.

With the post-blast team, the Yellowknife and Northwest Territories investigators and the Edmonton squad, McIntyre had fifty-three officers to coordinate during the first week. He had never commanded so many men, but he was pleased to see that resources weren't going to be a problem. Whatever he asked for he eventually got, whether it was more investigators from Edmonton, new wiretap machinery or a new $50,000 computer system.

As in any investigation, the first twenty-four hours were crucial, then the next twenty-four, then the next twenty-four. If a murder was to be solved quickly, history showed it would happen within that time. Clues and memories were still fresh in the first seventy-two hours. The murderer's behavior might be erratic.

As soon as he met the new members of his team, McIntyre packed them out the door to do interviews. As much as he could, he paired his experienced men with the raw local officers, preparing them to take over the investigation when the Edmonton men went home. Few of the Territorial Mounties had ever been involved in a murder investigation, let alone one of this magnitude. Few of them had ever taped an interview. Few had seen Special O teams, the observation units responsible for tailing the primary targets, or Special I teams, the groups that broke into the homes of suspects and installed telephone bugs. Only a few had ever developed informants.

While the local officers lacked experience solving major crimes, they were far from the dregs of the force. In fact, the Territories attracted a certain type of ambitious young man and woman. A transfer to the North increased an officer's salary, made it more likely that he or she would be promoted and made it possible to engineer a polar passage, a transfer back to the officer's home province after he or she had completed the mandatory three-year stint. Going north meant young officers wouldn't be stuck working their way up the twenty- or thirty-officer ladder at a midsized detachment, but could run their own show in a northern outpost. In those small towns of Déné, Inuit and whites, the lone Mountie was the only law, the only representative of the Crown. It was a fitting challenge for any hungry young cop.

After his night breaking up street fights, Corporal Dale McGowan reported to the third floor office of the homicide team. Before introducing himself to McIntyre, McGowan watched for a moment, soaking up the feeling of the room, the hum of knowledge and confidence. He was in awe. This was a big city unit. In that moment McGowan saw what made McIntyre tick, how the sergeant was comfortable being the man in the middle, easy with his staff, making rapid-fire decisions, then cracking a joke, nailing someone for the way he or she was dressed.

McGowan hesitated. He was a corporal, a senior rank for a street-level investigator in the force. He worried that McIntyre would give him too big a job, putting him in charge of four or five men. When he did introduce himself, he told McIntyre, "I'm no great hotshot, but I'm a good worker. I'm a horse with a proven track record, but not necessarily in this field. I'm just cannon fodder. You point me, you give me a job, and I'll go do it."

McIntyre laughed, then sent McGowan out to the mine site to join a team of officers interviewing the Royal Oak replacement workers, managers and Pinkerton guards. It was factory interviewing: one man in, another out, starting before breakfast and ending after midnight. The replacement workers were so upset they vibrated. They all understood they had taken a risk coming into Giant, but the blast had completely unhinged most of them. They wanted to fly out of Yellowknife as fast as possible. When McGowan went to the waiting room to call in a new man to interview, dozens of angry, anxious faces glowered at him.

Each replacement worker was asked for a personal history and an alibi, and then about his routines in the mine. The workers talked in the technical terms of their business, which the Mounties had to quickly pick up or they'd never get anywhere. McGowan soon learned the difference between a loki and a scoop, a man-car and a man-cage, shafts and drifts.

He got his most important insight into the crime three days after the blast. He was asked to go down into the mine to inspect the 50-scoop tram, the mine vehicle that shift boss Don Moroz had found out of place on the B-ramp at the door to the 575-drift on the morning of the blast. The RCMP now suspected that the murderer had used the 50-scoop in his escape from the mine. McGowan's job was to sort out what had happened by going into the mine with Moroz and CASAW line crosser Milan Tuma. Tuma had parked the scoop in the 712-scoop shop at 2:45 A.M. on September 18 at the end of his shift.

McGowan changed out of his street clothes in the C-dry, then got into mine coveralls and the necessary safety gear. To get to the 50-scoop tram, the three men had to pass by the blast site; McGowan could see Moroz was unnerved at the thought of returning. Still, Moroz agreed to go, determined to do whatever he could to help the police.

As they waited for the man-cage at the C-shaft, McGowan examined the place. Everything looked old and rusty, in need of a coat of paint at least. He wondered how sturdy the elevator was.

At the 750-drift, the three walked single file down the railway tracks. The tunnel reminded McGowan of the hallway of a dingy apartment. Just then, his lamp went out. It was against mine policy for a man to travel underground without his own lamp, so Moroz returned to the surface to get him a new one. The police officer stood alone with Tuma.

"I'll show you something," Tuma said, then shut off his own light.

The darkness was absolute. McGowan waved his hand in front of his face but could not see it. Even when he had shut his eyes in a dark basement room, he had never experienced such darkness.

Moroz returned with a fresh battery. They continued down the tracks. In the distance they saw the bright lights of the post-blast team's dig at the blast site.

"When we get there, we do not stop," McGowan told Tuma and Moroz. "We do not look around. We continue right through."

At the blast site, workers were digging down to the bedrock and picking through the debris. As they passed, McGowan looked at the pile of dead men. He had been told what to expect, that it was one man on the tracks, eight in the pile, but the sight appalled him, not so much because of what he saw, but because of what he didn't. All that remained was an anonymous pile of twisted limbs and parts of limbs—torsos, heads, shredded clothing, shredded flesh, splintered wood, splintered bones, cracked helmets and the remnants of mining equipment. It was hard to imagine that the shapes had once been human.

McGowan and the two men continued on, investigated the 50-scoop tram, then headed back, again passing by the blast site before heading out the C-shaft. Miners who saw the blast site were haunted by the carnage, especially if one of the anonymous corpses had been a friend. But McGowan saw the corpses as evidence, the victims in a murder investigation. It meant everything for him to see them. It put everything else into perspective. Suddenly all the complaints of the dispute—the self-serving talk of Peggy Witte, CASAW and the townspeople—became meaningless. Only this mattered. This spot, the bomb crater beside the tracks, this blasted man-car, the nine dead men. Who had come down here? That was the only important question. What makes a guy do this? Am I dealing with a total loony?

Asking himself these questions, McGowan felt like a homicide investigator for the first time. He had never aspired to such a job. He had always wanted to be a police officer, but never a big-city cop or a homicide detective. He grew up in Edmonton, but his family had its roots in rural Alberta. His farm cousins always knew the name of the local RCMP officer. They waved to him. He waved back. That's how McGowan saw himself, a community police officer, a small-town guy, a bit of a redneck, no tree hugger, no save-the-world type, just a good guy, helping out, solving problems and keeping the peace on the frontier.

His outlook had been shaped by his father's fatal kidney disease. When McGowan hit his teens, Norm McGowan had to go on dialysis. Norm needed eighteen hours a week on the machine. He had to quit his job. The family set up the basement as a mini-hospital, with a bed, TV, supplies and the dialysis machine. Dale's mother took a course on how to run it. Dale and his three siblings had to change filters, clean up and jab needles into their father's arm. The skin became as hard as wood from all the scar tissue.

Many nights when his friends were out partying, Dale was downstairs with his father, seeing how hard life could be, but also how tough a man could be if only he never got down and kept some humor about him. Norm never complained. At the hospital he always had kind words for the staff.

Norm died from complications while Dale was at the RCMP training depot. In his six months at Regina, McGowan learned the basics of Canadian law, court testimony, report writing, driving skills, shooting, karate, judo, police holds and ground fighting, the hand-to-hand combat where anything goes—blows to the eyes, the nuts, anything, the idea being if an officer is overcome, he's not only in danger himself, but he's endangered everyone else because he has a gun that could be taken away.

McGowan moved on from training to a posting in a rough métis settlement in Saskatchewan, then to a posting in the Alberta oil patch boomtown of Lloydminster. Along the way he learned a few new tricks; he spent nine months on court duty in Lloydminster, where he worked with Crown prosecutors and saw what was needed to convict. The thorough files were always the best. On the street he worked at staying calm, even when walking in on a rape or hurt kids and all he wanted to do was kick the living shit out of the offender.

Seven years back, he and his wife, Sheila, had decided to head north. There were 125 Mounties in the Yukon, 250 in the Northwest Territories. McGowan was sent to Fort Simpson on the Mackenzie River, a town of one thousand, mostly Déné Indians, then to Snow-drift, an alcohol-scarred community of 350 Déné on the southeast shore of Great Slave Lake. It was supposed to be a dry community, but there was lots of home brew made from yeast, raisins, strawberry jam and stick deodorant. They were the sweetest smelling drunks McGowan had ever met. After Snowdrift he went to Inuvik for a year, a hub community with a lot of whites and a lot of partying. McGowan earned his regular salary, plus $13,000 for a northern living allowance. It wasn't much when milk was $6 a liter, beer was $50 a case and a turkey was $75.

McGowan was promoted to corporal and sent to Baker Lake, an inland Inuit community in the Eastern Arctic. Baker Lake was the most traditional of the communities McGowan had lived in and the most pro-police. The Inuit still had clear memories of the RCMP help-ing avert starvation by bringing in food when the caribou hunt was bad. McGowan learned, however, that Inuit sexual mores were differ-ent here. It wasn't far back in the life of the community that there had been sex slaves. The village leaders carried themselves like the alpha males of a wolf pack. Men thought nothing of sharing their wives. *Agak,* the kissing of an infant's genitals, was not considered abnormal. Sexual assault was a problem in the town. Both a Catholic and an Anglican priest had been jailed. The town did have its own justice sys-tem where bad actors were shunned. Sometimes six men would go hunting and build two igloos, one for five men, and another for the one who had done wrong. In the middle of the night, the five would kill the other with guns and spears. The Inuit elders at Baker Lake still believed in walking off into a blizzard when they were no longer of any use.

In July 1992, McGowan was again transferred, this time to the plainclothes investigative unit at Hay River, across Great Slave Lake from Yellowknife. He and Sheila and their three kids had just bought a home and settled when the murderous blast occurred in Yellowknife.

McGowan's fear in the Giant investigation, the fear of every northern officer on the case, was that he would fail to measure up. For the Edmonton officers, however, the case was a chance to use skills they had been building for years. They were glad for the opportunity and confident they could solve the crime. The work gave all the Mounties the feeling they were players in an important story. It quickly became clear that this investigation was going to be the great challenge of each officer's life.

Inspector Don Watson's post-blast team worked at the bomb site for six days. In all, eighty-two yards of the 750-drift were scoured for clues. The RCMP team bagged five thousand artifacts from the site. They dug down to the bedrock at ground zero, but they found no trace of a tripping mechanism. For all the police knew the bomb could have been set off by a timer or by radio control, but explosives expert Jean-Yves Vermette decided it had most likely been activated by a trip wire of some type. The team found shreds of an AMEX bag and a piece of plastic with the letters *AFRA* on them, which had likely come from the word *MAGNAFRAC,* a type of stick powder used in the mine. This confirmed that the murderer had likely used both types of explosives.

The findings also included an important clue, an expended DCD blasting cap, found 118 feet north of the blast sight. Vermette guessed that the murderer might have used this DCD cap in a test blast, maybe to see if his batteries had sufficient power to fire a cap, which in turn would ignite the stick powder and AMEX. One other expended DCD cap was found near ground zero. It could have been the cap used in the actual bomb or maybe in a second test.

The investigators tried to see if it was possible to detonate AMEX by running a man-car over a bag. They loaded twenty-five hundred pounds of ballast into a man-car and gave it a go, but had no luck. Later they dropped a bag of AMEX eight feet to see if it would blow. It didn't. They added stick powder and dropped it. Still no blast. They added a blasting cap. Still nothing. They tried the entire series again, this time dropping the explosives from twenty-three feet. Nothing. The explosives weren't sensitive to shock. A derailment wouldn't detonate them. They had to be ignited by a blasting cap, at least one stick of powder and an electrical charge.

After a few more tests, Watson concluded in his report to McIntyre that the blast had most likely been set with two bags of AMEX, at least one stick of powder, a blasting cap and an explosive detonating cord called B-line. Wood fragments had been blasted into the hardrock ceiling above the site, leading Watson to conclude that the bomb had been covered up with wood.

The next step in the RCMP's investigation was to focus on the union. There were more than 150 remaining CASAW men and all of them were suspects. It was such a large number that the officers had trouble remembering the names of even the prime suspects. Corporal Dave Rodwell kept referring to Tim Bettger as Bittger and Bittinger and Battinger.

Corporal Ravelli, the crime analyst, studied the old strike files. His job was to take the old information and blend it with the new, turning it into what he called product—an easy-to-read, easy-to-understand, continuously updated chronological report on the case. As well as keeping everyone abreast of the latest developments, Ravelli had to study the material, looking for trends and links, trying to figure out what step the investigators should take next. In the first few days the list of murder suspects changed hourly. The flow of information was ten times faster than any other investigation Ravelli had worked on, but he'd never seen such hunger for that information either. McIntyre had to send reports to Ottawa, Edmonton and other RCMP detachments, as well as to every level of Canadian government—local, territorial, provincial and national. Every politician with a link to Yellowknife wanted the matter resolved as quickly as possible. The blast was already having fallout as politicians had to admit that they had been warned about the potential for this kind of thing, but hadn't been able to do anything about it.

McIntyre left much of the public relations work to Sergeant Dave Grundy, the information officer and media spokesperson. Because Grundy became the face of the investigation, the CASAW strikers came to hate Grundy the most.

McIntyre assigned Constable Bill Farrell to study the history of the strike to see if there was any link between previous crimes and the September 18 blast. After reading hundreds of pages of files, Farrell decided there indeed was a strong connection. His next task was to start getting together the paperwork for a Part Six, an application to bug the home telephones of thirty men and women connected to the union.

Some union men had suspected their phones were being tapped from the start of the strike. They were wrong. It was not so easy for the RCMP to get a wiretap authorization. Courts viewed the measure as an infringement on the right to privacy. Wiretaps were only permitted if the police had no other way to solve a crime.

Farrell believed a wiretap was justified in this case because of the nature of the crime. It was such a heinous act that it was impossible to imagine the murderer would come to the Mounties and admit he'd done it, not unless the police had something on him. Whoever set this bomb and the previous bombs at the mine wouldn't be running around bragging, but they might make a reference to the crimes at some point on the telephone, which would help crack the case.

A wiretap hadn't been authorized in Yellowknife in twelve years. There was no wiretap room, no trained monitors and no recording machines. No local Crown prosecutor even knew how to obtain a Part Six authorization. Farrell had to call up the Department of Justice in Ottawa to get help. Two prosecutors told Farrell that he had gone overboard in his request, that he couldn't prove his charges against the listed people. Farrell told them he didn't have to prove the charges, he just had to have a theory about the case that would lead to charges. Here, the theory was one of escalating violence. It became known around the office as the Progression Theory. It was straightforward: Al Shearing, Tim Bettger and numerous other strikers were part of a militant faction in CASAW. The police had no solid evidence, but they'd heard rumors that Bettger and Shearing were involved in the June 29 graffiti break-in, the July 22 satellite disk explosion and the September 2 vent shaft blast. They had started out throwing rocks and knocking over power poles, but the RCMP believed that Shearing and Bettger soon got angrier and bolder, setting off bigger and bigger explosions, until one or both of them decided to set the September 18 blast.

The Ottawa prosecutors didn't buy it, telling Farrell it seemed like he was on a fishing expedition.

"Fuck you," Farrell told them. "You're wrong."

He then called down to the Department of Justice in Edmonton, and the initial round of wiretaps was approved nine days after the blast. The RCMP's Special I operatives then broke into the strikers' homes and wired up the telephone bugs. At first the bugs were faulty. The CASAW strikers started to hear odd clicking noises on their lines. The problem was solved only after Farrell ordered new bugs from the U.S. Federal Bureau of Investigation.

The street-level investigators went to work interviewing the strikers, focusing on those men who were viewed as suspects or had been working the night shift on the picket line on September 18. The Mounties wanted to know what each striker was wearing and what he did that night, as well as what he had seen others wearing and doing.

One of those seemingly routine interviews was conducted on September 25, one week after the blast, between Constable Nancy Defer and CASAW striker Roger Warren. From her time working the strike line, Defer knew Warren wasn't one of the union hotheads, though he had been fired during the strike for participating in the June 14 riot.

Some of the union men were already acting hostile in their interviews, but Warren struck Defer as being the opposite. In fact, he seemed more open and honest than any of the other CASAW men Defer had interviewed. He was an older gentleman who appeared to have accepted the fact that something had gone very wrong, that this was no accident. He went out of his way to help out and even offered one interesting bit of information.

Warren wasn't physically imposing, just normal height and build. He had sharp features, a prominent beak of a nose, deep-set eyes, black, thick eyebrows and graying hair, combed back, bald on top. He was forty-eight and told Defer he had been at Giant for thirteen years. He mentioned he had seen a previous disaster at Giant. In 1987, he was one of the first men on the scene after an accidental blast that killed one man and blinded another, Warren's own partner Danny Mino. Defer noticed that Warren had tears in his eyes as he recalled the accident.

Warren said that on September 18 he caught a ride out to the strike line just after midnight with striker Max Dillman. Dillman dropped him off at gate six, the picket station at the north end of the strike line on the Ingraham Trail. Then Warren talked for an hour with six other strikers: Dave Madsen, Frank Woods, Brian Drover, Alex Mikus, Tom Krahn and another man named Alex. He told Defer he had on a khaki parka, denim coveralls, a Western-style shirt and green rubber boots.

Around 1:30 A.M., Warren said he headed out for a walk on the Ingraham Trail. It was a nice night, not too cold or windy. He was with Tom Krahn, going south toward Yellowknife. Warren told Krahn he'd join him shortly, but first he had to take a leak.

He started walking, then stopped to have a Pepsi and an Eatmore bar. Just then, he saw something odd—two shadowy figures walking in a businesslike manner on Giant Mine property back toward gate six.

Warren said he thought the two shadowy men might be Pinkerton guards, but he wasn't sure. They wore dark coveralls and hats with no peaks, unlike the ones the Pinkertons wore. "They were going at a nice clip," Warren said, "at a regular, pretty quick walk. They weren't trying to be surreptitious or nothing."

Defer found the information interesting. If these two men were CASAW strikers, they were on mine property when they shouldn't have been, and they were heading in the direction of Akaitcho, where the RCMP already knew the murderer had most likely entered the mine.

Defer went to get a map so Warren could mark where he had seen the two men.

"I never really made too much about it," he said. "I should have thought more, now that I think of it. . . . After all this, they could have been doing something like that [like murder]."

Warren described how he had continued walking. He noticed union leader Bill Schram, in jeans and his customary red jacket, either sleeping or reading at the gate five striker station. Warren said Schram didn't notice him. He said he kept walking until he got to picket gate three at the main entrance to Giant, near the C-dry, the headframe and the administration building.

Warren said he got on a bus owned by the strikers sometime after 2:00 A.M. He said the other union men, Dave Madsen, Leo Lachowski and Kelly Rhodes, were talking and sleeping. He said he talked with Kelly Rhodes. "Things were lookin' a little bit up for us," Warren told Defer. "These politicians were getting interested. That's one thing I remember mentioning to Kelly."

Warren said he and Rhodes fueled up a little Honda generator, then he went to sleep, waking up at about 5:00 A.M. His legs were a bit cramped from sleeping on the bus seat. None of the other men were up. He left the bus, walking back down the Ingraham Trail toward gate six.

"I went right straight there, basically, except the one time that I jumped down in the ditch there and got wet," Warren said, explaining to Defer that he heard a vehicle coming and he feared it was the Pinkertons. "I figured if they caught a guy like me out in the middle of nowhere, I might get myself hurt. Anyways, I hid in the ditch. I got a little wet in the process. Wet foot and I wet my parka and that and my knees."

Then, Warren told Defer, he kept walking along the highway, but he headed past gate six, carrying on because he saw a truck parked on a road on mine property with its parking lights on. He thought something might be up. He took a look, then decided to head back to gate six. Just then a truck came down the Ingraham Trail. It slowed down as it passed him. "He just took a couple of glances at me," Warren said, adding that he thought the driver was a Pinkerton security guard.

When he got back to gate six, Warren said he met strikers Brian Drover and Frank Woods. He recalled maybe mentioning to Drover something about the two shadowy men. After that, Warren said he hung around the line for another couple hours, then went home at about 8:00 A.M. His daughter asked him to drive her to work and he obliged. He then drove back out to the picket line and later talked to striker Terry Coe at gate six, again mentioning the two shadowy men.

"Can you think of anything else unusual that happened that night, Roger?" Defer asked.

"No. It was just calm. It was really quiet. That is the only thing that struck me as strange. It was really quiet, and there was very little traffic, so that's really about it. Probably fifty things I missed, but that's what I can remember."

The following day at the regular morning RCMP briefing, Defer heard that the man in the truck who had slowed down as he passed Warren on the Ingraham Trail at 6:00 A.M. was most likely Brian Broda, the mine's ore supervisor. Broda had been interviewed by Constable John Turgeron. Broda said that around 6:00 A.M. he saw a man walking on the shoulder of the Ingraham Trail. As he approached, he slowed his vehicle directly beside this person, but the man raised his hand to cover his face. Broda's description generally fit Roger Warren:

5'11", 180 pounds, no glasses, clean-shaven, wearing a khaki-colored camouflage outfit, a hat and no gloves.

Later that day, Defer called up Warren to ask for another interview. Warren seemed eager. "I'm glad you called," he told her. "I got some more information."

At the second interview, Warren told Defer that he and Rhodes hadn't refueled the Honda generator that night after all, that he had mixed things up with another night. Defer asked him about the truck driving by at 6:00 A.M. "When the truck came up behind, did you react in any way? Physically."

"I don't know. I can't really remember. It's quite possible 'cause the guy startled me. I mean, you're walking along there. There's a good chance I jumped."

"Did you ever bring your hands up to your face when the vehicle was going by?"

Warren said he had bad sinuses and could have been picking his nose. "My wife's always giving me hell for pulling on my nose and that."

"Did you in any way try to hide your face from the person who was driving by?"

"No, not intentionally."

Warren went on to describe what he did for the rest of the morning of September 18 in more detail, saying that when he headed back to the picket line after dropping off his daughter for work, he made a tour of the mine property on the Ingraham Trail. He noticed his car wasn't running so well so he pulled over to check his engine. After fixing the problem, he went to Nettie's for breakfast and then back out to the picket line, where he talked to striker Terry Coe.

After the second interview, Warren walked out on good terms with the Mounties. Indeed, Defer thought he might be a key Crown witness because of his sighting of the two shadowy men on mine property at 2:00 A.M. Such tips fueled the investigation, even if they weren't directly about the early morning of September 18. If the Progression Theory was correct, any information about any of the crimes committed by the Cambodian Cowboys, no matter how insignificant, could give the RCMP a better idea about the way Al Shearing, Tim Bettger and any other CASAW activists operated. It would also help to put pressure on the strikers.

Many strikers told the RCMP as much as they knew in their first interview, but others refused to cooperate. The investigators found themselves running up against CASAW's solidarity. The men had pulled together for months. Many of the hardcore strikers felt any admission to the RCMP would weaken the union's position. Already union president Harry Seeton was accusing the RCMP of harassing his men.

Some of the interviews were confrontational. Seeton had instructed his men to talk to the RCMP, but the Mounties could not convince many of the strikers that a murder had been committed, let alone that a striker might have been involved.

Many of the strikers wanted to tape their police interviews, but the Mounties feared the strikers would rush back to the union hall and play the tape, perhaps giving the murderer crucial information. Still, the investigators didn't dare ask the union executive members to put away their tape recorders. Seeton made his tape even though the Mounties offered to give him a transcript. He didn't trust them to give him an unedited version. He thought if the cops got frustrated and started yelling, they would cut out that segment.

In his interview, Seeton said he knew nothing about the blast. He said he was at the strike line until 1:00 A.M. on September 18, then drove Tim Bettger to the Polar Bowl tavern. He returned home himself, then had a snack, watched some TV and went to bed. He got up at 7:00 A.M. and went to the union hall, where he later learned of the blast. The blast was an accident, Seeton contended. Earlier explosions at the mine had likely been set by the Pinkertons or the replacement workers to make the union look bad.

Many of the strikers were full of bravado with the Mounties, every second word a "fuck" or a "goddamn." To get what they needed, the Mounties challenged them. Deprogramming, Corporal McGowan called it, peeling away the propaganda and rhetoric of the strike.

McGowan's own father had been a train engineer and a proud member of the Brotherhood of Locomotive Engineers. McGowan thought there was a place for a union, otherwise the capitalists would overrun things. But McGowan also thought unions had become too powerful and had come to protect a lot of lazy workers. His politics weren't that far off what many CASAW men believed, but McGowan still found himself quarreling with them. In a six-hour interview, he often spent the first two hours doing nothing more than deprogramming. He had to get them to focus on why they were sitting there: Did they understand what had happened, that one or more men had gone into that mine and set up a murderous booby trap? Did they know anything about it? Were they involved?

McGowan often made progress with a man only to find the striker suddenly slipping back into the unreality of the union's denial: "It was an accident."

"Hold it," McGowan shot back. Then he went through the evidence, the eyewitness accounts from miners like George Samardzija that no explosives had gone on the man-car, the fact that the blast came from beside the tracks, not from within the man-car, the fact that it was impossible to ignite AMEX in this manner, that the explosive was far too stable, that it had never happened before at any mine anywhere.

"Oh well," the striker would say, "they deserved it anyway. If they hadn't crossed the line, they'd be alive today."

"Hold it," McGowan shot back again. "This wasn't a little strike with some lofty ideals and we're going to take care of the scabs. This was the murder of nine people, not only nine people, but people who stood shoulder to shoulder with you and fought for that same cause, but for whatever reason, for family reasons or personal reasons, they made a personal choice to go back in there."

"Oh yeah, well, if Miss Piggy didn't bring in the scabs it wouldn't have happened."

"Hold it," McGowan said a third time. "You say you're a man, but you sound like some Nazi. You sound like one of those people who followed Adolf Hitler. But don't you think maybe today they look back and they think they did wrong? That's where I want you to put yourself. Get ahold of the big picture here. These men were human, not subhuman. They didn't deserve death."

While McGowan pushed them hard with his rhetoric, he was careful about what he said, never giving out a bit of evidence, always taking in as much as he could. Always in his head was the thought: This could be the guy. McGowan feared that one mental lapse could blow the case out of court on a technicality.

The Yellowknife officers had grown skins as thick as polar bears after the summer of abuse and mistrust on the strike line. But the Edmonton investigators had little patience with any refusal to talk. They didn't care about the strike, and they were used to people cooperating with them when it came to a crime as malignant as murder. The investigators had a word for the least cooperative CASAW men: knot-heads.

Relations between the union and the police were set back when an RCMP secretary printed up business cards for the newly formed homi-cide task force. It was customary to name a task force after the place where the crime occurred, so the secretary wrote "Royal Oak Task Force" on the first batch. When the union men saw the cards they laughed and scoffed, saying it only confirmed that the Mounties were working for Royal Oak. The RCMP quickly changed the official name to the Giant Mine Task Force, but the team ended up referring to itself simply as the Homicide Task Force.

The strikers constantly threw it at the investigators that they were working for Peggy Witte or Royal Oak or the government or the scabs. Constable Farrell came up with a reply to that statement, which many of the Mounties started to use in interviews: We are working for the nine dead men and nobody else.

Farrell told the strikers he had no hidden agenda. He wasn't out to prolong the strike, prove an accident was a murder or pin it on an inno-cent man. Farrell always wondered if the hate directed at him was just hollow rhetoric or if the strikers really meant some of the harsh things they were saying.

Corporal Ravelli had never seen such hatred for the police. Ravelli feared for his safety. He couldn't shake the thought that he would walk out the back door of the detachment one night and trigger a trip wire. He didn't trust anyone outside the third-floor task force office. He never went out socially except with other Mounties. One night they were having dinner in a nice restaurant when a wife of a striker came up and started screaming at them that they were all murderers. Ravelli asked the manager to have her removed, but he wouldn't. The Moun-ties had to phone in a complaint to get a uniformed officer to take her away.

Watch your back, was the word at the detachment. Don't go out alone.

All the Mounties took to parking their vehicles in lighted, well-used areas. Ravelli never went anywhere without his gun. He knew he was sometimes followed as he walked to his room a few blocks away in the Explorer Hotel. He was cautious about what he left out in his room. He knew some of the chamber maids were wives and girlfriends of the miners, and he feared they might snoop through his stuff.

The local officers worried about their homes. Constable Randy McBride always made sure to get up first and check his doors. He didn't want his wife to walk into some kind of tripping mechanism.

Sergeant McIntyre worried about the plainclothes men who were confronting the strikers day after day. One of them could very easily say the wrong thing to the murderer. If the man had killed once, what was to stop him now?

At the end of the day, each officer was drained. They had a nonstop diet of head-banging interviews, one in the morning, one in the afternoon, another after dinner. Other than the morning briefing, dinner was the only time the team got together. They tried to pick one restaurant and book a table for ten or fifteen, laugh, talk, eat, then get back at it. At 11:00 P.M., after the last interview or paperwork at the office, the out-of-town Mounties went back to the Explorer, the finest and priciest hotel in Yellowknife. The Mounties set up a floating bar, with four or five 26ers, pop, cheezies, chips. The bar moved from room to room. Afterward, the men hit the pillow and were out for the night, the adrenaline turned off like a tap.

To get away from it, Bill Farrell started going down to the Woolco to buy ties. He'd take his time, checking out each tie, always buying a few. It was mindless, but it relaxed him. His toughest moment came when the post-blast team was trying to figure out what type of ignition device had been used for the blast. McIntyre realized that no one had searched through the body parts for remnants of the trigger. The identifiable parts of the nine bodies had been released for burial, so Farrell, McIntyre and an Ident officer caught a flight to Edmonton where the unmatched body parts were stored. Five large pails were placed on a table. Farrell and McIntyre spent the day going through the bits of hair, flesh and bone. They found nothing.

A little dark humor might have helped Farrell and the other investigators, but on this case every officer noticed it was completely absent. Dale McGowan couldn't figure it out at first. Dark humor had been a part of his job since training school when he was shown pictures of corpses to see if he could handle it. Early in his career he had come upon a fatal traffic accident where a man with the surname Ratt had died. A more senior officer kicked the corpse, then in his best gangster imitation, sneered, "I told you you were going to get it, you dirty rat."

The comment upset him at first, but McGowan had since come to understand the humor. Yes, he was embarrassed to repeat the jokes later, but anyone who was there, who had to deal with gruesome death, knew it wasn't making fun—it was a way to keep doing the job.

No one made jokes about the nine dead miners, however. It was because of the magnitude of the crime, McGowan decided, but it was also because everyone knew that these guys got it dirty. Those who had crossed the line knew they were running a risk. They thought they might get punched out at the OK Economy grocery store, or they might get their homes vandalized. But nobody deserved to be stabbed in the back in the dark by a cowardly murderer.

The RCMP's initial list of prime suspects consisted of Shearing, Bettger and men who had been closely associated with the two strikers, such as miner Gord Kendall. The police knew Kendall was a radical, and he was known to have shown off photographs of the June 29 graffiti sortie, which he had helped organize. He was a heavy smoker and drinker, but still able to work as a miner. In his interview with the RCMP, Kendall shook when he first started talking, but he slowly calmed down. He handed over his photographs of the graffiti mission and said Shearing, Bettger and another miner, Art St. Ammand, were responsible for spray painting the 712-scoop shop. It was the first solid evidence the police had about their prime suspects breaking into Akaitcho, taking the same route that the murderer later took.

Kendall told the police that he feared that the men who had been in on the graffiti sortie—Shearing, Bettger, St. Ammand and driver Luc Normandin—were also involved in the murders. He told the Mounties that Normandin was the weak link. He said he'd seen Normandin sitting alone on the morning of the blast, looking worried and very scared. Kendall also told the Mounties that he feared retaliation if anyone found out what he had said to them.

Farrell took on the first interview with Tim Bettger, Target Two. Through the week, the RCMP's Special O surveillance teams had seen him, Kendall and Shearing meeting in Bettger's truck, talking over matters. Farrell's initial research told him Bettger was a good family man, a decent guy in many ways, but during the strike he had transformed into the fearsome Bear, a leader of the CASAW radicals.

Bettger knew that the Royal Oak faction and even other strikers were likely blaming him for the murders. When he came in to be interviewed, the first thing he asked Farrell was whether he had been fingered by a couple dozen people. As for his alibi, he told Farrell he'd been out at the strike line until midnight on September 17, then Harry Seeton drove him to the union hall. Striker Marvin Tremblett drove him home from there around 1:30 A.M. He watched TV until 3:30 A.M., then went to bed and slept until 10:00 A.M. He said his wife, Izzie, could confirm his whereabouts.

Bettger told Farrell he had become much more involved in the strike after the company had fired him. He denied that he had ever used explosives during the strike or that he had entered the mine illegally.

Farrell asked about the murder victims.

"I have trouble finding grief for these dead men," Bettger said. "The minute they turned scab I wrote them off anyway."

Farrell was taken aback by the interview. He wasn't prepared for the hostility that came from Bettger. This guy was angry enough that he could have done it, Farrell thought.

When Corporal Dick Bent, the RCMP's box man, or assignment officer, pulled out Al Shearing's file, Corporal Al McCambridge of Inuvik asked for it and got it despite being a northern officer with no experience as a homicide investigator. In the first ten days of the investigation, McCambridge had worked with McGowan and the others interviewing replacement workers and strikers. McIntyre quickly became impressed by McCambridge's hustle. If he gave the corporal a task, it was done as well and as fast as any of the Edmonton men could do it.

Al McCambridge had a pencil-thin build, 5'9", 140 pounds. He had never been able to get by with brawn, but he'd learned that his ambition and work ethic could make up for a lot. He was full of insecurities about failing, but he was also driven to succeed, which is why he wanted the chance at Shearing.

From strike-line reports, McCambridge read that on September 11, seven days before the blast, Shearing had got into a fight with Pinkerton security guard Edward Zembrycki, who went to the police. Zembrycki accused Shearing of throwing a long piece of wood at him in the parking lot of the OK Economy grocery store. The wood hit his elbow and his car door. When Shearing was arrested at the mine's main gate, he was found with a camouflage balaclava, surgical tubing for a sling- shot, pepper spray, bear bangers (loud explosives used to scare off bears), pliers, surgical gloves and a rifle clip containing five .22 caliber shells. He was sent to jail, then released on the afternoon of September 17, hours before the murderer went into the mine to set the blast.

Shearing agreed to come in to talk to the RCMP on September 28. McCambridge's main goal was to let Shearing talk and keep his own mouth shut. He wanted to give Shearing a chance to tell the truth if he was innocent, but he also wanted to get information that could later be checked. If Shearing had committed murder, he might give something away that McCambridge could use to hang him.

McCambridge had never met Shearing before. He saw that the miner was built much like himself, small and wiry. Shearing had on his jacket from Northwest Territories mine rescue. McCambridge was assisted in the interview by Constable Myles Mascotto. They started by asking Shearing about his background. Shearing said he was divorced with two kids, a son, Barry, who was twenty-one and not up to much yet, and a twenty-four-year-old daughter, Tammy, who was married with two kids. He said he was born in 1947 in Lewisport, Newfound- land. His dad was in the merchant marine. His mom was a drinker. She sometimes abandoned her kids, and they were all taken away. Shearing said he'd been in foster homes since he was nine months old. There were problems in his first home, but the second one was more stable. He stayed in school until grade eight, then went to work in the mines of Ontario in 1964. He worked as an underground mechanic in Timmins for eleven years. After he and his wife broke up, he came to Yellowknife, about fifteen years back.

"I was fighting for custody of my kids," Shearing told the cops. "It took me five years to finally get custody. Actually I got custody when I was up here."

"You did?" McCambridge asked.

"Yes, I was one of the five percent," Shearing said, meaning that he was one of five percent of divorced fathers who get custody of their children, a fact that made him proud.

At Giant Mine, Shearing said he worked on machinery all over the place, including a weekly check on a water pump at 738. To get to the pump, Shearing said he went down the C-shaft elevator, then took a loki down the 750-drift toward Akaitcho. The pump was about halfway to the remote ventilation shaft.

Shearing told McCambridge he'd gone down the ladders at Akaitcho on only a few occasions, but that was fifteen years ago. "I'd lose my way in there now. I wouldn't even know how to get around."

Shearing also said he had no explosives ticket and had never worked with explosives. Only when McCambridge asked Shearing about his mine rescue work did he become talkative. He said a man had to be resourceful and a decision maker. He was lucky, he said, because he wasn't afraid of heights. His team had twice won the Northwest Territories mine rescue competition and gone on to the nationals, finishing second one year, tying for first the other.

Shearing said he made $23.43 an hour, thirty cents an hour more if he was underground. It worked out to $58,000 a year before overtime, but Shearing said he was called out four or five times a week at night to fix something. In 1991, Shearing made $84,000. In the four months before the strike, he made $30,000.

"As a result of this strike how is your financial situation?" McCambridge asked.

"Shits."

The first tape came to an end. After McCambridge put in a new one, he switched gears in the interview, asking Shearing what he believed had caused the September 18 blast.

Shearing gave McCambridge the union's standard line that the blast was an accident. The miners were carrying AMEX, B-line and blasting caps, and when the man-car derailed, the explosives somehow detonated.

McCambridge asked if Shearing knew any of the dead men. Shearing said he knew Chris Neill, Joe Pandev, Spanky Riggs, David Vodnoski and Vern Fullowka from the picket line. He and Riggs used to go to the Elks Club or to the Right Spot stripper bar, which Shearing called the Wet Spot.

Shearing said he was a loner. He used to hang out with Terry Legge until Legge stopped drinking, but now he was closest to a few of his workmates.

McCambridge next asked about his alibi. Shearing said his latest court order stipulated he turn in his firearms and camouflage gear. At 6:00 P.M. on September 17, after he got out of jail, he said he went to the courthouse to hand over a black powder gun, two shotguns, cans of black powder and camouflage pants. Afterward, he went to the Polar Bowl, had a few beers and smokes and talked with striker Joe Ranger and a group of friends until about 11:00 P.M. Ranger walked him and Shearing's wife, Kara, home to their apartment. Shearing said he had a cigarette and a coffee, then went to bed at midnight. He got up at 7:00 A.M. Just before 9:00 A.M., he walked Kara to work, then went down to the union hall. When he heard about the blast, he tried to organize a mine rescue team.

McCambridge decided to test how honest Shearing was going to be. The Mountie wanted to push a button, as the investigators said, confront him with something the police already knew about his criminal activity. "When was the last time that you were down on the 750-level?"

"Uh, the last time I was on the 750-level?"

"Honestly."

"Honestly, yeah, um, let me see, it was two weeks, maybe three weeks before the strike that I was down there."

McCambridge knew from Kendall's information about the graffiti mission that this was a lie. A moment later he asked, "Have you ever thought about doing anything like this blast?"

"I've never been in trouble with the law in my life now, except for this strike here; only one time for not blowing on a breathalyzer. But besides this strike here, I never had nothing, and that's the way I want to be."

"Al, are you responsible for the murders of these men?"

"No. No. I hate to be even considered to be one that would do anything like this."

McCambridge next asked Shearing if someone had a reason for murder, what it might be.

"I don't know. Discredit the union, I suppose. That's the only reason, I would think."

"When the police find out who set the bomb, what do you think should happen to that person?"

"I think whatever the system, action should be taken up, and he should be castrated."

"Why do you think that?"

"Well, there is no need, like you say, for anybody to commit murder of nine people."

When McCambridge pressed Shearing on who might have set the bomb, he said that the Pinkertons had had the best opportunity. One rumor around the union hall was that a float plane took off from the dock at Giant property on Yellowknife Bay about fifteen minutes after the blast.

"Our problem, Al, is that with what you told us today, we have reason to believe that you are not being fully honest with us," McCambridge said.

"Why is that?"

"Well, we just have reason to believe that. There are some things that you told us here that we know aren't true."

"That's your prerogative."

"I'm just wondering, like, why would you want to hide anything?"

"What? I'm not hiding anything."

"You've never been down in the mine since the strike was on?"

"No."

"Never?"

"Never. Like I said, the last time I was down there was maybe two or three weeks before the strike."

"And that was the last time?"

"That was the last time."

Shearing said it would take at least six hours for someone to go down from Akaitcho to the blast site. If he'd done it, he said he wouldn't pick the 750 area because it was too hard to get to.

"Would you pick underground or above ground?" McCambridge asked.

"I wouldn't pick any of those 'cause I wouldn't do it."

Shearing went on to say he couldn't see anyone else in the union doing it either. If he had a number one suspect, it would be Peggy Witte.

"Why's that?"

"If she did want to get rid of the union, this would be a good way of doing it. . . . I mean, I've heard so many rumors about her, and we've done a lot of research on this woman—we have to because we have to try and find out what kind of woman we are fighting—and I would not put nothing past this woman."

If the September 18 blast was an accident, Royal Oak's shares would go down, Shearing said. If it was deliberately set, however, the shares would stay right where they were.

"I take it you are a very strong union supporter," McCambridge said.

"I wouldn't say I'm a strong supporter. I'm just strong in what I believe."

"And what exactly do you believe in?"

"I did vote for the strike. . . . I can't see myself taking these concessions on safety tours. . . . You're trying to make this thing safer, and they're trying to take this stuff away from us."

Shearing told McCambridge he didn't mind the men crossing the line because he had expected it. At the start of the strike, the union executive figured about eighteen to twenty percent of the men would cross. The only one of the dead men he said he felt sorry for was Joe Pandev. "I gotta feel sorry for him because he had that ten months until he retired, and I would not take that away from him. Go ahead and do it."

Shearing told the Mounties he'd be one of the last ten men from the union to ever cross the line. McCambridge asked who the other nine would be.

"Terry Legge would be one that wouldn't go across. I'd say the executive—Harry Seeton, Bob Kosta, Rick Cassidy, Rob Wells, Luc Normandin. There's actually about eighty to eighty-six people that would never cross that line. The rest just might."

Shearing said he hoped the RCMP would get some answers. "When you walk down the street it's 'There's a CASAW murderer.' You know, that don't feel very good."

Mascotto confronted Shearing with the idea that a lone wolf from the union might have done the crime.

"It could be," Shearing admitted. "There might be a maniac and you don't really know."

"Someone in this room could be a murderer," Mascotto said.

"No, I don't think so. No."

"See . . . the problem we're facing, Al, is that murderers don't have murderer written on their foreheads."

"You mentioned Terry Legge," McCambridge said. "When he gets drinking, he goes off the handle. What about him?"

"Yeah, but he's totally given it up for the last four or five years. He's never touched a drop," Shearing said, a smile coming to him.

McCambridge asked about it, and Shearing recalled seeing Legge on the news after the RCMP said the blast was murder. "He just blew off the handle and about ten minutes later, you know, that was it. You know, he just has to get it off his chest. That's Terry."

Shearing said the guys at the union hall had been sitting around for hours on end talking about what might have happened. One scenario was that maybe somebody had set something, but it wasn't supposed to hurt anybody. "But now, all of a sudden, you find out there is nine people dead and he says, 'Holy shit, what did I do?'"

Before Shearing left, McCambridge tried to convince him to submit to a polygraph lie detector test: "If I had the RCMP on my ass, okay, talking to me, I'd want to be eliminated. Okay, 'cause I don't need the hassle."

While he had no objections to the test, Shearing said he wanted a lawyer in the room and he only wanted to be questioned about the September 18 bomb. "Ask me if I done it under a polygraph and you'll get a negative reading."

Shearing left the interview, saying he'd call McCambridge or Mascotto the next day to set up a time for the lie detector test.

When he talked to a lawyer, however, Shearing was advised not to take the test. A few weeks later at the union hall, Shearing was overheard giving his advice on how to deal with the RCMP's requests for polygraph tests: "Tell them to go fuck themselves."

Chapter 7

POISON

Tracey Neill's parents, Ron and Roseanne Quintal, arrived at the Yellowknife airport late on September 18. Ron was appalled and astonished when he walked into Tracey's house and saw the video cameras in the living room and the other security devices.

"What the hell?" he shook his head. "You guys have been living like this?"

Tracey started to put the equipment away, but her mom told her to stop because they still might be in danger.

"No," Ron said. "We're taking it all down."

Tracey felt disoriented. After Jim O'Neil had confirmed that Chris was dead, she was only vaguely aware of the different people coming and going. Someone brought food. Someone else came to take Koni, the dog. Tracey was parched and drinking constantly, but she couldn't eat. She felt like she had to urinate every fifteen minutes. Late that night she started to throw up. She couldn't hold anything down.

The next day the house was constantly full of people gathering in the downstairs living room. Jim O'Neil came and went several times.

Tracey sat alone in the upstairs living room. Her mom answered the telephone in the kitchen and answered the front door. "No, Tracey can't talk right now," Roseanne said again and again. "She's sleeping."

Once, Tracey looked out the window to see Don Moroz drive by in his truck. Moroz had committed himself to contacting every one of the families of the nine dead men, but he couldn't find the courage to stop in to see Tracey Neill. He drove by twice. At last he stopped and knocked at the door. Tracey agreed to see him. They sat down on the pink couch in the upstairs living room.

"Were the guys carrying powder?" she asked.

"Oh no," Moroz reassured. "They can say whatever they want on TV, but they don't do that kind of stuff."

Tracey met with a few other people as well, all of them saying the same thing: Oh my God; oh poor Tracey. But Tracey didn't feel that way. No, not poor me. Chris is the one who is gone.

Tracey was caught up with one question: Where had Chris gone? If she knew that he had gone somewhere beautiful and peaceful, his death would be easy to take. But she didn't know that. If Chris had died before his time, she wondered if it meant he wouldn't rest until the time came when he actually should have died. What if he would have died at sixty or eighty? What would he do between now and then? If she ever saw him again in an afterlife, she wondered if she would have aged while he would still be young. She wished he could somehow contact her and tell her he was okay. That was all she needed to know. At night she wept and whispered, "Please just come back. Tell me you're okay."

Two days after the blast, Jane O'Neil set up a meeting between Peggy Witte and the widows. Witte had chartered a plane from Hawaii to get to Yellowknife. A number of the families arranged to drive to the mine site together to see Witte. The convoy stopped as it passed the CASAW picket station at the main gate. A mob got out of the trucks and cars. The one striker on hand ran into the picket shack. The mob tore down the pole with the CASAW flag, which had been flying at half mast, then tore down the placards on the Road of Shame. The signs were immediately taken to the local dump where a tractor buried them.

Witte poured coffee for the widows at the main office.

"I'm so sorry," she said to Judit Pandev. "What can I do to help?"

Pandev was no longer so mad at Witte. Her rage focused on CASAW. "These guys came back to work to keep the mine going," Judit told her. "Keep it open. If I have to come and work, I will come and work. I will sweep the sidewalk. I'll work just to prove to CASAW they cannot make us fear."

The other widows agreed with Judit, but Witte didn't need convincing. After meeting with the widows she held her first press conference regarding the blast. She told the assembled reporters she had come to Yellowknife to share in the grief of the community and the families. Her goal was to get the mine back up and running in no more than one week. She was now working on a safety plan with the RCMP, the Pinkerton managers and the Northwest Territories mine inspectors. If the mine wasn't operating within a week, Witte said she wouldn't sell it—she would shut it and flood it. One hundred and twenty-five jobs would be lost.

"Nine men have lost their lives to keep the Giant Mine open," she concluded in her speech. "Royal Oak will make sure their lives have not been lost in vain."

The questions from reporters focused mainly on CASAW's accident theory. Witte was asked how the miners on the 750-drift got their explosives. Her vice-president, John Smrke, answered, saying the explosives for the 712 work crew would come down the B-ramp on a truck, never down the 750-drift, certainly not in a man-car.

Asked if there was any hope of a resolution with CASAW, Smrke said the last time the two sides had met was two months ago in July, and it had then seemed to the federal mediator that there was no purpose in meeting again.

With her shareholders in mind, Witte sent out a press release saying Giant had 125 workers on site and work was going ahead. Gold was to be poured on schedule. Only $10,000 in damage had been done by the blast. For Royal Oak, dollars were still what mattered.

The RCMP were at last ready to take out the bodies at 2:30 P.M. on Monday, three days after the blast. A crowd of 150 gathered around the C-shaft's headframe. It was a mining tradition for the bereaved community to meet at the mine's collar, the main shaft entrance, when bodies came up. Miner Keith Murray saw Judit Pandev, Doreen Vodnoski, most of the widows, young and old, all crying, and all the assembled men crying, too. The widows had hoped to catch a glimpse of their husbands, maybe even to have a final touch. They had no idea about the state of the corpses. Linda Riggs and Norm Hourie's wife, Doreen, asked Murray what he had seen at the blast site. He told them.

A white van backed up to the C-shaft headframe building. The body bags were loaded. Mine superintendent Terry Byberg said the Lord's Prayer.

Afterward, Murray went to the C-dry washroom. For the first time since the blast, he wept. He beat his fist against the wall, cursed and swore vengeance.

Judit Pandev and her children followed the van to the airport. The bodies were to be taken to Edmonton for autopsies. The Pandevs followed the truck to the RCMP hangar, then drove back to town. Pandev's daughter, Maria Yee, agreed to talk to Marty Brown of the *yellowknifer*. "Sooner or later, whoever did this, next week, ten years from now, he's going to shake his head," Yee said. "His heart will pound so hard he'll think he's going crazy. And I want those pictures, I want those faces of my dad and everyone to flash before his eyes. I want him to go halfway crazy and die."

The mass murder of the nine men acted like a poison in Yellowknife. In a town where people had been proud not to lock their doors, many now did. They looked over their shoulders as they drove to work. They started with fear if they bumped into the wrong person at the supermarket checkout. The old Yellowknife was gone for many in town. The closeness and the innocence were gone. The closer anyone got to the strike and the murder investigation, the more likely the poison would infect them.

In the week after the blast, Dr. Ross Wheeler kept flashing back to the horror of the site. In the middle of a conversation, he'd forget what he was saying and even where he was. Though he had lived in Yellowknife for two decades, he felt like a stranger. Only in the emergency room did it feel right and good. This was one place that hadn't changed. He was competent there. He and his friends were doing good work. It was safe.

Talk of the blast consumed the town for a few weeks, but after that most townspeople had the good sense to avoid discussing it, at least in public. They knew it was dangerous to get drawn into the matter, especially when they could never tell where someone else stood. Some Yellowknifers embraced the union's theory that the blast was an accident. Most accepted the RCMP's word that it was homicide.

The frustration and disbelief of the townspeople was expressed in a letter written by Robert Slaven to the *yellowknifer*: "This isn't how Yellowknifers do things. Real Yellowknifers don't take jobs from each other. Real Yellowknifers don't commit vandalism. Real Yellowknifers don't screw their workers. Real Yellowknifers don't let what should have been a simple labor dispute tear their town apart. Real Yellowknifers don't kill each other. So if you're not a real Yellowknifer, then leave. We don't want you. We want our town back."

However much Yellowknifers wanted the poisonous dispute to end, their desire didn't matter to CASAW or Royal Oak. Neither side saw the blast as a reckoning. Neither admitted blame or past mistakes, at least not publicly. There was now no possibility of a rational settlement to the dispute, not while the toxins of hatred polluted the blood of the combatants.

At the Northwest Territories legislature, government leader Nellie Cournoyea appealed for calm. "Just because there is a criminal investigation underway doesn't mean there was union involvement," Cournoyea said.

Cournoyea criticized federal Labor Minister Marcel Danis for not coming to Yellowknife long ago to push for a settlement. In Ottawa, Ethel Blondin-Andrew, the Member of Parliament for the Western Arctic and a member of the opposition Liberal party, said the government had failed miserably. "Something more could have been done. . . . We could have taken extraordinary measures for an extraordinary situation."

Jim O'Neil was disturbed by such talk. He didn't want the government stepping in to end the strike, not now, not with his belief that someone in the union was a murderer. O'Neil sent a letter to Cournoyea, saying that if CASAW was allowed back to work, Royal Oak employees would feel endangered and would quit. "Please, for the sake of our lives and our jobs, keep politics removed from this sensitive situation and let the RCMP complete the murder investigation. We cannot let clubs, guns and terrorism control our politics or change law and legislation within our country."

O'Neil also decided to speak with the national news media drawn to Yellowknife by the blast. O'Neil's description of the blast site was the first eyewitness report of the event. He made a point of saying that he knew it was murder as soon as he saw it; it was one way for him to stick it to CASAW and its accident theory.

In order to reopen Giant Mine, Royal Oak had to tighten security around the thirteen main entrances. Keith Murray and other Royal Oak volunteers accompanied RCMP bomb squad members through the various drifts, shafts and raises of Giant, all the time looking for other booby traps. Every time Murray opened a door, he half-expected a bomb to go off.

The mine opened on Witte's schedule, one week after the blast, with the mine inspector's blessing. The next day, federal Labor Minister Marcel Danis announced a special mediator would be appointed to produce a report on the strike situation.

The first public memorial in Yellowknife had been held five days after the blast. It was put on by the firefighters for Chris Neill. One hundred people filled the church. An honor guard presented Tracey with Chris's fire helmet.

Neill's body was released by the medical examiner's office on Monday, September 28. It went straight to the funeral home. The director called to ask if the family would like to view the body. Tracey decided not to go. She hadn't gone to the collar to see the bodies come out. She had sensed that the damage to her husband was bad. She wanted to remember him the way he had been, and to see a body bag with Chris's name on it would upset her. Now she feared that a mistake might have been made, that maybe they had put Spanky Riggs' legs with Chris's body, since the two had the same build.

Tracey's father, Ron, went to see the body. When he got back, Tracey asked him if he was sure it was Chris. He said he'd seen Chris's hands, and Tracey knew it was him. Chris had distinctive hands with long, skinny fingers.

Neill's funeral was held October 2 in Calahoo, a town outside of Edmonton. Jim O'Neil read the eulogy. "Chris and I went fishing one day, and I flew to a place that I knew more for its beauty than its fishing qualities," O'Neil recalled. "We walked in the midnight sun along a wonderful riverbank in a valley of fast-running water. We walked for miles, and I learned about another quality of Chris Neill—his passion for the outdoors. We didn't bring home any fish that day, but I know that it was one of the best fishing trips Chris was ever on. The bonds of our friendship were strengthened. From that day on I made a mental commitment to my friend that I would walk a long mile for him because I knew him inside and out.

"In August, Chris and I returned to work at the mine, and we watched each other's back every step of the way. I always felt he worried too much about our safety, and he always phoned me to make sure I'd made it home safely. Today, I'm the one that wonders and worries about my good friend's destiny, and for Tracey. But I know that he is a big part of my life, Tracey's life and all the people that he touched with his smile, friendship, strength, hard work and dedication, and will be forever with us. I'm going to take a trip to my favorite fishing hole next summer and walk along the banks of that beautiful river valley. When I go home without any fish, I'll sit and recall the thoughts and memories of being there, and think of my good friend, Chris Neill."

Neill's headstone was put in a small country cemetery where many members of the Quintal family had been buried. Immediately after the funeral, Tracey, her family and the O'Neils flew back to Yellowknife for the city's memorial service for the nine men, which was scheduled for the following day, October 3, two weeks after the blast.

The city had already given $20,000 to a relief fund for the families. The city also put up a $20,000 reward for information leading to the murderer's arrest, a reward which quickly grew to $307,000, mainly from donations from Royal Oak and other mining companies.

Yellowknife shut down for the memorial. Banks, stores and government offices closed so people could attend the service at the Yellowknife Community Arena. The event was as much for the community as it was for the families of the nine dead men. Yellowknifers felt both sad and betrayed. This kind of thing might happen in Belfast or Beirut, but not here. The townspeople needed a catharsis.

Yellowknife's politicians and townspeople would have stopped the strike before it started, but they didn't have the power. They couldn't force the strikers to accept the tentative agreement any more than they could keep Peggy Witte from bringing in replacement workers. Through the summer Yellowknife's politicians had worked to make the federal government in faraway Ottawa understand that the strike was headed for disaster.

The townspeople were angry at what the mass murder had done to Yellowknife's reputation. They hated the national media going on about a town divided, a town out of control. At the memorial they wanted to show the rest of Canada that they were better than that. They could hold a community event and talk about healing and not descend to violence. They wanted to prove the poison hadn't got to them all.

The day was somber, cold and drizzly. A steady stream of people showed up for the ceremony. People didn't talk as they walked from the parking lot; the only sounds were footsteps and rain. Three thousand people filled the arena. The CASAW men and their wives didn't show. Many of them had wanted to go, but they decided it was best not to risk angering anyone.

A rock cairn had been erected with a miner's helmet set on top. A huge banner had been strung up as well: "For Our Miners." Jim O'Neil read that and felt as good as he had in months. All he had heard was scab, scab, scab, but here the townspeople were saying that the nine men weren't pariahs; they were part of the community.

The families of the dead men filled three long rows of seats at the front of the crowd. The widows looked frail and dazed. Most of them leaned on someone. It was the first chance for the townspeople to see their grief and ruin.

Each of the widows was asked to walk to the front and place a rose at the base of the cairn. Four clergymen got up to speak about healing and dealing with anger. The Gumboots, a local group, sang. Retired mine inspector Mel Brown read from Klondike Gold Rush poet Robert Service:

And when I come to the dim trail-end, I who have been life's rover
This is all I would ask, my friend, over and over and over
A little space on a stony hill, with never another near me
Sky O' the North, that's vast and still, with a single star to cheer me
Star that gleams on a moss-grey stone
Graven by those who love me
There should I lie down alone, with a single pine above me
Pine that the north wind whinnies through
Oh, I have been Life's lover!
But there I'd lie and listen to
Eternity passing over

Judit Pandev was happy to see that so many of the dead men's children had come. In the choir, she saw friends who had been at her and Joe's wedding. Tracey Neill noticed the children, as well as the many reporters with their notepads, cameras and microphones. She had never been interviewed before and decided she wasn't going to talk now. Her father urged her to reconsider. "I think you should. You have a lot to say."

Still, Tracey wasn't going to say anything, but then Sergeant Dave Grundy pulled her over when the service was done and told her Eric Sorenson from the CBC wanted to speak with her. Tracey agreed, but she told Sorenson she wouldn't answer any questions, just say what she had to say. She feared Sorenson might ask her about the union and she didn't want to get into that. As soon as she started to speak, Neill was surrounded by microphones and cameras. She felt the media drawing closer, smothering her.

"Chris and I were together for three and a half years," she said. "We had many hopes and dreams, and they all ended on September 18 when he was murdered. Chris and eight of his friends were doing what they felt was right for their families and their community. To the people out there who know what happened, please come forward. And to the people who are responsible for this, I just want you to know that if you were hurt underground or your house was on fire, my husband would have saved you. It's a hard time trying to come to terms with the way Chris died. But I don't think I'll ever come to terms with the cowardly way it was done. There are eight widows, eighteen fatherless children, grieving mothers and families, all just as innocent as the men that died."

Tracey thought she was saying too much, and, in the end, rushed off in tears.

The memorial helped the townspeople, but it wasn't enough for the Royal Oak faction. The line crossers and replacement workers still talked endlessly about going down to the union hall and beating any CASAW man they found. The line crossers were still getting their tires slashed and still getting hollered at in grocery stores. Cars were still getting painted. Fist fights broke out at the picket gate.

Many days the vengeful feelings were so strong that the working miners talked about grabbing clubs, drill rods and shovels and heading out to beat the strikers. One line crosser's dream was to take the mine's massive scoop shovel, drive out to the picket line, scoop up the strikers' bus and dump it into an open pit. Several times, mine superintendent Terry Byberg had to stand up on a chair to calm the men.

"Look guys, that's not going to solve it," Byberg said. "That's just playing their game and falling into their trap."

But the blast had also left many miners terrorized. Shift boss Don Moroz had gone back to work in the 712 area on the day the mine reopened. He took the man-car with his crew down the 750-drift. One man wouldn't get in, so he walked ahead of the others.

A foul smell started to come from the blast site. Flesh had been blown up into the cracks in the rock. A blanket of white mold had started to grow. It looked like a macabre undersea garden, hairy fungus creeping down from the ceiling. After the sickened miners complained long and hard, the corridor was washed with lime.

With the men back at work, Moroz had to make sure he didn't startle them when he made his rounds. A few of the men were so spooked that Moroz had to bang loudly on the pipes as he approached to warn them he was coming. One man always had to shine his light directly into Moroz's face to make sure it was him.

Many replacement workers who had sworn never to return to Yellowknife after the blast changed their minds. The same unemployment that drove them to cross the line in the first place pushed them to come back. But others who returned were just plain stubborn. They didn't want to let CASAW beat them. The miners and the managers grew much closer after the blast, all of them concentrating on working hard and safely. Each accident-free day and each ton of ore was deemed a statement that CASAW wasn't going to win.

Jim O'Neil satisfied his yearning for vengeance by driving across the picket line every day. It was his little fix, he liked to say, his shot of rye. The strikers had only to look at the rage and determination in his face to know they shouldn't try to slow him down. In the end O'Neil was glad no one tried; he knew he might have run him down or got out and fought him, and that wasn't his way. It wasn't in O'Neil's nature to hate. He was a friendly man but a worrier. An emotion like contempt was too much for him to handle. O'Neil also understood that if he hated one man, even the murderer, it would be that much easier to hate the next man and the next and the next one after that. He would become poisoned.

Still, O'Neil was haunted by the deaths and especially by the death scene. He could talk for hours to anyone about union politics or life in Yellowknife, but it was only after he had shared everything else that he could talk about what he saw on the morning of September 18, 1992. That sight had been unholy and all but unspeakable. O'Neil felt compelled to write down what he had seen. He and his wife, Jane, worked on a book about their experiences. They interviewed other people who had seen the carnage. While it was impossible to truly describe, it was important to the O'Neils that no one forget how and why these men had died.

At times O'Neil was filled with doubt about what had gone on during the strike. He knew he'd had the right to cross the line, but now he wondered if it was the right thing to have done. He shared his concerns with his boss, Noel O'Sullivan.

"Did I do the right thing?" O'Neil asked.

"I don't know," O'Sullivan said. "You can answer that, and no one can answer it for you."

O'Neil nodded.

"But, Jim, would you do it again?" O'Sullivan asked.

"No."

"Well, you've answered your question right there."

For his own security, O'Neil got a German shepherd guard dog and a Winchester Defender shotgun, which he kept loaded by his bed. O'Neil thought Chris Neill might have been on a hit list and he might be on it as well.

O'Neil understood that he and his colleagues needed to find something constructive to focus on, otherwise they would all be poisoned. The Royal Oak men eventually found it in their attempt to oust CASAW as the bargaining agent for the miners at Giant. They formed their own employee's association. The idea had originally come from Chris Neill. Neill had told O'Neil about such a group at a Crowsnest Pass coal mine. A few weeks after the blast, O'Neil called up the western office of the Canada Labour Relations Board to find out about the rules for starting a new association in the midst of a strike. He discovered that the laws were stacked against such a move. For one thing, CASAW couldn't be challenged until the strike was at least six months old, which was still weeks away. O'Neil also learned that if a decertification vote was held, the replacement workers weren't likely to be allowed votes. He could only count on the votes from the CASAW men like him who had crossed the line.

At first the new worker's group was made up of family members of the dead men, Doreen Vodnoski, Linda and Peter Riggs, Joey Pandev and friends of the men like Blake Rasmussen, Rick Titterton and O'Neil himself. They met at an isolated cabin on Great Slave Lake. O'Neil brought his guard dog, King, and his shotgun. Every time

O'Neil started his vehicle he wondered if he would be a goner. When he started going to more public meetings of the new group, the Giant Mine Employees Association, he took his wife's inconspicuous gray sedan instead of his red Toyota. He worried that someone would come into the meetings with a shotgun and start blasting.

After work O'Neil camped out in his office at home, sending faxes, talking on the telephone, going over documents, making photocopies. His three-year-old daughter, Katie, grew so sick of Giant Mine talk she put her hands over her ears and wept. "Don't talk about the mine anymore. I'm tired of that."

Even with the existing rules for a decertification vote, O'Neil thought his group had a chance. Royal Oak had now hired on some of the replacement workers as full-time employees to replace the union men who had been fired. Maybe they would be allowed to vote. And maybe he could sway the sizable group of CASAW men who were as disgusted as anyone with the September 18 blast.

O'Neil might be a big bag of nerves, he might be vilified from the union hall to the picket line, but he was determined to see it through. In any case, the CASAW men could hardly hate him any more than they already did. He'd had his neck out for months trying to change CASAW, and he thought this was the next logical step, if there was such a thing as a next logical step after your best friend and eight other men had been murdered.

8

THE SLEUTH AND THE ACE

Within a few weeks of the blast, Giant Mine foreman Noel O'Sullivan became convinced the murder had been committed by a lone wolf from CASAW, but not Al Shearing, Tim Bettger or any of the other Cambodian Cowboys.

O'Sullivan wasn't alone in trying to figure out who had committed the crime, but he proved to be more swift and sure than even the RCMP. He had one important advantage over the police in the hunt for the killer. The investigators had to take a crash course in the world of Giant Mine. O'Sullivan was the professor. The police didn't know the mine or the miners. O'Sullivan did. He knew all Giant's routines and practices. He had walked every drift and ramp, climbed every raise. He had dealt with every man at one time or another. The technical language of the mine was his second tongue.

While the police struggled to master this information, O'Sullivan leapt ahead. He focused on bits of inside information from strikers, Mounties, replacement workers and line crossers. He studied the various clues. He drew on everything he had picked up in his long and successful career in the mine.

After immigrating to Canada in 1965, O'Sullivan had first mastered the skills and rules of drilling and blasting, then moved up to management. He relished the chance to lead other men. He had no university engineering degree, only a grade ten education, but no one at Giant knew mining better than he did.

Before the strike, if O'Sullivan's name had been mentioned, almost any miner at Giant would have given the thumbs up. The men who worked underground respected him and told many stories about his career. Terry Legge liked to recount the time he was at the C-shaft headframe one day and was trying to open the big, heavy door leading to the man-cage area. Legge had to put down his tool bag to force open the door. When he finally got through, he ran into O'Sullivan.

"Noel," he had said, "for the love of fuck, can't you get this door fixed so a man can open it and doesn't have to fight with it?"

"No Sir," O'Sullivan had said. "There's nothing wrong with that door."

"Fuck, Noel, didn't you see what I had to go through to get in here?"

"Terry, if a man can't get in through that door, he shouldn't be working underground."

To O'Sullivan, the mine wasn't only a living, it was a testing ground, and it was as if he had been born to the challenge. He'd never been afraid, not in a mine, not when he was an orphan growing up on a farm near Cork City in southern Ireland. His own parents had died when he was four, one of cancer, the other of tuberculosis. He had been raised by his Aunt Kate, a strong believer, who stressed faith and a positive outlook. The Catholic church had remained the bedrock of O'Sullivan's life. In Yellowknife, he and his wife, Minnie, were volunteers at St. Patrick's Church. O'Sullivan was also the president of the Catholic school board and a member of the Knights of Columbus.

O'Sullivan had done every job in the underground, including the worst of them all, picking up the pieces after a man had fallen down a shaft or had been shattered by a blast. He had seen men killed from carbon monoxide poisoning. He'd seen them blinded and killed from drilling into a mishole, a drill hole still loaded with AMEX, which for some reason hadn't ignited during the central blast. Two years back he'd been on the rescue team when Peggy Witte's associate, Toni Borschneck, a female engineer, was killed in a freak accident. A fifty-pound piece of rock fell from a stope and crushed her skull.

To O'Sullivan, the accidents were just another day in the mine. He accepted them and went back to work. He'd had close calls himself, but luck and skill had always saved him at the last second. Once, he was clearing out an ore pass, a dumping chute for the muck; he got out moments before one thousand pounds of rock crashed down where he'd been standing. Another time, a man forgot to cordon off his blasting area and O'Sullivan had walked right into the explosion. Somehow, he remained untouched.

O'Sullivan's presence set younger miners at ease. The smartest of the greenhorns learned his ways, just as O'Sullivan himself had learned as a young miner from two tough old Germans in the nickel mines of Thompson, Manitoba. The Germans were serious, ambitious men, but also realistic. Mining was their livelihood. It was their past and their future. They would always have work, but only if they did things right. They said little to the young Irishman except that he'd better keep his eyes open and do what they said. O'Sullivan was impressed with their approach. They always did a job right the first time, and this became the heart of O'Sullivan's own code. He had no use for men who kept making mistakes, the ones who no matter how many times they repaired a piece of equipment couldn't keep it from breaking down again soon after.

O'Sullivan had never had much use for the union. When he was a miner he had never attended a union meeting. It was not that he disrespected the union or disliked strong union men, but he always said a union was like a doctor—good to have, bad to want.

Despite his misgivings about some of the lazier, more careless CASAW men, O'Sullivan kept on good terms with most of the miners. Through the first four months of the strike, he had kept up on almost everything the union was planning through his ties to the old-time miners. Between them and O'Sullivan was a bond stronger than any labor dispute. He had often stopped at the strike line to make small talk, just to remind the strikers there were human beings on his side of the line as well. Even so, the strike had made him dread going to work for the first time in his life.

On the day of the blast, O'Sullivan had had as many bitter thoughts about Royal Oak as he did about the union. He wished the upper management had paid more heed during the summer when he had pushed them to tighten security. Trying to get through to them was like talking to a wall, O'Sullivan thought, but that was no surprise.

He'd had reservations about Royal Oak since it took over the mine. The company's managers were adversarial and antagonistic, yet they expected everyone to work like demons to increase production. O'Sullivan thought it a strange way to do business.

O'Sullivan had disagreed with using strikebreakers. Peggy Witte must be getting bad advice, he thought. She obviously didn't count on how angry the strikers would be. She didn't see that sooner or later the strikers would retaliate against the replacement workers. A broken leg, a broken nose, a slashed tire, and how many men would stick around for a second helping? The company would constantly have to bring in new men. He and the other middle managers would have to train them.

Some of the ProCon workers were solid, but others had no business being underground. O'Sullivan labored to orient them and get them to work efficiently and safely. He and the other managers got little sympathy when production fell off. If the mine didn't pump out twelve thousand tons of ore a day, Witte and John Smrke could be pretty crude and rough.

"What the fuck is going on, you guys?" Witte railed at her managers at one meeting. "How come you're not making production?"

At the start of the strike, O'Sullivan and the other middle managers were promised they would be paid overtime as long as they kept the mine operating. If it meant they worked twenty days straight, they were told they'd still get paid. After the first month, however, Mike Werner told the managers that Witte would not sign their overtime checks. The managers could do little, except withhold any extra labor or quit their jobs, which many ended up doing.

From a few good friends in the union, O'Sullivan started to hear rumors about what the Cambodian Cowboys would try next. He reported them to his bosses, but they told him not to worry. They had hired the mighty Pinkertons and the mine was impregnable. O'Sullivan tried to tell them that they were wrong, that the Pinkertons weren't the force they were made out to be. Every morning at 5:00 A.M. when the cook shack opened, many of the security guards flocked to it like ravens, deserting their posts. Some of them fell asleep on the job.

The strikers were a much more determined group, O'Sullivan thought. They knew the whereabouts of all the Pinkerton patrols. They understood the mine far better than any security guard from the South.

They could poke and prod, waiting for the right night to do their business. They were running around in the dark as if they owned the place.

After the June 14 riot, O'Sullivan started to fear a break-in to the underground. He decided to do what he could on his own to secure the remote Akaitcho shaft, the easiest point of entry for the strikers. Akaitcho was an important emergency escape route so it wouldn't be wise to seal it. Instead, O'Sullivan took away the top two ladders leading into the shaft. He left them at the top of the landing so men could easily set them up again if they had to get out. Now the only way in was to shimmy down the steel cables running along the side of the shaft, which is what the Cambodian Cowboys did on their graffiti sortie. O'Sullivan thought they were crazy. One mistake and they would have fallen 450 feet.

O'Sullivan concentrated on other areas that he believed vulnerable: the mill's smoke stack, the vent shaft station and the hoist room. If they were destroyed the mine would have to close. If the strikers rigged a bomb at the base of the massive stack, the explosion might not fell it, but it would do enough damage to have the stack condemned. The hoist room, which housed the engines to run the C-shaft's three elevators, was isolated and vulnerable, as was the vent shaft station, where the mine's four air compressors were located. O'Sullivan appealed to his bosses for extra security, but got nowhere. He was told the Pinkertons made their rounds, but they couldn't guard everything all the time.

After the blast O'Sullivan tried not to dwell on past mistakes, but to focus his attention on the murders. After the dead men's families had left the property on the day of the blast, he sat down with mine superintendent Terry Byberg to go over things. Byberg mentioned that at about 9:40 A.M., before he had heard anything about the blast, he was driving along the Ingraham Trail. He had just come over a hill when he saw a car slow down, then stop on the side of the road. He recognized the car's driver as one of the striking miners. Byberg passed the man, then watched him in his rearview mirror. Byberg called up the Pinkerton station on his CB radio to report the man, but when security guards arrived, the striker was gone.

"I think it was the guy who worked in the 710 area," Byberg told O'Sullivan.

"Roger Warren?" O'Sullivan asked.

"Yeah, that's the guy. I saw him on the B-4 area, past picket gate number six. I thought he was putting something in his car. It doesn't make sense."

"Okay," O'Sullivan nodded. "That would be odd."

That was all O'Sullivan said, but he thought much more. Right then, he knew that Roger Warren was likely involved in the blast in some way. There was no other reason for Warren to be at that place at that time. O'Sullivan couldn't bring himself to think that Warren had set the bomb, but someone from the union had to have told the murderer where to go. An insider had to be involved in some way. Maybe it was Warren. Why was he on Giant Mine property just then? That was the last place a striker would want to be with the Pinkertons driving around. What was he doing right near a major entrance to the mine, the B-138 portal? Was he waiting for the murderer? Or maybe he had guided the hit man down and was there to somehow clean up his tracks.

But how could Roger Warren ever get involved in something like that? If anyone knew the code of the hardrock miner it was Warren, who'd had a long, productive and honorable career.

Warren was known at Giant as the Ace. If a shift boss had ten men like Warren, he'd have no worries. In O'Sullivan's mind, men like Warren created the wealth of everyone else at the mine. It was thanks to them that Giant's mechanics and electricians made an average salary of $77,000 a year. But the mechanics and electricians didn't live and die with Giant. They were just tradesmen. If they lost their job at the mine, they could find work anywhere.

But for a hardrock miner like Warren, the mine was everything. It was all he knew. He talked about little except his work. Some nights in the bar when he and others like him got together and started boasting about how much rock they could break, the joke was that the place had to be vacated because there was so much smoke in the air from all the blasting.

Warren was born December 17, 1943. He was one of five children from a working-class family in Milton, Ontario, just north of Toronto. He was a strong athlete as a kid, good enough to play Junior B hockey in the New York Rangers' farm system. He went to grade twelve in school. He was involved in petty crime and went to prison for stealing a car at one point. He had worked in two mines in Ontario and four in

Manitoba, starting in Thompson in 1968. Fifteen years back, he had moved to Yellowknife.

Warren met his wife, Helen Hyrnczuk, in 1968. They married in 1970 and had two daughters, Patty, born in 1971 and Ann, one year later. Patty worked as a hotel administrator in Peace River, Alberta. Ann still lived with her parents in Yellowknife. She was a government secretary, as was Helen.

Helen was a quiet woman, but she ran the house. She and Roger seemed a good match. He liked to tell her about what he was reading and she liked to listen. There was a lot of love between them. Warren often deferred to Helen's opinion.

Warren spoiled his two daughters. They got everything they want-ed, including his attention. Whatever they were involved in, he was behind them. He didn't take it well when his daughters rebelled a bit as teenagers.

Warren seldom hung out at bars, but had a few beers at home, or he and his best friend, Keith Murray, would polish off a bottle of rye. Warren met Murray when they were both working in Thompson. Though Warren was ten years older, the two had much in common. Both liked the outdoors, both were intelligent, both liked to read, both were devoted to their trade. Warren bragged that he could break more rock in a shift than any other man. When he and Murray became part-ners, Murray came to see that Warren wasn't off the mark with his claims, though Warren soon held out in bullshit sessions that it was his good friend Keith Murray who was at the top of the heap when it came to breaking a round.

Murray got all kinds of tips about the trade from Warren, but the main thing he picked up was Warren's obsession—how to blast out the right amount of rock, not too much, not too little. Warren hated seeing a drift that had too much rock blasted out. Not only was it messy, but it slowed things down. The scoop-tram operator had to take extra time to muck out the drift, which meant a man couldn't get back at drilling, which meant he made less bonus money.

Warren went home at night thinking about what he was going to do the following day, what kind of gear he needed, how he would cut and load the face with explosives. The work was anonymous. No crowd would ever see it, no critics ever praise it. Nevertheless, Warren strug-gled to make sure the floors of his headings were so smooth that a man could bowl on them. When the engineers inspected, Warren's and Murray's work was often perfect, just as it had been marked on the blueprints.

Both Murray and Warren had close calls. One day Warren drilled into a mishole. It blew up and a wicked burst of light flashed, but he wasn't hurt. Another day Murray was cleaning out muck from around an old shaft. Wearing no safety rope, he slipped into the shaft, a straight drop of 750 feet. A screen mesh hung from the side and Murray grabbed it as he fell. Warren came running, hooked a safety rope on Murray and dragged him up. Afterward, Murray didn't say much to his friend about it. What could he say? It was a close one; that's all.

Higher wages attracted Murray and Warren to Yellowknife. They went up in Murray's truck. When they arrived at Giant, Murray would have turned right around if he'd had the gas money. Giant looked run-down and dangerous. When the two men started work, though, they saw that Falconbridge treated the miners well.

In the late seventies, Warren and Murray usually made $60,000 or $70,000 a year. In the early eighties, Murray's salary got as high as $125,000 in one year. He spent it all on luxuries, booze, trips to the Bahamas or to Newfoundland to visit his girlfriend's family.

Warren had less expensive tastes. He was obsessed with building on his income. He worried about what would happen when he was too old to mine. He thought his job was aging him rapidly. He often told the other miners they should save their money because they wouldn't be blasting out a round every day at the end of their careers. Helen and Roger planned to retire to Winnipeg eventually, where both of them had family. Warren spent a lot of time reading about investments and plotting the couple's finances.

They rarely went out for dinner. There were no diamonds and furs for Helen. They rented a house at the Giant Mine townsite, but when the company decided to sell all the homes, giving first chance to the present residents, the Warrens decided to move into a cheaper apartment in town.

Warren would come home from work and nap, then read a book. He was a great reader and he loved to debate. He was up on current events and could get the best of most of his crowd. In an argument he would talk until he had silenced his opponent. He could be abusive and intimidating. If he put his foot in his mouth, he would bite it off rather than pull it out. He saw life in black and white, and was as narrow as the drifts he drilled. There were only two ways to do things and to think about things: his way and the wrong way.

He liked to go down to the Miner's Mess café to talk politics, smoke his Cameo cigarettes and drink coffee. He smoked heavily and had a hacking cough.

Murray and Warren liked to fish, hunt for moose and caribou, canoe and snowmobile. They traveled around in whatever clunker snowmobiles Warren was fixing up. He had a side business fixing them out of his garage. He never owned a new car, preferring to fix up old ones.

He played for the Old Blasters old-timers' hockey team. He wasn't a sports fanatic, didn't watch much on TV, but he liked to compete. He was a good skater and puck handler. If you were a defenseman, he could pull a tricky move and be by you in a flash. In fastball he was a crafty pitcher. He had lots of junk—drop balls, rises, curves—but he'd lost his heater. He hated to lose and usually won. If his teammates screwed up, Warren was furious.

In 1980, when CASAW first went on strike at Giant, Murray left to work at Con Mine. Warren took holidays, then went to work at Cadillac Mine for a while. Neither man was much of a trade unionist. Warren told Murray the only thing the union was good for was saving the jobs of slackasses.

Warren often blew up at other mine workers. He had a temper and could get pretty wild, throwing stuff around and screaming. Anything at all could set him off. If his machinery broke he ranted about the mechanics.

Warren had tried out as a shift boss for a time, but he didn't like to be responsible for twenty other men. If one of them screwed up, the shift boss could be taken to court and prosecuted. He was offered a full-time position, but turned it down.

Eleven years back, Murray had accepted a promotion to shift boss. Warren advised him to take the job, that it would be good experience. Yet Warren distanced himself from Murray after the promotion. Murray felt bad about it, but Warren had something against being close to anyone in authority. After a few years Murray was transferred to the open pit. He and Warren drifted apart.

Warren looked the part of the old-time hardrock warrior. Other men wore new yellow construction hats, but he kept his old-fashioned miner's helmet, a round, brown Fiberglass hat. His jaw was always plugged with Old Copenhagen tobacco. When he showed up to work, he wore jeans, a cowboy shirt, a baseball cap in summer, a toque in winter. He looked ornery and rarely talked to people going down in the man-cage.

He was at the top of the heap among mine workers. He could do any task, handle any piece of equipment, any drill, any loki, any scoop. Some miners were as good with explosives, but none was better. He had done all kinds of mining, from the old light-the-fuse-and-run-like-a-bastard to hooking up the rock face to the central blast. He always kept good care of his heading, making sure to extend the air and water pipes, the central blast line and the ventilation system. If somebody was sick one day, he could fill in anywhere at Giant. He didn't like it when he was switched over to a difficult project, however. He always bitched if he didn't get a good section of the mine where he could earn the maximum bonus.

Noel O'Sullivan's only concern with Warren was giving him a young miner to train. Warren didn't get along with people. To him, everybody was an asshole. He would tell greenhorns they were no damn good right to their faces. He referred to young miners as gunfighters; they drilled everything from the hip and made a mess. Instead of an eight-foot by eight-foot drift, they ended up with a ten by eight or ten by nine. Warren had run off a few gunfighters before he hooked up with Danny Mino, a young French Canadian, in 1985.

"Oh, you're going to work with the Ace," the other miners smiled at Mino when they learned of his new assignment. "Well, good luck."

Mino wasn't worried. "Work is work," he shrugged. He had been a scoop operator and contract drift miner in the past. He had about five years experience. His work wasn't as good as Warren's, but Mino thought he could hold his own and learn. The first day with Warren went well, but on the second day Mino was loading some holes with AMEX when he stepped on top of an air pump to reach his target.

"You're going to break the fuckin' thing, you stupid asshole," Warren said.

Mino said nothing, but walked back and turned off the air pump. He then confronted Warren. "Listen here, buddy, you don't need me to work, and I sure as hell don't need you to work, but if we're going to work together, we're going to get along. I don't care if you swear at the machine, I don't care if you swear at the wall, I don't care if you swear at yourself, but if you start swearing at me, you better have a goddamn good reason because I don't fuckin' need it. I'm not gonna play stupid with you here."

Warren looked down. "I like to talk a lot," he said. "I like to bark a lot. But I got no bite."

With the rules established, Warren and Mino got along well for the next two years. Mino made about $100,000 both years. He could see Warren was a proud man who enjoyed his trade and reputation. He liked being the ornery old Ace who was going to show everyone else at Giant how mining was meant to be done. If a tool didn't work, Warren called it a goddamn ornament and said it was good for fuck all except putting on a shelf as a decoration. Mino got a laugh out of that.

Each day started the same for Warren and Mino. They took the man-car down the drift to the scoop shop. Mino had a pop, Warren his cup of tea from a big metal thermos. The two men then walked to their heading and checked to make sure the scoop operators had taken out the muck from the previous day's blasting. If their work was shoddy, Warren blew up. "Goddamn son of a bitch! They get paid for this, and they don't do goddamn sweet fuck all."

Mino just smiled. Hearing Warren swear was like hearing him say, "Good morning."

After the heading was mucked out and the ceiling was checked for loose fragments of rock that might come crashing down, Warren and Mino washed down the face and looked for misholes. If they found one—which they rarely did because Warren knew how to pack a blast—they would circle it with paint, prime it with a new stick of explosives and blow it right away.

When they were at last ready to start the day's drilling, Warren painted the entire face, marking where each of the thirty to thirty-six drill holes would go. Usually he marked them about eighteen inches apart. Warren inserted a steel drill rod into the jackleg. The rods came in various lengths, from two to sixteen feet, depending on how deep a miner wanted to drill. On the end of the steel, Warren fitted a drill bit. The jackleg rotated and hammered, the bit grinding into the rock. Compressed air and water blasted through the middle of the steel and out the end of the bit.

The idea was to drill a pattern of holes so the rock face caved in on itself. The charges went off in sequences, starting in the middle, where three large reamer holes had been drilled and left empty. The blasted rock exploded first into the reamers, then into the empty space created by the first blast sequence.

Mino drilled the outside holes while Warren, the lead miner, drilled the cut, the holes in the center of the face. If the holes in the cut were drilled true, if they didn't intersect or shoot off in the wrong direction, the blast sequence would work and there would be no boot-leg, no unblasted rock. Warren almost always blasted right down to the buttons.

Warren taught Mino how to load the drill hole depending on the conditions. If the rock was hard he packed in more explosives because it would shatter like glass. If it was spongy rock, however, Warren used a lighter density of stick powder to get the right concussive effect.

Mino and Warren never went for lunch. Mino might have a pop and a sandwich at the face. Warren had his tea, maybe a sandwich. During breaks, Warren busied himself with a plastic ruler and pencil. He measured the geologist's map and calculated how much ore they had taken out, right down to the ton. At the end of the month, he might be off by ten to fifteen tons, but he always knew if there was a mistake on his bonus pay.

Sometimes Warren barked at Mino if he was drilling off target. Warren would grab the steel of Mino's drill and pull it over half an inch. Mino couldn't believe it, half a fuckin' inch! But that was the Ace: prickly, particular, a perfectionist.

After the holes were drilled, Warren and Mino reversed the throt-tles on their drills, the water blasting out the excess cuttings. The miners then used long poles to push powder sticks and the blasting caps into the hole. The long leg wires from the blasting caps stuck out of the face.

The two men used hand-held loaders to blow yellow granules of AMEX into the drill holes. Afterward, the leg wires were rigged up to the B-line, which is the blasting line. In turn, the B-line was rigged to a DCD cap, an electric-powered detonator.

With all the wires, the rock face looked like a jungle of spaghetti. Warren wired up the DCD caps to the main electrical power source, a line hooked up to the central blast. The work was done, the entire process taking three to four hours to complete.

Some days Warren had a lot to say to Mino. Some days he was sullen. If he wanted, he could talk a mean streak of mining stories. When Warren found out that Mino liked cars, they sometimes got going on that. Another subject was how the miners with connections to management got preferential treatment. The ass kissers always got assigned the best headings to drill, the drifts with nothing but milky stone, which meant there was no gold in that rock, and a miner could move as fast as his ability allowed.

Too often Mino and Warren believed they were assigned faces near an ore body. They started to drill and got the telltale signs, the rotten egg smell, the oily silt. The gold-rich ore was good news for the mine, but it was bad news for a drift miner. It meant the geologist would ask them to take out a small round so he could do his testing and see if they were hitting pay dirt yet. There was no money at that pace. Warren and Mino were usually in the top five best-paid miners at Giant, but because of the favoritism, they felt they couldn't make it to the absolute top.

On April 3, 1987, Warren and Mino's partnership ended. The two men had split up that week to work on different faces. The central blast had detonated Mino's charges, but for some reason, only the cut blew. All the outer holes were still loaded with AMEX. Mino cleaned out the top holes, but he couldn't get at the bottom ones. They were covered by muck.

With the help of scoop operator Vince Corcoran, Mino started to haul away the muck, Mino pulling away big chunks of rock with his hands, Corcoran using a hoe. Mino was about to say something to Corcoran when the blast went off. Corcoran was knocked against the wall. Everything went black for Mino. When he awoke he couldn't move and couldn't see. He thought his lamp was broken. In fact, rock fragments were embedded in his eyes.

Mino yelled for Corcoran but got no answer. Just then, he felt weak. He collapsed. He felt his face. His skin was wet with blood. His chin and eye seemed cut open. He knew his leg was broken.

Warren and shift boss Dennis Graham were first on the scene. Smoke filled the air. Graham called out, unable to see anyone.

"Hey," Mino moaned. "What happened?"

"There was an explosion," Graham said.

Warren found Corcoran, who lay face down against the wall. He was inert. Warren found no pulse. Graham left to get help, leaving

Warren with Mino. Warren saw one of his partner's legs covered with muck. Warren took off his jacket to warm Mino, then took off his shirt, and put it under Mino's head for elevation.

"You're going to be okay," Warren said. "You're going to be okay."

Warren was worried that a spark from the blast would ignite another mishole. The mine's policy was to stay away from a blast site for at least a half hour because of that possibility.

Mino slowly became lucid. He asked Warren why he couldn't see. Warren tried to change the subject, asking Mino what had happened. Mino said he thought he was hit by rock that fell from the ceiling. He didn't hear any blast, but he felt an impact. Warren tried to keep Mino from moving around too much. Any second he expected to see blood spurting. He held Mino's arms to keep him from touching his face.

"Where's Vince?" Mino asked.

"Dan, he's dead."

Mino was taken up on a stretcher, then to the hospital. Along with losing his vision, he almost lost his leg. He had to have skin grafts to save it.

Even after a coroner's inquest, no one knew exactly what had happened, except that maybe Corcoran's grub hoe had dragged a tape fuse across the ground and the friction had ignited it, setting off the AMEX. The mine stopped using tape fuses after the incident.

A few months later, Warren visited Mino at his apartment. Mino appreciated the visit from the old Ace. They talked, but they walked along the edges of what had happened in the accident. Neither really wanted to recall it.

Mino told Warren he was getting back into shape by going to the gym for physiotherapy. "If it wouldn't be for the damn eyes I could still go underground and drill another goddamn round."

"I got no problem believing you," Warren said.

They joked about sneaking into the mine one night and drilling a round for old time's sake.

After Mino's accident, Warren dutifully wore his safety glasses for the first time. Still, he felt he couldn't take it anymore. He quit the mine and went to work at a garage in Winnipeg that he co-owned with Helen's brothers. Within a few months, however, Warren saw there wasn't enough work for him. He gathered himself and returned to Yellowknife, first working at Con Mine, then back at Giant.

The mining business wasn't only working on Warren's nerves, it was breaking his body. His hands and feet ached. He needed a back operation. He had developed a condition called white hand from years of holding a drill. The broken blood vessels and damaged nerves made his hands painfully sensitive and turn white in the cold. Warren knew he was getting near the end of his time underground. Even so, he was still a big bonus earner. He made $92,184 in 1991 and $50,134 in the first four months of '92.

Knowing Warren's personality and the kind of money he made, Noel O'Sullivan couldn't see any reason for Warren to suddenly become a union activist, let alone a terrorist. Warren might be a bit haywire, he might hold a grudge, but he didn't seem like the type who would go crazy and plant a bomb.

Through the summer, when O'Sullivan saw Warren bickering on the picket line, he had wondered: What in the name of God got under his skin?

O'Sullivan knew that for trade unionists, line crossing was a betrayal as fundamental as the most serious breach of the hardrock miner's code. But was it enough to push Warren to murder?

O'Sullivan's wife, Minnie, often cried over the death of Joe Pandev and the other eight men, but O'Sullivan refused to be overcome by anguish or the urge for vengeance. He guarded his energy for the hunt. It burned in O'Sullivan's gut that the CASAW leaders were saying that the blast was an accident. The nine men were his men, too. They had died on his watch. The strikers were directly blaming him. He kept visualizing the union leaders claiming the investigation was a cover-up.

Maybe it was like they said, maybe miners do not kill miners, O'Sullivan thought, but some son of a bitch set that blast.

O'Sullivan kept Warren in mind over the next few days as he helped the RCMP in their investigation. The Northwest Territories Mine Safety Act stipulated that any visitor to the mine must be accompanied by a mine employee. The Mounties needed someone to go with them as they searched the underground for clues. O'Sullivan was deemed the best man for the job. He went down with a steady flow of police crews, guiding them, answering their questions, helping them understand the workings of Giant.

On September 22, four days after the blast, O'Sullivan took down

Ident officers Wayne Locke and Dan Stevely, the man who had found the unique footprints at the Akaitcho shaft. Locke had gone to the local Woolco and found a pair of boots with a print similar to those made by the Akaitcho boots. They were size eleven Kamiks. It was a popular name brand. Hundreds of people in Yellowknife would own such boots.

O'Sullivan, Stevely and Locke first went to the 712-scoop shop, which seemed to have been a center of activity for the murderer. After the blast, the miners had found a loki parked there when it should have been in a nearby charging station. The murderer had likely taken the loki down the railway tracks of the 750-drift to plant the bomb, then come back on the loki, leaving it where it sat. At the scoop shop, the murderer then picked up the 50-scoop and drove up the B-ramp.

Sergeant Locke spotted a perfect Akaitcho-style, size eleven Kamik footprint at the 712-cap magazine, where blasting caps were stored. The following day, Locke made a plaster cast of the footprint at the cap magazine.

O'Sullivan tried to think of where the murderer got his explosives. The most logical place was down the ramp road at the 907-powder magazine, a storage room for AMEX and stick powder. O'Sullivan and Sergeant Gary Christison traveled to the 907-mag, where they found a number of Akaitcho-style footprints. Christison roped off the area. It occurred to O'Sullivan that the murderer was right at home in this part of the mine and that before the strike Warren had worked here on the 712 crew. He would have got his powder at 907 and his caps at the 712-shop.

During the next two days the police and O'Sullivan followed the murderer's tracks in through Akaitcho and the 750-drift and out through the B-ramp and the B-3 area of the mine. The footprints proved easy to spot. They almost glowed in the red soil because of their freshness. There were no other remotely similar prints in the mine. O'Sullivan had never seen anything like them underground. In the mud the police could sometimes see an imprint of the distinctive, fragile Made in Canada symbol, complete with maple leaf. The boots had to have been new. If they had been used, the symbol and leaf would have worn off.

At the bottom of the Akaitcho shaft, the Mounties found a sawed-off pool cue coated with black tape, hanging from a nail. It looked like it might be a homemade billy club that the murderer had brought with him, then forgot on the way down. (The club was the one left by Art St. Ammand when he broke into the mine with Bettger and Shearing on the graffiti mission.)

After the trip to Akaitcho, O'Sullivan came out of the mine and ran into Peggy Witte at the C-dry.

"What did you find down there?" she asked.

"Nothing."

"If you had found anything would you tell me?"

"No."

"Oh, so that's what you think of me?"

"You said it Peggy, not me."

In fact, O'Sullivan and the RCMP team were now able to put together a theory of where the murderer had entered and exited the mine, as well as where he got his equipment and explosives.

That early morning of September 18, 1992, the investigators believed the murderer had slid down a cable to the first flight of ladders in Akaitcho, then descended the shaft. Twice the murderer had got lost as he made his way down the ladder system to the 750-drift. The Akaitcho shaft didn't go straight down to the 750-drift, but ended after a straight drop of 425 feet. The murderer found himself in the 425-drift. He had to locate a doorway farther down the drift that would lead to a raise or man-way, a long, angled shaft with ladders. The doorway to the man-way was only forty feet from the Akaitcho shaft, but the footprints showed that the murderer went past it and had to double back. After locating the doorway, he climbed down the ladder only to hit the 575-drift. Again he got mixed up. His footprints showed that he overshot the man-way, then doubled back. He found the door, then climbed down the ladder to his first destination point, the 750-drift.

The murderer had to know that the night shift went off duty around 2:45 A.M. in preparation for the central blast at 3:10. He also knew that after the central blast no one was allowed in the mine for at least thirty minutes. In fact, the mine would be all but empty until the morning shift came on at eight o'clock.

The murderer had to time his trip to make sure he didn't get close to the 712-scoop shop until all the miners had left. He also didn't want to be too close to an active mining area when the central blast went off; otherwise he would risk injury.

At Akaitcho, a sign pointed south toward C-shaft. The murderer headed down the railway track in that direction. He was careful to watch his step; even though the tunnel was flat compared with other areas of the mine, there were still potholes to step in and railway ties to trip on. A stream of water ran beside the track so the murderer kept to the middle. Old gloves and packages of sunflower seeds and chewing tobacco, the two favorite vices of underground miners, occasionally littered the drift's floor.

The central blast roared and the earth trembled, but the murderer was okay. The ventilation along the 750-drift was excellent so he wouldn't have to deal with smoke or noxious fumes.

It likely took the murderer about an hour to walk down the railway track to the 712-scoop shop. There, he picked up the 50-scoop tram and drove down to the 907-powder magazine. He put his explosives into the scoop's shovel, then drove back up the ramp to the 750-drift. He loaded the explosives onto the loki, drove down the track and rigged his bomb. He escaped, first on the loki, then on the 50-scoop tram. He could have driven the scoop all the way out of the mine on the B-ramp, but he must have decided there was too great a chance of meeting someone near the top. He left the scoop and walked off the B-ramp, heading along the 575-drift. Here the murderer's tracks were a continuous trail, disappearing on ladders, then resuming again on the next level. The prints went up through the mine to the B-138 portal, near the same spot where Roger Warren had been spotted that morning by mine supervisor Brian Broda and later by mine superintendent Terry Byberg.

The entire mission took about four hours, maybe a little less.

The police investigators often returned in the following weeks to check out parts of the murderer's route, but no one walked it as often as O'Sullivan. Sometimes he went on his own. One of his co-workers, engineer Gerry Wolf, made an interesting discovery at the 425-level of the Akaitcho shaft. While O'Sullivan and the RCMP thought the murderer had been lost for only a few minutes as he hunted for the manway, Wolf discovered that the murderer's footprints actually wandered off for about half a mile before coming to a dead end and heading back. It was obvious that whoever set the bomb had no knowledge of the tunnel system in the Akaitcho area.

Roger Warren had never worked at Akaitcho. O'Sullivan knew that. In his fifteen years at Giant Mine, Warren had had no reason to go there even once. O'Sullivan thought back to another clue left in the mud outside of the 907-powder magazine. From the tire tracks left behind by the 50-scoop, it was clear the murderer had parked the scoop tight against the left-hand side of the tunnel with the bucket down, just the way miners at Giant were taught to park a scoop. It was parked next to the wall so other vehicles could get by; the bucket was put down so the vehicle wouldn't roll. The murderer had done the same when he abandoned the scoop tram on the B-ramp at 575. A hit man from outside wouldn't do this, O'Sullivan thought, but Warren would.

As he followed the footprints, O'Sullivan wondered more and more about Warren. "Could it be him?" he said aloud. "Could it be Roger?"

Throughout the strike, Warren and O'Sullivan had always waved at each other when they passed on the Ingraham Trail or in town. After the blast, however, Warren changed. O'Sullivan still waved and tried to make eye contact when they saw each other, but Warren looked away and made no gesture.

O'Sullivan decided to share his suspicions about Warren with Keith Murray; he knew Murray would keep the confidence to himself. O'Sullivan listed some of the things that made him suspect Warren, such as Warren being spotted by Byberg on the Ingraham Trail. Then he asked, "Do you think that Roger would have the gall to do it?"

"Definitely," Murray said without hesitation.

Murray couldn't see his old friend as a union radical, but he knew Warren had enough anger in him to lash out.

With everyone but a few other old-time miners, O'Sullivan was careful never to identify his suspect. He knew that if he told one man what he thought, that fellow would pass it on, adding a bit of his own opinion. The next man would add a bit more, then the next a bit more, until the fifth guy would hear that the RCMP had just kicked down Roger Warren's door and made an arrest at gun point. Almost every miner had his own scenario about who had done it, who had a motive, who had the ability. O'Sullivan was appalled at the stupidity of some of the theories. He guessed that CASAW strikers were deliberately spreading bum information.

The RCMP continually returned to O'Sullivan to ask him what he thought about this striker and that striker, whether the person had the capability to set such a bomb, whether he had the nerve. O'Sullivan was hesitant to blame Warren. He decided he should apply the code he lived by in the mine to his present investigation; he wanted to get it right the first time. He didn't want to accuse someone, then find out later he had blown it. He never asked the police who their suspects were, but from their questions and from gossip around the mine, he knew the prime targets were Shearing and Bettger.

O'Sullivan had seen and heard enough to know that Shearing and Bettger were involved in other explosions and the graffiti break-in at the mine. If the two were so reckless as to plant a bomb at the vent shaft station, O'Sullivan decided they might be desperate enough to plant a bomb beside the tracks. O'Sullivan almost hoped it was these two, especially Bettger, whom O'Sullivan disliked.

But O'Sullivan had really liked Al Shearing. He knew of no man who was better in mine rescue. He admired Shearing's calm and fearlessness in a tight spot. Though he was small in stature, Shearing had a lot of guts. O'Sullivan had never seen the little devil back away from anything. He also respected Shearing for his work as a shaft mechanic. Still, the strike had ruined Shearing in O'Sullivan's mind. How could a man dedicated to mine rescue get involved in something like the vent shaft bombing? How could he take chances with the lives of others by setting such a bomb?

Neither Shearing nor Bettger would ever work at Giant again. They would likely serve jail time, and they might as well go down for the murders as well, O'Sullivan thought, but he was also sure they weren't the ones. To the RCMP, Shearing and Bettger's previous criminal activity showed they knew the mine, they knew how to rig bombs and they were getting both bolder and more radical. But to O'Sullivan, the graffiti sortie proved the two men could not be involved in the murders.

The route down Akaitcho to the 750-drift was almost like a funnel. It was possible to get lost, but it was far easier to stay on track, especially if a man had been down once before, as Shearing and Bettger had. There was no way they would have wandered off, trying to find the man-ways, especially not Shearing. With his mine rescue skills, he knew how to get around any mine. As for Bettger, O'Sullivan was sure he was too fat and lackadaisical to ever attempt such an ambitious plan on his own. It couldn't be him.

It was the murderer's route out of the mine, however, that provided the most convincing clues for O'Sullivan. The footprints always took the shortest route up and out of the B-3 area. The murderer knew paths that only a supervisor, a longtime miner or someone who had worked on the development crew in the area would know. Since they were both mechanics, Shearing and Bettger could not possibly know these shortcuts. Roger Warren, however, had worked along the 575-drift. Warren had also mined in the B-3 area.

The footprints in the B-3 area told O'Sullivan something else as well. The murderer's stride never seemed to change. Even after he set the bomb and was heading out, his stride was even, steady. If he himself had planted the bomb, O'Sullivan knew he would be running like a dog to escape. His heart would be pounding, his head swimming with doubt and fear. But the murderer kept plodding along, coolly picking his route, walking the ground he knew so well. The footprints weren't those of a scared rabbit, nor were they straight-ahead military style. They gave the impression of a side-to-side stride. How many men would have that kind of confidence? O'Sullivan could picture Warren now, walking along with that swagger of his, that calm, collected, easy manner, his shoulders drooped, swaying, his feet wide apart, a John Wayne kind of walk.

"I'm not wrong," O'Sullivan said at last. "Unfortunately I'm not wrong. I hope I am, but I know I'm not. There is only Roger that could be that confident."

O'Sullivan could even picture Warren considering the crime. All the hotheads in the union would be blabbing about blasting something underground, but most of them weren't hardrock miners. They wouldn't have the jam or the know-how to set off an underground explosion and get away with it. Warren would scoff at them. He would know they were full of shit, but he would feed off their hatred until at last he decided to show them what a real miner could do.

As O'Sullivan walked the route with the RCMP, he would occasionally point out the clues that showed Bettger and Shearing were innocent. "Look," he said to a group of Mounties walking one day in the B-3 area, "I know you guys are thinking Bettger and Shearing. Always remember they wouldn't know the shortcuts; they didn't work in this place."

The RCMP officers listened, but to them O'Sullivan's advice was just one bit of knowledge among thousands of bits. The police had trouble keeping up to O'Sullivan's walking pace, let alone his logic. Sergeant McIntyre and the other investigators were not dummies, but they were still grappling with Giant Mine's complexities. They didn't understand the significance of what O'Sullivan was pointing out. In fact, it seemed cryptic to them. Why couldn't someone have told Bettger and Shearing about the shortcuts? And, really, why couldn't they get lost on the way in? It sure seemed easy to get lost in this place.

A few weeks after the blast, O'Sullivan and Minnie went for coffee at the Tim Horton's, where they came upon Roger and Helen Warren. O'Sullivan didn't say hello, but made sure to take a seat close to the Warrens'. He tried to make eye contact. If Roger looks at me then everything will be okay, O'Sullivan thought. It will prove that I have the wrong guy, that Roger hasn't been looking at me on the highway because he feels a bit strange after the murders.

O'Sullivan kept looking. Warren never returned his gaze. It was as if a fierce wind blew at Warren and he had turned his head to brace himself against it.

After they left the restaurant, Minnie said to Noel, "That Roger looks old."

"If you had what he's got on his mind, you'd look old, too."

Minnie thought her husband meant the strain of the strike. O'Sullivan didn't elaborate.

A few days later O'Sullivan heard a rumor that Warren had suffered a heart attack. He told Keith Murray to give his old friend a call and find out how he was doing. The next morning O'Sullivan asked Murray what Warren had said.

"Well, if it was a heart attack, Roger is denying it. He says it was something else wrong with his chest."

"What else did he say?"

"He has to go back and give another statement to the police."

"Does that surprise you?"

"I guess not when he was seen where he was seen at the mine."

"How did he sound to you when he said he had to go back to the police? Did he say anything about why?"

"No, but he sounded kind of disturbed that they were bothering him."

"Well, Roger might have to go back a lot more times by the time he is finished."

A month after the blast O'Sullivan was again called on to lead an RCMP team along the murderer's route. With Sergeant Locke and Constable Ken Morrison, he went walking, the police carrying metal detectors in the hope of finding new evidence.

Alone with the two officers, O'Sullivan decided he should be more direct.

"So, are you getting close?" he asked Locke.

"It's tough."

"Well, the prime suspects are not the boys. You better go and check your statements."

"Why is that?"

"Your suspects are not my suspect. You should change your tactics."

"Well, the evidence we have doesn't indicate what you're saying is the case."

O'Sullivan shut up then. He didn't bother to name his suspect or explain his theory. He believed the police were being fooled, but he had confidence they would eventually get it right. He realized they were being swamped with theories. They didn't need Noel O'Sullivan to add his own. He had to be patient and have faith in the proper authorities. They would get it right in time. If they kept going over and over each CASAW man's alibi, inconsistencies would pop up.

O'Sullivan also kept quiet for another reason—it was an awful burden for any man to live with killing nine of his workmates, but it would be even worse to be accused of a mass murder you did not commit. As sure as he was that Roger Warren was the man, O'Sullivan knew there was a chance he was wrong. It was his prayer as well.

Chapter 9

THE MAGIC BOX

To find the murderer, the RCMP investigators first asked, "Who didn't do it?" In that category the Mounties put everyone in Yellowknife who had no knowledge of Giant Mine. Of the four hundred men who did, the police chopped any man who had an alibi and appeared to lack the motivation to set such a blast. Conspiracy theories aside, that eliminated every man in the Royal Oak faction. It also cut the vast majority of the CASAW men, the ones who had acted peaceably on the strike line. A group of forty CASAW men remained, some of them prime suspects, others peripheral. All had alibis, but something pointed to their involvement in the crime. In order to eliminate them, Sergeant McIntyre decided to rely heavily on the polygraph machine, the lie detector. The polygraph came to be viewed as something of a truth serum by the investigators. If a striker passed the test, only the most damning evidence would force the Homicide Task Force to take another look at him.

Two weeks after the blast, Sergeant Gerry Keane of the Edmonton polygraph section came up to Yellowknife to start the marathon round of tests on the strikers. Keane soon realized he'd need help. Sergeant Pat Dauk was brought up from Winnipeg.

The polygraph operators were an elite within the RCMP. They were considered the best interviewers on the force, so expert at extracting confessions they often got a man to talk even before he was hooked up to the machine. The threat of the polygraph was enough to make many liars tell the truth. The junior members of McIntyre's team spent hours watching and listening to the polygraph exams, then questioning Keane and Dauk, asking about the keys to effective interrogation and the secrets of the machine. A few of the Mounties asked to be tested to see for themselves whether they could beat the lie detector. In the test, the Mountie was hooked up to the polygraph, then told to pick one playing card from a hand of seven. The polygraph operator then went through the deck, asking if each card was the card the Mountie had selected. The Mountie was to answer negatively each time, even when the card he had picked came up. It was up to the polygraph operator to uncover the officer's deception. Without fail, Keane and Dauk succeeded.

The polygraph took advantage of the primordial fight-or-flight instinct. When a person trying to hide something was asked about a matter he didn't want to talk about, fight-or-flight kicked in, giving him a big jolt of adrenaline. The heart, blood pressure and perspiration monitors of the polygraph picked up even the most minute physiological reactions, even small increases in sweat or small decreases in the blood pressure at the tips of the fingers. These changes happened before a person knew it. They couldn't be controlled, at least not when there was something important on the line.

After seeing the machine operate, the officers believed that the polygraph was all it was cracked up to be, a ninety-nine percent accurate, murder-solving, soul-illuminating, knothead-busting marvel. The Magic Box, Sergeant Keane called it, and none of the investigators disagreed.

The RCMP were keen to get Terry Legge on the lie detector, not only because he was a suspect, but because he was a leader, a big talker, someone who would set a strong example for the other strikers if he took the test and passed. Sergeant Bill Code, assigned as the union relations man, went after Legge to take the test. Legge refused, fearing that his participation in the vent shaft blast might come out. Code told Legge that the police were only concerned about the murderous blast, not about any piddlyass vandalism, if that's what he was worried about. Legge was told he had already given a good interview to the police. They had checked out his alibi and it was strong, but the polygraph test would prove his innocence. It would be the period at the end of the sentence.

Legge decided to at least go down to the testing room at the Explorer and look at the polygraph. If I didn't do it, Legge thought, then what do I have to worry about? If the machine said I did it, then the machine is a crock.

Corporal Vern White escorted Legge up to Room 701, where Sergeant Dauk had set up shop. Rather than do the tests at the detachment, Keane and Dauk chose a room in the Explorer because it would be neutral ground and more comfortable for everyone. Dauk had tried to make the room imitate his drab polygraph testing room back at the RCMP's Winnipeg detachment. The window was closed and draped. There was nothing in the room but a bed, a table, two chairs and Dauk's machine, FactFinder II, a small, briefcase-sized metallic box of dials, meters and lights. If any striker was expecting an inquisition, he found to his surprise that Dauk and Keane were the most subdued RCMP officers they'd ever met, unless, of course, the machine told either officer that he was dealing with a liar.

Before he agreed to the test, Legge set his rules: he would talk about the September 18 blast, but he would not be asked about any acts of vandalism on the strike line. Dauk said that would be fine.

Legge was asked some questions about his health, both mental and physical. If he was under the care of a psychologist or psychiatrist, Dauk had to find out why. People with severe mental illnesses weren't suitable for testing. Likewise, if someone had heart troubles or high blood pressure, the results might be skewed.

Legge asked to be hooked up to the machine before he answered any serious questions, just to see how it felt.

Dauk asked Legge to sit down in the armchair, with pillows under his arms to keep them out from his body. Legge was then connected to FactFinder II. Probes were attached to his index and ring fingers to measure his sweat activity. Around his chest went two coiled cords to measure his breathing. A blood pressure cuff went around his arm.

Dauk tried the pick-a-card game on Legge, both to win over his subject and to analyze Legge's reactions in a nonthreatening situation. When Dauk guessed the right card the first time, Legge thought it was a fluke.

"Yeah, that was a good fuckin' guess."

"That was no guess," Dauk said.

The next time he looked at the cards, Legge didn't pull one out, he just went through them and picked one in his mind. Again, Dauk went through the deck and had Legge answer negatively to each card. As he answered, Legge tried to think about other things that made him mad and excited in order to throw the machine off.

After studying Legge's graph, Dauk again picked the right card. Legge was astonished. He had thought he could lie to the devil and get away with it.

If Legge had been a liar, he might have left right then. Of course, Dauk wouldn't have minded that; a man who bolted almost certainly had something to hide; the polygraph wouldn't even be needed.

After playing the card game, Legge was unhooked from the machine. He and Dauk finalized a list of questions. They then went through a trial run of the questions. The idea wasn't to surprise Legge with anything in the interview, but to get an accurate reading. If Legge was truthful, Dauk wanted to put him at ease, to help him feel good about the process. If Legge was a liar, however, asking him the questions ahead of time might get him to confess.

The police knew that many liars came in to take the test. About a third of all polygraph subjects were found to be liars. They often took the test as a last resort. Maybe the machine would say they were telling the truth when they denied the crime and they could walk away. If the machine got them, well, it got them. They were often tired of lying and running.

Liars tried all kinds of tricks, such as shaking during the test to throw off the monitors, or trying to disrupt their breathing pattern, or hiding a tack in their shoe, then jabbing their toe when a question was asked. They might visualize themselves floating on a cloud or try to dissociate themselves from the interview and not listen to the questions. Such stunts were almost always spotted.

Dauk hooked Legge to FactFinder II for the real test. He asked the questions, making sure to pause between each one, allowing Legge to settle so there would be an unaffected reading on the next question.

Dauk ended with two key questions: "Did you set the blast at the 750-level at Giant Mine on September 18, 1992?"

"No," Legge said.

"Do you know for sure who set the blast?"

"No."

After a few minutes, Dauk came back with the results. The lie detector said Legge was telling the truth when he denied he was involved. Legge was ecstatic. Afterward, he met up with Corporal White.

"I fuckin' told you I told the truth!"

At home Legge boasted to Claudia about his result. She was glad and relieved, but when she told him so, he blew up. "You're not a good wife! You should believe in your husband no matter what."

"What?" Claudia shot back. "You start acting like something that I can believe in. But you give me nothing to believe that you weren't involved. Nothing. When I hear people talk the way they talk and do the things they were doing. I have seen so much hate and just listened to so much hate that I have had it right up to here with hate."

Claudia wanted her husband to cut his ties to the strike completely. Her anger had reached its zenith. She was getting tired of Terry's lack of support around the house. He usually slept in, then went to the gym or the union hall. Claudia worked eight hours, then came home to cook supper, clean house and care for the three boys. She was always after Terry to help out at home, but he seemed to treat the strike like a holiday. He watched a lot of TV, endless reruns of *Star Trek*. She grew frustrated with Terry and told him the least he could do was help her go shopping.

"I don't want to go shopping."

"Why?"

"Everywhere I go I run into scabs."

"Oh okay. That's your excuse now. Before it was, 'I don't know how.' You just didn't want to."

One Saturday morning Claudia managed to drag Terry out to the supermarket. All the time they were there, however, he mumbled under his breath about scabs being in the next aisle or at the next checkout. Claudia thought: Okay, shopping by myself wasn't so terrible. She didn't know who the line crossers and strikebreakers were, and she didn't want to know. It made things easier around town and at work. She knew she might be angry with them, and she didn't want to feel that way.

Terry was always looking out the door at home, as if he expected a lynch mob to come for him. He worried that his jeep would be vandalized and told Claudia to be careful where she parked it. Claudia didn't understand why he'd ask such a thing at first, but then it hit home: they were living in two different worlds.

Claudia thought about leaving Terry, if not for good, then just until the strike was over. Their arguments got nowhere, just spun out of control. Why was this strike all-important? Why didn't he get a job someplace else? Why not do something else in Yellowknife? Did they have to wait forever before they could breathe again?

"I'm in it for the long haul," Terry told her. "Until the time where my kids are in danger or my survival is in danger, I'll keep at it."

Claudia started to see the whole thing as a poison, just like she and Terry when they fought and were so stubborn and neither would give until, at last, all the angry words had been spoken and they both felt drained. They knew they weren't getting anywhere so they stopped. The fight ended. Nothing was resolved, maybe, but at least they moved on. That's the way she hoped it would be with the strike and the murder investigation. It had to end eventually. At some point both sides would be too tired to keep fighting.

But Terry was still keen. This was a war, he knew that now, and he was in the middle of it. He might be flat broke, but he wasn't going to give up. No, he wasn't happy to see nine men die, but the union had nothing to do with that, as he himself proved with the polygraph.

At the union hall, he went about proclaiming his polygraph-approved innocence. He went from a doubter to as big a believer in the machine as any of the Mounties. He had little use for men who wouldn't take the test, and he was fearless in telling them so. One day at the bar he was with Shearing and Bettger, who gave the standard line for refusing to take the test: the lawyers had told them not to submit.

"That is bullshit!" Legge exploded. "I took it because I had nothing to fear! And if anyone else has nothing to fear they will take it, too!"

One by one, the CASAW strikers came in for a look-see at the magic box. Almost all of them agreed to be hooked up. Every one of them passed the test, proving his innocence, or at least that the results were inconclusive.

Many of the most influential men in the union took it—first Legge, then former union president Bill Schram, then Cambodian Cowboys Luc Normandin and Steve Cooper, then Tom Krahn, who had been at the picket line on September 18, then hardcore strikers like

Rob Wells, Gord Kendall and Jim Fournier, and, at last, Al Shearing's good friend Oscar Pond, who was part of Shearing's alibi for the evening of September 17 and early morning of September 18.

Dauk and Keane worked sixteen-hour days, conducting interviews, getting ready for the next interview and reviewing each other's work. They would independently mark each other's tests, then compare the results. Between the pair, they gave more than forty tests in four weeks.

During his examinations, Keane always told the strikers that the blast wasn't an accident, that he had been down to the site and he knew it was murder. If the strikers still wanted to believe the blast was an accident, that was their prerogative. Keane wasn't there to change their minds but to find out if they were involved in the crime.

The polygraph operators knew that everyone who came in to take the test was stressed, the heartbeat pounding at an above-average rate. They had probably had a sleepless night, thinking, God, I've got to do this tomorrow.

But Keane and Dauk weren't looking for that understandable nervousness. To compensate for it, the operator asked the subject some simple questions, such as "What day is it?" or "What city are we in?" That way, the operators could establish a base level for the various physiological reactions when the subject was being honest. During the real test, the operators looked for changes in that base level.

The polygraph operators were scornful of university tests that had shown the machine to be unreliable. Sure, if you asked a bunch of kids about their birthdate and you had some of them lie about it, the polygraph operators might make a few incorrect determinations. But what did that matter? What was on the line for the test subject? Nothing. There was no fear of being caught in a lie, no consequences. But if you tested a man who was facing accusations of molesting children or torching an office building or murdering, there was almost no chance he would be able to hide his guilt.

The polygraph had been used extensively for more than twenty years by the police, but the results had never been accepted by the courts in Canada. Dauk knew the machine wasn't perfect. There was an outside possibility someone could pass and still have knowledge of a crime. The operators erred in their judgments about ten percent of the time. In rare cases a person might be a nonresponder, someone who didn't show normal fight-or-flight reactions. The person might also have something else weighing on him or her that would affect the result.

The machine itself was one hundred percent accurate, just like any properly functioning scientific instrument like a thermometer or a microscope. It got precise readings. It was up to the operator, however, to interpret those readings, and sometimes the results were foggy. A truthful test graph looked completely different from a deceptive result, but some results were in the middle or all over the place. If an operator wasn't sure, he was allowed a margin of error and could score a test subject as inconclusive. An average of one in ten tests ended up that way.

A polygraph operator wanted to be positive before he cleared a man or damned him. The result of the test would greatly influence the investigation, taking the heat off of an honest man, turning up the burner on a liar. The burden was especially heavy in a murder investigation such as the one in Yellowknife.

For most miners the tests lasted about two hours for the pre-test, fifteen minutes for the test, then ten minutes for the polygraph operator to analyze the results. If a man was found to be deceptive, the officer would read him his rights, tell him that he had failed the test, then ask him why. The officer would push for a confession; the police had found that in half the cases where subjects had failed, they ended up confessing afterward.

Even if the CASAW men had nothing to do with any strike-line crime, many of them found the process an ordeal. Some started to weep when they passed. But the miners opened up to Dauk and Keane, talking about the agony caused by the strike and the murders. Miners who had called the dead men scabs on the line let go of their remorse and grief. Some of the dead men had been their friends.

A handful of hardcore CASAW men refused to take the polygraph, among them Shearing, Bettger and union leader Harry Seeton. Seeton gave the standard reason for his refusal, saying a lawyer had advised him not to take it and that he didn't trust the machine. Its results weren't admissible in court, after all. It wasn't completely accurate.

Along with the refusals, the main problem with the polygraph testing in Yellowknife was the high number of inconclusive tests, about one-quarter of the total. Keane believed there were a number of reasons for the high percentage, not the least being that he and Dauk were very cautious to either pass or fail anyone. Keane also thought they might be getting some skewed results because so many of the CASAW men had guilty consciences, not because they had murdered anyone, but because they were involved in other picket-line violence. The men with inconclusive results were asked to retest. Dauk and Keane were always able to pass all of them on the second go-around, with only one notable exception, striker Roger Warren.

Chapter 10

SOLIDARITY AND SUBVERSION

THE MOUNTIES investigating the blast pulled together every bit as tightly as the CASAW hardcore. If the strikers had the union hall and the Polar Bowl, the Mounties had the third floor of the RCMP detachment and the roving party at the Explorer. If the strikers refused to give interviews, the Mounties kept pressing them to talk.

By the end of the first month of the investigation, the roles of the investigators had become well defined. At the top was Sergeant McIntyre, the fixer. He got the officers whatever they needed. He arranged the surveillance vehicles, coordinated the coming and going of the out-of-town officers and guided each new step in the investigation. McIntyre kept away from direct contact with the union. He did no interviews. He had no strong feelings about Shearing or Bettger or even about the nine dead men. To him, they were names on files. He knew it sounded callous, but he had to stay calm, stay objective. The other officers had enough emotion to push the investigation. He had to keep everything in line, especially as the strain of the conflict with the strikers increasingly angered and wearied his team.

Most of the key investigators were raw when it came to murder investigations—right out of the package, as McIntyre always said, but he was starting to think they could handle the job. Already a handful of

Edmonton men had gone home, and McIntyre was asking more of the northern officers. He didn't like to explain himself more than once. "Lookit," he told them, "this is not a training exercise. This is the real McCoy."

But he tried not to make too much of mistakes. To him the crew was like an outboard motor; if you run it long enough it will break down. Nothing to fret over, especially not with this group. Just find out what had gone wrong, fix it, and steady as she goes.

McIntyre was pleased with the team's spirit. If someone did a good interview, the rest of the officers felt stronger for it. Still, the competition was fierce. The police force measured success by rank and by the job an officer had. This investigation was the ultimate job, and it would help down the road if an investigator stood out. The officers fed on one another, pushing themselves to work longer hours, to concentrate, to do good work. In the first months of the investigation, the officers worked straight through, rarely taking a day off even on the weekend, putting in twelve- to sixteen-hour days. McIntyre asked some of the officers to take time off when they got too tired and anxious, but they were so driven they looked at him like he had three eyes.

McIntyre's core group of investigators included Constable Randy McBride, the boxman, the file manager, an intense, edgy man, who had to soak up everything coming in each day, then spit it back at whoever needed to know; Corporal Dean Ravelli, the crime analyst, affable and sharp, who, like McBride, was a former standout hockey player; Corporal Al McCambridge, the dogged officer on Shearing's file; Corporal Mike Brandford, as hard a worker as any of the other officers, seemingly disorganized but always getting the job done, assigned to handling the RCMP's informants; Corporal Ken Murray, a longtime member of the Yellowknife detachment, a mine of information about the townspeople, a big, strong, easygoing but competent man, who had enough respect around town that he could get access to the hardcore CASAW strikers; Constable Bill Farrell, who handled the wiretaps and also some of the toughest interviews, a possessed, hard-nosed battler, who fought both his fellow officers and the CASAW strikers if he thought he was right and they were wrong; Constable Ken Morrison, Farrell's assistant on the Bettger file, the junior investigator, a university-educated man with a friendly manner and quick wit; Constable Nancy Defer, even-tempered, serious, as tall as most of the men on the team, who had worked the strike line through the summer and was in charge of the search warrants; and Corporal Dale McGowan, who was quickly earning a reputation as the best of the Northwest Territory investigators.

The final piece in the puzzle was finding someone to take over as unit leader from McIntyre, who was scheduled to leave in December. That person turned out to be Corporal Vern White, who had been serving at a one-man detachment in Lake Harbour, a town of 350 on Baffin Island. White was both large in size—6'2", 220 pounds—and ambition. White liked to be first in every line. He was bright, and had the savvy and drive McIntyre had seen in other good investigators. White looked the part of a tough-guy cop with his size, shock of red hair, eagle eyes and punched-in nose. He had arrived in Yellowknife on a two-week commercial crime training course shortly after the September 18 blast. Right away, he had headed up to the third floor to introduce himself to McIntyre.

"If you need a guy to do some interviews, count files—I really don't care what you want done, I'll give you a hand," he said. "I've got nothing else to do."

McIntyre assigned White some grunt tasks, such as watching video of the July 14 riot to identify strikers. White watched until he got a headache, but he was hooked on the case. He felt the power of the Giant Mine file, the adrenaline rush of coming in every day and seeing the unit at work. In his career he had worked on only two homicides. There was so much to learn, so much he had never done before. At the end of his course White was depressed at the thought of going home. "Lake Harbour has got no work," he told McIntyre. "It's not like when I get back I'm going to be busy."

"It doesn't matter. They say they want their detachment commander back no matter what."

Just before White was to leave, however, a Yellowknife divisional staffing officer offered him the job of primary investigator on the permanent Homicide Task Force. White was a senior Northwest Territories officer, he was available and he looked like he could handle it. He grabbed it and took over just before Christmas 1992.

He didn't know as much as the other men about the strike or about murder investigations, but he brought something just as valuable: his own roots in the mining industry. His father, Hector, had been a coal miner in Cape Breton for thirty-seven years. Hector had died of black lung disease only two years back. For his last ten years, he couldn't shower because the steam would make him gasp. Near the end, he was on oxygen day and night.

Every winter the coal dust turned the snow gray in White's hometown of New Waterford. It was a brawling, drinking town of ten thousand with thirty bars, but no hotels, motels or restaurants. The mines were dirty, cold, damp, primitive and dangerous, thick with coal dust and methane gas. The mine drifts ran for miles under the Atlantic Ocean. Saltwater dripped from the ceiling.

White had known many men who died in the mines. A blast had left a big scar on his father's face; Hector couldn't breathe from one side of his nose.

Hector was a devoted member of the United Mine Workers. After the union came in, he had seen his pay rise from a pittance. Vern grew up hearing talk around the table about the union's fight for safer conditions and hearing stories about the national president, Bull Marsh, who pounded his fist in meetings to shake up the company suits, and had half an ear, the other half chewed off in a fist fight. Whenever the company was trying something, it was the union that straightened it out.

In his interviews with CASAW's Newfoundland contingent, which included both Terry Legge and Al Shearing, White slipped into a heavy Nova Scotian accent and dropped the name of Bull Marsh. He told them he knew that miners depended on the unions to keep a mine safe. But the CASAW men pushed their accident–conspiracy theories on White, telling him what they had told every Mountie: "You don't know! You're not a fuckin' miner."

"Listen bud," White would shoot back. "I was in a coal mine when I was seven years old. I know what a coal miner does. I know what a union is. I know where you're coming from. But this is not a game for me. I've got a job to do here. I really don't care about this other stuff. I really don't care about Peggy Witte. I don't care about your strike. I don't care about anything except the fact that nine guys got themselves all over the side of a wall in that mine. You don't deserve for that to happen to you, and nobody can say that they deserved to die."

White could count on one hand the number of CASAW strikers who ever disagreed with him on that point, and once White had them agreeing, he had them where he wanted. "Well," he'd say, "if they didn't deserve to die, bud, we should be shaking hands and walking down the road here. Let's go get this guy."

White liked many of the union men. He thought they deserved better leadership than they got. But White's own feelings on the strike were less straightforward than the image he presented to the union men. If he were on strike, White thought, he might pull some of the same stunts. He'd chuck a rock at a man who was taking his job away. But in White's mind the Giant strike came about not because of any worthwhile issue, but because Harry Seeton and Peggy Witte could not deal with each other.

White loved to go head-on with the primary suspects and reveled in the verbal sparring with the strikers. He was a relentless, sometimes savage, competitor in every aspect of his life, an attribute he had picked up back in New Waterford. The big joke growing up there was, "I went to the fights and a dance broke out." When White got out of Cape Breton and started to meet men who had never punched a guy in the face in their lives, he couldn't believe it. Sometimes White had punched two different guys in the face in one day. He even enjoyed fighting. He got a crazy feeling, started shaking with adrenaline and tried to land as many punches as he could right off the bat.

He couldn't play any game for fun, not cards, not shinny hockey. If he lost he was the first one to shake everybody's hand and laugh and joke with the victor, but his mind was already working on how to win the next time.

In grade twelve he had left Cape Breton on a Rotary exchange, ending up as a boarder in a prosperous white Protestant neighborhood in Millington, Tennessee. The families took to White not only because he was a nonstop talker and storyteller, but also because he played ferocious defensive tackle for the high school football team. Once, he broke his nose in a game, and he drilled a hole in his mouth piece to keep playing. He tried to take out the knees of his opponents, hitting them low and to the side. It was the same in hockey. In a serious game, if there was a good player on the other team, White would try to fight him to take him out of the game.

White had joined the force when he was twenty-one, after taking a two-year business administration course at the College of Cape Breton. He wanted to be a Mountie because the work looked interesting and the RCMP were respected. In New Waterford, if your dad was a big man in town, the local police would let you off, but if a Mountie came around, it didn't matter who you were, you were busted.

At the RCMP's training depot in Regina, it didn't bother White when his instructors yelled in his face. He took it as another game to play and win. He scored well at courses on human relations, boxing and ground fighting. In one training fight he ripped his opponent's ear right down to the lobe.

He started his career in Stephenville, Newfoundland, a nice town, but too sedate for him. The first chance he got he transferred up to an Inuit village, Nain, on the Labrador coast. VietNain, the Mounties called it. Nain had only eleven hundred people, but an aggravated assault every week. Sexual assaults were almost as common. Ninety percent of the Inuit were on welfare. Half the houses didn't have plumbing so the shit piled up outside. Alcohol seemed to be in almost every home. The Inuit drank home brew, a hundred packages of bread yeast in a bucket with molasses and sugar peas. It was a yellow soup that stank like hell. Gas sniffing was also a problem. Sudden Infant Death Syndrome and Fetal Alcohol Syndrome were common. Sometimes people passed out in the cold and froze to death. One year Nain had Canada's highest per capita rate of violent crime.

White was so busy that the misery of the place never got him down. In February, 1985, he met his wife, Loretta, in Goose Bay, Labrador. Loretta's family was from Davis Inlet. After they married, Loretta moved up to Nain. For seventy nights in a row, Vern and Loretta didn't eat supper together because he was called out. He put in hundreds of hours of overtime every month, but didn't claim for it. It wasn't the thing to do if a young constable wanted to get a good assessment. White's performance appraisals were exceptionally good in his two years there.

After Nain, he applied to work in the Northwest Territories. He couldn't imagine going back to a quiet place like Stephenville. He was sent to Inuvik, where he got into plainclothes drug work. He became adept at working with informants, the flotsam of the drug trade. Most of the informants weren't turning in their friends, they were ratting on the competition.

White got into commercial crime work in Yellowknife, then took the Lake Harbour job. It meant a promotion to corporal, but there was little police work to do in the town, which truly was a dry community and had hardly any crime. White was free to spend more time with his two small daughters, Chelsea and Courtney, and also to help out around town, working with the Inuit art co-op and speaking at the school. Still, he hungered for action. When the opportunity came in Yellowknife, he grabbed it with a choke hold.

He loved the challenge. Throughout his career he had never felt he had worked hard enough. He recalled how one summer as a teenager he had worked cutting and laying sod. At the end of the day he'd stand back and look out at a new lawn. It had made him feel good, and at night he was drained and slept well. Police work was seldom like that, but this case took everything he had, physically and mentally, every single day.

The only thing that bothered White about the attitude of the CASAW men was their persistent attacks on the RCMP's credibility. Not only would they not take the RCMP's word that the blast was deliberately set, but they stuck to the notion that Peggy Witte and Royal Oak controlled the investigation. White told the strikers that the police had nothing to gain by saying anything other than the truth, but the strikers wouldn't believe him. Instead, they said it was obvious that the blast had been engineered by the RCMP, the government and Peggy Witte. All White could do was shake his head and tell them, "Look you're a sane man here; you can't talk this way. It doesn't make sense."

Many of the RCMP officers were growing tired of the CASAW denials. More and more, the investigators unloaded on any man who was believed to be withholding information: "Why are you protecting these guys? These murderers are hiding behind union solidarity. They're hiding behind honest men, behind the skirts of women and behind children."

The union struck back in early November, six weeks after the blast. Harry Seeton sent a letter to the RCMP Public Complaints Commission. He claimed that the union men had been subjected to discriminatory, intolerable treatment throughout the strike, and it had only worsened since the blast. Seeton charged that the RCMP had failed to investigate adequately the legitimate complaints of union members, which included death threats, assaults and the spread of anti-CASAW hate literature. All the union members had been requested by the executive to grant interviews to the police, and almost everyone had obliged, Seeton said, but still RCMP officers were using intimidation and other improper tactics.

The Mounties had few apologies for Seeton or any CASAW man. Sergeant Dave Grundy admitted there had been some mistakes in the handling of the labor dispute; on a few occasions the complaints of the strikers should have been handled with greater care. As for the murder investigation, however, Grundy said there was no harassment of anyone. The RCMP were just trying to find out the truth.

The Mounties kept after the strikers. Seeton himself was badgered for a follow-up interview. He ended up yelling at Nancy Defer to leave him alone. Defer said she didn't like his tone of voice.

"That's the only way you can hear," Seeton told her. "I'm not coming down for another interview. I'm not coming down for a polygraph. Leave me alone."

White knew his staff might occasionally push too hard. A few times the Mounties apologized to the strikers for something done or said, but White didn't fret. Who could go through life without apologizing now and then? In hundreds and hundreds of interviews, it was reasonable to expect that the investigators would sometimes go too far and say something offensive. In White's opinion the investigators should have received medals for the way they handled themselves, walking into a room with men some Mounties had known for years, only to be told that the dead men were nothing but fucking scabs and the Mounties were little better.

The RCMP's persistence at last started to crack the solidarity of even the hardcore strikers. More and more suspects eliminated themselves by passing the polygraph, including striker Gord Kendall, the mastermind of the June 29 graffiti sortie, who came in for his lie detector test in early November, six weeks after the blast. Kendall gave Sergeant Dauk some crucial information about the September 2 vent shaft bomb, saying that Bettger had admitted that he and a few others had set the blast.

Kendall also elaborated on the graffiti sortie. He said Shearing and Bettger gave him six blasting caps and fourteen pieces of stick powder, which they had stolen from the mine. Kendall said he destroyed the explosives. He claimed Shearing and Bettger told him they were thinking about stealing AMEX, putting it in the C-dry and hooking it up to the central blast. They'd all watch as the mine blew sky high. Kendall admitted he had talked about blowing up the mine himself.

At the union hall, word quickly spread that Kendall had blabbed. The CASAW strikers suspected he was helping the cops so he could get off on an arson charge; early in the strike, Kendall had allegedly set a shack on fire at the mine.

A few days later the RCMP got further confirmation from striker Conrad Lisoway that Shearing and Bettger had committed the vent shaft blast. Along with Legge, Lisoway had been a lookout. Lisoway told the police Bettger had supplied the timing device. Lisoway also said Shearing had taken down power poles by wrapping explosive B-line around them, then blasting a detonator cap with a battery.

The targets of the investigation were breaking down into two groups, men like Terry Legge and Lisoway, who grudgingly cooperated with the RCMP, and Shearing and Bettger, who not only refused to admit anything, but who were planning new attacks on the mine. The leaders of the Cambodian Cowboys carried on as if the September 18 blast had never happened, as if the strikers were still riding white horses. Their behavior only focused the investigators on them all the more.

Bettger seemed to be forever hatching new and violent plans. It was hard for the RCMP to tell if he was serious or just blustering. While the investigators knew he had set off bombs in the past, he wasn't doing anything now but talking trash and downing a few more power poles.

The Mounties learned about most of these plans through informants and electronic bugging. Listening probes were put in Shearing's apartment and in Bettger's garage and truck. Special O surveillance teams followed them constantly. Local officers did most of the observation, but they were helped by outside teams from Edmonton, Saskatchewan and Vancouver. The prairie officers knew how to blend into the Yellowknife crowd, but the Vancouver guys looked like tourists with their new jackets, gloves and boots.

Shearing saw less of Bettger in the months after the blast. The Bear seemed to have a new friend, Marvin Farris. Farris had been a hardrock miner at Giant for six years, though not a particularly good one. He was a thin, small man, thirtyish, with long dirty blond hair. He was a partier who liked to smoke pot and was a wanna-be biker, the owner of a Harley Davidson.

Farris and Bettger worked together hauling a few loads of chickens up from Grande Prairie for a Yellowknife dogsled trainer. On their trips, Bettger talked about his theory that the explosion was caused by Royal Oak. He told Farris that the police were wasting money trying to convict him of the offense, building a case on circumstantial evidence.

On November 17, Farris was at Bettger's house when the Bear talked about how he had tried but failed to make a land mine with two pieces of pipe, one fitting inside the other, a shotgun shell inside. A few days later, Bettger joked with Farris about getting back at Justice Ted Richards, who had earlier convicted him of breaching the injunction by going out to the strike line. One idea was to put weed killer on Richards' lawn. Another was to send kiddie porn to Richards' home.

Bettger mentioned one other plan to Farris, this one about blasting a power transformer with a shotgun and shutting down the mine. Farris had previously seen a freshly sawed-off 12-gauge shotgun in Bettger's garage. Bettger modified this plan a few days later, saying a team of strikers could go out to gate four, get past the security guards by blasting five shots into the radiator of their truck, then fire slugs into the hoist equipment and close the mine for a few days.

Bettger didn't know it, but everything he told Marvin Farris, Farris told the RCMP. Farris had become a paid informant after the blast, the most gaping fissure in the hardcore's solidarity. On the strike line Farris had been a picket captain. He had heard a lot of big talk about mischief, violence, setting off bombs. Some of it was just talk, guys taking credit for stuff they hadn't done just to look good. Farris believed that the September 18 blast was an accident, but he also knew men like his friend Bettger and Al Shearing had done more than just talk. One night Farris had overheard old Art St. Ammand at the Polar Bowl talking about the graffiti sortie. Farris wondered if maybe someone had gone haywire and set the bomb. While he admired Bettger for taking such an active role in the strike, Farris decided to rat on him and take the RCMP's money. His goal was to insinuate himself into Bettger's confidence by posing as someone who was ready for any new action against Royal Oak. Often when he met the Bear, Farris wore a body pack to record their conversations. A listening probe was also set up at Farris's house.

The task force investigators continued to try to convince Bettger to talk. The interviews got more and more accusatory. On December 8, Bettger met again with the Mounties and again told them nothing. Afterward, Farris tried to get something out of him, asking how the interrogation went. Bettger said it felt like being put through a sausage grinder.

"For what?" Farris asked. "Like blowing up the vent plant and the satellite dish and the graffiti excursion underground?"

"But I wouldn't admit to that," Bettger said.

"That's common knowledge."

"But I wouldn't admit that to them."

The winter of '92 brought with it the usual endless months of dark. The sun rose just above the horizon at 10:00 A.M., then set again just after 2:00 P.M. The investigators faced the coming of Christmas with no solution and the departure of their leader, Al McIntyre. The officers now realized the investigation wasn't going to wrap up in short order. A schedule was drawn up for the next six months. The officers at last could plan ahead for holidays, which made them feel better, but the realization that they still might be at it in six months was a blow.

McIntyre could see that his officers were getting a bit frayed, overreacting to small matters, getting into arguments. At the same time McIntyre had to leave. His last day was December 10. After that the plan was he'd only come up to Yellowknife every three weeks. A local inspector would oversee things while Vern White would run the day-to-day operation.

McIntyre wasn't happy to leave, but his family and real job were in Edmonton, and it was time to go home. He thought White had the tenacity and organizational skills to do the job. McIntyre also knew that because White had lived in Yellowknife for a time in the late eighties, he had local contacts.

After McIntyre left, the only out-of-town officers remaining were corporals Dale McGowan and Al McCambridge. The brunt of the pressure for getting results fell on White. He was a junior corporal in the RCMP, and there was some jealousy about his quick rise. Some officers said he was in a no-lose situation with the murder investigation. If he didn't solve it, what did it matter—McIntyre and his Edmonton boys hadn't been able to solve it either. If White did luck out, then he got big points.

White never saw it that way. He knew how complex the investigation was and how little experience he had. He never saw himself as the boss, just as another member of the team. He took longer to make his decisions than McIntyre. If White had to do a covert operation with an agent, he made phone calls to double check if everything was in order. He often called McIntyre for advice though McIntyre wasn't always giving it. He wanted to force White to take command.

Most of the officers on the task force thought well of White. He took over the system McIntyre had built and didn't screw it up. His drive helped propel the investigation. While some of the other investigators slowed down through December, he and a few others kept grinding. They were driven not only by the fear of failure, but also by the fear of another murder, that the mass murderer might kill again.

Some of the RCMP investigators believed the murderer's next target would be one of them. Every morning, the investigators took to looking around their cars for strange footprints in the snow. Al McCambridge didn't think the killer would go after a cop. It was one thing to blow up a man-car full of line crossers, but another to kill a Mountie. The bad guy certainly wouldn't want that kind of thunder coming down on him, both from the RCMP and everyone else in town. Another line crosser, though, someone like Jim O'Neil, would make a perfect target, McCambridge thought. He feared another killing all the more because he suspected the culprit would be his man, Shearing, the Night Crawler, and it would mean he had doubly failed.

McCambridge's suspicions about Shearing were kept alive by the reports coming in from the wiretap operators and Farris. In early December, Farris reported that Shearing and Bettger had talked about wanting to buy rocket launchers, about making missiles out of model rockets and about cutting the power lines if Peggy Witte refused to negotiate. The people of Yellowknife had soured on CASAW because of the power failures, but Shearing didn't care.

"Fuck the town," he had said.

McCambridge had been trying to eliminate Shearing as a suspect since the first week of the strike, but was no closer to succeeding. Nor was he much closer to proving Shearing's guilt.

As much as any Mountie, McCambridge loved being a cop. He was always a straight arrow, the son of a military man and a sea cadet himself. He had never smoked pot and always kept his hair short. He saw things simply and clearly: turn the key on the bad guys and keep the streets clean. He was never bothered by the abuse from the strikers. They could say what they liked; he wasn't going to stop investigating them.

Shearing believed Al McCambridge was obsessed with finding him guilty. But McCambridge always felt he dealt fairly and honestly with the striker. He told Shearing that his greatest wish was to take his file from the suspect pile and put it in the concluded file. "You don't have to help," McCambridge told the striker. "This is Canada; this isn't Russia. You're innocent until proven guilty. However, we're dealing with a mass murder, and there's no question it was a murder, and because of that we have to go above and beyond. We have to impose upon you the need to assist us in helping to eliminate you as a suspect."

McCambridge thought about Shearing's psychology. He realized that more than anything the striker wanted glory and craved attention. McCambridge believed Shearing secretly wanted to be the union's leader, but he knew he didn't have the smarts or the bargaining skills. Instead, he had become the Night Crawler, the union's man of action. He had gone from being a wallflower to the toast of the union. The battles with the RCMP and the Pinkies were a game to him, and he loved his camouflage gear and his slingshots. The June 29 graffiti mission had been the ultimate wild night out, complete with photographs to show off to the boys.

Shearing rose to the top of the Cambodian Cowboys, McCambridge thought, because he was able and fearless, but also easily manipulated. The smart guys in the union didn't do anything illegal themselves; they just pointed the Al Shearings of the world in the right direction.

If Shearing were truly a righteous union leader who cared only about mine safety and helping out the victims of underground blasts, McCambridge believed he would have acted differently after the blast. Shearing should have been the first to agree to take the polygraph test. The other union men would have followed his lead. In McCambridge's mind, Shearing had been given the chance to be what he always wanted to be, a leader, but he had failed. He thought it would play better with his union pals to snub the Mounties. He got attention by defying the RCMP at every step. He turned it into a game, trying to dodge the surveillance teams, picking up his telephone before he went to bed and asking for a wake-up call because he knew it was bugged. Every time he went the distance with the investigators in an interview and didn't confess to anything, it was a victory for him.

When other CASAW strikers tried to convince McCambridge of Shearing's innocence, they always brought up Shearing's initial reaction to the blast, how he had wept, then went about organizing a mine rescue team. McCambridge wasn't impressed. In fact, he started to see Shearing's rescue attempt in the worst possible light. Why would Al

Shearing want to go to the blast site? Maybe it was to see what the bomb had done. Maybe it was to destroy evidence. McCambridge studied the other suspects, but didn't see any of them having the credentials that Shearing had.

By the New Year the RCMP had cut the list of prime suspects from forty to about ten. While each of the ten had something pointing to him—most often a history of strike-line violence—all of them had things that made them look innocent as well, either a strong alibi, a history of cooperating with the RCMP, a passing grade on the polygraph or a feeling that the man simply lacked the extraordinary confidence and skill it would take to set such a bomb.

In McCambridge's mind Bettger had to be eliminated because he didn't have the courage to act alone. McCambridge knew Bettger was mechanically inclined and wouldn't be afraid of the bomb, but he also believed the Bear would get hopelessly lost if he went into the mine on his own. Bettger had always taken the man-car or a truck down the ramp to get to his work area.

As for Shearing, however, he had the balls, the know-how and the motivation to set the blast. He was an excellent mine rescue captain. He could find his way through the mine and handle the pressure of going alone. He wasn't a miner, but he could set up a simple explosive device, especially if someone else made it for him and told him how to set it.

McCambridge worked at checking out Shearing's alibi: that he had been in jail awaiting his charges for the alleged assault on the Pinkerton guard at the OK Economy; he got out on the afternoon of September 17; he helped a friend move; he went for drinks at the Polar Bowl; he went home with his common-law wife of three years, Kara Roderique, around midnight; he went to bed with Kara.

Kara's teenaged son, Mike, watched TV on the couch until 3:30 A.M. Shearing would likely have had to walk by him if he had left the apartment.

Shearing met with the police once, twice, three times, four times, always giving lengthy interviews. He never changed his alibi, and McCambridge could uncover no inconsistencies. But he didn't believe that Shearing's stepson, Mike, was reliable; the boy was half sleeping, half awake. McCambridge also believed Kara might lie. He had heard rumors that Shearing used to sneak out the window of their apartment during the summer to go do stuff. Maybe he had waited until Kara was asleep. He could move fast and it was just a ten-minute car ride to the mine site.

But why had no one seen Shearing out there? Why had no one seen his vehicle? McCambridge also wondered about the lack of physical evidence. Nothing, no boots or footprints, tied him to the site. Size eleven Kamik boots were much too big for him, though it was possible he could have worn many pairs of socks.

Early in the New Year the strikers stopped talking so much about the blast. They were again focusing on developments in the strike and on daily living. The police didn't like it. When Shearing was with Marvin Farris or talking on the phone, they wanted him talking about the crime, not about Peggy Witte or about fixing snowmobiles. To stir things up, McCambridge and the other investigators decided to play a game, planting a story in the media about the striker. McCambridge knew the story might generate talk between Farris and Shearing, and also between Shearing and Kara.

Kara had been interviewed by the police and disliked their continued focus on her husband. She was sure he was innocent. She might not like him appearing in a newspaper story and the two might quarrel about it. The police bug would pick up every word.

Shearing had been told in his interviews that he was a top suspect, and he hadn't been shy about spreading the news around the union hall. McCambridge believed that Shearing so loved the limelight and was so proud of his status as the number one suspect that he would likely talk to a reporter about it as well. The *Edmonton Journal*, the main outside daily newspaper sold in Yellowknife, was tipped off about Shearing's talk around the union hall. Reporter Greg Owens, one of the authors of this book, called Shearing. The striker opened up.

To Shearing, it was he who was planting the story. He talked about being harassed by the RCMP and gave his alibi. Kara Roderique was also interviewed. She said she could vouch for Shearing's alibi.

Just as McCambridge had guessed, Kara didn't like her husband telling the newspaper he was the prime suspect. She thought it sounded like he was bragging. She worried about the information getting out, but Shearing had no such fears. He thought he could take the heat.

The story appeared on the *Journal*'s front page on January 18, 1993, under the headline "Man Fears He's Suspected of Fatal N.W.T. Mine Blast."

"They told me I was the number one prime suspect and that was after six and a half hours in there with them," Shearing was quoted as saying. "They've got me guilty and I shouldn't have to prove myself innocent.

"I give them just as hard of a time as they give me. I tell them exactly what's on my mind."

John Lang, a representative of the Confederation of Canadian Unions, was quoted as saying that the Shearing case was a blatant example of the psychological rubber hose the RCMP were using on the strikers and union family members.

After the interview, the RCMP heard Shearing and Roderique squabble because she thought he was enjoying the publicity, but Shearing continued to deny that he had any involvement in the blast. Neither did he let slip anything significant with Farris. McCambridge hadn't uncovered the link he was looking for.

Shearing and Kara later agreed to meet and be interviewed by *Journal* reporter Marina Jiminez in early February, little more than four months after the blast. Jiminez met the couple at the Explorer. Shearing told Jiminez he'd now been interviewed by the police six times while Roderique had been interviewed three times and her son, Mike, twice. Shearing said he knew nothing about the blast or any other crimes. "They've come out and said I was like a boss man, snap your fingers and go do this. . . . They know if I've got something to tell them, I'll tell them. They told me if I take the polygraph they wouldn't harass me anymore."

"But they started telling people after they took the polygraph, they had to be hypnotized," Roderique interjected. "They're forcing their will on people and it's upsetting, especially when you tell them the truth. You tell them the same story three times. It's the truth, and in your heart you know it's the truth, and they still don't believe you. It's like calling you a liar."

Shearing said the RCMP hadn't adequately investigated the ProCon replacement workers. Maybe one of them set the blast to disgrace the union, he said. Either that or they were upset at guys like Norm Hourie, Joe Pandev and Chris Neill because the ex-CASAW miners were getting the cream-of-the-crop deals in the mine, the best money-making headings. "I think they should be putting their efforts some-where else, replacement workers or scabs. They're the ones who have the best access."

Jiminez asked Shearing how he was holding up.

"The investigation has been more stressful than the strike because I can deal with the strike. Two people got to sit down and talk. But with the RCMP, they'll tap your phone, they'll follow you all over town, fol-low the kids all over town. That's what they've been doing."

Roderique said she didn't like the personal nature of the RCMP's interrogations, such as questions about their lovemaking and whether he ever beat her. The police had even been asking her son's friends about them.

Despite everything, Shearing told Jiminez he didn't resent the police. "I have fun with them. When I get out of the apartment build-ing I check the street, and I know which car's not supposed to be there. So I'll pretend I'm walking towards the light, and this car comes out, he's got to pull out, he's committed now. After I see what the street is like, I just walk up to the corner and then I turn and walk back the other way. By the time he goes around the block, I'm nowhere to be found. I had one chase me around town here. I went in stores I had no intention of going in. In one door, out the other."

Roderique was less enthused. "Sometimes I feel like leaving town," she told the reporter. "It's not the same as it was. . . . The gossip is ter-rible. Al is the scapegoat for every little stupid thing, and every story, it's 'Oh, he's involved.' We'd like to get back to the simple way of living. Normal."

After talking to Jiminez, Shearing stopped giving lengthy inter-views to reporters and the RCMP. But McCambridge didn't give up. He wanted to get Shearing on the polygraph. At one point McCambridge persuaded Shearing to come down to the Explorer to see the polygraph and talk to Keane and Dauk. At the meeting, Shearing refused to sit in the chair next to the instrument. Instead, he sat on the end of the bed. McCambridge wondered what the chair was going to do to him if he had nothing to hide.

Shearing was never offered any deals about his strike-line crimes, such as the vent shaft blast. But McCambridge thought Shearing could likely have written a Get Out of Jail Free card if he had suggested a deal, then passed the polygraph.

Shearing explained his refusal to go on the lie detector to his old friend Terry Legge, saying it was like driving down the road: you're sober as a judge, but a cop wants you to take a breathalyzer and you don't want to take it. That was your right, wasn't it? And wasn't this the same?

The argument convinced Legge at first, but as the investigation focused more and more on the Night Crawler, Legge became impatient. He hated to see his good friend getting the blame. He believed the accusations were crap. He and Shearing had been friends for fifteen years. When strikers who didn't know Shearing asked Legge about him, Legge couldn't say enough good about him. Kids liked him, Legge said. Dogs liked him. Shearing was a do-gooder, a guy who would help a little old lady across the street.

The RCMP tried to get at Shearing through Legge. To persuade Legge to help out and to get him to realize the seriousness of the blast, Constable John Turgeron called him to the detachment and showed him a binder full of photographs. "This is what it's all about," Turgeron said and pushed the binder toward Legge. "You don't have to look at it."

"What the fuck is it?"

"It's the pictures of all the evidence, all the bodies. You've been very cooperative. You've persuaded a lot of guys to come and take the lie detector. But I want you to let the membership know that this is not a game. This is what it's about. The pictures are pretty gruesome, but if you want to look at it, go ahead. If not, don't look."

"No problem," Legge said, opening the binder. "I can handle that." He studied the pictures. "I got to admit to you, that is very disturbing; this is very devastating," he said at last. "It's a world of pain. But it still doesn't make it murder."

But Legge was coming to realize that the only way to prove it was an accident was to cooperate. It was the only way the investigation could get anywhere. He knew, for instance, that old Art St. Ammand had told the cops it was his billy club on a reward poster they had distributed, that he had left the billy club at the mine on the June 29 graffiti mission and that it wasn't linked to the murder.

The more Legge thought about Shearing's comparing the polygraph with the breathalyzer, the more he saw the argument wasn't sound. You're talking about the murder of nine men here! Not a fuckin' breathalyzer test!

At last Legge told Shearing it was time to go in: "You got nothing to worry about. There will be no charges. There will be nothing. All they want to hear about is this murder, but you guys resisting is fuckin' everything up. You're hindering the cops."

Legge told Shearing he could set up a meeting with White. Shearing agreed to go and talk with the investigator at the Red Apple restaurant, but he never showed. Legge later found out that Shearing had bumped into the Bear, who had persuaded him not to go.

Legge realized that Shearing liked playing a cat-and-mouse game with the Mounties. He'd see Al out on the picket line, bothering the cops, saying, "Even if I knew something, I wouldn't tell you."

Despite Shearing's attitude, Corporal White was starting to have big doubts that Shearing had set the blast. In White's mind, Shearing didn't seem the type who would kill anyone. He was too simple, too friendly. He might be acting guilty by lying about his involvement in the smaller blasts and refusing the polygraph, but maybe Shearing just didn't trust the Mounties. He probably believed that even if he was telling the truth, the polygraph operators would fail him and that would be as good as a confession.

As for Shearing's alibi, White believed Kara Roderique when she said that she and Al had slept together. The couple had been apart for a few days while Shearing was in jail. It was their first night together again. They'd have a lot to say.

White still hoped that the next interview might provide the key piece of evidence. With it, all the pieces of the Progression Theory would come together. The investigators had gathered so much evidence about Shearing and Bettger's involvement in other crimes that White expected something would tie one or both of them to the mass murder. Still, White knew he shouldn't be completely blinkered. In the end the police had nothing at all to link either Shearing or Bettger directly to the September 18 blast. Someone else could just as easily have set the bomb.

Chapter 11

THE
ENIGMA

Outside of the Cambodian Cowboys, the only CASAW men the investigators went back to again and again were the thirteen strikers who had worked the night shift on the picket line during the early hours of September 18. They were seen as potential witnesses. There was a good chance one of them had seen something that would make the difference in the case. The RCMP didn't know what that something was so they had to know every little thing that had gone on.

Corporal Dale McGowan and Constable Nancy Defer got the job, a stiff challenge. Almost all thirteen strikers seemed forthright about what they did and who they saw that night, but they had been out on the picket line for months. One night blurred into the next.

Of all the strikers who had worked that shift, the one who most interested the police was Roger Warren. Defer and McGowan knew that at 6:00 A.M., Brian Broda, a Giant Mine supervisor, had spotted a man fitting Warren's description walking on the Ingraham Trail, only a few hundred yards from the B-138 portal where the murderer had escaped from the mine. McGowan was also curious about Warren's admission to Defer in his first interview that he had seen two shadowy men, possibly CASAW strikers, on mine property earlier that morning at 2:00 A.M. McGowan was curious as well about the story passed on by old-time Yellowknifer Robert Carroll about Warren appearing nervous and distracted at Nettie's coffee shop on the morning of the blast. Carroll's story fit into the RCMP's feeling that Warren might one day be the chief Crown witness. If he had seen two buddies heading toward the Akaitcho shaft to break in and commit the crime, little wonder he was so agitated that morning.

Defer called Warren on October 16, one month after the blast, asking to see the clothes he had on that night. Defer told Warren they wanted to show the clothing to the mine employee who had spotted him.

No trouble, Warren said.

When McGowan and Defer arrived at Warren's apartment in a walk-up across from the union hall, Warren had the clothing ready for them: a pair of boots, a green ball cap and the hood from a khaki parka. The logo on the cap had been blackened in with a felt marker, along with the white trim on the boots; Warren said he'd done it so he could do ninja stuff out at the picket line. He said he didn't have the entire parka to give them, that he had spilled gas on it and had left it outside to get rid of the smell, but it had been stolen.

McGowan and Defer noticed that the boots were size eleven Kamiks, the same size and brand the murderer had worn into Giant Mine.

The two officers hurried back to the detachment with their discovery. Ident officer Scott McKenzie photographed the boots. McKenzie compared them with the casts and photographs of the murderer's boot prints. They were similar, except the soles of Warren's boots had numerous melt marks and cuts. With ink that could only be seen under ultraviolet light, McKenzie and Defer marked their initials and the date inside the boots. They wanted to be able to identify them in case they ever came back.

McGowan and Defer didn't bother showing the clothing to Broda, the mine supervisor. When they returned the articles to Warren, they made sure they didn't make a big fuss about the boots. They didn't want to tip off anyone that the police were interested in size eleven Kamiks. They didn't ask Warren what had happened to burn and cut the soles.

Warren was asked if he would dress in the clothing, then meet McGowan and Defer at the mine site. He agreed. On the Ingraham

Trail, the two officers had Warren show them where he had seen the two shadowy men and where Broda had seen him. McGowan took photographs.

The Kamik boots made Warren a suspect. Both McGowan and Defer thought they were extremely suspicious, and the two investigators decided that Warren should take a polygraph test. Before leaving him that day, Defer read him his rights to alert him that his status in the investigation had changed.

"Roger, did you have anything to do with murder?"

"No."

"Do you know who did the murder?"

"No."

"Do you know who planned the murder?"

"No."

"Were you involved in planning the murder?"

"No."

Defer marked his answers down in a formal statement, which Warren signed.

Three days later, Warren was scheduled to come in for his polygraph test with Dauk at the Explorer. That morning, however, Warren called up Defer to say he didn't want to take the test. He was worried about the machine. McGowan called back and managed to convince Warren to at least come in to check out the polygraph.

At 9:20 A.M. Warren met Defer and McGowan in the hotel lobby. They took him up to Room 701 to see Dauk, then went to monitor the interview, sitting with Keane in an adjoining room.

No tape recorder or microphone was visible in the polygraph room, but Dauk told Warren he was being taped. Warren was also told that the police viewed him as an eyewitness because of his sighting of the two shadowy men. Warren told Dauk he wasn't involved in the murders, that his hands were so bad he couldn't even climb down a ladder into the mine.

During the pre-test interview, Warren drank many glasses of water. Several times he had to go to the bathroom. He seemed willing to help out, but he also looked uncomfortable. Dauk pushed Warren to tell him if there was anything on his mind, especially something that might affect his polygraph test.

"This thing is ruining the town," Dauk reminded him.

"Truly, me too," Warren said. "My nerves are just shot right out the window."

When it was time to get hooked up to the polygraph, Warren refused. Dauk was even more suspicious then, especially about the boots and Warren's story about the two shadowy men. The polygraph operator decided to go right into an interrogation about the night and early morning before the blast. "Tell me what you saw. Tell me what you heard. Do you know, Roger, I've been doing this job for a long time? I've seen people in really tight spots. And you're in a tight spot right now."

Warren continued to waffle so Dauk pressed harder.

"Roger, are you a criminal?"

"I don't think so."

"I don't think so either. I'm convinced you're not. But what you're doing now is what a criminal would do. I'm very worried about that. I don't want you leaving here being suspected of criminal activity in this thing. Okay? Plain and simple. Because, Roger, if you don't tell me, the police are going to suspect you of criminal activity in this thing. Okay? Now I'm going to tell you something else: if you went down in the mine and set them explosives that killed those nine miners, don't talk to me. . . . If it's anything less than that, Roger, talk to me. Talk to me now. Tell me now because I don't think you're a criminal."

Warren said nothing. Dauk waited. Still nothing. Dauk could see that Warren was holding something in.

"Okay, if I've misread you, I guess you're a criminal. Because you fooled me, okay?"

Still nothing. Dauk kept pushing, asking Warren why he would not talk.

"There is no reason," Warren said.

"Yes, there is, Roger. Roger, there definitely is a reason. Is it because you were personally involved?"

"No."

"Then tell me what it is. Tell me what it is. Is it loyalty?"

"No."

"What is it then? What is it then?"

"Just fear of being implicated in this thing."

Warren told Dauk that when he had talked to McGowan and Defer he felt a terrible foreboding that they thought he had done

190 The Third Suspect

something, and he was getting the same feeling now. "My wife says, 'Don't go near this place.' Jeez, I think she was right."

"Oh no, Roger," Dauk said. "I hope not."

"You better realize there is a lot of fear in this kind of stuff," Warren said a moment later. "This is scary shit."

At last Warren gave a piece of information that appeased Dauk. The striker said he thought both of the shadowy men were strikers up to tricks against the company. While he hadn't clearly seen the faces of either man, he said he thought one of them was CASAW striker Conrad Lisoway, who was widely known as one of the Cambodian Cowboys. Warren let Lisoway off the hook a bit, saying he was sure Lisoway wouldn't do anything like that. He also said he'd heard that Lisoway had a solid alibi for the night before the blast.

Dauk left the room momentarily to speak with McGowan, Defer and Keane. He asked them if he should press Warren. They decided he shouldn't, that Warren might never agree to a polygraph if he were pushed too hard.

If Warren had hoped to end his involvement with the police by meeting Dauk, he had done the opposite. Dauk had taken a few hard shots at him, and immediately Warren had recoiled. The Mounties were now more interested in him than ever. Constable Farrell made an application to get a wiretap on Warren's house. The Special I officers installed it in early November.

The Warren file was going to be a difficult but crucial assignment. The investigator would have to balance Warren as a witness and a suspect, trying to get at the truth about the boots and the two shadowy men, but never upsetting Warren so much that he would refuse to cooperate. The officer would have to be the good cop and the bad cop at the same time. Sergeant McIntyre and Corporal White decided to give the job to Dale McGowan. He had as much intensity as any of the other investigators, but he set himself apart by being able to stay focused, to steadily hammer away day after day. His attitude was upbeat and he was never intimidated. He could persuade the strikers to do what the RCMP needed.

Corporal McGowan started to check out Warren, and he liked much of what he heard. Warren respected his profession and the police. He was both a skilled, hardworking miner and a good family man.

A few days after the meeting with Dauk, McGowan called up Warren's apartment, hoping to convince him to come in for a polygraph. Helen Warren answered the phone. She told McGowan that Roger was in the hospital. In the wake of his meeting with Dauk, he thought he might have had a heart attack.

Warren had gone down to the emergency ward at Stanton Hospital. He said he had a pain in the center of his chest and going up and down his arm. Dr. Andrew McMillan feared Warren had had a heart attack. He gave him oxygen and a nitroglycerin pill to open the blood vessels in the heart and get the blood flowing.

Tests later showed that Warren had not had a heart attack, but that every third beat of his heart was irregular. Dr. McMillan diagnosed anxiety as the likely cause of the problem. He prescribed a beta-blocker medication that would suppress the response of Warren's nervous system in times of stress, keeping down his blood pressure. Warren was released after four days, the problem seemingly under control.

When he got out, Warren went to the union hall where he talked about his problems with striker Marvin Farris. Farris later reported to his RCMP handler that Warren had seemed paranoid. As for the blast, Warren told Farris he'd been thinking about how the culprits might have escaped from the mine. He said they might have taken a scoop from the 750-level, then walked past the C-shaft, heading south along the drift, down to the A-shaft, at the complete opposite end of the tunnel system to Akaitcho. The murderers then stayed there overnight, Warren told Farris. They left the mine a full day after the explosion.

While Warren was in hospital, McGowan and Defer reinterviewed the CASAW men on the strike line, and at last the officers were confident they had down what had happened, including what Warren had done. Only one other striker claimed to have seen Warren after 1:00 A.M. on September 18. No strikers said they saw him from between 2:00 A.M. and 6:00 A.M. Four hours was ample time for him to be involved in a CASAW hit squad.

Striker Max Dillman confirmed that he gave Warren a ride to the picket line just before midnight on September 17. Warren was carrying a plastic grocery bag but Dillman had no idea what was inside. A number of strikers said they saw Warren at gate six—the closest picket gate to the B-138 portal and the Akaitcho shaft—after Dillman dropped him off. Warren had told Defer that around 1:00 A.M. he went walking down the Ingraham Trail, but no one said they saw him on the road and no one else claimed to have seen the two shadowy men. Striker Kelly Rhodes did say that he saw Warren at the strikers' bus at gate three, where Warren had said he slept from 3:00 to 5:00 A.M. But neither strikers Leo Lachowski or Dave Madsen, who were also at the bus, confirmed that Warren was there. Worse, striker Alex Mikus told the police that at 4:00 A.M. he dropped in at the bus. Mikus said he saw Lachowski, but he didn't see Warren, Madsen or Rhodes. Madsen and Rhodes were asleep at the back of the bus, so that made sense, but Warren had told Defer he was sleeping at the front. How could Mikus not have seen him?

None of this necessarily meant anything, but it struck McGowan as odd that striker Tom Krahn, who was out walking just ahead of Warren on the Ingraham Trail, also had missing chunks of time, but every time Krahn hit a new picket gate he was placed by one or two people. Krahn's alibi was confirmed again and again while Warren's was not. In fact, every other man at the picket line could be placed by someone else for the entire night, everyone except Roger Warren. His alibi was only as good as his word.

Another problem was Warren's claim that he had seen Bill Schram at gate five, either reading or sleeping. Warren even described the jacket that Schram had on. But Schram wasn't at the picket line that night. It was short, husky, graying Steve Cooper at gate five, not big, blond Schram. McGowan wasn't sure what this meant. It might be the same old blurring of nights and nothing more.

A number of men had seen Warren after 6:15 A.M. at gate six, and after that time every bit of his alibi was confirmed by others, right up until 9:30 A.M. when he returned to the picket line to see, as he put it, if the two men he had spotted at 2:00 A.M. had been up to anything.

Helen told her husband that the police had called for him. In early November, when Warren saw Dale McGowan at Tim Horton's, he went up to see him.

"I heard you're looking for me."

"Yeah, we want to know about that polygraph."

"I'm not going to do it," Warren said, adding that he was interested in helping out and clearing his name, but he wasn't taking a polygraph because of his medical condition.

McGowan asked Warren how he was doing, worried that the strain of being a Crown witness in a possible murder trial would be too much for the aging miner. Warren said he was fine. He agreed to come for another interview with McGowan.

The two met on November 5. McGowan's plan was simple: just lay out things for Warren, tell him the problems with his alibi, ask him about the two shadowy men and the boots, and ask him to help the police solve these puzzles. McGowan planned to make no accusations, just ask questions and give Warren every opportunity to explain himself.

McGowan told Warren that Mikus hadn't seen him on the bus. Warren said he really wasn't paying attention to times and he must have left at 4:00 A.M., before Mikus arrived, not at 5:00 A.M. as he had originally told Defer.

As for his belief that he'd seen Schram, Warren said Schram had been there almost every other night. He must have got his nights confused.

For once McGowan didn't have to do much deprogramming. Warren told him the bomb didn't do anyone any good. He admitted it was hard to believe the blast was an accident.

Warren said he was uncomfortable with Dauk, so much so that he saw black spots during the interview. But when he complained, Dauk took his health concerns to mean he was holding back.

Warren outlined his work history, saying he started in the business in the early sixties. Since that time, there had never once been replacement workers in a mine. He said he wasn't a big union guy, but wasn't happy about the strikebreakers and he wouldn't cross the picket line. He had been thinking of going to work at the in-laws' autobody shop in Winnipeg during the strike, but his hand was screwed up so he ruled it out.

McGowan asked Warren about the two shadowy men. Warren drew a picture of the one man he'd seen best. He said the guy had no mustache while Conrad Lisoway did. Now that he had thought some more, Warren said he was sure the man wasn't Lisoway after all.

McGowan cautioned that if the murderers knew Warren had spotted them on the mine property that night, he could be in trouble. McGowan told Warren he wanted to take care of him and his family if they needed it. But Warren wasn't worried. "I just can't believe it is one of our guys," he said.

McGowan asked straight out if Warren had committed the murders.

"No, I didn't do it. I don't know why I didn't stay home that night. I'll never fucking know."

At one point McGowan decided to risk a few questions about Warren's Kamik boots. Where did Warren get them? Why had they been burned and cut up?

Warren said he bought the boots a few months earlier at Woolco. He said he was standing too close to a bonfire one night when he burned one of the soles. He had to cut away the melted rubber, then decided to cut the other boot to make it match. When McGowan pressed Warren, the striker bristled and got up. "Why are you making such a big deal about my boots?"

Warren had his hand on the door, but McGowan explained that the police were making a big deal about every detail and this was just another. Satisfied, Warren sat down again. He said he wasn't even sure if he had worn the Kamik boots that night. He might have had on black rubber boots.

A composite artist was in town so McGowan asked Warren if he'd come in so they could do a sketch of the two shadowy men. Warren agreed. The following day he worked with Corporal Bruce Coats on the sketch. Coats found Warren to be very cooperative. Warren talked about drawing, saying that he, too, was an artist. When Coats showed Warren the finished composite, Warren said it was a good resemblance.

McGowan listened in on Warren's session with Coats and was displeased. Every time Warren described the two shadowy men some of the details seemed to change. To check Warren's story, McGowan started going out to the spot on the picket line where Warren claimed to have spotted the two men. McGowan went out under dark skies and under full moons, during storms and on clear nights. Each time he was struck by how little he could see. He had people stand where Warren said he saw the two men, but he couldn't make out any of the fine details Warren had talked about, such as seeing a clean-shaven man with a prominent nose. McGowan had perfect vision, too. It seemed impossible that Warren, a forty-eight-year-old man with glasses, had seen such detail in the middle of the night.

On November 10, McGowan was alerted to a key development in the Warren file. Conrad Lisoway, the man whom Warren was fingering on-again and off-again as one of the two shadowy men, passed his polygraph test. Lisoway already had a solid alibi and this confirmed his innocence.

McGowan felt more pressure now to get Warren on the polygraph. If Warren passed, McGowan could put aside his questions about the size eleven Kamik boots and concentrate completely on helping Warren remember more about what he had seen that night. McGowan called up Warren and told him he was the RCMP's best witness, but there were also things to implicate him as a suspect. He told Warren that some of the most hardcore union men, guys who had been doing all kinds of things on the picket line like Legge, Lisoway and Gord Kendall, had taken the polygraph and passed it. "Roger, this is the one way we can clear you. You take the polygraph and you pass, you're off the burner. Right now, you're still on the burner. Listen, when you talk to me, I can't tell if you're lying, but I'll put all my faith in the polygraph. If you pass, I will believe it."

Terry Legge also worked on Warren about the polygraph. Warren told Legge he had a heart murmur and didn't know if he should submit to it.

"This is foolproof," Legge told him. "It can't be beat and the cops aren't going to bother anyone anymore."

Warren was still against it, but Legge said the whole thing was giving the union bad PR. It looked bad that some guys were taking it, but some guys weren't. Sure, the lawyers were saying not to take it, that it wasn't admissible in court, but that was even more reason to take it. "If it's not admissible, then you got nothing to worry about. If you take it and fail it, then fuck it, you know it doesn't work. Turn around and take it again. And then if it still don't work, then you *know* it doesn't work."

When McGowan next called Warren in early December, the striker said he didn't know if his health would allow him to take the test, but he would meet with Dauk and Keane to discuss it. Warren saw the two officers on December 3.

"I'm going to get this stuff cleared up," Warren told them. "It's getting right on my nerves."

He described his condition to the two officers, and it was agreed that if he could get a consent form from his doctor he would proceed. At the same time, Warren was asked to fill out a questionnaire with his thoughts on the homicide. The first question read: "We are investigating the death of nine miners killed in an explosion in Giant Mine on

September 18, 1992, and we have reached the determination the explosion was deliberately set. How would you explain this?"

In reply, Warren suggested a scenario where the killer knew the miners would be late coming down on the man-car, so he set a bomb to blow up an ore train, six or seven ore cars pushed in by a loki and driven by one man. "This means probably no one would be hurt," Warren wrote. "But it would have been very scary."

Dauk called up a polygraph expert at the University of North Dakota to find out how Warren's medication might affect the process. The expert said Warren's reactions wouldn't be the best because the medication affected the heart, which the polygraph also measured. Still, after Warren brought in his consent form, Dauk and Keane thought it was worthwhile to go ahead. Warren's reactions might be delayed slightly, but they should still be there.

Keane tested him on December 5 at the Explorer. He read Warren his Charter rights, going to great lengths to make sure Warren was taking the test voluntarily. "We live in a good country," Keane said. "There are some things you have to do. If you get married you have to support your spouse. But you don't have to sit and talk with me now. You must understand what we say should not influence you. You are under no obligation to stay. The door isn't locked. You can leave at anytime."

Warren agreed to go ahead. Keane, as much as any other polygraph operator, had a calming effect on his subjects. He was a tall, neat man, with friendly eyes and a reassuring manner. He had the distinguished air of a man who designed luxury cars or managed an art gallery, not one who interrogated criminals.

Keane and Warren went through the questions Warren would be asked, then Keane hooked up his subject to FactFinder II. "I want you to sit perfectly still with your feet flat on the floor in front of you, looking straight ahead," he told Warren. "Often during the test I'll ask you to close your eyes just so that you can concentrate on what I'm saying so you are not distracted by other noises or any movement," Keane paused, then continued, wrapping the blood pressure cuff around Warren's arm. "Now, I will enter this air into the cuff. The air stays in the cuff during the entire test. You may feel a little tingling in your finger tips, but it's not going to be very uncomfortable at all. Once the air is in the cuff, I'm going to come over and I'm going to massage the cuff, just to stabilize the instrument. I'll do that now."

Keane checked the cuff, then went back to FactFinder II and started the test. Warren, as expected, denied any involvement in the blast,
but his body went into a defensive posture when Keane asked him the
question.

When Keane looked at the chart the results weren't clear. Dauk
studied it, too. He had never seen such a flat chart. Either Warren did-
n't respond to stress like most people, or he had popped a handful of
his pills before taking the test. Keane couldn't tell if Warren was truthful or deceptive. He noted that Warren generally had an open posture,
but didn't make a lot of eye contact. He decided to score him inconclusive. Keane wasn't happy with the result. He didn't think Warren had
set the bomb, but he did think Warren was holding something back,
and it was getting in the way of him being completely truthful.

Keane returned to the room and told Warren the result. "Roger,
look at yourself, look at what you're doing to yourself. You know what
I'm talking about here, don't you?"

"No," Warren said. "There is nothing bothering me. The only
thing bothering me is these endless interrogations and interviews."

"Am I interrogating you now?"

"Well, if I wasn't here I'd be doing something else."

"What would you be doing? Has anybody forced you to come in
here today? Are you being held here against your will at all, Roger?
Look at me."

"Well, you feel like you are."

Warren then told Keane that he had some new information on
Conrad Lisoway, that he'd heard rumors that Lisoway was responsible
for the vent shaft bombing. Warren said that this, along with him seeing Lisoway on mine property that night, caused him concern that
Lisoway was involved in the murders.

The latest admission followed a pattern: whenever Warren was
pressed, he threw out Lisoway's name and the specter of the two shadowy men. But why? The RCMP knew Lisoway had passed the polygraph and his alibi was strong. Lisoway did not set the bomb, but what
about the two shadowy men? Could they be some other CASAW strikers? Was Warren still protecting someone?

When McGowan heard the test result, it pounded home what an
enigmatic figure Warren had become and just how tricky his own job
was. Warren still had problems, no doubt about it. His status had not

changed one iota, and now it would be up to McGowan to get Warren on the polygraph again. Inconclusive wasn't good enough.

The RCMP waited until February 1993 to make the attempt. At the same time Crown prosecutor Ron Reimer told them they had no choice but to drop the wiretap from Warren's phone. Constable Farrell, who was handling the wiretap applications from Edmonton, got into a heated argument with Reimer. Farrell said Warren was still a suspect, that at the very least he knew something that he wasn't telling the investigators. But even Farrell had to admit that Warren rarely talked on the telephone and the tap had garnered no new information. From their surveillance the RCMP also knew that Warren never met with Shearing and Bettger. There was no legal justification for keeping the tap.

McGowan knew from police intelligence that Warren seemed to think he was out of trouble. An informant reported a conversation that Warren had had over a beer at the Polar Bowl with Art St. Ammand.

"We don't have to worry about getting into trouble," Warren had told St. Ammand. "They would never think of us laid-back guys."

A second polygraph test wouldn't be unusual, but each time a person took the test, the chance for an inaccurate result increased. The lie detector no longer got a fresh take on the key questions.

The polygraph was a pillar of the Yellowknife investigation, but some officers wondered if it had become a crutch. Gerry Keane talked over the issue with his colleague and friend, Sergeant Gregg McMartin of the Calgary polygraph section. McMartin told Keane that he didn't completely approve of the number of tests being done. The polygraph wasn't perfect science. It wasn't a fingerprint or a smoking gun. It was wrong about ten percent of the time. If the investigation was relying on forty tests, as many as four of them were likely inaccurate. The operators might clear someone who was actually involved.

The task force investigators were sold on the polygraph, but McMartin believed they didn't really understand it. He believed the best use of the instrument was to focus on two or three suspects, then hit them with it. FactFinder II was meant for a surgical strike, not for carpet bombing. Doing so many tests was just asking for trouble, McMartin believed. Where should they stop? There were 230 striking miners. Should they polygraph all 230 of them? Even if you put all of them on the machine, it wouldn't necessarily find the murderer.

McMartin also knew the investigation was aimed at two men, Al

Shearing and Tim Bettger. He wondered what would happen if these two ever did relent and take the polygraph. He knew if he were giving the test he'd feel tremendous pressure not to pass them, to score them inconclusive at best, even if their charts led to an interpretation that they were being truthful. And if they did pass, would the investigators drop these men as suspects? Not likely. Conversely, if someone other than Shearing or Bettger took the test and failed, the polygraph operator would feel pressured to pass him. "With the amount of testing you're doing, just really be careful," McMartin told Keane.

McMartin knew Keane and Dauk were in a bind and that he'd likely do as many tests if he were in Yellowknife. In the end Keane didn't think the test was being used inappropriately. Every striker tested was a good suspect for one reason or another.

On the Warren file, McGowan conferred with Dauk about a retest. Dauk was reluctant. Although Warren had only been tested once, he had been questioned by polygraph operators in detail three times. Dauk worried about how many times they could go over the material and still get an accurate reading. But he and Keane decided to go ahead.

To persuade Warren, McGowan offered to fly him to Winnipeg to visit his family if he would be tested there by Dauk, who had returned to his regular duties. The offer made sense to the Mounties because it would have cost just as much to fly Dauk up to Yellowknife.

Warren told McGowan he'd think about the offer. He said his wife was against him having anything to do with the cops. "I think as soon as you mention polygraph she'll go right out of it."

"Is that right?"

"Pissed off for days."

One week later McGowan went out to the picket line to find out if Warren had decided. Warren said he was against it, but McGowan didn't let it drop. The next time he went out to the picket line, he brought along Warren's longtime acquaintance, Corporal Ken Murray. Murray told Warren there was a lot of evidence against him and he should reconsider. Warren agreed to see Dauk in Winnipeg.

Warren told McGowan that he didn't want to be seen traveling with him. On February 13, 1993, almost five months after the mass murder, the two men flew to Winnipeg, taking the same plane but sitting in different rows. At the Winnipeg airport, Warren and McGowan were met by Dauk and his wife. Warren left in a rental vehicle; McGowan went with the Dauks. On their way home, Dauk's wife told him that Warren was a strange one. "There is something wrong with that guy. He wouldn't even look you in the eye."

Before the test, McGowan and Dauk went over McGowan's list of concerns about Warren, from Warren's odd behavior when Dauk had first pressed him on the cuts and burns on the boots to Warren's knowledge and ability to set the bomb.

Dauk started the interview with Warren by focusing on the purpose for meeting. "Why are you here?" he asked.

"Because my first test was inconclusive," Warren said.

"But what other reason? What's the actual underlying reason for your first test?"

"Well, because I am a possible suspect."

"You don't have to be here if you don't want to," Dauk said a moment later. "You don't have to talk to me if you don't want to. Right, Roger?"

"Yeah, if I didn't have to, I wouldn't be. I had a big argument with my wife. I can't have these guys running around thinking I did something like that, or that I had anything to do with it. I'm getting sick of it."

"Yeah, okay, so?"

"She told me this polygraph you got, we got other literature on it, different cases where guys confessed and everything else, and they found out later they had nothing to do with it. But they were so scared."

Nevertheless, Warren agreed to proceed. This time the interview and test lasted almost five hours. Dauk was astonished at Warren's reactions. He was asking Warren the same questions that Keane had asked, but now Warren's responses were much stronger, and they showed that he was being deceptive. He failed miserably. Dauk told him that his charts said he was the guy who had gone underground and killed the nine guys. Even so, Dauk told Warren he was scoring him inconclusive.

Dauk was new to the job, only a year at it, and he wanted to give Warren the benefit of the doubt. Before labeling a man as deceptive in an investigation for the murder of nine men, Dauk wanted to be one hundred percent certain, and he wasn't. His feeling was that Warren had sincerely tried to tell the truth. He had looked relaxed and open. It was nothing like their first interview back in October when Warren was shaken by the questions. He was strong in his denials, even if the machine said otherwise.

Still, Dauk knew Warren was almost certainly lying about something. "I want you to level with me, Roger," Dauk said in the post-test session. "Do you know who set that explosion in the mine? I believe you do."

"I told you and told you and told you, I haven't got a clue who went down in that mine."

To get something more from Warren, Dauk knew he had to give something, so he told the miner about the RCMP's suspicions about his size eleven Kamik boots. Still, Warren denied everything.

Afterward, Dauk and Warren met McGowan outside the test room. "So you're all done?" McGowan asked.

"Yeah," Dauk said. "Roger didn't have a good test today at all. Rog and I talked about certain things, and I told Roger that there was a footprint up by the Akaitcho shaft, which you guys are concerned about, and that footprint is a perfect match to his boots. Him and I went over the area of the boots and the bottom of the boots being distorted through burning."

"I didn't think they did match my boots," Warren told the officers. "So that's why I wasn't that concerned about it for a long time, till . . ."

"Today," Dauk finished the thought.

"Yeah, because I thought if they matched my boots I'd be long gone, locked up, throw away the key."

"Well, that shows you that's not the way we work," McGowan said. "We don't stop at one piece of evidence."

McGowan went on to say that some of the Mounties were suspicious of him, but that Warren's good attitude impressed all the investigators. "The way you come across to us and your cooperative attitude so far are indicative to me that you're still wanting to clear yourself, that you're trying to do what you can to get yourself out of the queue."

"It's getting to be a fucking nuisance," Warren said.

The next day McGowan decided it was time to open up even more with Warren. He told Warren of all the suspicious matters that still troubled him. Warren didn't budge. His denials were again forceful.

Before they got back to Yellowknife, McGowan wanted to try one final strategy. McGowan doubted that Warren could be hypnotized; Warren was extremely controlled, not the type to give himself up to the unknown of hypnotism. But McGowan asked Warren if he would meet with Dr. Allan Hayduk, an Edmonton psychologist who might be able to hypnotize him. The process could help Warren remember details about the night of the murder, especially regarding the two shadowy men. Warren agreed to try.

Dr. Hayduk had worked on about fifty major criminal investigations. Before going in, he didn't want to know much about Warren. His goal was to help refresh Warren's memory, not create false ones by inadvertently suggesting something to him. All Hayduk knew was that Warren had seen something the night prior to the blast on the strike line.

In their session, Hayduk never did hypnotize Warren. He started by asking Warren to think about the events of the evening of September 17 before he went out to the strike line. Hayduk's goal was to find several solid incidents of clearly remembered detail so he and Warren could build on them, the stronger memories helping Warren recall weaker ones.

Hayduk wasn't looking for deception. He assumed that Warren was trying to tell the truth. But Warren's behavior started to confuse him. It was unlike anything he had ever seen. Most witnesses who came to him had been desperately trying to remember details; Hayduk's first task was to help them relax, to go through the story one time before trying to hypnotize them. Warren seemed completely relaxed to Hayduk, but his story was extremely odd. He had very few clear memories about the evening of September 17 and the early morning of September 18. He kept going over what routinely happened on the strike line, information Hayduk didn't want to hear. He wanted specifics, not generalities.

Inconsistencies started to show up. Warren said he had bought cigarettes at midnight, then one hour later he was down to his last one. He said he had brought two cans of Pepsi because he didn't bring his thermos, but he hated Pepsi. He said he saw a flash of light around midnight, but later said it was around 11:00 P.M.

Hayduk started to think that Warren was talking about events from a number of different evenings. But when they got into the details of Warren's walk along the Ingraham Trail from picket station to picket station, the story suddenly was full of details. Warren appeared to be working hard to remember things, but Hayduk wasn't sure if Warren was actually remembering that night or reconstructing what he had said in his police statements about that night.

At one point Warren told Hayduk he saw two shadowy men on mine property. Hayduk decided he should go no further than this. Perhaps this was the detail the police were looking for. He didn't want to explore the recollection under hypnosis and perhaps give a defense lawyer something to jump on in court.

McGowan listened in on Hayduk's interview with Warren. It was more rehashing of what he had heard ten times already. When it was over, the two men returned to Yellowknife, the trip not wasted, but still not giving McGowan what he needed to close Warren's file.

Most of the Mounties had Warren far down on their list of possible suspects. At best he was the third suspect. Vern White kept coming back to the fact that Warren didn't seem the type to kill, that he had no past record of violence. Just as important, Warren showed no hostility toward the RCMP. He seemed forthright and pleasant, especially compared with the other suspects. He had been cooperative right from the start. Anything the RCMP asked, he would eventually do. Indeed, it seemed as if he was going out of his way to help out.

One strange detail did bother White: Warren went home around 8:00 A.M. on the morning of the blast, then returned to the picket line roughly ninety minutes later to find out if the two shadowy men had done anything. The story seemed odd. What did Warren expect to happen just because he saw two people on mine property ten hours earlier?

White knew Warren had the same boots as the murderer, but at most he thought Warren had lent his boots to the murderer. Maybe Bettger had asked to borrow the rubber boots because he had soaked his own leather boots on the graffiti mission and didn't want to do that again. Maybe Warren didn't know what the Bear's plan was and had unwittingly got involved in a terrible mess. Or maybe Warren fell asleep and the killer just took his boots. Or maybe he stood guard while the murderer went into the mine. That would account for the missing three to four hours in his alibi. Maybe Warren's polygraph result was inconclusive because he knew who the two men were on mine property, but he still wasn't ready to finger his union brothers Shearing and Bettger as the murderers of nine men. In any case, there was little left to do with Warren's file. McGowan didn't see him again for five months, not until August 1993.

Chapter **12**

SNOWED UNDER

T HE 940-MILE TRIP from Edmonton to Yellowknife took most travelers about sixteen hours, some of it hard going, but much of it on the best roads money can buy. The two-lane highway to the North cut through the farms of the Peace River country, then through the bush of northern Alberta. The road was mostly straight and smooth, with large, paved shoulders, and even across the border into the Northwest Territories where the shoulders were gravel a driver could push it to eighty miles an hour without much worry. Traffic was sparse and the Mounties rarely patrolled the section of highway between the border and Fort Providence on the western shore of Great Slave Lake.

During the first months of the RCMP's investigation, it was as if the Homicide Task Force was rocketing along these easy roads. All the officers clicked. They were making good time, seeing new things, charging ahead on an adventure. The pieces of the Progression Theory came together systematically. After the New Year, however, the investigators started to find the traveling rough. It was as if they had now ferried across the Mackenzie River and were going the final leg to Yellowknife—180 miles of gravel along the north shore of the Great Slave Lake with nothing but ruts, potholes and some knothead just up ahead, blocking the way, kicking up a blizzard of rocks and dust. Morale plummeted, and it got worse now that the Edmonton investigators were gone and the workload was still the same.

The task force members started to hear jibes from the regular detachment men about their overtime, but it didn't stop the investigators from claiming. Normally such big claims wouldn't look good when it was time for their annual evaluation, but the murder investigators believed that if they were expected to solve the case quickly, at least they should get paid for it.

None of the officers was eating or sleeping well. Many were drinking too much. Constable Randy McBride felt that each month of the investigation was taking a year off his life. Corporal Mike Brandford had four kids and Constable Ken Morrison had three, but both officers went for days without seeing them except when the kids were asleep in bed.

Constable Bill Farrell had desperately wanted to get home to Edmonton, but when he at last returned all he could think of was Yellowknife. Farrell went to his son's hockey game, but instead of sitting and talking with the other parents, he sat on his own, smoking, drinking coffee, staring at the ice, seeing nothing but the case. His head throbbed. At night he ground his teeth. He ate so poorly and exercised so little in Yellowknife that he had put on thirty pounds. He drank too much after work because he felt sorry for himself. His wife and teenaged kids were growing away from him.

Farrell had remained in charge of the wiretaps and was faxed twenty to forty pages of updates from Yellowknife every day. He had other work to do, but he found he couldn't concentrate on run-of-the-mill cases. He had to renew the Yellowknife wiretap applications every sixty days; he would never forgive himself if he missed a deadline, temporarily stopping the team from gathering evidence on a key suspect.

One day Farrell kept feeling the urge to call home to his son. He called three times, each time talking to the boy, but never remembering why he'd made the call. It was only later that he remembered it had been the boy's sixteenth birthday and that he had forgotten to wish him well, let alone buy him a present.

Even Vern White found it hard to keep pushing. When his primary assistant, McBride, went on holidays in February, White had to do McBride's job as well, reading all the pertinent files and preparing the court briefs. He had never been so burned out in his life. Every few weeks, he took a day off to sleep, but even then he dropped into the office for an hour or two.

Task force members were starting to feel as if they were down three games to one in a seven game series, but White knew that as team leader he couldn't let them think they would fail. Fear pushed him now. He knew he was lucky to be working on the case, but that meant nothing to him if they didn't find the bad guy. The last thing he wanted was for everyone to say Vern White had investigated but failed to solve the biggest mass murder case in Canadian labor history.

The high stakes of the case and stress of dealing with the strikers spilled over every day in the office. The investigators vented the tension on one another. Most of the men got derogatory nicknames. Al McCambridge was Hamster because of his small stature. Ken Murray got tagged with Raven because of the way he ate. A few of the men joked with Nancy Defer about a nickname that Bettger had given her, the Bull Dyke from Hell.

The officers spent the first part of every day cutting each other down, picking on Ken Morrison for his ties or Vern White for his punched-in nose or Dale McGowan for his ever-increasing bald spot. Any one of them could be skewered for getting fat and looking run-down. God help anyone who wore two different socks to work.

When Gus Garry, an expert from the United States Bureau of Alcohol, Tobacco and Firearms (BATF), came up to do a psychological profile of the killer, the investigators were expecting a hotshot in an Armani suit. Instead, Garry walked in looking like the dopey cartoon character Elmer Fudd, wearing a big hat with flaps, pants tucked into his socks and clodhopper boots. Here was a guy who needed a shot, and McGowan started in, slamming Garry's tie.

"Holy smokes!" Garry smiled. "Just like a task force down south. Basic task force mentality."

When the third floor office got to be too much like a locker room, Constable Nancy Defer felt isolated. She thought the joking was more cruel than funny. She worked long hours but didn't glory in it like some of the guys. A few times Defer let the others know how she felt. Arguments flared up.

But other officers reveled in the atmosphere. Corporal Al McCambridge worked as long and hard as anyone and never missed a chance to go out for an after-hours drink. He believed that the put-down humor broke the tension, that senior guys like White and McGowan would slash a guy for his tie, but they weren't above taking a good hit themselves. It made them feel like they were in it together.

McCambridge's wife, Allison, was back in Inuvik. The family was supposed to have been transferred to the small Arctic settlement of Fort Good Hope in November 1992, but that was on hold while McCambridge investigated the mass murder. He didn't want to leave until he had resolved the Shearing file. If he ever felt down and lonely, McCambridge looked at the photo on his desk of Allison and their one-year-old daughter, April. They were dressed up for a Christmas party. He tried to tell himself he was doing it for them, but when he was honest, he realized this wasn't entirely true. Allison was at home and pregnant, alone with April, confined to their apartment in the twenty-four-hour darkness and minus forty-five-degree temperatures of the Inuvik winter. When Al came home every second weekend, it seemed that all he did was sleep and do laundry. Allison started to feel like a single mother living in a northern hellhole. She tried not to develop a grudge. As the months dragged, however, she started to question things. I know they've lost nine families, she thought. I know their nine men aren't coming back, but my husband is still alive. So why isn't he coming back to me? Why do we all have to suffer?

Her frustration started coming out in tearful phone calls to her husband. When McCambridge got off the phone, he always felt like a schmuck, but when he looked around and saw the other guys feeling the same way, that somehow made it easier to deal with.

In the end it was just Al McCambridge and Dale McGowan at the Explorer. In some ways, they were both in cop heaven, not having any responsibility except to the biggest case of their careers. They didn't have to go home and play with kids or change diapers or clean up after supper. They could spend every minute of each day working on the case, from 7:00 A.M. to 11:00 P.M. They could brainstorm endlessly with people who were equally obsessed.

By the New Year, however, the life was starting to feel empty. McGowan looked in the mirror and didn't see himself. He had always played sports and exercised, but not in Yellowknife. He looked five years older. He had never gotten sick before, but now every bug that came through the office got him. His diet was restaurant food: pizza, clubhouse sandwiches, fries and gravy.

He was told he was free to return home to Hay River any time. He was a valuable team member—nobody knew more about Roger Warren than he did—but if he wanted to be with his family, it was his decision. The offer was tempting, but neither McGowan nor his wife, Sheila, discussed it as an option. Sheila believed her husband was doing what he was meant to do. The case was too important to let go, and until Christmas at least, it seemed like the investigators might crack it at any moment.

McGowan had always seen himself as someone who did his work but who also pulled his load with the household chores and caring for his children. Still, in Yellowknife he knew he had to shut down the part of himself that was a family man. He saw some of the other guys killing themselves with guilt over abandoning their families. It was stopping them from concentrating on the task at hand. McGowan realized that he had to let go. He had to be like a train moving on. Later, when the bad guy was caught, he'd rehook.

When they had decided to get married, McGowan had told Sheila that his job would be harder on her than on him, but she was only twenty-one then, madly in love and naive. She'd had no idea that something like this might be in store. McGowan had worked hard to prepare her. He always worried about what might happen if he was killed on the job. "I have to make you independent," he told her. "I don't want to think that if something happens to me you won't be able to go on, you won't be able to keep everything together."

While McGowan was in Yellowknife, Sheila worked hard to set up herself and the kids in their new home in Hay River. When she talked to her husband on the telephone, she tried not to burden him too much with her problems. She felt like the glue holding everything together. While he felt guilty for being away, she felt guilty for being exhausted and short with her kids.

Dale McGowan and Al McCambridge fell into a schedule of working twelve days on, two days off, taking turns going home on weekends. The first time McGowan came home, his kids jumped all over him. As his arrivals and departures became routine, however, the kids treated him like another piece of luggage. At the dinner table, the talk swirled around but rarely included him. It wasn't out of rudeness, McGowan knew that. It was just that the kids and Sheila had become accustomed to him not being there. Still, it hurt.

McGowan had always played and roughhoused with his kids, but now he had no energy. He had never been one to sleep on the couch, but that's all he wanted to do. Almost always, he slept poorly.

"So how'd you sleep last night," Sheila would ask him.

"I didn't," he'd say. "I just can't turn it off. I can't work fourteen- or sixteen-hour days from Monday to Friday, then come home Friday night and turn the switch."

He sat down to watch TV or talk to Sheila, but his mind was in Yellowknife. His memory about the case was phenomenal, but if Sheila told him something, he didn't always retain it.

"I'm suffering from Alzheimer's," he joked.

Sheila worried about their children. Amanda was seven years old and had always been a happy, self-confident girl, but now she was easily upset at school, especially if Sheila was ever late coming to pick her up. Amanda started to have hysterical crying fits. One day Sheila came home late and found the little girl sobbing in her room.

"What's the matter?" Sheila asked.

"I'm afraid that something will happen to you," she said. She thought she had been abandoned by her daddy, and she couldn't stand it when her mom wasn't around.

After he heard about Amanda's outbursts, McGowan tried to explain to her why he had to be in Yellowknife. "Do you understand that there are nine people who are dead and these are daddies? Just like you have a daddy, these guys are daddies. These guys are never coming home to their kids. I come home. And I'm gonna come home one of these days for good, but right now you have to understand that your dad has to be gone for a little while."

The two boys, Michael, five, and Daniel, two, were also affected. Michael had always been quiet, but now he became even more withdrawn. Daniel craved male attention. When Sheila took him to Michael's hockey games, Daniel was all over the other fathers, wanting to play and talk or just sit with them.

McGowan never told Sheila much about his work in Yellowknife, except to say it was like a jigsaw puzzle with a million little pieces. She found herself focusing on any news story about murder. She thought about the people involved, the police officers, the victims. All of them were suffering, she knew that now. In her Christmas cards that year, she joked: "I feel good because I haven't abused my children, I haven't had an affair and I haven't become an alcoholic."

The main thing keeping the couple going was their late night talks. McGowan would be in bed at the Explorer, sleeping uneasily, unable to turn off the investigation. A drunk would crash down the hallway and wake him up. Unable to get back to sleep, he'd call Sheila, even if it was 3:00 or 4:00 A.M. He knew she wouldn't have kids hanging off her then and they could really talk.

"I hope you don't mind that I'm phoning," he said.

"No, I want you to phone. If you need to talk to me for whatever reason, no matter how small it is, or just to hear me, that's fine."

McGowan could talk about what was on his mind, bounce stuff off her. He had never been one to really open up about his feelings, but for the first time he told her everything in his heart. He needed to talk to someone about what he was going through.

So often he came out of interviews with strikers and felt like he'd had it, that he was tired of all the crap. Why would he set himself up in an eight-by-eight interview room with a guy who he knew he was going to end up in a shouting match with? Why put up with the endless confrontations? McGowan tried to rationalize it, thinking, This guy is a bigger dink than I am.

One thing that helped keep him strong was the reward poster with photographs of the dead men, the blasted man-car and the billy club found at the bottom of Akaitcho at the 750-level of the mine. After the toughest of his interviews, he always needed to look at it. He read the nine names: Joe Pandev, Vern Fullowka, Norm Hourie, Arnold Russell, Robert Rowsell, David Vodnoski, Shane Riggs, Malcolm Sawler, Chris Neill. He studied their faces. He thought about his own dangerous work and hoped that if something ever happened to him someone would work as hard to solve the crime as he was working now.

In January and February 1993, winter hit hard as always. Even so, Yellowknifers rarely complained about the minus forty-degree temperatures. The weather wasn't an imposition like a cold spell in a southern city such as Toronto, Calgary or Vancouver. Yellowknifers knew that every single year between September and May they would freeze. Anything warmer than minus thirty degrees and most people were prepared, even keen, to head outdoors, as long as it wasn't windy.

Yellowknifers respected the weather. They bundled in parkas as big as down quilts. They rigged their cars with automatic start-up mechanisms, which were activated from the warmth of a house, a shopping mall, a restaurant or a bar. It was common to go down a street and see two or three empty, idling cars, some locked, some not. Townspeople didn't fret too much about their cars getting stolen. After all, there was only one way out to civilization. Where was a car thief going to take the vehicle? Fort Rae? Hay River?

The city had public transit and eighty taxis, one for every two hundred Yellowknifers. There were no downtown tunnels and only one pedway, but people who complained about the cold were considered somewhat odd and wimpy. What did they expect? If outsiders whined about the cold, they were met with hostility. No Yellowknifer liked to hear that a person would have to be crazy to live in such a place. It was hard enough to deal with the weather without facing insults as well. The cold air burned in their lungs, but it made them feel alive. The northern lights danced with such intensity that hundreds of Japanese tourists visited the city in the blackest days of winters. To the Japanese it was like seeing Niagara Falls in the sky. They went back to their rooms at the Explorer and had sex, believing that the magic of the lights would bless their child with intelligence.

Winter brought the townspeople of Yellowknife together, locking families in their homes, pushing together the singles crowd at the various restaurants or bars: the dining room lounge at the Explorer and a downtown restaurant called the Office, both specializing in outrageously priced drinks and Arctic delicacies such as char and caribou; the Right Spot, a strip club until it burned down, reopening as a sports bar; the tiny, intimate Float Base pub; Giorgio's, for heaping portions of home-cooked Italian food dished out by Mama Meraglia herself; the fish-and-chip place, Bullock's, located among the strange assortment of shacks, mansions, airplane hangars, marinas and tourist shops of Old Town on Yellowknife Bay; the Bush Pilot's Brew Pub, with its Arctic brand beer and an airplane wing for a bar; the blue collar Polar Bowl, next to the CASAW union hall, a sports bar that brought in all the big closed-circuit boxing matches; the Gallery, which had live music; the trendy Monkey Tree restaurant; the trendier downtown Bistro; and, of course, the Gold Range, or the Strange Range as Yellowknifers called it, the town's oldest and most famous bar, which had the look and feel of a skid-row pub, but was packed with a cross section of bureaucrats, miners, engineers, Déné, Inuit and whites.

The Homicide Task Force investigators got to know all the bars, though their favorite hangout ended up being the Monkey Tree, located in a shopping mall in the newer residential section of town, the restaurant farthest from the union hall.

The investigators had few people to turn to except each other, and they spent many a late night eating, drinking and obsessing about the case. But just as the claustrophobia of the investigation was peaking, good news came from Ottawa. A full-time inspector was going to be appointed to the task force. Team members hoped Sergeant Al McIntyre would get promoted from Edmonton, but it was never a sure thing because Ottawa was making the call. McIntyre dearly wanted the job, so much so that Dale McGowan decided to have some fun. Putting on his best French Canadian accent, he called up McIntyre in Edmonton, with Vern White listening on another line.

"Yes, Sergeant McIntyre," McGowan said. "This is Inspector Fillion, officer staffing, Ottawa.

"Oh, yes Sir."

"Yes, we are filling that position in Yellowknife. Have you been expecting my call?"

"Well, as a matter of fact, I have, Sir."

"You have? You've been expecting my call?"

"Well, I thought I might get one."

"Well, I just want to tell you in reviewing the files before us that you're probably not the best one for that job."

McGowan thought he heard McIntyre's chest heaving.

"Yes," McGowan continued. "We have decided . . ." and here McGowan paused, ". . . that Dale McGowan of Hay River is the best guy for that job!"

McGowan and White howled with laughter, then sang, "You're so easy, so easy, yeah, yeah. You're so easy, so easy, yeah, yeah."

"Good-bye," McIntyre said, hanging up.

He called back in an hour. "You guys will be happy to know the paramedics have left," he said. "They patched me up pretty good, actually."

In the end McIntyre did get the promotion. The team had its leader back.

At the same time, the investigation took a turn, the Mounties now focusing on Tim Bettger rather than Al Shearing. Bettger had always been number two on the list, but the Bear moved to the forefront because of a new bit of evidence from CASAW striker Luc Normandin, who at last talked to the RCMP because of a guilty conscience.

Normandin was a carpenter at the mine. He was short, but strong, a French Canadian and a practicing Catholic. Normandin wanted the police to solve the crime, but he feared that if they arrested Al Shearing, they'd be arresting the wrong man.

Just after Christmas, Shane Riggs' sister, Linda, had been drinking at the Gold Range with David Vodnoski's widow, Doreen. The two saw Normandin at another table drinking with some friends. Linda relished confrontations with the CASAW men. She hoped they might get rattled and admit something. She decided to send over a round of drinks to Normandin and his friends, telling the server to say the drinks were courtesy of Spanky.

Normandin decided to approach the hostile women. He told Linda that he felt bad about Spanky, that he had been a friend. Linda kept after Normandin, accusing him of the murders. Normandin told her he had nothing to do with the killings.

"I know you know who has done it," Linda shot back.

Normandin put his head down and walked away without replying.

One month later he went into the RCMP detachment to talk to Nancy Defer. He was on the verge of tears and appeared to have something important to say, apparently regarding some conversations he had heard. But Normandin told Defer that he feared his family might be in danger if he said anything. Defer had to pull every sentence out of him. He left without divulging his secret. A week later Defer went back to him. Again he refused to talk. Still the RCMP pushed, and a few weeks later, at the end of February, five months after the blast, Corporal Ken Murray finally succeeded in getting Normandin to talk.

During the interview, Normandin again appeared anxious. He told Murray that he feared a union brother would give him hell for dealing with the police. Or maybe someone would take it out on his family. But Normandin said his knowledge weighed heavily on him. He wasn't sure what to do, but he had a theory about who had killed the nine miners. He said he might be wrong, but if he was right he wondered if he would have to testify.

Yes, Murray said, if it was that important, he would.

Normandin laid it all out. On September 13, 1992, five days before the fatal blast, Normandin said he gave Tim Bettger a ride out to the strike line. Bettger told Normandin he wanted to stir things up, maybe set a booby trap explosive on a bridge at the mine. A Royal Oak or Pinkerton vehicle driving over the bridge would trigger the blast.

Normandin told Murray that he had asked Bettger if the blast would hurt anyone in the truck. Bettger said he didn't care because they were all scabs anyway.

Normandin didn't want anything to do with the plan. But later on the picket line, he had heard Bettger talking it over with striker Conrad Lisoway. Normandin waited for something to happen, but he heard nothing that night or the next night. He decided to approach Bettger and ask what had happened. Bettger told him nothing had come of it, but he had something else planned. A few days later, the nine men were killed.

The plan Luc Normandin described to Murray came to be known among the strikers and the investigators as the Flying Truck Scenario. For the Mounties it was the single most compelling piece of circumstantial evidence that tied Bettger to the September 18 blast. The Mounties could place him in the middle of a plot to use a trip wire device to blow up a truck. If the plan wasn't intended to kill, it certainly showed a reckless disregard for the truck driver's safety. The investigators realized that the plan could have been nothing more than the same bravado they had seen from Bettger ever since the bomb had gone off. But the timing of this particular plan made it seem like the penultimate scheme in the Progression Theory.

Yes, it looked like Bettger had waited until Shearing got out of jail on September 17 to enact his trip-wire plan underground, but he only waited because he needed Shearing's okay, not because he needed Shearing to go into the mine and do it. It was Bettger's bomb. He would set it. Nothing seemed beyond the Bear anymore.

Chapter 13

A MURDERER AMONG US

F or Yellowknifers there was no easy cure for the poison of the strike and the mass murder. All its victims could do was fume and curse, vent and weep. Marriages broke up. People left town. Some had breakdowns. A few people closest to the strike attempted suicide. Questions about the blast plagued both the CASAW and Royal Oak factions: Why can't they see it was an accident? Why can't they see it was murder? Who did it? Who is to blame? Will someone blame me?

There were no answers for the widows and relatives of the dead men either, but they found some solace in the months after the mass murder by writing letters to the *yellowknifer:* "You cannot go around and pretend that you will get away with this murder," Shane Riggs' mother, Carol, warned the killer. "Believe what I say. Your time is coming. If not in this life, in another."

Carol spent the months after the blast living at her daughter Linda's trailer in Yellowknife. One night Carol picked up the telephone to hear an angry voice say, "Traitors deserve to die." Carol screamed and dropped the phone. Linda mentioned the incident in a letter to the newspaper, then added: "You know it just seems that all you ever hear or see is the strikers being shafted. As far as I'm concerned, they have this city wrapped around their pinkies."

And David Vodnoski's widow, Doreen, wrote: "I have read so many letters and articles that are pro-union and anti-union. My letter is nei- ther. I am writing to say, 'Cut the crap!' The fact still remains nine lives have been lost."

The Royal Oak miners continued to fight off the poison through their attempt to decertify CASAW. Royal Oak management supported the new association. Pamphlets for the new Giant Mine Employees Association (GMEA) were freely distributed around mine property. The association signed up members in the company's parking lot, and the association hired its lawyer, Israel Chafetz, because Jim O'Neil remem- bered that mine superintendent Terry Byberg had said Chafetz was a good labor lawyer.

One day during the sign-up drive in November 1992, the mine's secretary handed O'Neil an envelope with $5,000 in it, all twenties and fifties. "We are a group of CASAW members who feel that you can do something to change things around and help us," read the note inside. "We entrust you with this money in the hopes that it might be of some assistance in helping you."

O'Neil asked the secretary where she got it from.

"It was dropped off on my desk," she said.

O'Neil suspected that the money had more likely come from Peggy Witte than anyone in CASAW. Another possible donor was some pro- Witte member of the Yellowknife business community. A while later, the GMEA got another mysterious cash windfall. An anonymous busi- nessman called up, asking for the GMEA's bank account number, then deposited $4,800. O'Neil liked to think the money wasn't necessarily from Witte. CASAW had a lot of enemies.

The GMEA got another mysterious boost during the group's sign- up drive: a mailing list with the names and addresses of every CASAW member. O'Neil found it, seemingly by chance, in the photocopying room of Royal Oak's main office. The list was an organizer's dream. O'Neil could now get to the CASAW men without having to go through the union hall.

To convince men to sign up, O'Neil berated CASAW for being autocratic and for protecting a group of lazy, hardcore radicals. But his strongest argument was simpler: Someone in that union is a mass mur- derer.

The striking miners responded by labeling the GMEA a scab association. "Once someone crosses the picket line they become sub-fuckin'-human," Harry Seeton told Peter Cheney of the *Toronto Star*. "A transformation takes place. They go lower than a reptile."

In the end almost every man working at Giant signed on, but the GMEA signed up only a few CASAW strikers. The union still had a majority of the men, even if the Canada Labour Relations Board allowed the replacement workers to have a say in the decertification vote.

The strikers had less luck finding a way to combat the poison. They were sick with hate when they saw replacement workers boldly walking about town, shopping at the supermarket, going to restaurants and bars. The Posse, a group of union miners from both Giant and Con Mine, went out looking for the Royal Oak men. Scab-hunting, the locals called it. The Gold Range was the easiest place to fight and remain anonymous because it was so crowded. One night in early November brawls broke out at three bars.

Townspeople couldn't believe that the violence was back just two months after the blast. City council members signed a proclamation condemning the violence: "People 'hunting' people in order to vent violence upon them is not a sign of a civilized society. Yellowknifers have reached their limit of tolerance and will not be held hostage by a few who employ coercion and intimidation to reach their goals."

On the Canadian Broadcasting Corporation's national radio morning show *Morningside*, Mayor Pat McMahon said, "I'm disappointed, disillusioned and I think the feds had better get their act together in a heck of a hurry or there's going to be more people that are going to get killed in this whole thing."

The only antidote for the CASAW men was to cling to the issues of the strike. They held tight to the notion that the strike and the mass murder were unrelated, that the strikers could go back to work before the RCMP's investigation ended. No one paid any attention to them except to demonize them, they believed. They were just a group of ordinary men, they contended, not some highly trained, fanatical force of evil terrorists.

Through October, November and December of 1992, Peggy Witte pretended to negotiate with the union in order to appease federal mediators and the Canada Labour Relations Board. The talks were a sham. Witte had no economic interest in ending the strike. She paid

her replacement workers less than the unionized men, so operating
costs at the mine were lower than they had been. As long as the murderer was at large, Witte felt justified in taking this position. If CASAW
came back, the killer might return as well, walking the same underground tunnels as the men who had been his prey. The mine would
become a time bomb. More men would almost certainly die.

The CASAW men waited anxiously for the report of special mediators Don Munroe and Vince Ready of Vancouver, who had been
appointed by the federal government to have another look at the matter. Their report came on November 25, two months after the mass
murder. Ready and Munroe told Federal Labour Minister Marcel
Danis that the two groups were far apart, with a number of matters
separating them: CASAW's membership turning down the tentative
agreement, which Royal Oak took as a great blow; Royal Oak using
replacement workers, taking away the economic incentive to settle; fallout from the September 18 blast; the decertification bid by the GMEA;
and both parties remaining far apart in their collective bargaining
demands. The biggest obstacle, however, was the fate of forty-three
strikers fired by Royal Oak, which included the likes of Al Shearing,
Tim Bettger, Conrad Lisoway, Roger Warren and Terry Legge. The
union said all of them must be rehired in any deal. Royal Oak said they
had to be cut loose by the union before negotiations would even start.
This final issue would never be solved through negotiations, Ready and
Munroe told Danis. Both parties had to submit to an arbitration
process voluntarily on each of the forty-three cases.

"We will be blunt," the two mediators wrote. "As a matter of law
the dispute between these parties is essentially private in nature. But as
a matter of fact, the public fallout from the dispute has been enormous
and, at least in our experience, unprecedented. Both sides owe it to the
surrounding community to take a serious and tangible step toward a
resolution of this seemingly intractable dispute."

If there was any cause for hope in the negotiations, it was that after
the blast both sides had brought in experienced, reasonable negotiators,
Bill Heath for Royal Oak and Heimi Mitic of the Canadian Auto
Workers for CASAW. Heath, a management troubleshooter from
Ontario, gave Royal Oak an outsider's perspective. He also worked
hard to improve the company's reputation, meeting with Yellowknife
politicians and civil servants, getting to know Mayor McMahon, the

deputy ministers of the government, the various reporters, playing a weekly squash game with RCMP Superintendent Brian Watt.

Under Heimi Mitic's direction CASAW's membership voted in early December to accept Ready and Munroe's report, including the arbitration clause for the forty-three fired men. But just before Christmas 1992, Witte said she could not accept arbitration on the fired men. In a letter to her employees, she wrote: "I hold as sacred my responsibility to you and to your families, and it is for that reason we have taken the step of rejecting the mediator's report. Not now nor will I ever do anything to jeopardize the health, safety or security of any Royal Oak employee."

After Royal Oak rejected Ready and Munroe's report, the Minister of Labour took the unusual step of appointing an Industrial Inquiry Commission into the strike, a move that Yellowknife politicians had been calling for since the summer. Ready and Munroe would lead the commission, and they would have greater power. They couldn't force a settlement, but they could subpoena witnesses and documents to their inquiry, which they scheduled for the end of January 1993.

Despite the mass murder and labor turmoil, the Canadian business community's take on the Giant Mine situation was almost entirely positive. Giant was producing as much gold as ever but at a slightly lower cost. The company's stock continued to rise. Witte was cast as a tough, plucky woman, who stood up to a pack of macho, radical miners, and a campaign of laudatory publicity came soon after the mass murder. First was a letter to the *yellowknifer* by longtime Yellowknife writer Erik Watt, who was then working as publicist for Royal Oak. Watt started his letter by recounting how he had inadvertently seen Witte in private on Monday, September 21, the day the nine bodies were brought out of the mine. She hadn't cried in front of the grieving families, but Watt saw tears running down her cheeks. While Witte was being called a cold, cynical union buster, Watt said he'd known a very different person since he first met her at a bush camp in 1988 when the Colomac gold mine was being developed. "She proved to be a human dynamo who left me gasping in her wake as she tore about that rugged chunk of real estate (there were no roads there then), and a sharp promoter whose enthusiasm couldn't help but rub off on those she met.

"Among the two dozen people crowded into the leaky Colomac exploration camp she was quite literally a figure of worship. It wasn't hard to understand why. She was 'Peggy' to everyone in camp, and she had time to listen to anyone who wanted to talk to her. She was just as much at home in the bush as in her Vancouver office, and her quarters were as Spartan as anyone's. She expected people to work hard, but she worked harder than any of them and obviously enjoyed it.

"She's tough all right; pussycats don't run gold mines or twist wrists with high-powered financiers when money's tight. But she's a decent human being, too, and she cares for people."

In December 1992, Witte received a more important boost from corporate Canada's organ, the *Financial Post* magazine, a publication her shareholders might read. Gord McLaughlin's profile on Witte ran under the headline "Tough Enough." The article showed Witte as driven, charismatic, sometimes ruthless. It did little to suggest that this attitude was anything but admirable. McLaughlin concluded: "So far, Witte has exceeded expectations, answering only to shareholders and to an intrinsic lust of achievement. And if you don't like her extreme methods or survivalist motives, that's just tough."

In no article did Witte ever admit that she might have made a mistake by bringing in replacement workers. But then, even if Witte did believe she might have helped set in motion events that culminated in mass murder, any public admission from her would have been played up by CASAW. It also would have been dangerous legally. If Witte was ever sued for negligence in regard to the deaths, a lawyer could use such an admission as proof of her guilt.

The hard, polarized attitudes of both sides left no room for any public displays of remorse or goodwill, as a group of Yellowknife citizens discovered when they tried to build a monument to the nine dead men. The idea came from sculptor François Thibault, who had been a miner himself. Thibault knew the strikers, line crossers and some of the dead men. On the day of the blast, he felt the pain when a friend of his, a shift boss at the mine who had been underground, came to him for consolation. The man was shattered.

Soon after, Thibault found himself doodling a sketch of the C-shaft headframe of the mine. He realized that a monument based on the sketch could be made for the nine men and others who had died in Territorial mines. Thibault went about organizing the project, approaching the city, the Territorial government and private businesses. The gesture wasn't meant to take a side in the dispute, he told them, just to do something decent. His message was well received.

Thibault built a refrigerator-sized, stylized headframe with an eternal flame fueled by an underground 450-pound fuel tank. The statue was shown to the public on January 14, 1993. The plaque read: "North of 60 Mining Memorial. To commemorate the men that perished on September 18, 1992. Chris Neill, Norman Hourie, Arnold Russell, David Vodnoski, Shane Riggs, Malcolm Sawler, Josef Pandev, Vern Fullowka, Robert Rowsell. And to all who have lost their lives in the mining industry."

The monument was put in downtown Yellowknife in front of the Northwest Territories Mine Rescue building, across from the RCMP detachment. As soon as the CASAW supporters saw it, the tempest started. Thibault was visited at his crafts shop by men and women who berated him for this monument to the scabs. The following day, Northwest Territories government workers took off the plaque, replacing it with one that read: "To all those who have lost their lives in the mining industry." John Quirke, deputy minister of public services, explained to reporters that the government had not known the plaque would refer to the nine men by name. It never would have supported the monument if it had known. Because the monument was on government land, the plaque had been changed.

Thibault was furious. He spoke to a number of bureaucrats, saying he thought he'd made it clear to everyone what the monument was all about. The government officials gave him a new reason for the change in the plaque's wording: everyone knew there was a murderer on the loose; what was to stop him from putting a blasting cap in the monument, taking out the fuel tank and blowing up a quarter of a city block? More people might die.

The officials suggested to Thibault that as a last resort he could try to work things out with CASAW. Thibault visited the union hall. Terry Legge met him at the door and asked what he wanted. Thibault told him he wanted to talk about the memorial. "Why are you so against it?" he asked.

"You're making these fuckin' guys out to be some kind of martyrs or they died a normal death," Legge said. "These guys didn't die honorably. If they wanted to die honorably, die on the fuckin' picket line."

Inside the hall Thibault tried to reason with an incensed throng of CASAW men. He told them he wasn't in it to piss anyone off, but for humanitarian reasons. He didn't want to blame anyone. The plaque didn't say these men had been murdered. It said they had perished. "Come on, guys," he exhorted. "These are people you used to hunt and fish with, for Christ's sake, and drink beer with them, and now because they've crossed a picket line, you don't want this monument? Well, if you don't want it, there you go. I'll fuckin' pull the pin on it right now."

Thibault left the union hall resigned to defeat. At home he continued to get calls from CASAW supporters, but also from relatives of the nine dead men. Both sides agreed on only one thing—Thibault had betrayed them. A few of the widows raged at him. Thibault tried to explain to them the potential for a disaster. "It's just too dangerous right now. There are some loose cannons out there." The attacks of the family members were the most painful blow to Thibault. He had done this for them, but now they despised him.

The dedication was held Sunday, January 17, four months after the mass murder. The families, mine workers and the media gathered at the monument. The Mayor spoke, making no mention of the controversy, saying it was important to remember all the miners who had died in accidents. Thibault spoke next, but was interrupted by Linda Riggs, who asked why the names were taken off the monument. Thibault tried to explain, but Linda and the other relatives of the dead men only got angrier.

Afterward, Linda spoke to the assembled media. "Even the mayor talks like these guys died by the hand of God," she said. "Well, they didn't. They were murdered. All nine of them were murdered, and that was the original reason why Thibault, out of the goodness of his heart, did this. He was dedicating it to those nine men. It's just politics and it's got to stop because us family members are getting tired of it."

In the following weeks, people glared at Thibault as he shopped and while he waited in the lineup at the bank. He often didn't know who these angry people were, which side they were on, but they seemed to be everywhere. At home his wife, Caroline, finally told him he had to stop answering the phone. The calls were driving him crazy. There was no way he could adequately explain himself to the factions. They were beyond reason. Thibault hated to walk by the monument. At first it made him angry, but then he only felt empty and sad.

While Thibault resigned himself to what had happened, Tracey Neill fought on to have the old plaque put back up, even if she had to battle long distance. After the blast she had moved to Rocky Mountain

House to live with her parents. She much preferred it in the small, central Alberta town. She could walk downtown and no one looked at her, no one crossed the street, no one muttered. She liked to be on her own with her thoughts, and Rocky Mountain House allowed her solitude. She spent much of her time going for walks. She didn't think about going back to work. Like the other widows, she received a $50,000 life insurance payment and a monthly worker's compensation check of $1,306. The Neill's home in Yellowknife had also been paid off through life insurance. Tracey sold it and planned to buy her own home in Rocky Mountain House.

At Christmas she had visited Chris's grave and talked to him and wept. She talked about him all the time with her mom, dad and brother. She kept in touch with Jim and Jane O'Neil, who told her the investigation was focusing on Shearing and Bettger. She vaguely remembered Al Shearing, how mad he was when Chris's team beat his team in mine rescue. As for Bettger, she had no idea.

After the monument fiasco, Tracey tried to contact a number of Yellowknife politicians, but her calls never made it through. Instead, she wrote a letter to the *yellowknifer*, which appeared at the end of January.

"CASAW's objections to the naming of the nine men killed on the monument is another example of their continuing efforts to dehumanize the victims of the September 18 explosion. They portray these men as scabs or replacement workers. They do not want people to realize that six of those men were members of their own union who, after being fed up with the violent nature and questionable motives of their union, made the difficult choice to cross their own picket line.

"Apparently, there was concern that if the plaque was not changed the monument may be blown up. Being that there is a large propane tank within the monument, should it be exploded a large area of Yellowknife and many lives may be lost. Now, considering that there have already been three explosions in connection to this strike and that there may be murderers on the loose, this is a very real concern. But it is also terrorism. This city and our government should not allow themselves to be held hostage by terrorists. The politicians have once again bowed to the pressure of the union at the expense of the families of these men."

The monument debacle made Judit Pandev all the more keen to leave town. She had wanted to stay until the murderer was caught, but she was becoming too fearful. She was stared at on the street. People mouthed the word *bitch* at her. They gave her the finger. She studied people walking by and wondered: Are you one of them or not? She hated every last one of the CASAW men, but since she couldn't identify them all, she ended up suspecting and hating everyone she saw. Her bitterness affected her health. She started to have nightmares. She shook uncontrollably. She couldn't sleep through the night, just looked at the clock every hour. She started to take sleeping pills at night, tranquilizers in the day. In bed she felt like bugs were crawling over her. In the shower she felt like she had hairs all over her back. Her hands and knees ached from arthritis. Along with the sleeping pills, she took anti-depressants, insulin, high-blood pressure pills, high cholesterol pills and anti-seizure pills. At times she envied Joe and the eight other men. They were dead. All their problems were over. The only thing keeping her going was her responsibility to her three children and her infant granddaughter, Kayla. She'd had a falling out over the money from the inheritance with Joe's three kids—Joe Jr., Ivan and Maria.

In the end Judit was saved when Peggy Witte and Royal Oak agreed to buy her house so she could leave. Judit moved to the town of New Waterdown, Ontario, outside of Hamilton, leaving behind the town she had lived in for thirty years.

Through the winter of 1993, two government agencies—the Industrial Inquiry Commission of Ready and Munroe and the Canada Labour Relations Board—worked through the various issues of the strike, but made little progress—not that progress could be made. No government organization would be so bold as to end the dispute while the murderer was at large. Both agencies held hearings in Yellowknife, Ready and Munroe calling witnesses in late January, the Labour Board in early March. Both times, the CASAW men and the Royal Oak miners half expected some sudden resolution to the strike, the strikers praying for such a result, the replacement workers and line crossers fearing it. Not only did the Royal Oak faction fear working with the CASAW strikers, but many of the replacement workers realized that the end of the strike would mean the end of their jobs. They feared that whatever Peggy Witte said about not allowing CASAW back, at some point the bottom line would prevail; she'd see it was best to quit wasting time and money on the dispute, settle things and get on with business.

At the Industrial Inquiry Commission hearings, the union held that the company had tried to break the union from the start while Witte again said she wasn't going to negotiate until the issue of the forty-three fired men was dealt with once and for all. As she spoke striker Amos Simon yelled out, "You're the real murderer, Peggy Witte!"

Mine foreman Noel O'Sullivan also testified for Royal Oak. He said the two groups of miners, replacement workers and strikers, could not work together until the murder was solved. It would be too dangerous otherwise. "Where better to settle a score than underground where there are no witnesses?"

O'Sullivan said it would be better to shut the mine than bring the men back together again. "I cannot see this anger disappearing overnight. No Sir. I don't think this anger will disappear in my lifetime."

After his testimony shift boss Gord Edwards, one of O'Sullivan's confidantes, came up to him. "Jeez, you should have seen Roger Warren when you mentioned the murder of September 18," Edwards said. "His jaw just about dropped off of his chest."

"Really," O'Sullivan said. "Isn't that interesting."

At the conclusion of the hearings, Ready and Munroe decided they could go no further until the Labour Board made a final decision on the GMEA's decertification bid. Before the Labour Board hearings in March, the GMEA made a move in the propaganda war. Jane O'Neil wrote a three-page essay called "A Murderer Among Us" about how the nine dead men had first been labeled as scabs, dehumanized, then murdered. "It is thought that once the arrests are made the town can start to 'heal,'" she wrote. "This is an extremely optimistic view. . . . The aftershocks of this tragedy will not be as widely spoken of as the murders, but they will have a devastating effect on many of us who were touched by this strike.

"Some people seem to feel that things are calming down already, but that is far from the truth. The anger and sorrow are so deeply ingrained, and how can things 'calm down' when we know that there is a murderer among us."

Jane gave her husband the essay to read. O'Neil thought it was good enough to use and ran off two thousand photocopies. Along with a crew of helpers, he delivered it around the community, putting it in apartment lobbies, faxing it to the media, tacking it up on posts, even sending a copy to Wolverine Sport, the business of CASAW strike coordinator Dale Johnston.

At the Labour Board hearings, O'Neil was attacked for his cozy relationship with Royal Oak. When O'Neil took the stand he made an accusation of his own: that before the strike Harry Seeton had threatened to kill scabs and their families. In his testimony Seeton denied having said this, responding not only to Jim O'Neil's allegation, but to the anti-union feelings typified by "A Murderer Among Us": "This is what is so hard for us to live with here during this dispute. We're branded as a bunch of murderers. The union is branded as a bunch of murderers. No one has apologized to us in this community for that.

"It seems that everything that happens here and everywhere we go, we have this finger pointing at us. I'd just like to express how hard it is to live here. We want to see this investigation finished and the culprit brought to justice as much as anyone else."

The hearings ended, but the board made no immediate decision about whose vote would count in the decertification bid. It set no deadline for when it would reach a decision either. Again, the process was stalled.

The strikers had now been off work for ten months. They had lived with the fallout from the murderous blast for six months. Many strikers faced a grim truth: it was either leave town, get other jobs or lose their homes. The men made $4.28 an hour in picket pay, but rent in Yellowknife was the highest in Canada, with a two-bedroom apartment going for $1,054 a month and a single for $848.

The situation had by now overwhelmed almost every striker who had been involved in any criminal activities. If they hadn't yet confessed, they felt intolerable pressure to do so, if only so the RCMP would know they had nothing to do with the mass murder. But still Al Shearing and Tim Bettger held out.

Chapter 14

THE SECOND SUSPECT

HUNDREDS OF SUSPECTS, hundreds of interviews, thousands of exhibits, conspiracy theories, Bettger, Shearing, Lisoway, Warren—it was up to RCMP crime analyst Dean Ravelli to bring everything into a package. In February 1993, he put out a three-hundred-page report on the murder entitled *The Royal Oak Giant Mine Multiple Homicide*. Ravelli also produced a multicolored flow chart, which displayed all the major suspects, events and pieces of information in the investigation. With the chart someone new coming in would need about an hour to understand things. In the end the chart grew to be twenty-one feet long.

Ravelli came up with three theories about the Giant Mine homicide. The first was that the explosion was the direct result of an order from the union executive, a theory held by many replacement workers and line crossers, but largely discounted by Ravelli and the other RCMP investigators. The second theory revolved around a group of radical union members who felt the executive wasn't doing enough. They took it upon themselves to push Peggy Witte into negotiations, setting off a number of small explosions, then the September 18 blast. This was the Shearing–Bettger Theory, the Progression Theory. Ravelli named his third hypothesis the Lone Wolf Theory. It went that a lone union man had set the bomb. He hadn't involved anyone else and hadn't told anyone else.

In late February Inspector Al McIntyre brought in two outside experts, RCMP Inspector Ron McKay and BATF Special Agent Gus Garry, both experts in drawing psychological profiles of criminals. From the details of the crime, they tried to infer the psychology and personal history of the criminal. After studying the case file and traveling to the blast site, both Garry and McKay came to favor the Progression Theory, just as most of the investigators did. The only difference was that McKay and Garry favored Shearing as the bomber while the investigators focused on the second suspect, Tim Bettger, basing their suspicions on Luc Normandin's story about the Flying Truck Scenario.

Tim Bettger was thirty-seven and a heavy duty mechanic. He grew up working off and on in his parents' radio and television repair shop in the town of Rosthern, Saskatchewan. The Bettgers were solid, honest people. Tim's sister became an RCMP radio operator. After high school Bettger worked as a mechanic in various prairie cities. He had moved to Yellowknife six years back and got on at Giant. His wife, Izzie, worked at a Yellowknife restaurant, Our Place. They had two kids, fourteen-year-old Jake and twelve-year-old Tina. The couple was careful with their money and owned their own house. In the year before the blast, Bettger made $75,000. In the four months before the strike, he made $37,000.

Bettger liked to work in his garage at home. He wasn't a big drinker, but occasionally smoked pot. At Giant he had a mixed reputation. He was a skillful but slow worker and not very popular with his workmates. He didn't like to share his tools. He had a big ego when it came to his work and thought he was better than the other mechanics.

At the beginning of the strike, Bettger fell right in with Shearing and the other Cambodian Cowboys. He became a guard for the union executive, meaning he parked his mammoth frame at the union hall's doorway and glowered at anyone who entered.

Bettger proved to be far more difficult for the RCMP to handle than Al Shearing. Along with Harry Seeton, he was the strongest voice against any union man taking the polygraph. He agreed to be interviewed a number of times, but he held that it was a basic right not to have to submit to a polygraph. He said he had no confidence in the machine. In Bettger's mind the RCMP weren't conducting an honest investigation. It was nothing more than a relentless pursuit of him and Al Shearing. He started to fear that the Mounties might try to plant evidence and arrest him for a crime he hadn't committed. "There's a couple of us who have been really giving them hell out there, and we're gonna get the blame," he told his union buddies.

Constable Bill Farrell had handled Bettger at first, but when he returned to Edmonton, his assistant, Ken Morrison, took over. Morrison always got a laugh out of the way Bettger talked. It seemed like Bettger had a thesaurus in his back pocket. He used three sentences when three words would do and never hesitated to use a long word instead of a short one.

Morrison believed that Bettger was the killer, although he wasn't as vocal about Bettger as Corporal Al McCambridge was about Shearing. The RCMP had learned from striker Gord Kendall about Bettger and Shearing's shopping trip to Vancouver to buy materials for their bombs in the summer of 1992. Using records from VISA, Morrison and the other investigators pieced together the trip and Bettger's various purchases.

Morrison's biggest doubt about Bettger's guilt was the lack of evidence for the early morning hours of September 18, 1992. Bettger had an alibi. Nothing linked him to the picket line, let alone the blast site.

Bettger had had his fill of the RCMP, Farrell and Morrison in particular, a few months into the investigation. But if the investigators had any thoughts of letting up on the Bear, they were dropped because of his continued plotting of violence against Royal Oak's security guards and property. Bettger continued to discuss many of his plans with Marvin Farris. At $800 a week, the RCMP thought they were getting good value from their informant. He got as much information as any undercover officer could have at a fraction of the cost. On December 30, 1992, Bettger and Farris snowmobiled past Justice Ted Richards' home, the same judge who had convicted Bettger for a minor breach of the strike-line injunction. "There's where Judge Bean lives," Bettger had told Farris, then added jokingly, "All we would have to do is cut the phone line, then the power line, then boom, nothing left but a crater. If you really want to fuck him up, just take out his wife and kids."

On another snowmobile trip, Bettger told Farris about a previous break-in at the mine. The first few ladders at Akaitcho had been removed, Bettger said, so they had to slide down a cable. They walked along the 575-drift, then climbed down the ladders of the Muir raise to the 750-drift and the 712-scoop shop.

"Is this the trip that involves the artwork?" Farris asked, referring to the June 29 graffiti mission.

"Yes."

A few weeks later, Farris asked Bettger how many times he had been underground.

"Just one," Bettger said.

Bettger also talked with Farris about a plan to shut down the mine for at least thirty-six hours by knocking down a number of power poles. He explained that he was trying to round up other union men for the plan, but it was getting more difficult to find help. Another plan entailed Bettger and his group ambushing a security truck, then pulling out the guard and beating him until he needed a partial body cast. The attack would send a message to anyone thinking of coming to work at Giant. Farris asked Bettger how they'd get the truck to stop.

"Best way to get him to stop is to put a 12-gauge slug through his rad."

Farris told the police that Bettger might expect him to go along on the beating of the security guard. Bettger also wanted Farris to help out downing power poles. Farris thought he'd have to lend a hand if Bettger was ever going to trust him completely. It was decided that Farris could accompany Bettger on his power pole missions, but he should try not to take part. As for hurting the security guard, if the plan ever came close to fruition, Farris would conveniently have something to do out of town.

While Bettger talked trash about hurting property and people, he never seemed to follow through. It occurred to Morrison that Bettger didn't have it in him to set up a lethal bomb by himself. When he set the vent shaft bomb, he was side by side with fearless Al Shearing. Unless he had a crowd behind him, Bettger seemed unwilling to take any action. Morrison balanced that observation against the changes in Bettger's personality that had occurred since the strike had started. Bettger hadn't been a very outgoing person before. Now, however, he was something of a leader. Events had put him at the center of the most violent strike in Canadian history and the biggest RCMP investigation in the country. He was a somebody, Tim Bettger, the Bear, not just an anonymous nobody in a dingy old gold mine. He saw the battle in historic and grandiose terms. It was Canada versus the United States. He wasn't a striker who had done a few stupid things and was obstinately getting in the way of the investigation of the murder of nine men; he was a brave, innocent man trying to fight the overwhelming, corrupt misuse of power by the courts and the police. To Bettger, the investigation was like the strike: all about rights, his rights, what was fair and just for Timothy Alexander Bettger.

Maybe Bettger's sense of right and wrong had gotten so out of whack during the strike that he'd grown into someone who could set such a bomb, Morrison thought. But just when he had convinced himself of this, Morrison came up with a new doubt. Bettger was so hostile to the police, so defiant and contemptuous. He seemed to have no fear of them. The behavior didn't fit with a mass murderer trying to avoid detection. If he himself had killed the nine men, Morrison knew the last thing he'd do is piss off the investigators.

Morrison and the other Mounties respected Bettger's wife, Izzie, and the couple's strong marriage. Izzie was judged to be a friendly, moral woman. She appeared to have something special with Tim, a warm, trusting relationship. Izzie knew her husband was a suspect. From the strange clicking on their telephone, she had to know they were under surveillance. Their kids, Jake and Tina, were harassed at school. Some kids called them murderers. At work Izzie picked up the telephone to hear an exploding bomb sound from a Wile E. Coyote cartoon. She knew her husband had done a few things on the picket line like slash tires, but she believed he was innocent of any major crimes. She was committed to standing by him through the strike.

The RCMP sent undercover officers to talk to both Izzie and Shearing's wife, Kara Roderique. One agent booked the seat next to Izzie on an airplane flight. But none of the operations paid off with any important new evidence.

The police continued to try to get at Bettger and Shearing through other CASAW men such as Luc Normandin and Terry Legge. After his polygraph test in October 1992, the RCMP had dropped Legge as a suspect, but they refused to leave him be until he admitted his involvement in the vent shaft blast. Not only would an admission strengthen the Progression Theory, but if he was still holding back about his role in the vent shaft blast, maybe he was holding back something even more important.

The RCMP's breakthrough with Legge came about because of his growing trust in Vern White. The two men had a slight connection: White's wife, Loretta, was from Goose Bay, Labrador, Legge's home-town, and Loretta's father was one of the closest people to Legge's best friend and brother-in-law. White was a fellow Maritimer and had mentioned to Legge that he had worked in Nain, Labrador.

The two men went to the same gym, Bodyworks, and chatted after workouts. White started out talking about the polygraph, knowing that Legge approved of the test. In time they argued about Legge's belief that the murder was an accident. To convince the striker, Ken Morrison and Corporal Ken Murray called him in and laid out all the evidence. They astonished Legge with their knowledge of the vent shaft blast. They had every detail down, including the identity of all the main players, Bettger, Shearing, Lisoway and Legge himself. Legge read something else into the meeting, an implied threat that if he didn't confess to his part in the vent shaft blast, he'd be tied up in Shearing and Bettger's conspiracy to kill the nine miners. Legge still didn't think Shearing and Bettger were involved. He could understand them not wanting to admit anything and possibly face charges. He felt the same way, but by not admitting to his part in the vent shaft blast he realized he was playing the same dangerous game as they were, withholding evidence in a murder investigation.

Before saying anything to the RCMP, however, Legge decided he had to call up Bettger. Bettger told him that he didn't want to talk on the telephone.

"Don't be so fuckin' paranoid," Legge said. "Don't worry about them. Fuck them anyway."

"Well, that's okay, but we shouldn't be talking on the phone."

"Tim, I have been in for an interview, and I'm going to come clean with them."

"Well, you do what you have to do," Bettger said. "But I wish you hadn't spoken to them at all."

"Well, Tim, Jesus, what are we supposed to fuckin' do? I got three kids. I got to live in this town. I got to do my best here. And we're talk-ing about the murder of nine men here. You are going down for these murders whether you did it or not. You know that."

"I believe that the cops are going to try to pin it on me."

"Not only are the cops going to try to pin it on you, they're going to build a case around you."

"I believe that, but I got nothing to worry about. I didn't do it."

"Sometimes that's not enough."

"It doesn't matter. Just don't talk to these guys. Don't talk to them. They're fishing."

"Tim, they're not fishing. If they said it was Terry Legge, Tim, and this one and that one, they weren't fishing. They had the four of us down pat. How did they know?"

"Doesn't matter. You don't have to tell them nothing."

"That's easy for you to say, but if I don't, they're going to charge me with impeding a murder investigation; they're going to charge me with covering up a murder investigation. It's time we laid all the cards on the table."

"You do what you have to do."

While Bettger was determined not to talk, Legge hoped he could persuade Al Shearing. Legge called him.

"Al, we been friends a long time," he said. "I want you to come with me. Let's go down to the cop shop, and we tell everything, every fuckin' thing.

"Terry, I'd like to, but I can't," Shearing said.

Legge couldn't understand his refusal. Legge had known Shearing for sixteen years. They had been great friends, but in the short months of the strike, Shearing and Bettger had forged a closer bond. Shearing would not defy his new friend.

Legge went to work out at Bodyworks and again found himself sitting next to Vern White, who as usual turned the conversation to the murder investigation. White told Legge that he knew Shearing and Bettger had bought the parts for the vent shaft bomb at Lee Valley Tools and the police had figured out the timing device had come from a clock.

"Yeah," Legge said. "It was a small, black one. Square."

"Really?" White said, astonished that at last Legge had told him something.

"Yeah."

"Yeah? If I showed you a picture, could you pick it out?"

"Sure."

White set up a meeting with Legge. On March 16, almost six months to the day after the blast, they got together in White's car. White had a tape recorder, but he saw Legge didn't want him to turn it on. White knew it didn't matter because he was wired and the conversation was being monitored by officers in a nearby van. White wanted a tape because he worried that Legge might be like some of the other union guys, making outlandish claims after an interview, maybe even putting in a formal complaint. The covert recording also gave the RCMP a record of the conversation in case Legge admitted something.

White showed Legge three pages of pictures from a Lee Valley Tools catalogue. Legge picked out the correct clock mechanism, then told White about his involvement in the vent shaft bombing. The only detail he left out was Conrad Lisoway's participation, though he did admit that Lisoway may have been out at the line that night.

White told Legge that he was going to be needed as a witness. Legge said he could never do that, but White told him he would have to testify, that he would get a subpoena compelling him to come to court, but after that he couldn't be charged with the offense.

"I don't care about that!" Legge said. "If you want to put me in jail, put me in jail, but you won't put me in jail for nine fuckin' men. That's all I care about."

With the evidence building against Bettger, White decided to turn up the heat. First, the police issued a press release to the local and national media with some information from Special Agent Gus Garry and Inspector Ron McKay's psychological profile of the killer. White didn't put much store in the psychological profile. He knew the technique was helpful in multiple sex crimes, but the blast was a one-shot affair, unless, of course, it was related to the previous bombings, which is what Garry and McKay believed. Indeed, the profiles were so specific that they might as well have named Shearing and Bettger.

"The profilers have concluded that the bombing of the satellite dish on 22 July 92 and that of the air vent intake shaft on 1 Sept. 92 were committed by the same person or persons who killed the nine miners on 18 Sept. 92," Garry and McKay wrote, then went on to outline the RCMP's Progression Theory, how the explosions got bigger and more sophisticated on each occasion.

"When profiling an offense involving more than one offender it is the dominant personality that is described. In cases where two strong personalities are involved, there may be components of both found in the offender profile.

"The dominant offender in this case will be a white male with an estimated age in excess of thirty years. His childhood years will reflect a disruptive rearing environment. He will have a deep-seated need to seek respect. While he may present a face of confidence, he suffers from well-hidden insecurities.

"The anger which perpetrated this offense is mostly depersonalized and is directed at 'Scabs' generally and not toward individual persons. . . . The victims represented not persons, but objects upon which he could focus his anger while carrying out an act that would demonstrate his importance to his peers.

"The prerequisites required to complete this crime would be extensive knowledge of mining operations generally and long-standing experience and geographic familiarity with this mine in particular."

The Yellowknife media made much of the release, as it was the first public declaration of the RCMP's Progression Theory. Editors and reporters were also excited that someone trained at the FBI's famed Quantico, Virginia, violent crime analysis unit had worked on the Yellowknife case.

The next phase of the Mountie's offensive was to stage confrontations with the two prime suspects. Since neither man would come in anymore for interviews, Vern White and Al McCambridge decided they should get in their faces out on the street. The drop-ins were strategic; the RCMP hit Shearing and Bettger before the two suspects were scheduled to meet up with one of the police informants.

Shearing got the treatment first. White, wired with a body pack, walked up to him on a downtown street, then ripped in: "Hey, Al, you blasted the vent shaft, and I know where you bought the stuff."

Shearing denied it, but he walked around town with White and listened to what White had to say, which was the police's goal.

The investigators next went after the union executive. Harry Seeton had always said publicly that the union had nothing to do with any of the bombings. It was time he was confronted with the truth about the vent shaft and the satellite dish, as well as Bettger's Flying Truck Scenario.

The RCMP's union liaison, Sergeant Bill Code, set up the meeting with Seeton and his vice-president, Rick Cassidy. White felt Seeton would continue to deny everything, but he sensed Cassidy was realistic enough to know the blast was murder and, hard as it was to admit, someone from the union must have been involved. The two CASAW leaders came down to the RCMP detachment. White told them about the vent shaft information, then got into the Flying Truck Scenario, describing how only a few days before the fatal blast Bettger was known to have been plotting with Conrad Lisoway to set up a trip wire on a bridge to knock over a Pinkerton truck.

"What did you say?" Seeton cut in.

Before White could answer, Cassidy repeated the story, but added more information.

"Rick, you actually had a little bit more than I knew," White said.

"Well, Conrad called and told me that," Cassidy said.

"What did you say to me?" Seeton again asked.

"Well, Rick just told you," White said. "Obviously, it's not a secret here."

"Well, that's it!" Seeton snapped. "That's it. I'm out of here."

Seeton left, and Cassidy followed him out the door. They argued in the hallway before leaving. The next day White called up the CASAW office with an offer: if Shearing, Bettger and their buddy Joe Ranger, a fringe member of the Cambodian Cowboys, would agree to go on the polygraph, and if they all got positive results, White would issue a public statement saying just that. The CASAW men considered the offer. There was some talk of bringing in a neutral polygraph operator to run the test, instead of an RCMP man, though an RCMP tester would be allowed to monitor things. But in the end nothing came of the plan.

White now decided to drop in on Bettger. He told Bettger much of the same information, adding a few more details about their shopping trip to Vancouver. Farris later reported that Bettger was shaken up by White's visit.

The information from Luc Normandin and Terry Legge enabled the police to make their boldest move yet. At 10:00 A.M. on March 30, Vern White and Ken Morrison knocked on Bettger's door. White read Bettger his rights and Morrison gave him a copy of a search warrant signed by Justice Thomas B. Davis. The police were free to search Bettger's house for the next eleven hours, whether Bettger liked it or not, based on his suspected involvement in the ventilation shaft blast.

Bettger made a point of saying he'd talk to other officers, but there was no way he'd talk to Morrison. "It gets the hair up on my back that he's even in my house," the Bear told White.

Morrison felt good being there, so much so that he searched the living room in front of Bettger. All along Bettger had acted like the police were picking on him, like he had done nothing wrong. This gave Morrison a chance to show Bettger otherwise, that the police were justified in being so intrusive, walking right into his house, but doing it legally.

Along with White and Morrison were ten other officers, including explosives expert Jean-Yves Vermette, an Ident photographer, and a handler with a dog trained to find explosives.

Al McCambridge also helped out, though his wife, Allison, had given birth just five days earlier and planned on coming home that afternoon. (The couple had transferred to Yellowknife in early March.) McCambridge ducked out of the search long enough to get her home and resting on the couch, the baby safely in the hands of his grandmother, who had come up to help out. A moment later he was back out the door and off to Bettger's place.

The RCMP searched the house and garage, the storage cabinet behind the garage, the shed, the dog house, Bettger's GMC pickup truck, boat trailer, boat, camper and two Chevy Citations. They found a circuit tester, a balaclava, camouflage clothing, flares, arrows, a sawed-off 12-gauge pump-action shotgun, four timing devices identical to the ones used at the vent shaft blast, credit card slips, written material on building bombs, lots of firing line, pliers, a hash pipe, a roach clip, a bag of pot and a trip-wire device made from a clothespin and wire. The RCMP installed a listening probe in Bettger's house.

Through the day the union hall buzzed with news that the Bear's house was being searched. Soon the local media stood outside of the house. *yellowknifer* reporter Doug Schmidt called up Seeton, who said he wasn't pleased with the way the search was being handled. Seeton described the RCMP officers as "Swatlike with bullet-proof vests."

"He's a mechanic," Seeton said. "I'd hope they'd find some pliers."

Seeton said the union had contacted a lawyer for advice. "I'll tell you we still feel strongly a public inquiry should be held. They've concentrated their whole investigation on the union, and this more or less confirms that."

As the search went on, Bettger called up Vancouver criminal lawyer Glen Orris. Bettger refused to talk to the *yellowknifer,* but the following day he granted an interview to Lee Selleck of the pro-labor newspaper *Press Independent.* Selleck named Bettger in his story. It was the first public notice that the Bear was the focus of the murder investigation. Bettger said his home had been plundered. "The search was calculated to intimidate. I told [Morrison] I wanted to watch what they were up to. He didn't permit me to do that.

"They walked all over the place with their boots on. . . . They were encouraging me to leave, but I didn't think that was a good idea and neither did my wife.

"They abused it, but it's still my house. We're getting advice on a whole range of complaints on the search and other things."

Bettger told Selleck that he had to get someone else to pick up his kids, Jake and Tina, from school. He said both kids had been called murderers. "When you've raised nonviolent children, they don't like confrontational situations, and they're finding it hard to walk away. Because of the school-yard crap they have to put up with, we're considering relocating them.

"When you raise them to have a respect for the law and they see abuses like yesterday, they see a hypocritical situation."

The RCMP thought the search was a nine out of ten with an unexpected bonus in the clothespin trip line, which tended to confirm Normandin's story about the Flying Truck Scenario. Still, it wasn't a ten out of ten. The investigators couldn't make an arrest. All the items could just as easily have been used on the other explosions, not the big one. In future interviews they could tell the other strikers that Tim Bettger was a terrorist, but they couldn't say that he was a murderer.

When the RCMP confronted Bettger the following day with what they had found, he claimed the items were to be used to make a clock. As for the trip-wire mechanism, he said he had used such devices on Pinkerton security guards. He hooked them up to lights. When the Pinkies tripped them, they were momentarily blinded. It annoyed and frightened them.

Bettger repeated this story about the trip wire and the lights around the union hall. He also shot off flash cubes in peoples' faces and handed them clothespins, making a joke of the search. But Marvin Farris reported to the police that none of the strikers remembered using such trip-wire devices against the Pinkertons. Some of the union men were beginning to wonder about Bettger, including striker Rob Wells, another leader of CASAW's Newfoundland contingent.

One week before the RCMP searched Bettger's house, Wells and his four-year-old son had been cleaning up his tent trailer, the same trailer that had been out the previous summer at the picket line. Wells had brought it home after the September 18 blast because he feared it might be trashed by replacement workers. As Wells and his son cleaned it, the boy handed him a bag. Inside, Wells found four pieces of dynamite taped together and wired to blow. At once, Wells hid the explosives in his shed. He went into the house to vomit, sick with visions of what might have happened if his children had found the bomb and it had gone off.

Wells talked to Rick Cassidy and the union's lawyers, trying to decide what to do with the bomb. On April 2, three days after the search on Bettger, Wells decided to hand it over to the Homicide Task Force. He got in touch with Vern White. White came over at once. He had no idea why Wells was calling and was worried about the striker's strained tone. White wired himself with a body pack for the meeting, figuring that if he got ambushed at least someone could come into the house and drag him out.

At the meeting, Wells told White about the bomb, but didn't hand it over. Wells recalled that on September 19, one day after the fatal blast, he went out to his trailer at the picket line where he saw Tim Bettger with a plastic bag. He told Bettger that if there was anything illegal in the bag to get it the fuck out of his trailer. Bettger shuffled around the trailer for a while, then left with the bag. Wells said he had forgotten about the incident until he found what looked to be the same bag with the bomb inside.

The evidence against Bettger seemed to be coming together, but again the tent trailer bomb wasn't enough for an arrest. In fact, it could fit into a theory that Bettger was not the killer: first, Bettger talked to Luc Normandin and Conrad Lisoway about the Flying Truck Scenario; then a few days later he told Normandin he had called off the attack on the Pinkie truck and was thinking of something else; someone else set the September 18 blast before Bettger had a chance to do anything, and he'd been left to dispose of the bomb in Wells' trailer—if in fact it was Bettger's bomb. The RCMP had no conclusive proof of that yet.

White decided to go back to Terry Legge one final time. He knew Legge was still holding back that Conrad Lisoway was involved in the vent shaft blast. White showed Legge a list of the items seized in Bettger's house.

Legge was scared and confused. Four timing devices? A trip wire?

What the fuck can you use that shit for? There was only one thing. Jesus, a fuckin' trip wire!

He thought he knew Bettger, but maybe he didn't. Bettger did seem to have a bit of Rambo in him. One spring when the mine had been threatened with flooding, someone had to go down to a lower level and fix a pump. Bettger volunteered. He showed up in the head-frame in a wet suit, a big knife stuck to the side of his leg. Legge thought Jaws himself wouldn't stand a chance against big Tim.

During the early days of the strike, Legge recalled how there had been nothing Bettger wasn't game to attempt. The truth was, Bettger scared Legge a bit. He didn't know how far the Bear would go.

Legge decided to tell White about Lisoway's role in the vent shaft bombing. He told White that he had nothing more to give and that he would go to Al Shearing one more time to talk about coming clean.

When Legge got home he called up Lisoway in Saskatchewan and told him that he had told the police everything. Lisoway said it was okay (he had already confessed his role in the vent shaft). Next, Legge met with Shearing.

"I'm worried, Al," he said. "It's possible that maybe Tim did it. And Al, I don't know if he did or didn't confide in you, but if he did, you can confide in me, but I'm tellin' you, you tell me and I'll take care of it. I'll turn him into the cops myself if he did the murders."

"I know Tim really well," Shearing said. "Terry, he didn't do it. I can assure you he had nothing to do with the murders."

"Well, even if he didn't, Al, it's got nothin' to fuckin' do with it anymore. This is not a game. They're going down for it. Tim is going down for it."

"Terry, there is nothing there. There's just nothing."

Legge's biggest wish was that Bettger would stop listening to the lawyers about the polygraph. If the Bear took it, Legge knew Shearing would follow him in like a lamb and do the same. If both were cleared, Legge believed he would be off the hook himself. There would be no murder trial so he wouldn't have to testify about his connection to the vent shaft blast.

Now that Legge had completely unloaded to the RCMP, he decided to tell Claudia about his role in the vent shaft bombing. "We knew what we were doing," he assured her. "There was no people around. We made sure of that. We didn't want to hurt anybody."

The Yellowknife city skyline, a city of 16,000 in the Land of the Midnight Sun. Here, residents said, the gold was paved with streets.

After contract negotiations with Royal Oak Mines Inc. failed, the Canadian Union of Smelter and Allied Workers (CASAW) Local 4 went on strike May 23, 1992. For the first time in more than fifty years, replacement workers were brought in. Inflamed by this action strikers erected the Road of Shame, naming each man who crossed the picket line. Warren claimed he slept in this bus on the morning of the mass murder.

Strikers on the picket line confront a worker as he crosses the line. Such confrontations escalated from name-calling to rock throwing to rioting on mine property.

Soon after the strike began, the picket gates became littered with graffiti, including this example directed at the American president of Royal Oak, Peggy Witte. Tensions on both sides of the strike escalated as more and more strikers elected to defy their union and return to work.

Royal Oak's tough and con-
frontational president, Peggy
Witte, broke a fifty-year
precedent in the Canadian
mining industry by bringing
in replacement workers. She
was named Woman of the
Year by Chatelaine *maga-*
zine and Mining Man of the
Year by Northern Miner,
but to many striking CASAW
men she was known as Miss
Piggy, the woman they loved
to hate. Both she and the
CASAW executive would
later be found to have failed
to bargain in good faith.

The Giant Mine site with the main office at the bottom center, the high tower of the
C-shaft headframe left of center, the C-dry (the long building) at the center and the
Ingraham Trail curving behind in the upper left corner. Peggy Witte bought the
bankrupt mine in November 1990 at a cut-rate price.

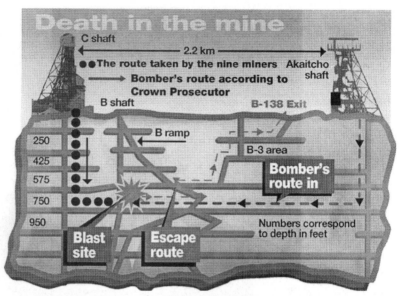

In the early morning hours of September 18, 1992, Roger Warren entered Giant Mine through the remote and unguarded Akaitcho shaft and set his bomb on the 750-drift. He exited through the B-138 portal near the Ingraham Trail. The mission took approximately four hours.

The secluded Akaitcho headframe where the murderer broke into the mine. After the September 18, 1992, fatal blast, the RCMP would find the distinctive prints of size 11 Kamik boots leading from Akaitcho into the mine. Roger Warren later presented the police with a pair of Kamik boots with the soles defaced. But when he confessed, Warren insisted he wore different boots into the mine. The Akaitcho headframe was also the entry point for the Cambodian Cowboys' graffiti mission.

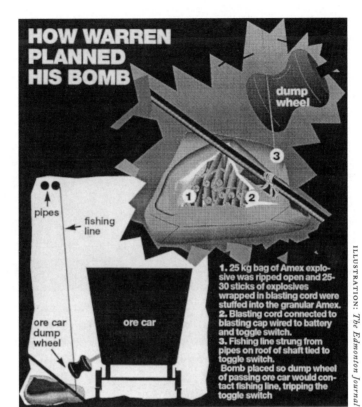

ILLUSTRATION: *The Edmonton Journal*

Roger Warren's bomb on the 750-drift killed nine replacement workers and line crossers. In his confession he insisted it was rigged with a vertical trip wire designed to be triggered by the dump wheel of an ore car, not by a car carrying men. The exact nature of the triggering mechanism was never discovered.

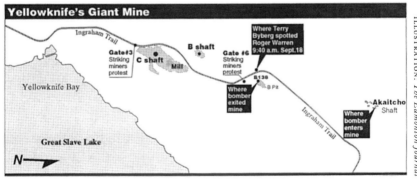

ILLUSTRATION: *The Edmonton Journal*

After exiting the mine, Roger Warren was spotted near the B-138 portal close to the Ingraham Trail by mine superintendent Terry Byberg.

PHOTO: DALE BRAZO, *The Toronto Star*

Roger Warren on the strike line. He was known as the Ace, one of the best miners in the North. He was a perfectionist, a fierce competitor and prone to fits of temper. But he was also a strong family man who loved to read and argue politics. Warren earned over $100,000 a year as a miner at Giant.

PHOTO: GREG SOUTHAM, *The Edmonton Journal*

Two days after the blast, CASAW president Harry Seeton, in the foreground, held a press conference to decry the RCMP's initial handling of the investigation. Seated at the far end of the table, facing the camera and wearing a hat, is Roger Warren, there at the union's request to answer media questions on explosives.

PHOTO: GREG SOUTHAM, *The Edmonton Journal*

CASAW president Harry Seeton refused to accept that the blast was murder, insisting instead that it was an accident caused by miners carrying explosives in a man-car in violation of mine regulations. This view was widely promoted by CASAW and is held by some to this day. They have raised $25,000 for the Roger Warren defense fund.

PHOTO: THE ROYAL CANADIAN MOUNTED POLICE

By studying the blasted hulk of the man-car, RCMP experts could determine that the explosion came from outside the car, which contradicted the union's accident theory.

Royal Oak staged a photo opportunity for the media to demonstrate that a man-car carrying eight men and pushed by a driver on a loki could not also carry a large amount of explosives.

Striker Terry Legge lashes out at a suggestion that the blast was homicide, shouting that it was an accident. The photo came to symbolize the animosity on both sides as the union and Royal Oak dueled in the media with their competing theories about the cause of the blast.

After the blast, the anti-union faction of replacement workers and line crossers tore down CASAW's flag at the main gate of Giant Mine. Three union men, including Roger Warren, facing the camera and wearing a hat, hoist the flag again. The union's motto was "We will last one day longer than Royal Oak."

During the winter of 1993, hate literature was rampant in Yellowknife, including this anti-CASAW piece. As the investigation wore on, both sides became increasingly polarized in their views. A breakaway group of replacement workers and line crossers attempted to challenge CASAW as the legitimate bargaining agent for Giant Mine workers. The breakaway faction received generous anonymous cash donations.

Is CASAW Worth It?

My Father Got Murdered In Yellowknife!!

PHOTO: GREG SOUTHAM, *The Edmonton Journal*

CASAW men Conrad Lisoway (left) and Rick Cassidy. Roger Warren strongly hinted to police that Lisoway was illegally on mine property in the early morning hours before the September 18 bomb exploded. Warren's allegation was a lie meant to deflect attention from himself. However, Lisoway was a member of the Cambodian Cowboys and participated in the September 2 vent shaft bombing.

PHOTO: GREG SOUTHAM, *The Edmonton Journal*

Al Shearing, the Night Crawler, an excellent worker who became the RCMP's prime suspect, is arrested by Constable Bill Farrell for criminal activities at the mine site, including the bombing of the vent shaft.

Tim Bettger, the Bear, the RCMP's second prime suspect in the murder, is arrested by Constable Ken Morrison for his participation in the vent shaft and satellite dish bombings. Bettger and Shearing formed the core of the Cambodian Cowboys, a group of the most militant CASAW strikers prepared to use violence to provoke an end to the strike.

Jim O'Neil stands with the shotgun he purchased to protect his family. O'Neil and Chris Neill became close friends and confidantes after they publicly denounced CASAW and returned to work at Giant Mine. Worried about his friend's safety, Chris Neill called Jim every night after work. On the day of Roger Warren's sentencing, Jim O'Neil left the courtroom with tears in his eyes. "I'm a mess," he said.

Chris Neill's widow, Tracey, is supported by her mother, Roseanne Quintal, after attending Chris's memorial service. Neill had become increasingly disillusioned by CASAW's militant rhetoric. He crossed the picket line in early August 1992 and was killed seven weeks later. Neill was a volunteer fireman; Tracey was given her husband's fire helmet at the service.

Judit Pandev with pictures of her and Joe. Judit had already lost one husband in a mining accident, and Joe was only months away from retirement when he crossed the line and was killed. Judit would later attend court every day during Warren's trial. Immediately after the verdict, she said, "I'm grinning like a monkey from ear to ear."

The monument built by sculptor François Thibault was originally intended to honor the nine men who were murdered in Giant Mine. When it provoked further controversy between union and Royal Oak factions it was eventually rededicated to all workers who had died in Northwest Territories mining accidents.

Inspector Al McIntyre, veteran homicide investigator, led the RCMP team in the thirteen-month hunt for the mass murderer. It was the second most labor intensive investigation in RCMP history, involving more than 300 police officers.

PHOTO: GREG SOUTHAM, *The Edmonton Journal*

Sergeant Vern White, second in command, the son of a Cape Breton coal miner, helped drive the investigation forward. Strikers at Giant Mine hated White's aggression, prompting one striker to call him a "scum sucking son of a whore."

PHOTO: DAVID STAPLES, *The Edmonton Journal*

Corporal Dale McGowan, who handled the Roger Warren file. McGowan was viewed as the best of the local investigators. An even-tempered, persistent man, he never let Warren off the hook. Roger Warren's attitude toward him proved instrumental in helping the RCMP break the case.

Noel O'Sullivan, foreman of the underground, was a legend at Giant Mine. After the mass murder he formed his own theory about the crime and vowed to catch the killer. Using his firsthand knowledge of the mine and miners, he came to focus on Roger Warren as the prime suspect.

Polygraph expert Sergeant Gregg McMartin, seated behind Factfinder II, the lie detector, studied the transcripts of police interviews with Roger Warren and became convinced of the miner's guilt. Known as a master interrogator and sometimes brilliant performer, McMartin provoked Roger Warren's confession during a marathon interrogation session.

PHOTO: GREG SOUTHAM, *The Edmonton Journal*

PHOTO: GREG SOUTHAM, *The Edmonton Journal*

Prosecutor Peter Martin of Calgary persistently challenged Warren with the web of lies woven around his activities in the early morning hours of September 18, 1992. With Martin pitted against Orris there was, as one reporter commented, no absence of testosterone in the courtroom.

Roger Warren's lawyer, Glen Orris of Vancouver. A large and imposing man, he fought hard to characterize Warren as a deeply troubled man who, under the intolerable pressures of the strike and criminal investigation, falsely confessed to a grizzly mass murder to bring an end to the strike.

PHOTO: GREG SOUTHAM, *The Edmonton Journal*

When Roger Warren was escorted into the courtroom by RCMP Sergeant Jim Barr on January 26, 1995, to receive a sentence of life in prison with no parole for twenty years, Warren said he felt like he was "going before Judge Roy Bean." His only comment after receiving his sentence was "Ah fuck it."

Claudia was angry but relieved. It sounded like a fiasco, but she consoled herself, thinking everyone makes mistakes and it's best to face up to them. But at the union hall, many men were furious about Wells handing over the bomb and Legge talking to the RCMP. The CASAW hardcore thought Legge was a weasel and a weak link, that he'd been pressured by Claudia into becoming a snitch. With his neat, short hair, nicely trimmed mustache and pro-police attitude, Legge might as well be a cop, some of the hardcore said, especially with the way he worked out at the gym with White every day.

Legge hated the gossip. He believed anyone who snitched should be horsewhipped. He tried not to care that others thought poorly of him. He told himself that it wasn't true, that he had been up-front with Bettger and Shearing before talking to the RCMP. Nobody put money in his pocket. He wasn't making any deals. He was ready to go to jail for what he'd done. He was no fuckin' snitch, and if he heard that someone had said he was, he confronted him. Legge still felt at home at the union hall, but he decided he wanted to get out of town. He spent time out at his cabin at Lake Chedabutco, then worked for three weeks as a camp cook, earning $300 a day.

To press their advantage the Mounties decided to release more information from Special Agent Garry and Inspector McKay's psychological profile to the media. "The offender's wish to be seen as a hero would spur him to actions that would normally only be thoughts by most people," the release read. "He would readily accept encouragement toward violent ends and would relish any praise resulting from his actions.

"Being mission oriented regarding this crime, it is felt he failed to appreciate the social abhorrence, not only from the community, but also his peers as he felt he would be righting social injustice by his act.

"Being of an opportunistic nature, he will capitalize on the natural tendency of those close to him to rely on denial even in the face of strong and reasonable suspicion of his involvement. His inner conflict continues to bother him in that if he denies participation in the crime he loses the image enhancement he has sought all his life.

"He takes great pleasure in hearing, talking or reading about the crime and his philosophy in this regard is 'the best defense is a good offense.' By proclaiming innocence to a wide audience he can draw attention to his 'achievements' while attempting to create doubt in the minds of his peers and accusers.

"The maturity of this offender suggests that at some point he will come to the realization that he has been manipulated by another and this will cause strain in their relationship."

Again, the media jumped on the release, but the RCMP were disappointed to find the second release had little effect on Shearing and Bettger. In fact, it backfired. The two men joked about it at the union all, saying the only thing the RCMP forgot to mention was that the little guy had a mustache while the big guy had a beard. Even so, on April 7, the day the release came out, Shearing and Bettger took the advice of the union's lawyers and resigned from the executive.

The RCMP still lacked evidence that broke either man's alibi and put him at the strike line in the early morning of September 18. Ken Morrison decided to again go over Bettger's alibi with his wife, Izzie, and their two children, Jake coming in one day with his mom, Tina the next. Izzie was present while both children were questioned. After he was done with the kids, Morrison went over the story again with Izzie: Tim got a ride into Yellowknife that night from the picket line with Harry Seeton, then sat in the Polar Bowl bar for about an hour, then got a lift home from striker Marvin Tremblett. Izzie was sleeping by then, but she said she heard him come in around 1:30 A.M. He started up the microwave. Around 3:00 A.M., he turned on their light and got into bed. Izzie told Morrison she was annoyed because Tim was cold.

Morrison didn't know if he should believe Izzie. He decided he had to hit her with everything the police knew and suspected about Tim. He told her that down the road, without any doubt whatsoever, her husband was going to be arrested, whether it was for the vent shaft and satellite dish bombings or for the murders. He was going down big time, Morrison told her, and it was time she started to look after herself because obviously he wasn't doing it. Izzie started to cry and left the interview room.

Morrison felt bad afterward. He knew Izzie was a fine person, but he also believed he had done what was necessary. She had to know what was up with her husband, otherwise she might never realize how serious the matter was and might never tell all she knew.

Morrison's treatment of Izzie outraged the Bear. A few days later, Ken Morrison and Dale McGowan were at the McDonald's restaurant. McGowan had his burgers and was getting ketchup and a straw when he spotted Bettger.

"How you doin', Tim?"

"Good," Bettger said.

McGowan went to sit down. A moment later, Morrison ran into Bettger. "Hi, Tim. How's it goin'?"

Bettger glared at Morrison. "Eat shit and die, motherfucker."

"Oh, I guess you don't want to talk then."

The encounter left Morrison shaken. He knew now that it was personal, that Bettger hadn't said anything to McGowan, but had singled him out. It bothered him that Bettger was lashing back in such a way, trying to get him to look over his shoulder. But it had worked. At night Morrison started to make doubly sure his doors were locked.

Vern White was also worried about Bettger's outburst against Morrison. He knew a number of union men were starting to detest him and the other investigators. White had a hard time getting to sleep. He, too, checked his house to make sure it was secure. He felt like a predator guarding its lair.

The investigation was now in its seventh month. The investigators went over and over their evidence, trying to find something they might have missed. Twice, McIntyre brought in RCMP homicide investigators from the outside to review the file and maybe find that blind spot. Instead, the Yellowknife team was told it was on the right track; it just needed to keep at it. But what more could be done?

White and McCambridge kept confronting Shearing and Bettger. White would walk into Bettger's garage and keep talking until he was ordered to leave. He always left his card. White still considered Bettger the most likely suspect. Among the Cambodian Cowboys, Bettger was the talker and the instigator. It was Bettger who built things, not Shearing. Yes, maybe Bettger built the bomb and Shearing put it in the mine, but White kept thinking back to something one of the CASAW guys had told him: "Bettger didn't let anybody play with his toys."

Bettger was overweight, arguably too fat to pull off the mission on his own, but White knew Bettger had made the same trip down Akaitcho to the 712-scoop shop on the June 29 graffiti mission. The murderer's route out of the mine was a bit convoluted, and it would be unfamiliar territory to Bettger, but maybe somebody made a map for him.

White looked for a hole in Bettger's alibi, but all he found was evidence that Bettger wasn't the killer. For one thing, Bettger's truck was broken down at the time of the fatal blast. It had needed a new fuel pump. White thought that maybe he had used Izzie's Chevy Citation, but after interviewing and reinterviewing the people out at the strike line that night, not one of them ever mentioned seeing a Chevy Citation, let alone Tim Bettger. Bettger had also come home from the picket line at midnight, instead of just waiting around out there. None of it made sense if he was the killer.

There was also Izzie's confirmation of the alibi. White didn't think she was lying. After her run-in with Ken Morrison, White had gone to her for a follow-up conversation. She had insisted her husband had come to bed that night. "I'm telling you, Vern, I will not tell you a lie," Izzie had said. "If he was not home that night I wouldn't tell you that he was."

White started to think that maybe Izzie didn't really know. She thought she remembered, but she really didn't, and when Tim told her what had happened she backed him up, not wanting to call him a liar. But if Izzie was right, Bettger's alibi was solid up until 3:00 or 3:30 A.M. It didn't leave much time to get out to the line, go down Akaitcho, set the blast, get out and get home again.

White went to an Ottawa company that took satellite photographs and, by chance, had taken an image of Yellowknife at 4:00 A.M. on September 18, 1992. He hoped he would be able to pinpoint all the vehicles near the Akaitcho shaft at that time. When he got the photographs, however, they were so blurred he couldn't even make out buildings, let alone vehicles. It was on such points that the Homicide Task Force had now stalled. New information only trickled in, then stopped altogether, save the usual reports from Marvin Farris. The investigators spent more and more time sitting around the task force office, files stacked high on their desks, coffee cups, pizza and donut boxes, computers, pens and pencils all over. They tried to think up new plans and argued about the various suspects. Only one thing was becoming clear: If they couldn't agree on who the murderer was, how could they ever convince a jury?

Chapter 15

PLEASE COME HOME

THE WIDOWS and closest relatives of the dead men lived in a twilight world of murder survivors that no one untouched by the poison in Yellowknife could easily understand. The widows were scarred and haunted by their losses. They were pierced with the terror and mystery of the crime. They saw ghosts in everything: the smell of a man's soap, the sight of a man's razor, a stranger with a familiar walk or profile or hair color. They drifted in and out of a fantasy world where they danced and made love again with their men. They talked, held hands and worked out the problems that hung over them. In their worst moments, they descended into nightmares of the Giant underground and the blast at 750. A silent trip in the dark, the cataclysm, then pulverized wood and steel and flesh. Few of the widows had been able to look under the cloths at the funeral home to see the remains. They could not bear to know what had happened, but it was what they wanted, second only to the return of their men. Did he die quickly? Was he okay now? In their nightmare visions, each searched the 750-drift for her man amidst the carnage, hoping to find him with no wounds, dead, but peaceful and intact.

The mass murder poisoned Doreen Hourie most strongly. She lost her memory and struggled to keep her sanity. Her husband, Norm, had been a lifelong packsack miner, a drill and blast man who traveled from contract to contract across the mining country of Canada: Thompson, Manitoba, then Sicamous, British Columbia; Mika Dam, British Columbia; Balmer Town, Ontario; Kamloops, British Columbia; Stewart, British Columbia; Wawa, Ontario; LaRonge, Saskatchewan; Ross River, Yukon; Wells, British Columbia; Duncan, British Columbia and finally Yellowknife.

Norm lived for his work and talked of little else. He was a workaholic, a calm, quiet man, a light drinker. He spent his free time on hockey, curling, woodworking and Doreen. He was her provider and lover. She never took a full-time job, just part-time cooking and cleaning because when Norm came home from his latest contract he wanted Doreen all to himself.

Both he and Doreen had been divorced when they had got together. She had two teenaged boys, Johnny and Jimmy, from her first marriage while Norm had two adult children, Trevor and Darla, with a granddaughter on the way. Norm was fifty-three years old in the summer of 1992. Doreen was sixteen years younger, a petite, pretty woman, only 4'11" and one hundred pounds, with light reddish brown hair. Norm wanted to look good for her. He did fifty to a hundred push-ups a night. Shortly before his death, he had looked in the mirror and boasted, "Jeez, this isn't the body of a grandfather."

Norm's union job at Giant was to be his last contract. He'd already had one operation on his hands, but they continued to ache. He and Doreen planned to settle in Vernon, British Columbia, on Lake Okanagan, where they owned a house.

Norm had never been big on unions, but getting on at Giant meant he had to sign on with CASAW. When contract talks came up, he was unimpressed. He thought the pro-strike forces were bullying weak-minded men into supporting them. He was astonished that men would let loudmouths sway them on such an important decision. When he heard Royal Oak was going to keep the mine going with replacement workers, he decided to stay on. He helped set up the barrack-style beds in the makeshift C-dry dormitory for the incoming replacement workers.

Norm's brother Allan also worked at Giant, but he wouldn't cross the line. Allan went to work at Yellowknife's Con Mine instead. He kept telling Norm that someone was going to die before the strike ended, that's how ugly it was, but Norm never believed him. He was so easygoing himself that he couldn't believe other people could get riled up enough to kill.

Norm lived at a series of houses and trailers in the old Giant Mine townsite. By mid-June, he believed things were calm enough for Doreen to come live at the camp as well. She had a job lined up, $12 an hour to clean the various houses where the men lived.

On the evening of June 14, Doreen got on a helicopter at the airport and flew into the camp. She and Norm immediately went for a celebratory dinner at the cook shack. Norm sat down to a big steak while Doreen had her tea. Outside she started to hear distant chanting. It was the men on the picket line, holding some kind of rally. The roar got louder, rumbling like the waves of Great Slave Lake when the wind shrieked in from the north. Suddenly a rock smashed against the cook shack. Another crashed through the window. One of the replacement workers peeked out to see that the strikers had ripped down the fence and were charging onto mine property. Wild screaming erupted all around. A smoke bomb went off. The air horn at the strikers' bus wailed again and again. The Pinkerton security guards ran away to safety. In the cook shack, some of the replacement workers cowered under the dinner tables while others locked the doors at either end, just in time to keep the strikers out. The CASAW men hammered at one door. They broke in just as Norm and Doreen and the other Royal Oak employees hurried out the other.

Doreen tried to keep up with Norm. A rock hit her, then she caught an elbow in the throat. She saw just the flash of the man who had attacked her: dark, wild eyes. Norm yelled at her. She ran crazily toward the bush behind the main office. Twigs cracked and cut her. She was sure she was being chased. At last she could hear only her own breathing. She was alone. She stopped running. She looked around and saw other panting men and women. At last she found Norm. He limped on a sprained ankle but was otherwise okay.

After the riot each man on Giant Mine property was assigned a gate to go to if trouble broke out. The men were told to have a stick handy to defend themselves.

"Everything will be fine as long as we're together," Norm told Doreen.

While living on Giant Mine property, they always had a room to themselves, which was better than most. Six or eight replacement workers lived in most of the small homes while as many as thirty-two Pinkerton security guards crammed into the mine managers' large cabin. Some slept in closets.

Doreen had to cross the picket line every day. She took orders from the workers and went to town to do their shopping. She never had any trouble from the CASAW men. She smiled and said nothing as she waited for them to get out of her way or remove the board with the nails sticking up.

Off shift, the replacement workers read, played Ping Pong, went for walks and watched videos. No drinking was allowed and little was done. A camp cook got drunk one night, went out to the picket line to mouth off and was fired the next day.

The CASAW strikers were outraged at Norm for being one of the first of the union men to cross the line. The union's vice-president, Ken Cawley, would see Norm walking by and get on the blowhorn. "Hourie, you'll never leave here alive! You're a dead man!"

Norm just waved back, but in midsummer when Cawley died in a car crash, Norm had little sympathy. "I guess that's one less guy to worry about," he told Doreen.

Doreen felt okay as long as Norm worked the day shift. She didn't feel safe if she was alone at night. The explosion at the satellite dish upset both her and Norm because it was so close to their home at the townsite.

By the end of August, things were calm enough that Norm and Doreen could easily drive to work across the picket line. They decided it was time to get out of camp, and rented a trailer in Yellowknife. Norm started working part-time as a shift boss, and Doreen worked in the company store. She was getting to know most of the replacement workers. Life seemed almost normal, but then came September 18.

Doreen lost her mind and her memory that day. She only started to get them back seven months later in April 1993. When she came to, she was told that Norm was dead, that he had been murdered in an explosion at the mine. Doreen could remember the strike, but as for Norm dying, no, that couldn't be true. She remembered seeing him go off to work that day, just like he always did. She was sure he would come home to her eventually, just like he always did. Doreen was home in Vernon, so that meant Norm must be out on a contract. If he wasn't in

Yellowknife, he was somewhere else. He'd call her when he had a minute. He was pretty busy, after all.

No, her family told her repeatedly; there would be no call. Norm wasn't coming home. He was dead. He had been cremated in his hometown, little Grand Marais on Lake Winnipeg. Doreen had been at his funeral. Norm's ashes were in the urn that she had on the dresser in her bedroom. After the funeral she and her youngest son, Jimmy, then sixteen years old, had gone to live with her sister, Sharon, in Kamloops. Jimmy was still there with Sharon.

None of it made sense to Doreen. She simply didn't remember the months of sitting alone in the bedroom, Sharon helping her to dress, getting her tea, cigarettes and what little food she would eat. At last, when it looked like she would be okay on her own, she was taken to her home in Vernon, where she could be close to Darla and Norm's infant granddaughter, Carly.

Even as Doreen started to remember the past, she had trouble keeping track of the present. She still lost time, lost track of the days and months. She had trouble recalling what she had done the previous week. It still seemed to her as if Norm had just left her. She went out a few times and found herself searching the streets for Norm. One day she saw a man with Norm's red hair in the parking lot at McDonald's. She followed him until Darla called her back.

If Norm was gone, then why did she feel him everywhere around her? When she lay in bed she could feel him beside her. She curled up in his arms. She kept out his shaving stuff for his return.

Slowly, however, she lost hope. Overwhelming, troubling emotions started to wash over her. She started to feel frightened. She got down on her knees and begged. "Please come home. Please come home."

When the phone rang, she didn't want to answer it. She cowered when someone knocked on her door. Maybe it was someone phoning to tell her Norm really was dead, knocking on the door with the bad news that he really was never coming home. She hated it when people told her that. She didn't want to hear it. Still, her family kept repeating it, and they wouldn't say it just to hurt her. It had to be true.

One day she went to the bank and started to bawl at the teller's wicket when she saw Norm's name on their account with $50,000 in it. Insurance money, she was told. She refused to touch it. What was this, some friggin' lottery? Lose your husband, win some money?

Doreen's confusion about what had happened was replaced by pain and anger. If she couldn't have Norm, she would have revenge. She thought more and more about the murderer. He was out there somewhere, breathing the same air, looking out at the world, maybe holding his wife close. Doreen focused on that man and the circumstances that had created him. She raged against CASAW. Why hadn't they been honest with Norm? Why didn't they tell him it was a live-or-die vote, that if he crossed that picket line he would be risking his life? He would never have gone back to work if he'd known he was going to die.

The numbness of her memory loss had saved Doreen from the pain that she now had to handle. She hated herself. She knew she was poisoned. She could no longer sleep through the night and would wake up every hour, only to stare at the clock. She pulled at her hair and dug her fingers into the palms of her hands. Her doctor prescribed sleeping pills. She could hardly move after taking one, but still she would sleep for only a few hours and then wake up feeling like she hadn't slept at all. She'd take another pill and go back to sleep, then wake again to feel pain in her stomach and chest, as if someone were squeezing her from the inside until she couldn't breathe.

Terrifying seizures came upon her. She started to feel shaky and itchy, as if bugs crawled up and down her body. A stabbing pain shot up from her foot. She was hot, then cold. Everything inside raced so fast that she feared she might come apart. If she was driving a car and a seizure came upon her, she had to stop and get out. Her doctor prescribed anti-seizure medication. When she felt herself losing control, she swallowed the pills until she slowed to a standstill.

She had to remind herself to try to eat. When she did take something, she usually vomited it up. She got by on Ritz crackers, toast and tea. She lost ten pounds. She felt guilty putting food in her mouth. Why should she go on living and eating when Norm could not?

At night Norm continued to live in her dreams. He would get out of his truck and they'd hug. "Nobody would believe me," she'd say. "I've told everybody that you would come home and nobody would believe me."

She slept in Norm's pajamas and wore his sweatshirts during the day. She kissed his picture and told him that she loved him and missed him, and she wept. When she traveled she always brought the wooden urn with the engraved geese that contained Norm's ashes. She was afraid that if she left the urn the house would burn down. She planned an escape route to get the ashes out during a fire. She had a towel near the dresser in case the urn was too hot to handle.

The only thing that kept her grounded was her relationship with her new granddaughter, Carly. Darla went back to work and Doreen was in charge of the little girl through the day. Doreen didn't have so much time to fret. She showed Carly photographs of Norm.

"Where's grandpa?" she asked.

Carly learned to point at his picture.

Doreen's family and friends noticed that she seemed to be getting better, so they pushed her to make new friends. "You're young, Doreen," they said. "Go on with your life." Doreen felt she was a reminder to them that Norm had been murdered. It wasn't Norm and Doreen anymore; it was just Doreen. At family functions there always seemed to be an empty seat next to her.

She talked to Norm and wrote him letters. She told him how big Carly was and what the baby had done today. She asked him for help with their boy, Jimmy. In her darkest moments, Doreen wanted to kill herself, but she knew her death might set off a terrible chain reaction among her children. She knew that Jimmy especially was suffering and struggling. He, too, had had trouble accepting that Norm was gone. "It sure seems like Dad is on a long contract, hey, Mom," he said to Doreen.

Jimmy was in school in Kamloops. He rarely came to Vernon. He felt overwhelmed when he returned home to his father's house. "I can't stay," he told his mom when he did visit. "Dad isn't here. Everything is Dad's here."

Jimmy's clothes started to look ragged. He needed a new pair of runners. Doreen asked him about them, but he said he couldn't buy new things, he didn't want to go shopping, that was something he'd always done with his father.

He had never been an outstanding student, but now he started to fail. He skipped classes and for the first time told lies to cover up. He said he was at the dentist's or on a job interview. Doreen worried. She knew that without school Jimmy would have it tough, especially because she couldn't help him much. "Dad's not here," she told him. "We don't have any safety net anymore."

Doreen decided that she had to find out more about Norm's death.

She called up the funeral home in Manitoba. The director told her that Norm had no body to speak of. On the coroner's report, however, it said that from the neck down Norm's injuries were unremarkable. What did that mean? What was the truth? Was he not there anymore?

Doreen also wanted to know exactly what had happened to her on September 18, 1992. She went to a hypnotist to try to regain her lost memories. She had no trouble thinking back to any happy memories from the summer of 1992, but when she came to the day of the blast she started to shake and cry. After the sessions she vomited.

She called up her friends in Yellowknife and asked them what she had done that awful day. They told her she had been frantic, running around, confronting the men who were coming up from the underground, asking, "Did you see Norm? Did you see Norm? Did you see Norm?" On the day the RCMP took the bodies out and shipped them to Edmonton, she learned she was at the collar with the rest of the widows, but she was excited. When she heard the men were coming out, she thought it meant Norm was finally done his work on mine rescue and she'd see him. She didn't know why everyone else was carrying on and crying. Norm was coming home. The RCMP hid the bodies being loaded into the van so no one ever saw them. To Doreen, this was proof that Norm was all right. "See, I told you this was a waste of time," she had said. "Norm is still down there. He's just waiting to come up when the time is right."

Doreen thought more and more about the other eight men who had died. She was the only one of the widows who knew them all because of her work at the mine site. She could picture each face, even the faces of the three replacement workers. In Yellowknife these three got little attention. They were outsiders, in town for only a few weeks, then gone. There were no grieving widows, no severed associations. But Doreen had got to know the three men, friendly Malcolm Sawler, and the more quiet Robert Rowsell, and Arnold Russell, as happy-go-lucky a man as you'd want to meet. The night before the men had died, she recalled how Arnold had come to see her at the store in the C-dry. "All the guys are going to town tomorrow to buy you something really sexy for Norm because you've been so nice to us," he had told her.

From her Yellowknife friends, Doreen heard about the other widows. The ones who did the best were the ones with young children. The mundane, arduous tasks of daily living kept them in the present.

They had work to do. If they didn't do it, no one else would. Their husbands were gone. That was final. It couldn't be any more real for them than having to care for one or two or three young ones all on their own. Some of them had to continue with their jobs. Each of the widows was paid $1,306 a month from Worker's Compensation, plus $269 for each dependent child. Along with the $50,000 of life insurance money, a sum of $4,120 was paid out to each of the twenty-three wives and children of the dead men from the Yellowknife Victim Relief Fund.

Doreen's Yellowknife friends also told her about the RCMP's investigation and about Jim O'Neil's group trying to take over from CASAW. The first significant decision by a government agency regarding O'Neil's group came in early May when the Canada Labour Relations Board at last ruled on the bid to decertify CASAW. The Labour Board said that CASAW still represented the miners at Giant. However, the board said Royal Oak hadn't controlled and manipulated O'Neil's group and the replacement workers at the mine had the right to vote on the union's leadership. As of January 1993, CASAW had the support of 185 men while the Giant Mine Employees Association had only 160 men, so CASAW was still on top.

Though his group had failed to gain control of the union, O'Neil celebrated the decision. It was the first time in Labour Board history that replacement workers had been given a vote. Hoping to press his victory, O'Neil said that the GMEA would apply again to decertify CASAW.

With the Labour Board's decision, Don Munroe and Vince Ready of the Industrial Inquiry Commission said they could now accept CASAW as the bargaining agent for the miners, and it was time for both Royal Oak and CASAW to put forward new bargaining positions.

On May 12 the strikers got some good news made all the sweeter because Peggy Witte was the cause of it. Early in the strike Witte had claimed that the mine was working at full capacity. Labor regulations stated that if a company got up to eighty-five percent capacity during a strike, the striking workers were entitled to collect unemployment insurance. Many of the men got big backdated pogey checks. Harry Seeton got $8,000.

The union made another complaint against Royal Oak to the Labour Board. CASAW's lawyers said the company had failed to bargain in good faith, mainly over the issue of the company's insistence that no man who had been fired during the dispute could ever come back to work.

On May 23, the first anniversary of the strike, about two hundred CASAW supporters marched on Giant Mine, chanting antiscab slogans and defying the court injunctions limiting the number of men at the gates. At the main gate the strikers unveiled a new billboard that named Jim Gauthier, a CASAW executive who had helped negotiate the tentative agreement and then crossed the picket line, as the Scab of the Year.

A number of the widows wrote letters to the *yellowknifer* for the anniversary, including Tracey Neill. She criticized CASAW's leaders for issuing death threats early in the strike. "While CASAW members sit on the picket lines in Yellowknife congratulating themselves on lasting a whole year, as other unions, citizens and politicians pledge their support to 'the cause,' remember the nine men who were killed, remember the bombings, the vandalism, the intimidation, fear and terrorism. My husband Chris Neill was murdered. Open your eyes and take a good hard look."

Doreen Hourie also wrote to the newspaper, but the *yellowknifer* wouldn't run her letter. When Doreen called up to ask why, she was told the letter was full of hearsay. In the letter, Hourie had attacked the union for inciting violence against the replacement workers, then concluded by asking, "When this investigation is all over and CASAW members are found guilty, will the faithful CASAW followers pick up their signs and march around town shouting, 'Yes, we killed those miners Sept. 18, 1992!'? And carry them high yelling, 'We tried hard to hide our murderers!'?"

Throughout the summer of 1993, Doreen fixated on the police investigation. She had no deadline for the RCMP to make an arrest, but she knew they had to lose some interest over time. She prayed the Mounties would not give up on the nine men, and she tried to keep her faith in the task force. But it was hard to have so much riding on the work of a group of men and women she didn't know.

She bought the paper every day and flipped the TV channels, hungry for any news. Like the other widows, she lived for the Friday phone call from Nancy Defer, who had the task of regularly updating the widows. But when Defer kept giving Doreen the standard line about the police wanting to dot every *i* and cross every *t* before making an arrest, Doreen finally blew up. "How many fuckin' *i*'s and *t*'s are there?"

Norm had always made a good salary, about $75,000 a year. Now Doreen was getting by on a few hundred a week. All the things she could afford before were out of reach. She made do, but had no more expensive little treats, not that the lack of luxury bothered her much. Instead, it was just another reminder of her loss. She didn't need Norm's money. She needed him. The world was large and lonely, but Norm had filled all the empty places inside her. He had made her feel beautiful. He had loved her for who she was, with all her faults. She believed she would never again have that feeling, and that is what hurt and scared her the most.

Chapter 16

THE
BLITZ

B Y MAY 1993, the eighth month of the investigation, even the moderate CASAW men had had enough of the RCMP's requests for follow-up interviews. Indeed, the moderates had again rallied around Al Shearing. The union men were united in their anger when Shearing was sentenced on May 11 to six months in jail for two strike-related incidents: on August 11, 1992, Shearing had been found on mine property with a slingshot; and on September 11, 1992, he had stopped a Pinkerton security truck in the parking lot of the OK Economy, then thrown a stick, striking a guard in the arm.

To the strikers, the six-month sentence was another example of the court's pro–Royal Oak stance. The Northwest Territories Federation of Labour had a convention in Yellowknife a few days later, and dozens of delegates marched in protest up Yellowknife's Main Street, Franklin Avenue. They rallied before the courthouse.

"The court systems are not friends of working people," Darrell Tingley, president of the Canadian Union of Postal Workers, told the crowd. "The system supports the rich."

Harry Seeton wrote a letter of complaint to Territorial Justice Minister Stephen Kakfwi. He called the justice system warped and biased. "In our view, there is a strict law for CASAW Local 4 and no law for Royal Oak. . . . The unfair punishment inflicted upon Mr. Shearing simply inflames the frustration already felt by our members."

Shearing appealed the sentence. It was reduced by two months, but through the summer the Night Crawler had his first lengthy stay in jail.

The CASAW executive cut off all formal contact with the Mounties. The final break happened after Superintendent Brian Watt suggested in a letter to a Quebec labor leader that CASAW's executive had accepted that the blast was deliberately set and that the RCMP were appropriately investigating it.

Seeton wrote a scathing reply: "The CASAW Local 4 Executive has NOT in any way accepted the fact that the explosion was the result of a deliberate criminal act. We have NOT been shown any evidence that it was done deliberately. All we keep getting from the RCMP is—It was not an accident! It was not an accident!

"Finally, we do NOT accept that the police are appropriately investigating the incident as a multiple murder. We have told them on several occasions that we feel they are concentrating solely on the union in their investigation."

Yellowknifers lived for the summertime when the sun didn't set until 2:00 A.M. and rose a few hours later. At last people got outside to hunt, fish, sail, hike and picnic. The town was full of a strange and joyous energy, people coming out of the bars at midnight, seeing the sun still in the sky, and suddenly feeling ready to keep talking and partying through the sunlit night.

The Homicide Task Force investigators, however, found no respite. They were still confined, reading over files, arguing, brainstorming, making plans that never seemed to lead anywhere and confronting union men who were increasingly hostile. The investigation that looked like it might wrap up before Christmas, then before the winter was over, now looked like it could drag on for years.Officers began to fear they might never solve the case. They had lived in a cocoon for more than six months. They had neglected their families and their health. Everything outside the case had been put on hold, and this would likely continue.

The main pick-me-up for McIntyre and his officers was to drive out of town, then hike for an hour over the hardrock to a favorite fishing hole, Secret Lake, which had been stocked with trout. The officers coated themselves in bug grease and put their socks over their pants so the biting black flies couldn't crawl up. The Mounties fished through the evening into the early morning. They always caught something. To finish up, they cleaned the fish and had a shore meal. They felt better afterward, but the fishing trips were all too few, only a handful through the summer.

The investigators got one other boost when they left their third floor office at the detachment to get their own office at the Centre Square Mall. They moved partly to get more space, partly to get away from the distraction of working in a large office where everyone wanted to know what they were doing.

To get to the new office for an interview, a striker had to walk through the mall's main floor, past a Gramma Lee's restaurant and a lottery ticket center, then up either the elevator or a stairway. On the second floor the striker saw the Yellowknife public library on his left, the door to the task force office on his right. The door was locked. It had an intercom and a video monitor for security. The office was L-shaped, and the strikers only saw the front section, where the police had set up a waiting area and two adjoining interviewing rooms, complete with hidden recording equipment. A polar bear skin hung on a violet wall, a color chosen by Nancy Defer. The main office was around the corner. The investigators sat face-to-face, desk to desk, in a bullpen area— Morrison, Defer, Murray, White, Brandford, McCambridge, McGowan and McBride all packed in tight. McIntyre set it up this way so the officers would always be plugged into the latest news. Only McIntyre had his own office. On the bullpen's wall he'd added his own touch, two little porcelain busts, one of Sherlock Holmes, the other of Dr. Watson.

Along with the new office, McIntyre wanted a new perspective, another outside opinion. He asked for a Crown prosecutor to come in to look at their evidence and answer a few questions for the team. Was there any chance they had enough to lay charges? Could they get the case through a preliminary hearing to trial? Could they convince a jury? If not, what did they still have to do?

McIntyre had a particular prosecutor in mind, Peter Martin, an outstanding lawyer from Calgary with whom McIntyre had worked on a number of murder trials. In McIntyre's opinion, Martin was the best in the business, a thorough, unrelenting and able man with a special knack in the courtroom for thinking on his feet.

Martin came up for a week in mid-June to look at the evidence firsthand. After his review he made it clear that he needed either a confession or evidence to break the alibi of a prime suspect and place him at the scene of the murder. The Progression Theory was only circumstantial and would never convince a jury, not when the first two suspects were at home sleeping with their wives when the murderer was setting the blast. Martin's lack of enthusiasm for the case against Bettger and Shearing disappointed the investigators. They felt like they had written the most important exam of their lives and received only a slightly above-average grade. The mark was sobering.

Christ, Vern White thought, we can convict Shearing and Bettger on all the other stuff they did, like the vent shaft blast, and as for their graffiti mission, it's got to be the best-investigated break and enter of all time. But, really, how much closer are we to laying murder charges that could stick in court? We must be missing something. But what is it?

The investigators came up with a new plan code-named the Blitz. The idea was to show the strikers the information the police had gathered on the search of Bettger's house and a photograph of the four sticks of explosives found in Rob Wells' trailer. The police also planned to release some of the information about the murderer's route in the mine, including the fact that he had left footprints at the Akaitcho shaft. But the police wouldn't tell everything. They held back a few key pieces of evidence—things that only the murderer and the police would know. If a man ever confessed, he'd have to know the bits of hold-back evidence or the police would know that he was making up his confession.

In many ways the Blitz was just like everything else the police had done, getting in the strikers' faces, making them realize the seriousness of the matter, but this was the first coordinated, all-out bombardment since the start of the investigation. The police wanted to show the strikers how strong the case was against Bettger.

Five Edmonton investigators came back up to Yellowknife to help out. The bulk of the work was done on three days, June 16–18, nine months after the deadly blast. One of the twenty-odd strikers targeted was Marvin Tremblett. Tremblett was a key part of Bettger's alibi. He had always maintained that he had driven Bettger home from the Polar Bowl at 1:30 A.M., and the RCMP believed he was telling the truth. He had passed his polygraph test. But Tremblett was a big talker at the union hall, and since one of the goals of the Blitz was to keep the strikers focused and talking about the murder, working on an opinion leader like Tremblett was essential.

Defer and Constable John Turgeron, one of the Edmonton men, showed up as Tremblett was cleaning his garage.

"Look, I got nothing else to tell you guys," Tremblett said as soon as he saw the Mounties. "I gave everything I had. Seven interviews. A lie detector test. If I knew who killed those nine people you wouldn't have to come knocking on my door; I would turn them in. I wouldn't care if it was my father."

The officers told Tremblett they had new information.

"I don't even want to hear it!" he said. "I've had enough. Just leave me alone. You guys from day one have marked it as union, and I believe some day it's going to come where you guys will have to say, 'It's not a murder. We looked in the wrong direction. It's an accident.'"

Defer told Tremblett he was wrong, that this was a murder and that the RCMP's two suspects were Al Shearing and Tim Bettger.

"Listen, if you got that much evidence on both of them, arrest them."

"No, we can't," Defer said. "We're looking for some more pieces to the puzzle."

The officers kept talking, telling Tremblett what they knew, even if he didn't want to hear it, outlining the evidence against Bettger and Shearing, then showing him the photograph of the bomb. Defer told Tremblett that one day the RCMP would be proven right.

"If that's the case I will personally come and say, 'Hey, I should have listened,'" Tremblett said. "But I'm sick of this bullshit of the RCMP coming to my door and calling me into their office and trying to push it down my throat."

Tremblett was especially upset about the allegations against his buddy, Al Shearing. Shearing was no longer so cavalier about the Mounties' attention. He had been to jail for the slingshot and parking lot assault incidents (though he was out at the time of the Blitz while the case was on appeal). Shearing realized it was no longer a game, that McCambridge would never give up, not unless he admitted what he had done, and he still wasn't prepared to do that.

Tremblett and the other strikers saw Shearing as a victim, and the RCMP's insistence that he was involved in the killings outraged them. Tremblett wasn't impressed with the items found in Bettger's garage either. Of course, they found some old junk! Tim's a mechanic. The RCMP seemed so keen to manufacture something that Tremblett decided if he was ever going to be convinced this was a murder, somebody would have to get up on the witness stand and say, "I done it."

While the RCMP only infuriated Tremblett, they did convince other strikers to give more information about the various crimes at the mine. Luc Normandin provided another tidbit about the Flying Truck Scenario. He told them that Bettger had wanted to pull off the caper while Shearing was in jail. The RCMP would be mystified, Bettger believed, and might start to doubt that Shearing had been involved in any of the other bombings.

Ken Morrison wanted the chance to hit the Bear with the Blitz package, but he knew Bettger would just slam the door in his face. McGowan and White did it instead. While Bettger admitted nothing, he did tell the officers he was going to Vancouver to speak to defense lawyer Glen Orris, whom he had earlier contacted during the search of his house. At last the investigators got lucky—none other than Marvin Farris planned to accompany Bettger on the long drive to Vancouver. The RCMP planned to wire Farris for transmission. They hoped Bettger might unload on his traveling companion, as so often happens on a long trip. The Blitz would certainly give Farris plenty of reason to talk about Bettger's strike-line activities.

At 3:00 A.M. on June 18, the darkest time of the night, Farris and Bettger headed out of Yellowknife. Sure enough, they started talking about the police investigation.

"The cops are no longer saber rattling," Bettger told Farris. "They are brandishing."

"I wonder what would happen if we would have done the pig and not the underground blast," Farris said.

"I've often wondered that myself."

Bettger started talking about the Flying Truck Scenario, telling Farris that if the plan had worked the Pinkerton truck's front wheels would have tripped the line and the truck would have been thrown off the bridge into a stream.

"I'm listening and observing different people right through this whole thing," Farris said. "On September 17, you and Conrad went out to gate two to pull the Flying Truck Scenario. But for some reason or another, be it too much heat, it was called off."

"Something like that," Bettger nodded. "I'd have to get right under the bridge. Someone would have to stand watch. Conrad was too nervous. Why did you think it was Lisoway, anyway?"

"I'd been listening to Roger Warren one night, and he said he was sure it was you and Conrad that did something," Farris said, thinking fast. "Roger almost called out your name. He didn't believe it would alert the guard."

"Did Roger actually know it was me?"

Farris replied that Warren seemed pretty sure it was Tim Bettger and Conrad Lisoway.

"Where did Roger say he saw us?"

Farris said he wasn't sure, but he thought it was out by gate six.

Now that he had Bettger focused on the night of the murder, Farris brought up the RCMP's Blitz and how the police were saying the evidence pointed to him as the killer. Bettger told Farris he had nothing to do with the blast. The cops were putting him in a vise, he said.

In Vancouver, Bettger said the same thing to Glen Orris, telling the prominent Vancouver defense lawyer that he had nothing to do with the homicide in any way, shape or form, but nevertheless might soon need a good lawyer.

On the trip home to Yellowknife, Farris again brought up the night of September 17, asking Bettger if he had been with Lisoway on mine property.

"No," Bettger said. "He was probably out there, but he was not with me."

Again the RCMP's effort had been thwarted. Bettger had been in a spot where he might at last open up, but when he did, he again denied he had anything to do with the murder. Was he lying? Or were the investigators wrong?

In July 1993, the Homicide Task Force came up with a new plan, one that grew out of the interview with Luc Normandin during the Blitz. Normandin had mentioned that Bettger had planned the Flying Truck Scenario to divert attention while Shearing was in jail in September 1992. The RCMP's idea was to get Farris to suggest another such operation now that Shearing was in jail again. Farris agreed to try the plan, but he was starting to get nervous. At a July 14 union meeting, Edmonton defense lawyer Brian Beresh told the strikers they could apply to get access to the sealed warrants to search Bettger's house. The warrants would list the names of the RCMP's informants.

Nevertheless, Farris hit Bettger with the new plan as they traveled

to Edmonton two days later to watch motorcycle races. Farris told
Bettger that he was thinking about blowing up a powder magazine in
the mine. He would make sure to time the explosion so it occurred
while Shearing was still in jail and Bettger was out of town. The blast
would confuse all the people who believed that Bettger and Shearing
were responsible for all the blasts at the mine, Farris said.

Bettger liked the idea. He told Farris he would be out of town at
the end of July to attend a wedding in Saskatchewan. Meanwhile,
Shearing would be in jail until July 30. On the sixteen-hour drive to
Edmonton, Farris and Bettger worked out the details, deciding how
the bomb would be built and set up. Farris was to travel into the mine
through the B-138 portal. He'd rig up explosives in a powder magazine,
setting the bomb to detonate when the central blast went off. The mission would take no more than twenty or thirty minutes. No one would
likely be hurt, but the blast would be massive.

Of course, Farris and the RCMP never intended to blow up anything. Farris was to hook Bettger on the idea, but then Farris would say
he'd only do it in order to clear his two good friends Tim and Al. He
wouldn't do it to clear the name of any other striker. He had to be sure
that the mission was necessary, that Bettger had in fact set the September 18 blast and really needed such a bold diversion to cover for him.
Bettger would have to confess to him.

Bettger and Farris returned to Yellowknife on July 19. During the
next week they went about with their final preparations and discussions. On July 27, the two men went out riding on their motorcycles,
then sat down to rest on some rocks. Bettger told Farris that the new
plan was perfect, that it would shut down the mine. Farris agreed, but
then sprung the trap. "The only way it's going to happen is if it's a
cover for you or for Al."

Bettger refused to give Farris a straight answer about the matter,
but he said it was so perfect that they should do it anyway. Farris told
Bettger he'd have to think about it.

Again the RCMP had come far, but Bettger didn't give them what
they needed. The Bear's continued denials to Farris were starting to
concern the investigators. How tight do you have to get with this guy
before he tells the truth?

The police had been wired into the inner worlds of Bettger, Shearing and dozens of other CASAW members and supporters for almost a

year, but had yet to hear the key phrase. They had listened in on husbands and wives fighting, eavesdropped on tired, drunken, angry exchanges, but not once had they heard any strong accusations or admissions of guilt.

Before making another push on the first and second suspects, the investigators decided that they should first clean up other matters, especially the Gord Kendall, Conrad Lisoway and Roger Warren files. If Bettger or Shearing were ever arrested, these three men had enough against them that the defense could wave their files in front of the jury, saying that one of them might have set the bomb. If they weren't eliminated as suspects, they might represent a reasonable doubt in a trial.

Kendall had been one of the first strikers to tell everything he knew to the police. He had also taken and passed the polygraph, but the RCMP had new information saying Kendall was going around blabbing that he was linked to the mass murder.

Kendall had moved from Yellowknife to Surrey, British Columbia One night, he had met two strangers, Gary and Sharon Jeeves, at a bar. He allegedly told the couple that the dead men were scabs and deserved to die, so he went into the mine, set up a bomb and murdered the bastards. He allegedly claimed he and two other men set the bomb. Gary Jeeves went to the police with the story. The police ran a few undercover operations to see if they could find out more from Kendall, wiring Gary Jeeves on one occasion, then having a Mountie pose as a sympathetic union organizer and going to drink with Kendall. It quickly became clear that Kendall knew nothing about the real blast. The RCMP also knew that Kendall wasn't out on the picket line that night. If his name ever came up at a trial, they could easily shoot it down.

Conrad Lisoway's case was more serious because of his tie to the Flying Truck Scenario. Defer, White and McGowan teamed up to travel to Porcupine Plains, Saskatchewan, where Lisoway now lived and worked in the oil patch.

Lisoway had earlier admitted his role in the vent shaft bombing and had confirmed Luc Normandin's story about Bettger approaching him with the Flying Truck Scenario. Lisoway had also passed his polygraph. But one of Lisoway's answers during the test concerned the investigators. FactFinder II scored Lisoway as inconclusive when he was asked if he knew for sure who had set the September 18 bomb. The result meant one of two things: either Lisoway had a strong suspicion about who had set the bomb but didn't know for sure, or Lisoway really did know and he was lying when he denied it.

The investigators decided to push Lisoway hard. Based on Roger Warren identifying him as one of the two shadowy men, McGowan accused him of being out on mine property in the early morning hours of September 18.

"No, I wasn't," Lisoway said.

"Yes, you were," McGowan insisted.

"That is bullshit. That is bullshit. You guys are wrong."

"It's not us. It's somebody said that they saw you on the property walking at 2:00 A.M."

"That person is wrong. He's bluffing."

"But he's saying that. Why would he say that? That's why we're here. That's why we have come all the way from Yellowknife to Porcupine Plains. Why would he say that?"

"Who would say that?"

"Well, I'm not gonna say."

"Well, it's not that old miner, Roger, is it?"

McGowan was astonished. "Where'd you come up with that name?"

"Well, because we talked about it a day or so after. He was asking me some questions about that. He said he thought it was me."

On the way back to Yellowknife, McGowan kept thinking about how Lisoway had come up with Warren's name. What does it mean? Why would Roger Warren talk to Lisoway just a few days after the blast about being out there?

McGowan had no answers, but another incident in late July 1993 gave him and the other investigators another push in Warren's direction. Mine foreman Noel O'Sullivan was leaving work early to attend a school board meeting when he saw McIntyre and McGowan driving away from the mine site back to Yellowknife. O'Sullivan knew both men well by now. He decided to catch up with the two and give them a hard time, something he had held off doing until now. He was fed up with the RCMP chasing Shearing and Bettger. O'Sullivan had made up his mind about Warren's guilt ten months earlier, and nothing he had seen or heard since had changed it. Why the hell couldn't the RCMP solve it with all their resources when he and a few other men at the mine could just about put their finger on it themselves?

As O'Sullivan followed the two officers, he could see them looking back at him in their rearview mirror. He trailed them into the parking lot of the RCMP detachment. He stayed in his truck and rolled down the window.

"Come here," he called out. "I want to talk to you."

McIntyre appeared reluctant to stop, but McGowan came over.

"Lookit," O'Sullivan told the Mountie, "I got to talk to you. You guys are chasing two rabbits. That's all they are is rabbits. They are out there for a reason. They know more than anybody who the suspects are, and they're using that because you guys think it's them, and it's not them. It's time you bring in Roger Warren and squeeze him some more."

"Yeah," McGowan said. "We believe he's implicated, but we don't know if we have enough."

"Christ, you have to have methods at your fingertips to be able to help you. You've got to be able to put the heat on him. You guys are trained for it."

O'Sullivan told McGowan his theories about the murderer's route, how no mechanic like Shearing or Bettger would know the shortcuts the murderer had taken on his way out. Most of what O'Sullivan said wasn't news to McGowan, but it was all circumstantial, not the kind of thing that would convince a jury.

McGowan was already planning to reinterview Warren. He had wanted to hit Warren during the Blitz in June, but Warren had been away with his wife, Helen, on a six-week vacation in the United States. The RCMP went ahead and got a warrant to seize Warren's size eleven Kamik boots from his apartment. On the warrant, Tim Bettger, not Warren, was listed as the suspect in the murders, the theory being that Warren had lent his boots to Bettger.

McGowan hoped that the seizure of the boots would again show Warren and every other union man that the investigation hadn't stopped, that more and more hard evidence was being amassed. McGowan knew that Warren wouldn't keep quiet about it.

Seizing the boots also allowed the police to examine them at length for the first time. McGowan and Defer made a key discovery. Warren had always said he accidentally burned the boots by standing too close to a bonfire, then cut off the burned material, slicing away until the soles of the boots matched. McGowan now saw that wasn't true, that some of the cut marks were melted, meaning the boots had been cut, then burned. It was a small thing, but why would Warren lie about it?

Warren got the news that his boots had been seized from his daughter Ann, who had been home during the RCMP's search and seizure. She told her dad about it when he called from Wyoming. She told him that Bettger's name was on the search warrant. Warren told Helen about it, saying, "Boy, these guys are way out in left field."

In early August, McGowan called Warren for an interview. He told Roger he wanted to talk about the seizure of the boots and some other new developments. McGowan hoped that Warren would at last admit who the two shadowy men were, especially if they were Shearing and Bettger.

On August 6, Warren met with McGowan and Defer at the new Homicide Task Force office. They chatted about the strike. Warren said he was now working forty hours a week on the picket line. McGowan then went over Warren's Charter rights and asked if he had heard anything new about the blast and the police investigation. Warren said he'd heard something about the bomb in Rob Wells' trailer. "The last time he'd seen it, Tim Bettger had it," Warren said. "That was one pretty shocking thing."

Warren said it made him wonder about the search warrant and what connection the police thought he might have to Bettger.

"What do you think we took the boots for?" McGowan asked him.

"I wasn't sure. Just needed comparisons. It was when I seen that stuff about Tim on there, I couldn't make too much sense of it 'cause I can assure you I never had anything to do with those guys. Pulling stuff like that . . . I just never was in on any of that stuff, which I'm sure you must know."

McGowan set things out clearly to Warren, saying he was a knot in the rope when it came to the investigation. There were still things that made him look like a suspect, McGowan said. "We have to do the best we can to clear some of these matters up. I have to know beyond a doubt that Roger Warren didn't have anything to do with this."

"I told you before that I didn't. I don't know what else I can do."

McGowan told Warren that the RCMP were now looking for minor players in the whole thing. It would be best for these minor players to come forward now rather than be implicated later. "You can rest assured that with the cooperative nature that we receive, we would do what we could for the person."

Warren said the only other thing he might have seen that early morning of September 18 was a truck at 4:30 A.M. while he was walking along the road.

McGowan tried a new tack, saying, "If somebody had something to do with this and came out, how do you think the union would perceive him?"

"Well, he's a real piece of scum," Warren said.

"What if a person . . . was the first one to come across and take down the people that are really involved. How do you think the union would perceive him?"

"Oh, you mean, like, would they consider him a traitor? I doubt it."

"Would he be a hero because he solved the matter?" Defer said.

"I think so."

McGowan brought up how Conrad Lisoway had guessed it was Warren who had told the RCMP that he was out on the picket line at 2:00 A.M. Warren denied ever talking directly to Lisoway regarding his concerns over the two shadowy men. But a few days after the blast, Warren said he did tell a few other union men about seeing the two men; Lisoway might have overheard something.

"Did you borrow your boots to anybody that night?" McGowan asked.

"No."

"Did you go underground that night?"

"No."

"Did you assist anyone in any capacity that night to do that offense?"

"You'd have to know this stuff by now."

McGowan listed the facts against Warren, the fact that his boots matched the footprints at the Akaitcho shaft, how he was an excellent, capable miner, how some guys had heard him uttering threats on the picket line against the scabs. Defer told Warren that one striker reported that Warren had once said he knew how to commit the perfect murder.

Warren said he didn't remember ever saying that, and that McGowan and Defer should look at a person's past record: he might use some outrageous rhetoric, but he had never kicked the shit out of anyone. He didn't agree with men crossing the picket line, but he didn't want anyone to get hurt. Right from the start he said he wouldn't do anything like that, and he barely knew Bettger and Shearing. "I thought they were pretty retarded. I know they were doing a lot of run-ning around out there."

The Mounties moved to the information in the Blitz package. They told Warren that they knew everything about the other explo-sions: who had done them, how they were done; and a real pattern had developed. They set forth their theory—how Shearing and another striker took out power poles, how Art St. Ammand, Shearing and Bettger went on the June 29 graffiti mission and stole sticks of powder. Luc Normandin drove them to the line. Next, Bettger set a fire near the dump, and then in July he and Shearing loosened the bolts on the satellite dish and set off a bomb, hoping to blow the dish off the hill. Warren was told about Shearing and Bettger's trip to Vancouver to buy six clock mechanisms and about the vent shaft blast, with Bettger, Shearing, Lisoway and Terry Legge teaming up to set the bomb. Next, McGowan told Warren about the Flying Truck Scenario, how the plan didn't come off, but Bettger told other strikers that he had something better planned. McGowan said the search of Bettger's house uncovered a clothespin trip-wire device.

"I never would have thought about something like that," Warren said, then added he had heard that the trip wires were used for setting off flashbulbs if anyone walked by.

There was a common denominator in all the illegal activities, McGowan said. Shearing and Bettger used men like Luc Normandin, Terry Legge, Art St. Ammand and Conrad Lisoway. McGowan said he wanted to make sure Warren wasn't like them, an unwitting helper.

McGowan then decided to push a button, asking Warren to explain again how his Kamik boots had been defaced. Warren repeated his story. He said he first wore the boots at gate six about a week before the blast. A bunch of young women came out that night. They played music and had a bonfire. Warren said he stood around the fire. He smelled something and looked down to see he was standing on a metal screen, which was red-hot from the blaze. His boots were stuck to the screen. When he examined them the next day, he saw the bottoms were melted and full of rocks. He cut off the melted pieces, making sure both boots were the same.

The answer was a turning point. For the first time McGowan was convinced that Warren was lying to him. His story about the defaced boots was crap, McGowan was sure of that, but there Warren sat, arms folded as usual, gazing to the side as usual, sticking to his story about the boots, lying as if it was the easiest thing in the world. Maybe Warren wasn't a murderer, but McGowan had no doubt that he was dealing with a deceptive man.

McGowan again confronted Warren with the things that implicated him—the boots, the three hours in his alibi that nobody else could account for and his wet clothes.

"That's why you're still here," McGowan reminded him.

"I don't know what I can do to clear this shit up," Warren said. "It doesn't seem to do me much good to try to cooperate."

McGowan reminded Warren that his cooperation spoke to his innocence.

"Well, what do you want me to say? Like I've told you, it's got nothing to do with me. This is where I was, and this is what I did. The best I could, I could corroborate it and that's it."

McGowan told Warren that the boots really bothered him. They looked like they had been intentionally altered and that they were cut, then burned, not the other way around as Warren continued to claim. This told him that the boots were the ones that went down in the mine. Either Warren had them on that night in the mine or someone else did. The modification could mean someone was trying to hide something, McGowan said.

"Do you agree they're pretty damning things?"

"Yeah, it looks to me, if you look at it in that light."

McGowan told Warren the boots were going to be sent to a crime detection lab. Warren had no problem with that. He went so far as to guarantee that they were not the boots that left the tracks in the mine. "My boots were never more than fifteen feet off the road. They were never on the property. Not a chance."

To end the interview, McGowan promised to get back in touch with Warren when the results from the crime lab were in. The interview was one of McGowan's last duties for the Homicide Task Force. Now that McCambridge had transferred to Yellowknife, he was the last of the outside investigators still in town. His bosses in Hay River wanted him back. At last it was time to leave. He wasn't really needed in Yellowknife anymore. The investigation had started out with five hundred files, but it was now down to forty. The local investigators could handle it.

Enough is enough, he said to himself. I'm going to try to get a life.

Before leaving, however, McGowan wanted to help put in place one last plan on the Warren file. Through the debates about which of the CASAW suspects had done it, McGowan never went too strong in any direction. He was a show-me guy. If the evidence wasn't clear, he wasn't one to jump to conclusions. He never liked to say how he felt about a suspect; he just said what he knew.

So much of the evidence pointed in so many different directions that he didn't know what to conclude, but now with Roger Warren it was clearly time to change the approach. Warren had been playing the game too long, pointing his finger at Conrad Lisoway, screwing up on his polygraph tests, lying about his boots, changing his description of the two shadowy men so often that now they were the image of Al Shearing and Tim Bettger. McGowan felt burned. For the first time he argued that someone should go after Warren aggressively. "He's got to be hardballed by somebody," McGowan told the other investigators. "Somebody has got to have the ability to walk in and say, 'Bullshit!'"

Chapter 17

FOOTSTEPS OF THE MURDERER

A T THIS POINT, the authors of this book become players in the story. On September 18, 1993, on the first anniversary of the mass murder, we wrote a story for our employer, the *Edmonton Journal*, called "Footsteps of the Murderer." It detailed the RCMP's working theory on how the murder was committed. The story wouldn't be worth mentioning, except that it created a furor among the national news media and came to play a key role in the investigation and the subsequent murder trial.

The idea for the anniversary story came as a result of *Journal* reporter Marina Jiminez's interview with Al Shearing. Shearing gave Jiminez a transcript of his first interview with McCambridge on September 28, 1992. After we read the transcript, it was clear that only ten days after the blast the RCMP already had a picture of the murderer's route through the mine. If we could understand where places like Akaitcho, the B-138 portal and the 712-scoop shop were, we could figure out the murderer's route through the mine and write a story. It looked both challenging and worthwhile. The mine had always seemed a frightful, confusing place, but the story would explain it. It might also perform a public service. Shortly after the blast, we had interviewed trackman George Samardzija, the last man to see the man-car. He had told us there were no explosives on the car. His disgust with the union theory was strong. His eyewitness testimony convinced us. We realized that by writing about the murderer's route, by making it real to Yellowknifers, the union's insistence that the blast was an accident would be seen for the delusion that it was.

We approached the RCMP just as Inspector McIntyre and Corporal White were certain the investigation needed a boost. They had had their surveillance teams cut back. McGowan was gone. The Blitz had come and gone. No one was talking. There was nowhere else to go with Farris. The local media seemed to have lost interest.

McIntyre and White knew that much of the information we wanted for our story was already out in the community, released to the strikers during the Blitz. The two officers agreed to point us to places where we could find it, as long as we agreed not to identify them. They believed they were making a deal with the devil, as they distrusted the media, but it fit in with their strategy of keeping the strikers focused on the murders.

Before heading to Yellowknife, we telephoned Tim Bettger to ask for an interview. Bettger agreed to meet us. We expected him to tell us his story about the RCMP harassing him, but when we arrived at the union hall and held out our hands in greeting, he snarled, "I'm not going to shake your hands. Parasite number one and parasite number two."

For our interview, he took out his own tape recorder and trained a video camera on us. A pack of strikers looked on, chuckling at Bettger's tactics. Bettger was asked why he was so hostile when initially he had sounded like he would be glad to talk.

"It was the whole entire presentation of the horrible situation last fall that bothered me and the way that you guys carried it," he said, referring to stories we had done in the weeks following the blast. "That's all I have to say about that."

Bettger said he wouldn't talk about the police investigation, but if we wanted a story we could write about the dangerous levels of toxic chemicals in the various emissions from Giant Mine. He said the problems had been around for decades, but he blamed them on Witte. "It is my opinion that if you want a story what you should do is document the process being carried out by an economic terrorist, the person who has threatened the region with economic ruin if she doesn't get her

way. Every time the government says that she can't have this or somebody says she can't have that, she says, 'Oh, I'll shut the place down.'"

Bettger had little else to say. The meeting left us shaken. Bettger
was a huge man, bearded, with dark, angry eyes. He radiated hostility,
not just toward Witte, but toward us. It didn't take a great deal of
imagination to conclude that this man had the rage in him to kill. For
the rest of our stay in Yellowknife, we felt the paranoia that the RCMP
and the Royal Oak line crossers had known for almost a year.

Bettger was also becoming increasingly hostile toward the RCMP.
He would be talking on the telephone to a friend; then after saying
good-bye, he would send a message to the police monitors: "Vern
White is a scum sucking son of a whore!" or "You hear that, you rotten
fuckin' bastards!"

The first time he heard about this, White thought it was funny, but
after a while he wondered if Bettger was cracking. White was even
more alarmed when he came back from a short, out-of-town trip to
hear that surveillance teams had spotted Bettger parked momentarily
in front of his house late at night. White didn't want to alarm his wife,
Loretta, so he didn't tell her. He was a bit scared himself, despite
knowing that Bettger was always watched. He thought Bettger was
becoming brazen.

We contacted a few other CASAW strikers for our story, including
Rob Wells and Terry Legge. In a brief interview Wells confirmed to us
that he had found the bomb in his trailer. Legge told us about his part
in the ventilation shaft bombing. He said he was near his limit. "This
past year and a half have been the worst years of my life. I've been bor-
derline sometimes, I'll tell you that."

He and his family had had to sell their trailer home and move into an
apartment. The bills were choking him to death, he said. He hoped
Bettger or Shearing would never be charged with murder so he'd never
have to admit to the vent shaft bombing in court. "If it's a murder trial,
then the shit's going to hit the fan. And I'm not talking about murder; I'm
talking about the shit's going to hit the fan about all these other things."

We also tried to contact Roger Warren. From the Yellowknife
courthouse, we had obtained a copy of the search warrant the police
had used to seize Warren's boots. It seemed odd that the boots were at
Warren's apartment while the police believed Bettger was the killer. In
our talks with the RCMP officers, not one of them had ever mentioned

Warren's name. When we asked about the boots, we were told that Warren had likely lent them to Bettger. We gave Warren a call, but he wasn't home. He seemed to be a bit player, so we left it at that.

Even before the first draft of the story was completed, Harry Seeton faxed a letter to *Edmonton Journal* editor Murdoch Davis urging him to ensure that the anniversary article would be balanced. "We emphasize that our members and their families have suffered serious hardships in the past as a result of sensationalized stories which serve only to inflame emotions during this difficult time."

We finished the initial draft of "Footsteps of the Murderer" on September 15. It was sent out on the computerized Southam/Star news network to the daily newspapers of Vancouver, Montreal, Ottawa, Calgary, Toronto, Hamilton and other smaller Canadian cities. A note on the story said it was embargoed until September 18, 1993, meaning that no other newspaper could publish the information until then, the same day the *Journal* would print it. The story had an editorial note on top, which newspapers were to run: "This story describes the RCMP's working theory of how two striking miners committed the murder of nine men at Giant Mine on Sept. 18, 1992. The account is pieced together from court documents, union, company and RCMP press releases and interviews with mine officials, striking miners, miners who crossed the picket line, explosives experts, RCMP and FBI psychological profile experts and confidential sources. A key document is a 126-page transcript of an RCMP interview with a striking miner, given to the *Journal* by the miner.

"The *Journal* knows the names of the two suspects. To protect their identity, the names will not be published. To confuse Pinkerton security guards during picket-line skirmishes, the striking miners used nicknames over the CB radio such as Cambodian Cowboy, Night Crawler, Sidekick, the Ghost-Rider, the Bear, Timber Man, Bubba and others. In this story, the two suspects will be referred to by the fictitious nicknames of Coyote and Goblin."

The story began: "In the early morning darkness, the Goblin put his homemade bomb in a knapsack, got into a vehicle with Coyote and headed out of Yellowknife. Tonight, the two men weren't out to do mischief, as they had been on other nights. Tonight, they were out to kill."

The story went on to detail the history of the strike and how the Goblin and the Coyote had shopped for material for their bombs in Vancouver, then set up the explosions at the satellite dish and the vent shaft, the main elements of the Progression Theory, which was well known among the key players in Yellowknife. The story then detailed the Goblin's route through the mine and his construction of the bomb. "According to an explosives expert, the trip wire was likely attached to a small piece of wood, or some other piece of non-conductive material. The Goblin had inserted the piece of wood between the jaws of a clothes peg; the wood kept the pegs from snapping shut. Electrical wires were wrapped around both pegs. When the man-car hit it, the trip wire pulled out the piece of wood, snapping shut the pegs, connecting the wires, completing the circuit of the battery. The electrical charge activated the detonator, which ignited a stick of explosives and the AMEX."

The second half of the story detailed the battle between the RCMP and the union, dispelled the union's theory that the blast was an accident and detailed the pain not only of the friends, family and co-workers of the nine men, but also of the innocent CASAW men who had lived with being called murderers. It described what some of them thought should be done with the murderer should he be caught.

"Hang him high," said Terry Legge.

"You plug him in, I'll pull the switch," said Marvin Tremblett.

"Castrate him," said Al Shearing, a reference to the suggestion he'd given McCambridge in their first interview.

The story ended with a description of the tension inside the mine: "The place haunts mine workers. Longtime mine handyman George Samardzija can't get the face of his best friend Joe Pandev out of his mind. Now when Samardzija passes the blast site he says aloud the names of Joe and of David Vodnoski and the other dead men. And Samardzija asks, 'Who killed you, Joe? Who the hell did it?'"

The main legal issue was contempt of court. No one had yet been arrested for anything. For all we knew, arrests might never be made. Still, if Bettger or Shearing ever did get arrested, the story might prejudice their trial. After consulting with the paper's lawyer, Allan Lefever, we decided that as long as we sufficiently blurred the identity of the two prime suspects, the contempt concerns were minimal.

We realized we might be criticized for helping the RCMP, but that would be to suggest that working with the police was our main motivation and that the RCMP's aims were somehow wrongheaded. In fact, the investigators wanted to put pressure on the mass murderer of nine men. Nothing was wrong with that.

The *Journal*'s plans started to unravel on September 17 when *Toronto Star* reporter Peter Cheney was handed the *Journal* story by an editor and asked to get reaction from Yellowknifers. His sidebar story was to run with an edited version of our package. Cheney tried to get a comment from the *yellowknifer*'s business editor, Bill Braden, a trusted source. Braden said he couldn't comment on something he hadn't seen. Cheney agreed to fax him the story if Braden would stand by the fax machine, then keep the story to himself. Cheney didn't know that the *yellowknifer*'s editors had been calling around the Southam newspaper chain for several days, trying to get their hands on the story.

When Braden got the fax, he gave it to editor Bruce Valpy. Publisher Jack Sigvaldason was also sent a copy. Sigvaldason's first reaction was to call up his wife and tell her to lock the doors and think about hiring a security guard. He feared there would be violence in the streets when the story came out the next day. To ready his community for the *Journal*-induced apocalypse, he had his editor, Valpy, order *yellowknifer* reporters to provide copies of the story to the government, CASAW, the RCMP and Royal Oak.

The *yellowknifer*'s staff had been pressured for many months by Harry Seeton and the CASAW executive, who wanted Yellowknifers to forget the investigation and focus on the labor dispute. After all, the Mounties knew what the evidence was, not anyone else. Let them solve it if they could. In Seeton's opinion it was no use for the newspaper to keep up the endless speculation. It was just making people crazy.

The *yellowknifer* had done an excellent job of covering the Giant Mine strike, but stories and editorials on the murder investigation had become scarce by September 1993. The turning point for the newspaper had been the first anniversary of the strike in May, when it ran several accusatory letters from the widows, including the one from Tracey Neill. Seeton had responded at once. His rebuttal letter ran in the following issue. "How much longer is the *yellowknifer* going to permit people to call us murderers in their paper? Where is their sense of community responsibility? Are they trying to create more injury or death that will then be attributed to this labor dispute?

"I don't know what kind of hell Tracey Neill is going through as a result of losing her husband, but it must be terribly hard. However, I never had anything to do with the death of him or the other eight men.

"The burden of being called murderers on the street is more than we deserve. We do not need the additional stress of being labeled the same in the newspaper."

After Seeton's letter appeared, the newspaper's coverage took on a different tone. In June 1993, for instance, when the *yellowknifer* reported on the Blitz of the CASAW men, the story didn't mention that each of the men hit was a CASAW member, and that all the information in the Blitz package concerned a handful of union men. The link between the murder and the union was no longer drawn in news stories.

Al McIntyre and Vern White got their copy of the *Journal* story the afternoon of September 17, 1993. They were as astonished at its contents as anyone. They hadn't expected it to be so graphic and detailed. They knew what little they had told us, but the story included far more than that. They hadn't expected Terry Legge or Rob Wells to talk. Most of all, they were surprised by what we had gathered from other confidential sources, sources we still cannot name.

At the union hall, Terry Legge was horrified to find that he was named in the article, especially in relation to his role in the vent shaft bombing. He immediately called us in Edmonton to ask that his name be dropped. He had never requested anonymity during our interviews, but he wasn't used to dealing with reporters. He was so distraught and had such fears for the safety of his family that the *Journal*'s editors decided Legge's request was reasonable. The same deal was made for Rob Wells after his wife called up with her fears.

We hoped these would be the last changes, but the union sent the story to their defense lawyer in Edmonton, who faxed it to Crown prosecutor Peter Martin in Calgary. Martin was uneasy with the piece. He contacted the *Journal*'s Lefever to talk about his concerns that the story might affect a future trial. After Martin's warning, *Journal* editors Murdoch Davis and Michael Cooke had three options: kill the story, run it as it was and perhaps face contempt charges, or drastically alter it. We agreed on the last option. Any link between the RCMP's two prime suspects and the union was taken out. The fact that the Goblin and Coyote, now called Suspect 1 and Suspect 2, were union men was taken out of the story. One quarter of the text was chopped.

In Yellowknife, the Saturday *Journal*'s circulation went from the normal run of seven hundred to sixteen hundred. At the memorial ceremony at Giant Mine, the gathering was more upbeat than it might have been. People ran out to buy as many copies of the *Journal* as they could. Many of them saw a copy of the original, unedited story, which was quickly being photocopied and spread around town. Rather than shrieking for blood, the group at Giant Mine was encouraged by the new information. Noel O'Sullivan gave a short speech. "You have to leave the authorities to act and the culprit will be brought to justice," he said. "The hammer is about to come down."

After the *Journal* article appeared, Tracey Neill called up Al Shearing to ask him what he thought about it. They had a polite, uneventful conversation.

On Monday, everyone at the *Journal* still wondered how the story was leaked to the union, Peter Martin and the other authorities. Valpy's front-page newspaper editorial that day answered our questions. Valpy said he didn't believe the story should run as it was written, so the story was released to various authorities. "That the story was well-researched and written was undeniable, but it was also dangerous. Naming a person would put him in immediate danger. The story also drew unfounded connections that appeared highly prejudicial, not only to any upcoming trial, but also to many innocent union members."

At the *Toronto Star*, when Cheney found out what had happened, he at once owned up and offered to resign. He was turned down. Cheney faxed Bruce Valpy a letter: "I suggest that you rethink your role as a journalist. It is not your job to decide that the work of others is harmful, and block its publication."

After finding out that Valpy had attempted to censor the story, Murdoch Davis and *Journal* publisher Linda Hughes decided that the situation shouldn't stand as it did. Portions of the story that were taken out of the original were run in the following Saturday's newspaper, mainly the description of the bomb and the section on the union's conflict with the RCMP.

Along with each of the thirteen hundred *Journal* copies sold in Yellowknife that day came a letter from Davis in which he called Valpy a censor. Davis also wrote an editorial, explaining what had happened to the *Journal*'s original story and why the paper was running more information now. "This isn't just a vandalism case or even some 'routine' murder. . . . This was one of the most heinous crimes ever committed in Canada.

"Deluded perhaps by a sense that the union struggle is more important, that union solidarity is more important, or the denial that clings to a false hope that there was no murder, some people in Yellowknife are protecting the guilty. If getting the facts out might cause one such person to stop the denial and give his or her evidence to the police, then our journalism will have fulfilled one of its many roles in our society. Hiding the facts only serves to continue the denial. And to protect a mass murderer."

Some of the CASAW strikers were furious both at the *Journal* and at Vern White. They believed that White had orchestrated the entire thing. Still, the article had one redeeming feature in their minds. Until now they could only speculate about what the RCMP really thought about the blast. It seemed each one of them had been told something different.

The *Journal* story only increased the feeling of doom among the strikers. They were facing another bleak winter. Men were starting to drink heavily on picket duty.

While no resolution to the strike or murder investigation seemed close, more of the court cases against the strikers were being resolved and not always to the union's liking. Two strikers were convicted for an incident during the riot, James Fournier getting three months for breaking a security guard's rib with a rock and James Mager getting fifteen months for hitting the same security guard with a stick and wearing a balaclava onto mine property.

At the same time, the Industrial Inquiry commissioners, Vince Ready and Don Munroe, released their final report to Bernard Valcourt, the Labour Minister. They found a possible solution to the strike, based on the tentative agreement from April 1992, the deal the CASAW men had once voted down. Ready and Munroe couldn't force CASAW or Royal Oak to respond to their suggestions, but they made sure neither the union nor the company could ignore them without facing some consequences. "Neither side should be permitted to treat this report as being simply another chapter in a dispute without an apparent ending. In our view, if either party approaches this report in that unproductive manner, it should be seen as raising serious issues of good faith. Very simply, it should not be countenanced."

The strikers voted ninety-four percent in favor of accepting the recommendations in Ready and Munroe's report, but Royal Oak rejected them. Peggy Witte spelled out her objections in early October. "We have a general sense that CASAW members are involved in the murders and related violence," she wrote to the Labour Minister. "We have great concerns about returning to the bargaining table with people who for all we know at this time may be involved in the murders or one or more of the smaller acts of violence against the company."

Witte's comments were reported in the *yellowknifer* on October 13 under the headline "Charges First, Talks Later." The mood on the picket line was as down as it had ever been. In one shack, strikers Roger Warren, Al Barrett, Cal Williams and Blaine Lisoway, Conrad's brother, stayed up all night talking about politics, cars and the *yellowknifer* and "Footsteps of the Murderer" articles. At one point Lisoway and Warren talked about going into business together with a car wash and wheel alignment shop. Lisoway said they might as well do it. "We'll probably all be in wheelchairs before we go back in there, unless they catch the ones who set the blast."

No one said a thing in reply. At last the reality of the mass murder gripped the strikers. They now understood that if the murderer wasn't caught, there would be no end to the strike. No CASAW man could deny it any longer, not even the murderer himself.

Chapter 18

THE THIRD SUSPECT

INSPECTOR AL MCINTYRE knew that his investigators could get too close to their files and miss something important. Through the first year of the investigation, he had often brought in outside experts to review the case. At first, outsiders such as Special Agent Gus Garry and two experienced RCMP homicide investigators from Calgary and Vancouver had agreed with the team that the Progression Theory was right, that Tim Bettger and Al Shearing were the most likely suspects. But as the first anniversary of the blast came and went, the outsiders started to contradict the task force's theory. Crime analyst Lloyd McLeod, who had taken over from Dean Ravelli on the case, came to believe in the Lone Wolf Theory.

McLeod's view wasn't clouded by the hate that had grown between Bettger and the police. Indeed, if McLeod disregarded everything that had happened from the beginning of the strike to the night before the blast, if he concentrated only on the night of September 18, there was only one strong suspect: Roger Warren. Warren didn't have a confirmed alibi, he had the right boots and he hadn't passed his polygraph tests.

It was now even more important to clear up the Warren file. After hearing that Warren had lied in his August 6 interview with Dale McGowan and Nancy Defer, McIntyre agreed that Warren should be hardballed. McIntyre and McGowan also agreed that an outsider should do the job. The outsider might be able to get the things McGowan hadn't been able to get from Warren, answers to questions like: Did you wear the size eleven Kamik boots that night or did you give them to someone else? Who were the two shadowy men you claim to have seen? But if Warren reacted badly to the pressure, McIntyre wanted to have McGowan on hand and on good terms with Warren. If Warren bolted, McGowan could reel him back in, saying, "You're right, Roger, that guy was an asshole."

McIntyre called up RCMP headquarters in Ottawa and asked for a list of the top RCMP interrogation experts in Canada. In the end the shortlist contained the names of three men. The Yellowknife team chose Sergeant Gregg McMartin of the Calgary polygraph section. McGowan liked what he heard about McMartin, that the sergeant could go hard in an interview, but could also be subtle. This was important with Warren, a well-read, cagey, strong-willed man. Warren wasn't likely to be intimidated.

Gregg McMartin was known as a master interrogator, a driven, sometimes brilliant performer. He was two years from retirement, but only forty-three years old, a veteran of twenty-three years on the force, but still physically and mentally at his peak. He was a successful man from a successful family. His father was a sawmill owner on Vancouver Island, one brother a music producer in Australia, the other brother, the superintendent of the RCMP's Langley, British Columbia, division.

Gregg McMartin had first worked as a uniformed constable in a number of small Alberta detachments: Jasper, Fort Chipewyan and Breton. His skill as an investigator got him a quick promotion to a plainclothes unit in the southern Alberta city of Lethbridge. From there, McMartin was promoted to corporal and headed up the General Investigation Service in Stony Plain, an oil patch town outside of Edmonton. It was 1980, boom time in Alberta, and the work never ended. McMartin was at the office every weekend trying to catch up on paperwork. His kids grew up playing on his office typewriter.

In 1985, McMartin joined the RCMP's Edmonton target team, which focused on career criminals. They waited for a bad guy to get out of jail, then watched him, knowing full well he would soon try to pull something. McMartin watched many major crimes come down and busted the bad guy in the act. It was his ultimate high, a huge adrenaline rush. In the end, however, the danger of hounding such men was too much for him. He only felt comfortable when he had his snub-nosed revolver with him. After three years on the team, he was also tired of all-night stakeouts. He still liked taking down bad guys, but he needed regular hours.

McMartin saw the Calgary polygraph section as a perfect blend. He took the polygraph course in Ottawa in 1988, then settled in to spend his days traveling southern Alberta, hooking up both the guilty and the innocent to FactFinder II and trying to separate the two.

He loved the work. He was fascinated with the dynamics of a confession. When a suspect told him something incriminating, he always wondered what had made him talk, especially when the guy knew he would go to jail if he opened his mouth. McMartin came to believe that people were driven to confess. Maybe it was just too hard to keep lying. They had to let it out, and he tried to use this need. He knew that sooner or later the bad guy was going to tell someone about what he had done—his wife, his friend, his priest. It was McMartin's job to make sure the guy also told him. McMartin loved to be the first one to pry out the secret. It was a thrill to know that the person had confided in him, an RCMP officer. It was a testament to the power of his persuasive abilities. He never felt guilty when he got someone to confess. These were bad guys, not innocent bystanders. They had done wrong. They should confess. They should go to jail.

McMartin enjoyed exposing liars and felt awful if he couldn't get them to confess, but he enjoyed protecting the innocent, too. He often dealt with men who were falsely accused of a crime, perhaps a father in a messy divorce accused of sexually abusing his children. McMartin was always thrilled if he could help a good man get out of the biggest trouble of his life.

McMartin was asked to do the Warren interview, then got a call from Corporal Al McCambridge in late September, shortly after the anniversary of the blast. McCambridge gave McMartin the rundown on the problems in the Warren file, mainly that Warren had seen the two shadowy men on the picket line, but was refusing to identify them. McCambridge told McMartin that the two men were most likely Al Shearing and Tim Bettger, the prime suspects. However, Warren had the same kind of boots that the murderer wore into the mine. If Warren didn't come clean, it would be hard to arrest Shearing and Bettger because Warren could be hauled into court as the number one defense witness and give the jury a reasonable doubt.

McMartin asked McCambridge to send him transcripts of some of the team's interviews with Warren so he could study them. He then called up Calgary prosecutor Peter Martin.

"I'm going up to interview this guy," McMartin said. "Anything for me?"

Martin said no. "With your experience, we want to see what you come up with and how you feel about this guy."

Martin seemed to have faith in him, but that made McMartin worry all the more. He saw that Warren had been interviewed eleven times, twice while hooked up to the polygraph. What could he get that the other interrogators had missed?

McMartin called up his colleague, Sergeant Gerry Keane of the Edmonton polygraph section. The two had earlier talked about the great number of polygraph tests being done in the investigation. McMartin knew Keane had tested Warren in December 1992. Keane said many of the same things McCambridge had said. Keane also advised McMartin to read the *Journal*'s "Footsteps of the Murderer" article to get a quick overview of the situation.

Finally McMartin called Sergeant Pat Dauk of the Winnipeg polygraph section, who had done the second test on Warren in February 1993.

"I got deceptive charts on the guy," Dauk told McMartin. "They were lying charts." Nevertheless, Dauk said he gave Warren the benefit of the doubt and had scored him as inconclusive. Like Keane, McCambridge and almost everyone else, Dauk believed Bettger and Shearing were the most likely killers.

When the transcripts arrived from Yellowknife, McMartin went to work dissecting them with a technique known as Scientific Statement Analysis. The technique had been developed by Avinoam Sapir, an ex-Israeli police officer, who had degrees in criminology and psychology. Sapir, like most officers, always had a gut feeling when he was being told lies. He knew truth often had a certain ring to it, just as a lie did. He wondered if there was an analytical way to find out what caused these gut feelings, if there was something different about how an honest person told a story compared with a liar's tale.

Through his research Sapir found several tip-offs to help police

officers uncover deception. The tip-offs were subtle, verbal tics, uncon-
scious ways of speaking that seemingly meant nothing. But again and
again, Sapir found that when people were telling a true story based on
a real memory, they spoke differently from when they were making
something up.

Some of his findings were common sense. If a suspect failed to
answer a question, that was an easy sign of deception. Or if the mother
of a recently abducted child talked about the child in the past tense, it
might show that she knew the child was dead. In a real abduction the
mother would hope the child was alive and refer to the child in the
present tense.

In an alleged rape, if the victim said she was "asked" to take her
clothes off, Sapir would wonder why she used such a gentle word for
such a violent situation. Or if a rape victim said, "We got in his car, we
went out to the field, we got out of his car, we took our clothes off and
he raped me," Sapir would wonder why she used "we," a pronoun that
implied collaboration, instead of saying, "He got me in his car. He took
me to a field. He took me out of the car. He took my clothes off. He
raped me."

Sapir found that statements composed of real memories had more
sensory detail than lies and more of the jumbled quality of real life. In a
true story, one action would often lead to something that might seem
unrelated. A liar's story on the other hand had few feelings, outside
occurrences or complications.

Real memories were generally told in simple language, in the first
person and the past tense. A true statement would go: It was raining so
I got in the car. I went to the store, I bought some things, I got back in
my car and went home.

If a liar told the same story, he might not put himself in the middle
of it. He'd leave out the pronoun *I*, saying: It was raining. Got in the
car, went to the store, bought some things, got back in the car, then
went home.

Or a liar might change *I* to *you*, saying: It was raining so I got in
the car and I went to the store. You could drive there in about five minutes. When you got there you could buy some things. . . .

In case after case, Sapir found that liars changed to the present
tense, likely because they were making it up as they went along, thinking in the present, not the past. For instance, a liar might say: It was

raining so I got in the car. I'm going to the store, then I'm buying some things.

A liar might even leave out such an obvious fact as it was raining that day. Or a liar might talk about getting in his car, driving his car down the street, then suddenly refer to the car as his vehicle. Why make such a change? They were all small things, but if there were enough of these verbal tics, Sapir knew there might be a problem with the statement. It was just like reading body language. If someone crossed his arms it meant nothing. But if someone crossed his arms, never made eye contact and looked down and to the side at critical times, it might be a sign of deception.

The hardest thing to spot was when a liar left something out. A robber might recount his entire day, telling the truth about everything he did, but omitting the thirty minutes when he robbed the bank. Sapir found that liars sometimes tipped off omissions by using words or phrases such as *started, began, continued, proceeded, completed, and then, after that*. Someone might say: I went to the store to go shopping and bought some things. After that, I got in the car and went home. Using Sapir's theory, an investigator could conclude that between buying some things and getting in his car, this person may have done something he wasn't mentioning; otherwise he wouldn't have needed to say "after that."

McMartin took Sapir's courses in Detroit and Los Angeles. It made sense to him, putting into a formula many of the things he himself had noticed in interrogations.

To do a proper statement analysis on a two-page statement could take him eight hours, but McMartin had found the work paid off, particularly in the case of Lucie Turmel. Turmel, a cab driver, was stabbed to death in Banff, Alberta, in May 1990. It was a big case for the Mounties, the Rocky Mountain resort's first murder. For eighteen months the RCMP slogged away, but failed to make an arrest. McMartin wasn't involved in the case, but one day a young officer brought him a statement from a peripheral suspect named Ryan Love. The officer said he'd heard McMartin speak on statement analysis and thought Love's statement had some problems. After his analysis, McMartin agreed, so much so that he wrote a report saying Love was the killer. The investigation changed course to go after Love. For months afterward, McMartin worried that statement analysis might be discredited if Love wasn't the man, but DNA testing proved McMartin had been right. Though he never confessed, Love was convicted of Turmel's murder.

The Warren file contained hundreds of pages of interview transcripts. McMartin looked for a section when Warren spoke at length and without interruption about his alibi for the early morning hours of September 18, 1992, how he walked up and down the picket line, saw the two shadowy men and slept for a time in the picket bus at gate three. In McGowan's interview from November 5, 1992, McMartin found a three-page section that was perfect. McMartin photocopied it, then used colored highlighters to mark important points. In the end the three pages were a mass of colors, almost every word marked up, some of them circled.

McMartin used a green highlighter for names. At a quick glance, he could see when various strikers like Tom Krahn, Leo Lachowski, Brian Drover and Kelly Rhodes came in and out of the story.

Every time Warren said "I" McMartin circled it in red. There were enough red circles in the end to see that Warren consistently put himself in the middle of his story.

With a yellow highlighter, McMartin marked when Warren prefaced a sentence with a qualifier. The three pages became a sea of yellow. Instead of saying, "I did this, then I did that, then I did this," Warren invariably said, "I think I did this, and then we usually did that, and then I guess I did this, but I'm not sure." To McMartin, this showed that Warren didn't believe his own story.

But a few sections appeared to be real memories. At one point Warren talked about taking a leak by the roadside when a little car went by. That kind of detail—the unrelated memory of the car triggered by Warren's recollection of taking the leak—was something a liar wouldn't likely think of. Still, McMartin wondered if Warren was simply recalling something that had happened a week or a day before the night in question.

With a blue highlighter, McMartin noted every time Warren explained one of his memories. Instead of just telling a story, it seemed that Warren often felt he had to justify himself. The most suspicious blue section was when Warren said he jumped into a ditch to avoid being spotted by a security guard. He said he fell in a puddle and got wet. McMartin wondered about the strange detail. Why does he have to justify an unimportant matter like getting wet unless perhaps he got wet in the mine? Maybe he was worried that other strikers had seen him wet in the morning and he felt he had to explain it away.

At the end of his analysis, McMartin concluded that something was wrong with Warren's statement, but it wasn't until he got to Yellowknife and immersed himself in the file that he came to any conclusions. He flew up on Tuesday, October 12, 1993, thirteen months after the deadly blast, one day before the *yellowknifer* published its story about Peggy Witte's outright refusal to negotiate until the murderer was arrested.

McMartin was met at the task force office by Dale McGowan, who had come up from Hay River to help him prepare. On McMartin's first night in town, McGowan took him out to the picket line to the spot where Warren said he had seen the two shadowy men. McMartin realized then there was no way Warren had seen these men in such detail. It was far too dark. So why was he lying? Was he trying to protect someone? McMartin doubted it. You don't protect someone you didn't see.

At the office, McMartin holed up in a small coffee room, a Pepsi machine humming in the background. For twelve hours the following day, he pored over Warren's statements. Every hour his suspicion grew stronger. He became increasingly convinced that Warren's alibi was a complete crock, and if Warren was a liar, he could also be a murderer. McMartin knew this feeling went against the investigation; when he looked for information on Warren in the hundreds of pages of court documents already prepared for the homicide, he found him mentioned only once.

McMartin asked the investigators what they thought of Warren. Though some said he might have lent his boots or stood lookout, no one said Warren was the guy. Many of the task force investigators were no longer open enough to think that the criminal could be someone other than Shearing and Bettger. Staff Sergeant Lloyd McLeod, the one officer who did consider Warren the prime suspect, kept his thoughts to himself. "I've got some feelings on this, but I don't want to bring that out with you at all," he told McMartin.

Reading and rereading the transcripts, McMartin found something odd in Warren's polygraph interview from December 1992 with Gerry Keane. Keane had asked Warren to tell him what had happened the early morning of September 18.

"Do you want me to tell what I've heard or what I know?" Warren had answered.

"Tell me everything that happened," Keane had said.

What a strange reply, McMartin thought. Was Warren letting on that he knew more than what he had heard?

Again and again, McMartin found times when Warren was deceptive under questioning. In his notes McMartin marked each question with DNQ, for Did Not Answer Question. More and more, McMartin started to come out of his room to talk things over with the other investigators. "Holy shit, guys," he said. "There is nothing in here that is supporting that this guy didn't do it. I've got major, major problems."

Many of the officers razzed him, but McGowan was pleased to see McMartin's growing suspicions. McGowan's hopes were high that this approach was going to finally get some answers. He kept telling McMartin that he had no doubt Warren was somehow involved, even if he wasn't at all sure that Warren actually set the bomb.

To help sort through the conflicting stories and opinions, McMartin listed his concerns about Warren:

1. Roger knows the mine shaft.
2. Can handle explosives.
3. Has made the walk before.
4. Has failed the polygraph test.
5. Lying about description of two guys.
6. Has the same boots.
7. Deliberately alters boots.
8. Lies about burning boots.
9. Is wet.
10. Cannot account for over three hours.
11. Making up alibi by obtaining times from other people who were there and what they were doing.
12. Next accounted for by person at gate six and person (murderer) used the B-138 exit.
13. Goes back in the morning. Knew that something was going to happen.

After more study, McMartin found a few more items that cast doubt on Warren, including his strange behavior at the restaurant, which was reported by Yellowknife old-timer Robert Carroll. Then there was the fact that Warren didn't mention seeing the shadowy men walking on mine property to any of the other strikers at 6:00 A.M. McMartin knew that strikers went out walking on mine property all the time. They got a kick out of sneaking onto the mine site to take a crap, their little protest against Royal Oak. There was no reason for Warren not to tell the other guys about the two shadowy men, especially since they seemed suspicious to him.

As for the shadowy men themselves, McMartin decided Warren had most likely made up the story as a smokescreen. He had tried to deflect suspicion onto his union brothers, such as Conrad Lisoway. The plan had worked. Warren had kept the RCMP jumping for thirteen months. He had side-tracked investigators, polygraph operators and psychological profilers alike, McMartin thought. On the other hand, the smokescreen had also drawn attention to him. It was in many ways the rash act of a guilty man. If Warren hadn't said anything about the two shadowy men, the RCMP would likely have never kept coming back to him so often.

On Thursday morning McMartin had finished with the major transcripts. But since the story of the two shadowy men seemed like such a key, he got hold of the transcript of Warren's meeting in November 1992 with RCMP composite artist Corporal Bruce Coats. For McMartin, this transcript turned out to be the most damning of all. Warren's description of the two men was full of inconsistencies and made-up details. Warren started out describing the two men, saying things like: "Looks like me, wearing dark clothes, fifty-sixty-seventy feet away . . . Pretty dark . . . Just a quick glimpse . . . 5'8" and 6'1" . . . One guy is 180 pounds . . . Tall guy was skinny . . . Other guy is built like me . . . Upper part seems bigger . . . Other guy, hair was blond or gray . . . Main feature I saw was his chin and nose . . . Nose came straight up above, slightly bent . . . The guy had big hips . . . There was a blond mustache, two collars turned up, end of guy's nose rounded."

McMartin knew it was difficult for a witness to accurately describe someone at the best of times, but here Warren was talking about two men he had apparently seen for a flash from at least fifty feet away in the pitch dark of a northern night. And yet Warren claimed he could see that one guy had big hips and a rounded nose, slightly bent. It had to be bullshit. If this story had really come from memory, it would be far more consistent. The details wouldn't keep changing. McMartin had no more doubt. No way in the world did Warren see anyone out there. At last McMartin came out into the task force office and told the other investigators, "I'm saying he did it. It was Warren."

"Well, go get 'em tiger," a few of the investigators laughed. "If you think it's him, let's see."

But now that McMartin had reached his conclusion, crime analyst Lloyd McLeod felt he could speak up. "Well, you know I've got to agree with you," he said. "I've got problems with a few things with Warren."

With McMartin ready to go, McGowan called up Warren to see if he'd come in for an interview. "I've been out of town at Hay River for a while, but I'm back for a couple days. Would you like the results of that thing with the boots?"

"Yup," said Warren.

An RCMP footwear expert had studied the size eleven Kamik boots under a microscope in his laboratory in Edmonton. The expert's observations backed up what McGowan and Defer had seen with the naked eye, that the left boot had been cut, then burned. Melt marks interrupted the cuts (the expert couldn't tell the order of the cutting and burning on the right boot).

For some reason, it appeared that Warren had no fear of the lab test. Even if he had been lying about burning and then cutting the boots, he seemed certain that he did not wear the size eleven Kamiks on the night of the blast. He said he was working the night shift on the picket line, but agreed to come in the following day, Friday, October 15, at 2:00 P.M. McGowan didn't mention anything to him about McMartin.

The night before the interrogation, McMartin talked on the telephone with Al McIntyre, who was in Ottawa for a week of meetings.

"So what do you think?" McIntyre asked.

"He's your guy."

There was absolute silence.

"What do you mean the 'guy'?" McIntyre said at last. "Are you saying he's the guy who planted the bomb?"

"Yeah. I am."

"What about the other two guys? What about Bettger and Shearing?"

"I don't know and I can't say. I haven't even looked at that."

"Well, yeah. Okay, bud. Good luck on your interview."

McIntyre was excited about McMartin's conclusion, but he had been through enough highs and lows in the investigation not to get too optimistic. McMartin had his suspicions, but McIntyre couldn't take them to court.

McMartin planned to confront Warren, tell him straight out that he was a liar and a murderer. He didn't want to fudge his accusations, as the police had always done in the past.

Roger Warren did this, McMartin told himself. If he brings up the two guys, I will not believe him. I will not be sidetracked.

That night, McMartin also called up Gerry Keane in Edmonton. Keane told him how Warren might react after he was accused, that he might shut down, crossing his arms, looking away and refusing to say anything.

McMartin's own belief was that after he accused Warren, Warren would swear at him and immediately leave. But if Warren did stay, just sat there saying nothing, McMartin wanted to be ready. After reading the psychological profile report from Inspector McKay and Special Agent Garry, McMartin understood that the murderer might have a hard time confessing because of the hardship he had caused his union brothers. The killer would feel conflict because he had murdered for the good of the union, but it had backfired. Now he couldn't tell any-one about it.

McMartin decided he'd put a few scenarios to Warren, such as per-haps he had set the bomb but hadn't meant to kill. McMartin wanted to show himself as a person who could understand any act, who could understand that in the murderer's mind on September 18, 1992, it was the right thing to do to commit this crime. McMartin believed even the worst criminal was still a human being. The criminal had a reason for doing his crime, and if McMartin could show the bad guy that he understood, the bad guy might just talk about it. McMartin had learned to be observant, to watch body language, the eyes, head, arms and feet, searching for any sign that the person was responding to what he was saying. He didn't so much break down criminals as open them up.

He wrote down a list of themes he might use with Warren, psycho-logical bombs he would drop again and again if necessary to show Warren that he could no longer lie. Warren might have killed because he didn't agree with people crossing picket lines, McMartin thought. Maybe Warren was angry because a replacement worker took his job. There was so much frustration, and then he got fired for his part in the riot. He could never go back to work.

McMartin knew that if he could find the right key with Warren, the door to a confession might open. He'd done it with child molesters in the past. He never yelled at them or called them perverts. He appealed to them to get help, to end their torment. If that didn't work, McMartin tried saying the sex had only happened because the little kids had come on to them. Once he suggested to a guy that he grabbed young girls' breasts because they didn't know about breast cancer and he wanted to check them for lumps. Sometimes McMartin's suggestions were appalling, even absurd, but if they got a guy to confess—as they did with the breast groper—McMartin was satisfied. His attitude was: Tell it to the judge, you fool.

It would be the same with Warren. If he wanted to say he set the bomb, but didn't intend to kill, that was a huge step forward. It might not be the whole truth, but maybe the investigation could prove that the murder was actually premeditated. McMartin had been a police officer long enough to know that there were few crimes where the whole truth came out, where the motive and the actions of the criminal were fully known. Even in confessing, most criminals continued to lie. They tried to make themselves look better than they were. But McMartin also knew that it was right to suggest to Warren that the crime wasn't as heinous as everyone believed. So often things like that were true. Maybe Warren really hadn't planned to kill anyone. McMartin didn't know, but he vowed to himself he wouldn't stop until he found out.

Chapter 19

CORNERING THE THIRD SUSPECT

I N THE MINUTES before Roger Warren arrived at the office of the Homicide Task Force, crime analyst Lloyd McLeod gathered the investigators together to take a poll.

"Who thinks Roger did it?" McLeod asked.

"No, he didn't do it," Vern White said. "But he could be involved because he knows who those two guys were."

Ken Morrison agreed with White. Gregg McMartin voted yes, as did Nancy Defer, who was no longer sure about Bettger and had come to accept McMartin's viewpoint.

"I don't know if I want to vote," Dale McGowan said.

"You have to," the others insisted.

"Well, he was there, he was there."

"No, no, you got to pick one."

McGowan voted that Warren wasn't the killer, but he continued to hold that Warren was involved.

Sergeant McMartin was tense now. Maybe he'd been shooting his mouth off a bit too much, he thought. He tried to cover himself, say-ing, "Lookit, if it's not him, I'm going to be very surprised. Hopefully he's going to be able to do some explaining."

Roger Warren showed up as he had said he would. McGowan

greeted him at the door, then ushered him into an ambush. McGowan sat Warren down in a waiting area that the investigators had prepared as carefully as a stage set. They had stacked four empty boxes, each with its own label: Warren, Shearing, Bettger, Court Documents. On wall dividers, photographs of the soles of Warren's boots and footprints from the mine had been tacked up. An Ident man had put red lines on them, as if to point out various similar features. The RCMP also posted photographs of the blasted man-car.

McGowan was trying something he'd seen in a training course. In fact, the red lines were meaningless, just a ruse. The idea was that an innocent person would immediately react, asking what was up with the boxes and photographs. For a guilty person, however, the exhibit reinforced that the police were still after him. It also softened him up for what was about to come.

Warren was left to sit alone in the staging area for a minute. McGowan returned to find him standing, hands in pockets, examining the photographs. McGowan brought him into the interview room and introduced him to McMartin. Warren saw a neat-looking man, dark hair, six feet tall, 185 pounds, with an intense, inquisitive expression. McMartin was dressed in a shirt and tie. He carried no weapon. The room was spare: bare white walls, three chairs, a desk and a telephone.

McGowan went over Warren's Charter rights, telling him he had a right to a lawyer and that if he couldn't afford one he could get advice from Legal Aid. McGowan next said that McMartin had been working closely with Peter Martin, the special prosecutor from Calgary, and he wanted to clarify a few things. In truth, McMartin had spoken to Martin only once. McMartin had concocted the story about working with Martin in order to explain to Warren why someone would be up from Calgary to interview him. He also wanted Warren to believe he knew more about the case than he did, so there would be no bamboozling him. He certainly didn't want Warren to know that his knowledge of the strike and the main investigation came from a lone *Edmonton Journal* article.

After McGowan left the interview room, McMartin faced for the first time the suspect he had been studying for a week. He saw a middle-aged man, balding, with dark, deep-set eyes, dark eyebrows and a sharp nose. He wore a black ski jacket, a buttoned shirt and a ball cap. At once, Warren took up his standard position, arms and legs crossed, chewing gum, eyes looking off to the side, rarely making eye contact.

"I want to thank you for coming in, Roger," McMartin said. "It's good that you came in."

The police officer started out by making small talk, asking Warren about his mining experience and about his pension before working back to the investigation. He told Warren he'd like to go over again what he had done on the night and early morning before the blast. McMartin knew that people could remember twenty to thirty percent more detail if they were asked to visualize an event, to think hard about it, and that is what he did with Warren. "Any details that you could leave out could be the one little piece in the puzzle, obviously. So I'd like you to tell me everything that you did, everything that you saw, everything that you heard, everything that you felt, the environment, people, vehicles, everything at all that you can remember. Would you be able to do that for me and just go through her again?"

Warren spoke for the next thirty minutes. McMartin said nothing the entire time. His silence was deliberate. He wanted what police call a pure version statement, an uninterrupted, unaffected recollection. McMartin knew that if he broke in to ask questions, Warren might shape his answers, saying what he thought McMartin wanted to hear. By asking leading questions, McMartin would also risk creating a false memory, making Warren believe he had seen something when it had only been suggested to him.

In a way it was fun for McMartin to sit back. He didn't have to nail Warren. Warren did it himself, just by talking. McMartin again heard the tip-offs that showed Warren didn't believe his own alibi: "I can't remember . . . I'm pretty sure. . . It might have been . . . It seems . . . I'm pretty sure. . . Apparently . . . I must have . . . I think." Warren used fifty-three such qualifiers as he described his actions from the time he left the other strikers at picket gate six at around 1:00 A.M. to the time he returned to the same picket gate just after 6:00 A.M. His description was particularly littered with qualifiers any time he talked about being around other people.

However, when Warren talked about spotting the two shadowy men, then later about jumping in the ditch and getting wet (the two things McMartin was sure had never happened), he was completely straightforward. He went from using endless qualifiers and expressions of uncertainty to having none at all. The stories were straightforward, but too straightforward. They lacked the slightly wonky, jumbled quality of real memory.

Near the end of his recollection, Warren explained that he hadn't been spotted walking on the Ingraham Trail by anyone else because he was afraid of the Pinkertons. "They'd never hurt anybody that I can remember, but who wants to be out in the middle of nowhere and those guys come along? So guys were sort of acting like Daniel Boone there, you know, staying off the road. Like, you seen lights coming, get off the road."

At last Warren stopped talking, his story complete.

"Going back to the two guys that you saw. Who did you think it was?" McMartin asked.

Warren gave the description he'd been giving to the police for a year: a skinny fellow, with a Roman-type nose, filled out on top, looking somewhat like Conrad Lisoway, only Conrad had a mustache and this fellow was clean shaven.

McMartin went on to press for more details about the alibi, each time asking Warren if he got these details from talking to other strikers about what had gone on that night. Warren waffled, never denying the subtle accusation, but not admitting to anything either.

Three more times McMartin asked Warren for descriptions of the two shadowy men, digging deeper into the story. Warren rattled on, giving more and more detail, but somehow the picture never got any clearer. McMartin decided to spring a trap. He wanted to throw out something completely absurd to see Warren's reaction. Since Warren had said that the upper bodies of the two shadowy men seemed somewhat large, McMartin asked him, "Could it have been women? Being bigger on top?"

"Oh, I never thought of that," Warren said. "It's possible. Yeah, it's possible."

Jesus, Roger! McMartin thought. What a bunch of garbage!

He decided to press Warren on his suspicious behavior, asking why he had returned to the picket line that morning, even before anyone knew about the blast.

"Just basically, probably a little bit of curiosity from that," Warren said, referring to the two shadowy men.

McMartin repeated the question. When Warren waffled, saying he used to go back many mornings for no particular reason, McMartin asked the question one more time, this time with an edge to his voice: "Why did you go back in the morning, that morning?"

"I am not even sure if actually I just really had a reason. I did it on a lot of occasions. I went out there."

McMartin had had enough. He'd given Warren his chance to explain things but had only heard the same old evasions. "First of all, Roger, I don't believe you, okay," McMartin said, looking directly at Warren. "I don't believe anything that you are saying. . . . I know that a lot of people have said that they believe what you have been saying, but maybe not believing about the boots or about these two people or whatever. Roger, what you have been saying is not the truth. What it comes down to—and I'm talking about the people that you saw, Roger—that's not the truth. About going into the mine, that's not the truth either. With your boots, that's not the truth either. And what that comes to, Roger, is that it is not what happened. We all know what happened. But it is why, and why things happen."

McMartin kept his eyes on Warren, expecting an outburst. Indeed, Warren's first reaction was fury. He wanted to punch McMartin right through the wall, but he kept his rage locked inside. Warren held his position, eyes down, arms and legs crossed, unmoving. I've got the right to remain silent after all, he thought. I'll just not give this prick anything.

McMartin was astonished at Warren's lack of movement, but also enlightened. This was not how an innocent man would act. But he still feared Warren would bolt at any moment, so he kicked into his understanding mode, presenting the first of his ideas about why Warren might have set the bomb: "I guess the sad thing about this was that when it all did happen, when everything first started, there was a good reason. I'll tell you something, every time that we do something, it is the right thing to do. Do you know why? Because we do it, it is right. That's why. Maybe a minute later, maybe an hour later, a day, a week, a month, a year, we may sit back and say, 'God, why did I do it?' and not even be able to really truly understand it. . . . I don't know if this was done as a premeditated thing to blow people up—and God only knows you've seen death before down in the mines, and what that is like—or whether or not it was done solely not expecting people to be down there. I have no idea. I would hope like hell that it was done because there weren't going to be people going down in there, and it becomes a tragic goddamn accident, and because of being caught up in the rush, the adrenaline, and everything else that is going on—these guys piss you off, a person often gets very frustrated with these guys going across the line, you've worked all your life for something that you really believe in—and all of a sudden guys do things."

Warren was free to leave the room at any time, but McMartin continued to talk so Warren wouldn't have a moment to take up that option. And still Warren sat unmoving. McMartin thought he had better make things clear again. "I have no doubt whatsoever, I don't have any, that you are the person. You are the person that did this. Where I said it becomes so very important is to be able to understand why because without that, what happens is that people misunderstand, don't they?" McMartin said, then told Warren that setting the bomb must have seemed like a good idea. "It shows that somebody is a man, somebody can take the ball and run with the bloody thing and do something. However, as time goes by, what happens? Everybody all of a sudden starts filtering away. How many strikers are there roughly?" McMartin asked, wanting to draw Warren into the conversation because he needed some sense of how Warren was taking this.

"What do you mean?" Warren said, as if he had just woken up.

"When it first started. When the strike first started."

"One, two hundred and some, two hundred and twenty maybe."

"How many strikers have we got now?"

"I don't know. Maybe 120 or something like that?"

"So it has just about been cut in half. Guys are moving away. Guys have gotten new jobs, going and working. And you know what? It is going to keep going like that. . . . It looks like you guys are at an impasse because you sure as hell have been for a year." McMartin then returned to his themes, telling Warren he should talk about why he set the bomb because maybe it wasn't set to kill anyone and only he could clear that up, then moving on to the idea that he acted for the cause, he did it to send a message, but now he was isolated.

At last Warren cut into McMartin's monologue. "You guys are arresting me, you mean?"

"No, we are not arresting you," McMartin said. He told Warren that he was simply advising him where the investigation was. McMartin listed the lies that Warren had told—the two shadowy men and the boots, which the forensic lab test had shown had been cut, then burned, not the other way around.

When Warren insisted that the boots had been defaced just as he had described, McMartin changed his tack. "Who are we dealing with?" he asked. "Who is Roger Warren? Who is Roger Warren? I don't believe for a moment that Roger Warren is a Clifford Olson—not for a second—who doesn't give a shit about anybody or anybody's feelings or what he does."

Nevertheless, McMartin told Warren he was still accountable for what he had done and should apologize. "Maybe it does take a man to be able to say, 'Okay, Jesus, this has gone on long enough, I'm sorry.' Are you a man or not? I have no idea. I don't know you. But I would hope that you are."

"If you guys are that convinced of this stuff, I am just wondering why I am not arrested," Warren repeated, this time sounding more sure of himself, more sure that he was free to leave.

McMartin told Warren that the police were in no rush, that he wasn't going anywhere. "This could go on for another six months. Who cares? I mean, it is already done. It's like the water that is under the bridge." McMartin kept up his barrage, telling Warren that Peter Martin and the Attorney General's Department were still studying the case.

Just then, Warren interrupted. "I have to pick my daughter up and take her for a therapy appointment."

"At what time?" McMartin said, deflated.

"Right now, actually. I should be there."

McMartin asked Warren if he would come back later because he had more things to tell him. Warren said he'd return in about ninety minutes, at 5:30 P.M. The striker got up and left.

McMartin was sure Warren was gone for good. He'd be crazy to return. He must be so relieved to be out of here, McMartin thought. Besides, what does he really have to worry about? I didn't hit him with any hard evidence, just accusations, the same stuff he's been brushing off for thirteen months.

McMartin consoled himself with one thought—Roger Warren set that bomb. Warren had the right to remain silent, but McMartin took the silence and Warren's lame responses as an admission of guilt, one that would never play in court, but was nonetheless convincing to him. "I didn't get any denial whatsoever," he told Dale McGowan. "He is the guy that killed the miners."

McGowan wasn't completely sure, but he knew something was different with Warren. McGowan had listened to the interview on a speaker in the monitoring room. Warren had always denied accusations put to him in the past, but not this time. McGowan believed that Warren had bolted to escape the pressure and gather his thoughts. He thought Warren would return. "If Roger Warren tells you he'll be back, he'll be back," he told McMartin. "He's never said he's going to do something, then not done it."

"Well, if he does come back, he has to come in that door and tell me I'm full of shit or maybe say, 'I talked to my lawyer and I'm not going to stay around.' He's got to come back in and do something."

McGowan and Defer set out to follow Warren. They wanted to see if he actually was going to take his daughter to physiotherapy. They were surprised when he did. Afterward, Warren drove home, sat around, then went to pick up Helen from work. He told her about this guy in the interview accusing him of the murders. On their way home, Helen asked him to stop at the Centre Square Mall because she had to get money from the bank. Warren went to buy a coffee, but he was still so rattled from the interrogation that he realized he didn't have any money to pay for it. He told the cashier his wife would come back and pay. When Helen returned, Warren told her he had decided to go back up to see the Mounties for a minute. "The guy said he had something to tell me."

McMartin was astonished when he heard that Warren had come back to the mall and was having coffee with his wife. At the task force door Warren surprised him again. Warren issued no strong denial or challenge. Instead, he walked into the room and sat down in his chair, striking his pose, arms and legs crossed, eyes down. It was as if he was challenging McMartin to keep blasting away and see who could last the longest.

McMartin asked Warren about his daughter's therapy, then decided he should pick up the interview where he had left off. "You are worried about where all this is going to go, or what it is leading up to?"

"What you were talking about here?" Warren said.

"Yeah."

"Well, of course I am concerned."

McMartin started rolling out his themes again, stressing that he believed Warren wasn't an evil man, that he didn't intend to kill. "I don't see the type of guy in front of me that people are gonna have to say, 'Oh my God, here comes Roger Warren! Lock the door! Shut the windows!' That's not the case at all. We're talking about a one-time incident where there is a lot of emotion involved, where there's a lot of frustration involved, where there is a lot of pressure on you and stress on you. . . . Maybe I am wrong, but I don't think so. I don't think so at all. What do you feel is the best way to deal with it, Roger?"

"Well, if I was that convinced somebody's guilty of something I'd just arrest 'em and lock 'em up."

"Well, yes, you know, it may happen, Roger. But I'll tell you something: I don't think that's fair to the person either. That's not fair to you." McMartin explained that it would look better to everyone, even the judge, if Warren confessed so they could understand what had happened. He kept up his even-tempered, persistent prodding. He spoke almost without pause for more than an hour. All the while, he kept a close watch on Warren to see if he reacted in any way. Warren continued to sit still, his stance closed and defiant. McMartin hoped his talk would be like a commercial, the endless repetition finally convincing Warren to buy into one of the themes and confess. McMartin rumbled on, one theme, then another, then another. The Mounties listening in the monitor room—White, McGowan, Defer, McLeod and Morrison—grew anxious. It was the strangest interview they had ever heard. Why was McMartin droning on?

Shut the fuck up, Gregg, McGowan thought. Let Roger talk.

But McMartin continued to pound away, his voice full of conviction: "The most natural tendency for any human being is that when we've done something that we know isn't right, we tend to run away from it. It only becomes wrong when maybe we keep on running and say, 'Screw the world.' Now people put on the brakes and say, like, 'Who are we dealing with? Maybe we are dealing with a hardened criminal. Maybe we are dealing with somebody who doesn't give a damn about anybody or anything.'"

Nothing seemed to move Warren so McMartin decided it was again time to push him out of his silence. "If it wasn't meant to be, it's important to understand that," the police officer said. "Let me ask you this: Was it meant to be? Am I sitting here going way off? Am I being snowed? Was it meant to be? Is that who it was directed at? Hey? Am I the one that's totally out in left field?"

Warren coughed.

"If that's the case, I'll be eating a lot of crow, I guess, but I've eaten crow before. I've been snowed before, but I sure as hell don't think I am here. Was it directed at those guys? Were you after the men? Were you after Joe? Hey, is that what it was?"

Warren coughed again, then said, "I don't see what the point is. Like, what's the difference? Something happened. A bunch of guys are dead. If you're gonna nail somebody for it, fuckin' nail the guy!"

"No, no, Roger. That's not fair. You know that. You know why?"

"You got nine guys dead," Warren continued. "You got about eighty people fuckin' affected directly. Now some guy's gonna come up with an excuse for this, and everybody's gonna feel sorry for him? Like, not too fuckin' likely."

"No, no, no, no, no, no, no, no, no. I'm not suggesting that for a moment that people are going to feel sorry for him. I haven't said that. . . . Nobody is going to walk up and just shake your hand and say, 'Congratulations.' Jesus, we are all responsible for our actions. However, it becomes important to understand that, so it can be dealt with, Roger. You know that and so do I. . . . You are a human being, and all human beings have some compassion. We all do, Roger. And all I am saying is that it becomes important to understand what was going on here. Was it directed at those guys or not?"

Warren continued to sit, silent and defiant.

"Maybe I am being snowed and I am way out in left field and you want to play the game," McMartin said bitterly. "I don't care. I don't care. It is not my guts that are being torn apart. . . . I can go back to Calgary and my words are, 'He didn't give a shit. Take it from there. You guys do what you have to because he doesn't care. Why should anybody else?'"

A moment later, McMartin returned to his understanding mode, but now he added a new twist, reminding Warren of the accident where Danny Mino was blinded and Vince Corcoran killed. "You couldn't take it with one person. I sit back and look at that and say, 'He did not intend it with those nine miners. I can't believe it for a moment that he intended that.' Am I wrong? Can you be a man yourself, Roger? Can you at least even admit it to yourself? Am I wrong? Hey? Can you not be a man yourself and say, 'Goddamn it, I am sorry.' Or you can't say those words because you don't care. Is that what it is? Am I wrong about that with the miners? You could not live with yourself, knowing that it was going to happen. Could you? Eh?"

"No," Warren said. "I wouldn't be able to."

"No, I know you wouldn't be able to," McMartin said, at last feeling a rush of excitement from Warren's slight admission. "So it was an accident. It was done, but it wasn't for the people there. . . . By even just being able to admit that, like what you just did, is a little segment of being able to start that healing process in yourself. Yes, the end result was tragic, and you didn't mean to, but it wasn't as if it was a deliberate act to be able to laugh in the face of those miners' families. That was never done. It was never done and never will be done. Was it done up the way that they said that it was? Eh?"

"Well, the way those guys say that it was done, if that was done like that, then somebody deliberately tried to murder somebody. Because anything going down the track, even a guy walking, if there is something strung across the track, it's going to kill the guy when it goes off."

"So it wasn't done the way that they said?"

"I'm just saying, if it was done the way they said, then it was deliberate."

"Yeah, you already told me that it wasn't for the miners' sake, so it tells me that they are wrong in their thoughts of how it was done. That's obvious."

"I am just saying . . . if I deliberately was responsible on purpose of killing nine guys, they would have been gone a long time ago. Poof or something, you know."

"Yeah, and I know you are telling that it wasn't done purposely for nine guys," McMartin said, sensing he was one step from getting Warren to talk. "How was it, Roger? Be a man, Roger. Take the big step. Let's cut the bullshit so that we can say that there wasn't a game, that there wasn't any bullshit. It's obvious, very obvious now, yes, it wasn't done against the miners. So that I know that it wasn't set that way. Exactly what are you saying?"

"There are quite a few things I've heard said," Warren said. "I heard one thing here said today that those footprints down there are my boots."

"Yeah, they are."

"Guaran-fucking-teed they're not!"

"No, you're wrong."

"Guaranteed!" Warren said. "Those boots that you guys took out of my house, those boots?"

"What boots are they?"

"My green Kamik boots, size eleven."

"What prints are in the mine?"

"How in fuck do I know? But I know they are not mine."

"Roger, Roger, now you are going back to lying again."

"You guys are lying to me. Everybody. I've heard it about five times now around the union hall, this and that, that the guys are always looking for size ten boots, not eleven boots."

"No, no, no, no. Roger, Roger, Roger, Roger. I don't understand. All of a sudden, now what are we doing here? It is like a fish out of water. What kind of man are you? What kind of a man are you, Roger? Eh?"

Again, McMartin felt deflated. He thought he had Warren, but this business with the boots had somehow got in the way.

Roger Warren felt as strong as ever now. He was sure he wore size ten Kamik boots that night to the picket line, and if the RCMP were so stupid as to insist he had on the size elevens, it only showed they didn't know what they were doing.

From McMartin's patter, Warren was beginning to understand that if he said the bomb wasn't meant to kill that the charges didn't have to be first degree murder. The option appealed to him, but he didn't trust McMartin and didn't believe it was true. If he was going to confess, he needed to know for sure that he had no other option. "You have got to think of your wife," he told McMartin. "You got to think of your children."

"Yes, okay, I agree."

"Look, even if I was hypothetically going to make a decision about something like this like you're talking about, without getting advice from lawyers and all kinds of bullshit, which I have never done. . . . The state is going to take its penalty. Anybody involved in this kind of stuff I guarantee is going to get ten years. You are going to have probably somebody there trying to prove you did do something deliberately. Even if you could prove you didn't and it was accidental, it's still an act of terrorism using explosives. I'm sure you are going to get the mandatory ten to fourteen years for that."

McMartin took up Warren's new issues, offering him an inducement to confess, explaining that there were different charges for murder, depending on the intent of the killer and whether or not the act was planned and deliberate. "I am not suggesting here for a moment that you wouldn't be going to jail because you will. All right. The thing is, if it is manslaughter, if it was that this explosive was not set the way that they are saying, or it was not deliberately set to take out these miners . . . if that is what the truth is—and I am only interested in what the truth is—there is a variety [of sentences]. . . . When a guy is sentenced to ten years, how much time is he going to have to serve? If he shows that he is not cold, not callous, he is sorry for what happened, they look at that. What happens? Maybe a guy serves a few years, and then is able to come back out into society and again say, 'I'm sorry for what happened.' When you say people don't give a shit, Roger, you are so, so wrong."

McMartin then went on another lengthy soliloquy, rehashing his themes, but Warren still wasn't moved. "The only thing I'm afraid of is, I don't want somebody tricking me into an admission of something and then I found out later I didn't have to admit that," the miner said.

"Roger, nobody is tricking you into an admission. Nobody is tricking you."

"'Cause I don't want some lawyer to come along after and say, just hypothetically, 'Fuck man, you're doing a lot of stuff here you shouldn't have did.' You always hear those horror stories, you know—the one guy that cooperated the most with the police in Ontario in that little girl's murder there, that Lemay or whatever his name was, Paul Lemat," Warren said, meaning the unjustly convicted Guy Paul Morin. "They put him in jail, then they took him back out again. I understand it wasn't you guys, it was the O.P.P. [Ontario Provincial Police] or whatever. But that was one of the only guys in that whole community that ever, ever cooperated with the police, you know, in that particular case, and who gets nailed for this thing? The guy."

A moment later, Warren reiterated his main concern. "I can't understand how I could ever prove that it wasn't deliberate."

"Who knows what's here in your mind?" McMartin asked him. "Only you. Right? Only you. I am only asking you what the truth is, Roger. And I am not going to sit here for a moment when you tell me the truth and say, 'Fuck you.' I will not. I will not."

"But the bottom line is, one wrong word and it's don't pass go, go straight to fuckin' jail," Warren said. "It's pretty serious."

McMartin was growing frustrated. He never yelled at Warren, but he raised his voice. The debate continued until Warren said, "I've been doing some heavy thinking about this kind of stuff. Well, if I'm not under arrest I'm gonna leave."

"Can I just get you just to wait here a moment," McMartin said, then got up and left. He had lost Warren once before that day and didn't want it to happen again. It occurred to him that one of Warren's worries right then was that his wife, Helen, had been waiting for him downstairs for almost two hours.

McMartin brought in Nancy Defer, then told Warren that Defer could pick up Helen and take her home.

"So I guess you answered my question," Warren said. "You are arresting me?"

"No, you're not under arrest, not right now," McMartin said, then set off again with renewed energy. He had managed to keep Warren in the room, and now it was like he was just warming up. He'd go as long as it took—five hours, eight hours, ten or eleven, as long as he had an audience. Still, he could not convince Warren that there were any sane reasons to confess.

"Well, I'm refusing to comment anymore unless I'm arrested, and even if I'm arrested, I'm not commenting without a lawyer," Warren said.

"Okay, you want to play the game then?"

"It's not a game! A guy's got to protect himself, partner. Holy fuck!"

"From what, Roger? From what?"

"Well, I'm going on a lot of faith here. If I had a lawyer present, if there is any details to be brought out that you are talking about, and mitigate and whatever," Warren said, fishing for the possibility of a lighter sentence.

"Is it easier for you to talk about it with a lawyer sitting here?" McMartin shot back. "I mean, we'll get ten lawyers here. I don't care."

"I'm just saying—"

"Is it easier for you to sit down and to be a man and to take that step?"

"Oh, so you're saying 'be a man.' I'm fucked."

"I'm sorry, I'm sorry for what happened."

"Half this fucking shit that happened in this fucking place should never have happened because seventy-five percent, twenty-one million people in Canada are protected from this fucking shit, you know."

Warren was angry now, speaking in the voice of the picket line. But at first McMartin didn't understand Warren's point. "I'm sorry," he said. "I'm not following you."

"The use of replacement workers. They're not allowed in three provinces. One has ten million people, one has eight and one has three. That's twenty-one out of twenty-seven or twenty-eight million. That's seventy-five percent of the population."

"What are you talking about?"

"I'd put a little guilt on the people who caused that, too," Warren snapped.

"Yes, I have no doubt about that whatsoever," McMartin said, at last catching on.

"I don't really feel that I'd really be guilty about this shit. I feel terrible as everybody else does about anybody ever getting damaged or hurt. I said that from the start about the whole fucking strike. I mean, I'm not going around smacking guys with fists or clubs or anything else, and I don't think a lot of other guys ever did that."

McMartin knew that if Warren was worked up about this, he had better use it. He himself was no trade unionist. Unions had tried to organize his father's sawmill, but the men and women didn't go for it, a fact that made his father proud. But if this is what turned Warren on, McMartin was willing to use it. He started to mimic Warren's angry, menacing voice. "Those fucking guys shouldn't have been down there," he said. "They shouldn't have been going in and, in fact, it probably would've never happened if the Northwest Territories had a law prohibiting it."

"Exactly," Warren said, then raged about the lack of antiscab legislation. "When you're involved in this kind of stuff, like, only one person is going to take the fuckin' rap for it," he said, then added, "You see, you probably didn't see it, there were a lot of people interviewed here around the eighteenth, and a lot of them said they don't condone violence of any kind, but they blame the owner of that mine."

"Peggy White, is it?" McMartin said, betraying his ignorance.

"Witte," Warren corrected.

"I'm sorry."

"Witte. Which was surprising to me."

McMartin agreed that the people had blamed Witte for the blast, but he said the unfortunate thing was that Warren's fellow strikers were leaving town now, abandoning the strike. "And the other unfortunate thing is that it [the bomb] still didn't stop those pricks from going in there."

"Actually, that is like a total fucking disgrace anyways. I think it's a black mark on the history of fucking Canada," Warren said, then added that about forty of the union's men had crossed the picket line.

McMartin continued to mimic Warren's arrogant, bitter voice. "I couldn't think of anything more bloody frustrating than to have those guys keep going down like that. Is that all it was, to put an end to all this? And I'm gonna tell you something, I'm gonna talk about it, man,

I'm gonna tell you something—it takes a hell of a goddamn man to do what the hell you did to stand up against a company like that, and not only stand up against a company like that, to stand up for what takes place in this country. I mean, it's like going to war for a country and to stand up for what you believe in. That's a hell of a thing, Roger, it really is. You had a lot of guts. The only bad thing about the whole damn thing is that it didn't stop, and if that doesn't stop them, what the hell ever does? But, you know, maybe because of this, maybe the end result is that we get the goddamn government involved, and to say, 'When guys are out doing something legal, like on strike, you don't bring in scabs to undermine the guys that are doing things legally.'" A moment later he added, "Maybe we can change things in this country. It's a different kick in the ass to a few politicians and to a few people."

"That's the way it happened in Quebec," Warren said, and now McMartin and he were in sync, so much so that if a politician had walked into the room right then, McMartin himself would have taken a swing at him.

"I'm sure that there is a lot of guys, a lot of strikers who admired . . . what you did," McMartin said.

"They admired it?" Warren said, disbelieving.

"Admired the balls that you would have to do something to try to put an end, to be able to stand up, like nobody else could, and say, 'This is bullshit! We gotta put an end to this!'"

"I don't think anybody admired that."

"Maybe not admiring what the end result was, but for what you did for the cause and maybe to be able to get something changed in this bloody country to give some politicians a kick in the ass. . . . What went on that night, Roger? What went on that night? What took place?"

"I'm just saying that if anybody wiped out nine guys, anybody like me hypothetically wiped out nine guys, I'm fucking telling you right now I wouldn't be even fucking around, I'd just go out and gas myself. Something gentle so my wife wouldn't have to fucking look at a mess."

"If it was deliberately done?"

"That's what I'm trying to tell you. I think most sane people would act the same fucking way."

"Okay, if it wasn't deliberate, then what was the thought that was going on? Roger, cut out the bullshit here with the hypothetically. For

Christ sakes, I mean, we're playing like a little kid, playing a fucking game. Right. You're a goddamn man. I'm a man. We can sit and we can talk. What was going on up there?"

"Look, to me this is like fucking being drilled in an inquisition."

"Well, it's not. I'm just asking you."

"I'm not under arrest, but I can't go."

"Do you want to go?"

"I don't want to fucking answer something."

"Do you want to go?"

"Right at this particular moment anyways," Warren said, and now he had lapsed out of his angry voice. He was completely rational again, weighing the pros and cons of confessing, and still not convinced there was any benefit for him to go ahead.

"Why?" McMartin asked. "Why don't you want to answer at this particular moment? . . . Now I guess I'm really sitting here being caught. Where? I don't know where. We're talking about the scabs shouldn't have been there and damn it, this was a way to stop them. But we're also talking that it was not deliberate to them. I guess, what we're talking is real conflict here, like, I can't see where they go together."

But at last Roger Warren could. Warren the problem solver, the one who plotted ahead exactly what he'd do at work the next day, the one who loved to calculate how much rock he had broken, the one who loved fixing snowmobiles and outwitting hitters in fastball, that Roger Warren had at last figured out a solution to this problem. And as McMartin said, even if he confessed he might come out a winner. He might avoid getting a life sentence, and he would escape the torment of the investigation. He could subvert Peggy Witte. The strike could end. Maybe there would be antiscab legislation. He would be like the phoenix rising from the ashes, he thought. He would be destroyed, but he would win.

Warren began his confession.

"What it is I'm talking about is a guy can set something up underground whereby an ore car, hypothetically an ore car going by, could get smashed against the wall. An ore car's got steel that fucking thick. There's not going to be much happening with an ore car. You can set something up for an ore car because an ore car has got something on it that no other fucking car has, a fifth fucking wheel."

"Maybe someone might get hurt," McMartin said, grasping the main point, "but they're not going to be killed."

"There wouldn't be too much chance of it if that happened because the fucking motor is back fifty, sixty feet where the guys are, you know what I mean?"

As soon as Warren started giving his hypothetical plan, the Mounties in the monitoring room got down on their knees to say a team prayer. Throughout the investigation, whenever McIntyre had been hit with a big problem, he grabbed the bridge of his nose with his thumb and index finger and said, "Jeez, jeez, stress headache, stress headache." The other investigators had started to imitate him, calling it their team prayer, and now they prayed for all they were worth.

"He's right there!" McGowan said. "He's right there! Take him!"

McGowan asked the monitor to start taking notes and to set up another tape recorder just in case the master tape failed.

In the interview room McMartin asked Warren if he could go grab a photograph of a mine car.

"There's nowhere in here you can smoke, eh?" Warren said.

"You want to have a smoke, go ahead, have it, have a smoke. I'll grab you an ashtray if you want, but can I grab a picture of the car so you can show me what the hell you're talking about?"

"Yeah."

McMartin came back with a photograph of a man-car and a pop can for Warren's cigarette ashes.

At last Warren could look at McMartin and not feel anxious. Warren seemed playful, relaxed, euphoric almost. It was as if he were a teacher who loved his subject and was sharing it with a prized pupil. For the first time, he made eye contact and held it. When the details came, they came gushing. He started talking about how a man could set up a bomb, stringing the trip wire from the ground to the ceiling beside the tracks, not across the tracks as the investigators had been suggesting. That way, the device would allow a man-car pushed by a loki to pass. An ore train, however—five or six or seven ore cars pushed by a loki—would detonate it. Warren explained that each ore car was hinged and had a dump wheel or dump arm sticking out from the side, which was used to lift the box and dump the muck down the ore pass. As an ore car passed the bomb, the protruding dump arm would hit the trip wire beside the track and ignite the explosion.

Warren drew a picture of the ore car, his bomb and the 750-drift to help explain. He said there would be a number of massive ore cars between the blast and the driver of the loki. The driver would be back far enough that he would survive. "Fucking hare-brained," the old-time miner said, then added in a moment, "Like when somebody thinks if something was done deliberately, sometimes stuff can be done that doesn't seem to be deliberate."

"Yeah," McMartin said.

"Tragic shit happens sometimes."

"Roger, I'm glad you told me that."

In the monitoring room, the Mounties whooped and hugged and smiled and laughed and shook hands. McGowan felt electric. The killer was his man, his file, and he had seen it through to the end. Still, he made an effort to calm down. He pulled away from the celebration to think. He knew he would be going into that room to drag out more details. He tried to concentrate on what Warren told McMartin.

The bomb was set with a fishing line trip wire, Warren said. When the bomb's switch was tripped, it ignited one bag of AMEX explosives and about thirty sticks of powder. The only way Warren could see the man-car triggering the blast was if somehow something was sticking out from the side.

"Why didn't you come out and tell us this before?"

"Fear," Warren said.

"I guess so. Okay."

"Bullshit aside, why else, for fuck sakes?"

"Okay."

"I felt horrible about the fucking guys. I still do. I can't barely sleep sometimes."

"I know. I can understand that, Roger. I can understand that. But it's so good to understand that it was done."

"I wasn't even gonna do that," Warren said, dropping the hypothetical and putting himself in the middle of the story for the first time. "I was gonna go out to the fucking mine shaft and fuckin' really fuck that shaft up with nobody in it. Of course, but how you gonna do this shit by yourself? Who wants to involve somebody? I ruined my whole life. I ruined 120 or 140 guys that are left. They're fucked. What else can you do? Fuck."

"But it wasn't meant to be," McMartin said, then delved deeper into Warren's story, using the map from the *Journal*'s "Footsteps of the Murderer" article to help explain his route through the mine. Warren told McMartin he thought explosives were going to be hauled on the 750-level that day. "I figured, you know, with the car, the fucking thing goes off, the company is gonna be in a lot of fucking shit. It's gonna be an unexplained fucking explosion."

Warren next detailed his initial plan to blow up the C-shaft. "I was gonna take a couple bags out there, go around the shaft and take three or four rolls of fuckin' lead wire, go back, put them on the motor, boom! But then I got fuckin' scared. I should have. Fuck."

McMartin asked about when Warren defaced the boots. Warren said he did it a few days later. "But those aren't the fuckin' boots," he insisted. "They aren't."

"They're not? Why did you cut those boots up then?"

"They aren't the fuckin' boots I was wearing. I wore boots like that but a smaller size. Why lie? It's a waste of time now."

"You've got me confused. So, in other words, your other boots are also cut, too, then?"

"No, I just threw them away."

"Where'd you throw them?"

"I burned the fuckers."

"Where?"

"Oh, way the fuck out by Cameron Falls."

Warren explained that he later cut up and burned the soles of the size eleven Kamik boots that he showed the police because he was afraid. It was stupid, but he wasn't thinking. He said he threw out his jacket as well because it had mud on it.

McMartin knew the next step would be to get a videotaped reenactment of Warren in the mine. McMartin thought about going with Warren on the trip into Giant, but then he gave his head a shake. Lookit, he told himself, these guys have been at this for thirteen months. They know what is going on and I don't. It's time to bring in McGowan.

"I'll be right back in a second," he told Warren, then got up to leave. "You took a big step, Roger. I congratulate you for it."

Chapter 20

RETURN TO 750

W HEN DALE MCGOWAN walked into the room, he saw a
Roger Warren he had never seen before. Defensive no more,
Warren leaned back in his chair, his feet on the table. He
looked McGowan in the eye.

"Couldn't tell any more fuckin' lies," he said. "Simple decision."

McGowan now had no doubt that Warren had set the blast, but
Warren had lied and lied and lied, and now that he was confessing,
McGowan wanted him to prove that he had done it, prove it beyond
any doubt. Warren had to tell him things only the murderer and the
police knew. Warren had to show that he hadn't just talked to the real
murderer and for some unfathomable reason decided to take the fall for
him. McGowan also wondered if the bomb was really set the way Warren was now saying. And he wondered if someone else had been in on
the plan. He took over the questioning from McMartin. "I'll tell you
right off the bat, before we get going away, I didn't think that you were
the type of guy that would intentionally do something like that,"
McGowan said.

"No," Warren said.

"And I knew something was churning in you so it's a good step for
you."

McMartin listened for a few minutes, then excused himself. McGowan asked Warren to go back and describe what he had done from the time he arrived at the picket line on the evening of September 17, 1992. Warren told McGowan that he hadn't necessarily planned to set the blast on that night, but he was feeling good standing around talking to the other guys at picket gate six. All the other men started to fade away, so he decided to go for it. He left gate six and walked right to Akaitcho. He never went to the bus at gate three, as he had always claimed. He believed he could get away with the story because he knew everybody on the bus would be sleeping so deeply that a man could kick them and they wouldn't wake up; he was doubly sure of this because he'd seen them drinking earlier that night at the union hall.

Warren said he'd stashed some gear in a satchel under some brush earlier in the evening. A few weeks before, he had fashioned a light out of a bicycle lamp and a six-volt battery. In his bag he also had fishing line for the trip wire, a toggle switch for the bomb, two nine-volt batteries and a hard-hat, the same one he'd had on during the June 14 riot. After he set the blast, he told McGowan he packed all his extra material into the satchel, drove seven to nine miles out of town and threw it into a swamp.

Warren said he picked Akaitcho because he didn't think there would be a security guard there. He had scouted it out a few days earlier. He broke into the shack protecting the shaft by climbing on a drum and through an open window, just as the footprints had suggested to the police. A piece of plywood covered the shaft. Warren said he lifted it, climbed in, then jammed his hunting knife into the plywood in order to pull it back over the shaft, concealing his entry.

Warren told McGowan that he climbed down about four hundred to five hundred feet to the first level. He walked back through the drift because he couldn't find the man-way that led from the 425-level down to the 575-level. This fact was a crucial piece of hold-back evidence. Only the police and a few people at Giant Mine knew the murderer's footprints showed he had gotten lost there. Warren also said he got lost at the 575-drift looking for the man-way, another key match between his story and the hold-back evidence.

After climbing down to the 750-drift, Warren said he walked toward the 712-scoop shop. He was close to the shop when he heard the central blast go off. For a few minutes, it was smoky. He walked to

the 712-charging station, where he picked up a loki. He drove it to the
712-scoop shop. There, he got on a scoop and traveled down the ramp
road to the 907-powder magazine. He pulled a bag of AMEX and thirty
sticks of powder off the shelves. He put the explosives in the bucket of
the scoop. On the way up, he realized it was past 3:00 A.M. He told
McGowan he feared he was running out of time if he wanted to set a
bomb at the C-shaft. "I said, 'Holy shit, if I go out there and start
fuckin' around and somebody comes down there, a mechanic or something, after this central blast clear-out, I'll be out in the fuckin' shaft,
you know. What am I going to do, eh?' So that's when I got the idea,
'Well, fuck, maybe I can set this up so just the fuckin' car can set it
off.'"

At the 712-cap magazine, Warren said he got three DCD blasting
caps and about ten to twelve feet of B-line detonator chord. He loaded
his explosives and other gear onto the loki, then headed south down
the 750-drift toward C-shaft.

He wasn't sure if his nine-volt battery had enough power to charge
the DCD cap, which would then ignite the B-line, detonating the rest of
the explosives. About fifty feet from the blast site, he said he stopped to
do a test. He rigged a DCD cap to a battery and a toggle switch, stuck it
in a hole in the wall to absorb the shock, then triggered it. The cap
blew. "I says, 'Oh fuck, these things'll work.'"

The test blast was another piece of hold-back evidence, matching up
with the detonated cap that explosives expert Jean-Yves Vermette had
found north of the blast site. Vermette had guessed that the murderer
might have used it to test his battery. Now Warren had confirmed it.

Warren next described to McGowan how he had set up the bomb
in order to ensure that a man-car pushed down the tracks by a loki
would not trigger the bomb, but that an ore car would. Warren said he
traveled past the blast site to a spot where the dump wheels of ore cars
always banged the wall, leaving behind a mark. He took a stick and
measured how far that mark was from the tracks. He used that mea-
surement to gauge how far from the tracks he should set the trip line.

To build the bomb, Warren said he found a length of drilling rod.
He dug a hole in the muck, then anchored one end of rod in the
ground, wedging the other end up against the wall. He taped his toggle
switch to the rod. He put tubing from his snowmobile hose over the
toggle switch to extend its length and give it more flexibility, then

attached string to the tubing. He ran the string straight up to the high pressure water and air pipes on the drift's ceiling. He tied the string there. Next, he wired the nine-volt battery up to the toggle switch and to the lead wires of the DCD cap. The triggering mechanism was complete. Warren tested it, pulling on the string. The DCD cap detonated. He replaced the spent cap with his third and final cap.

Finally he prepared the explosives. He cut open the AMEX bag and stuck in the powder sticks. He wrapped one of the sticks with B-line detonating cord.

Warren checked the circuit of his toggle switch with a continuity meter. He wanted to make sure that the circuit wasn't complete when it was off. If it had been complete, and Warren had failed to check, he would have instantly vaporized himself when he clipped the explosives and the triggering mechanism into the DCD cap. "I checked the thing and everything was safe," he told McGowan. "Which is fuckin' scary, hooking that up, but I hooked it up. Nothing happened. Then away I went. I was pretty fuckin' happy. I figured I did sabotage, but I was stupid." Warren said he had no thoughts that his device might catch a man-car. "I wasn't even half worried about it. I figured, 'Well, fuck, it'll knock the car off.' Then after, when I got into the fucking daylight and took my daughter to work—holy fuck, what if somebody gets killed here?"

Warren said he couldn't figure out what set it off—maybe the man-car vibrating the tracks.

To get out of the mine, Warren said he took the loki north up the drift to the 712-scoop shop. "I was gonna just put the fuckin' scoop away, and then I said, 'Holy fuck, I gotta walk all the way up this fuckin' ramp!' And I said, 'Piss on that.' So I put fuel in the scoop right there 'cause the fuel gets low and I was scared, eh."

Gassing up the scoop wasn't hold-back evidence, but it was the kind of small detail that McGowan knew would later make a difference.

As he drove out, Warren said he started to worry that he might come upon a couple of big security guards or miners, then be faced with fighting his way out; maybe he could have battled them fifteen years ago, but not now. He told McGowan that he decided to leave the scoop at the breakthrough door to the 575-drift and take a less traveled way out of the mine.

"How did you park it?" McGowan asked, looking for one more piece of hold-back. The RCMP knew that the scoop had been backed next to the wall, so other traffic could get by, then left with the bucket down, textbook parking procedure for a miner, ensuring the scoop wouldn't roll away. Sure enough, Warren described this exact procedure. Next, he described how he had walked down the 575-drift and decided to save time by heading out the B-3 area of the mine, instead of leaving through Akaitcho. The B-3 exit was riskier than Akaitcho; B-3 was an active mining area, but Warren was so exhausted that he went for it.

A steel gate covered the B-138 portal exit. He crawled under, but got wet in a puddle. He ran up behind the portal, over a hill, through the scrub trees, ending up back on the Ingraham Trail just a few hundred yards north of picket gate six, where he had started out that night. He pulled a garbage bag from his pocket, packed up his gear and left it in the bushes.

Warren said that the reason he returned to the mine that morning was to collect the bag. When he parked on the Ingraham Trail, he said he saw Terry Byberg drive by. Warren opened the hood of his car to make it look like he was having car trouble. "I looked all around and nobody was around, and I just made a mad dash and grabbed that shit, threw it in the trunk and took off."

McGowan knew that one of the things that would prove Warren's story was to develop a paper trail of bills and receipts from Warren's purchases for the bomb. McGowan went through each item, asking Warren where he got it. Warren said he got his boots and six-volt battery at Woolco and the fishing line and the tubing from Canadian Tire. Other odds and ends were bought at stores ranging from Radio Shack to Bumper to Bumper.

Warren told McGowan he acted on his own. "I was gonna even involve somebody, eh. And then I said, 'Fuck, I can't talk about that to anybody.'"

He said he didn't think what he was doing was that major, so he didn't expect such a massive investigation. He was only trying to commit sabotage, not murder. He hoped it would be investigated by the mine inspector, not necessarily the police.

McGowan told Warren that one consolation for the whole thing was that people could start to grieve properly. "You've lived with this for a little over a year now, and it's gotta be tough on you. And it's no doubt tough on families as well."

"I wonder if my wife knows about this now," Warren said. "Fuck me."

"I don't know. Have you ever discussed anything with her?"

"Not really."

"What do you mean 'not really'? Did you tell her that you—"

"Well, she knew I had some plans to do something, and she just asked me if I did anything, and I said, 'No.'"

"What kind of plans were you discussing?"

"Well, I was, you know, talking about how a guy should do this and why don't they do that. But that day she asked me about it, I don't think she even wanted to know. I kept everything covered. I never told her fuck all. . . . She was in no fuckin' way involved."

"Okay," McGowan said. "Have you talked to anyone, anyone at all about any particulars at all as to what happened?"

"Oh fuck no. Tell anybody that I did it?"

"Or even an insinuation, kind of?"

"Oh fuck no. Not this kid. Not this kid."

McGowan went back to Warren's alibi, asking what he and the other strikers had discussed about his whereabouts that night.

"You know," Warren said, "guys asked me, 'cause they knew I'd been missing, eh, they said, 'Jeez, you want us to say you were here?' I says, 'Fuck partner, the truth will set you free.' I remember telling that to Frank Woods and a couple of guys, that Brian Drover. Like, I didn't want to involve anybody. Like, after this, you know, I had felt about a quarter of an inch high. If it would have been just the fucking cars blasted, even if a guy had a broken wrist or some fucking thing, I wouldn't really have cared too much."

As McGowan questioned Warren, he tried to concentrate on what was being said while at the same time thinking ahead to all the areas that had to be covered. He knew everything he said would be dissected and analyzed in the adversarial atmosphere of a courtroom. He would have to answer for everything he did. He wanted to treat Warren as well as he possibly could. He thought McMartin had used a lot of bullshit and rhetoric on Warren, but he hadn't gone too far and hadn't breached any of Warren's rights. To make sure of this, McGowan asked Warren, "Did you feel that you were threatened or had to say something, anything, on fear of a threat or a promise?"

"Not really."

"Okay, what do you mean 'not really'?"

"Not really a threat. It's just the guy said, you know, basically, like you're fucked anyways. I could've still probably caused a lot of trouble for you guys. You'd have to go and fuck around and prove this and prove that, who knows? There was, like, quite a few circumstances there. If there were any less I probably would have said, 'Fuck, I'll probably fucking fight things.'"

"Yeah."

"I'm sick of fighting. Fuck it. And I'm sick of talking to guys about it and trying to act like you're innocent. . . . I tell you, I was out hunting and I was thinking of giving it the old crack, and then I said, 'Pretty yellow fucking thing to do, leaving your wife there, holding the bag.'"

"You swear up and down that there's nobody else involved?" McGowan asked again a moment later.

"No."

"All this heat and direction that was paid to Tim and Al were for—"

"I know I couldn't fucking stand that much longer either. But I was fucking positive that they'd never arrest those guys 'cause I'm sure those guys would never do something like that. They might do something this stupid—but . . . anybody knows that they wouldn't have. They wouldn't know how to do it. They'd never do it."

McGowan asked Warren if he wanted a coffee. Warren said yes, a bit of cream and a touch of sugar. McGowan left Warren alone in the interview room.

The task force office was now full of investigators, with more being called in all the time. Gregg McMartin was surrounded, all the officers firing questions at him, including Superintendent Brian Watt. The first and most repeated query was: "Do you think these other guys are involved in it?" After thirteen months, no one could easily drop Shearing and Bettger, except for McMartin.

"I don't know," he said. "We got one set of footprints in the mine. We got one guy saying it was me and only me. And one guy who has given back all the hold-back. Are these other guys involved? I don't know if they helped plan it, but they sure as hell weren't down in the mine."

Every officer who had been part of the investigation met the news of Warren's confession with as much disbelief as relief. Ken Morrison called up McCambridge, who was on holiday with his wife, Allison, in Florida. Morrison woke McCambridge up and told him the news.

"Bullshit," McCambridge said. "Tell me something that only he would know, something new."

"McCambridge doesn't believe me," Morrison said to the others, then handed the phone over to Superintendent Watt.

"Al?" the superintendent said.

"Sir?"

"You know the hours I work—I wouldn't be here if it wasn't true."

"Yes Sir. Do you want me there?"

"No, we have the guys coming in from Edmonton."

Even though Vern White had been in the office and had listened in as McMartin broke Warren, he felt no joy. As the primary investigator, this should have been White's crowning moment. For months he had thought about it, dreamed about it and wondered how he would feel, how great the excitement would be. Yet somehow the confession was an anti-climax. He thought this huge weight would be off him. It wasn't. He had no feeling of relief at all. He wondered if it was because he disliked Tim Bettger, but he knew that wasn't it. No way would he want to arrest the wrong man.

Maybe it was like shooting a moose, White thought. You pull the trigger and that's when all the work begins. All White could think about was how much was ahead of them, getting everything out of Warren, then getting the court case together, rewriting everything they had done.

Superintendent Watt asked McMartin what the next step should be.

"The first thing is someone has got to go in and arrest him," McMartin said. "We have to now arrest him for the murder."

It might make Warren angry and uncooperative, but McMartin knew there was no choice. He had not arrested Warren because he didn't know the investigation. For all he knew, everything in Warren's confession was baloney. But now that McGowan had nailed down the details, it was time.

The Mounties had one other consideration. If McMartin's interview was found to be inadmissible in court, everything McGowan got from Warren might be inadmissible as well, the fruit of a poison tree. However, if the RCMP went in, read Warren his rights and told him he was under arrest, but he still kept talking, it would be a brand new show. It would also reinforce that his entire statement was made freely and voluntarily.

Though Warren was confessing to manslaughter, Gregg McMartin doubted that part of the story. Warren's description was strong and consistent, it sounded like the truth, but he'd had thirteen months to come up with it. It would have been just as easy for Warren to use the same trip-wire device, and instead of stringing it vertically, set it across the tracks. Even if he set it from the ground to the ceiling, he was still saying the bomb had eighty-five pounds of explosives. Warren was an experienced enough miner to know that this amount would almost certainly kill the driver of an ore train. The charge had to be murder, McMartin thought.

The Mounties hoped Warren would agree to travel into Giant Mine to reenact the crime. A second officer would be needed to guard Warren on such a trip. White went back into the room with McGowan.

"This is Vern White," McGowan said to Warren as the two officers entered. "He's the primary investigator on the matter. . . . There will be just the two of us dealing with you from now on. And I know you haven't met him."

"Vern," White said, "just call me Vern, Roger."

"There's certain formalities that we'll proceed through," McGowan continued. "One of the things is that I'm obligated to indicate to you that you are under arrest for murder and that I'm going to go over your legal rights and legal obligations." McGowan looked for a reaction, but saw none. He then repeated Warren's rights, asking again if anyone in authority had made any threats or promises that made him talk.

"No," Warren said. "Nobody did that."

McGowan had to make sure that Warren was completely willing and able to go on the reenactment. McGowan knew how a defense lawyer might try to make it look in court: here you have this poor old man, bad back, bad hands; you verbally pound him in the interview room hour after hour, drag him through the mine, walk him three miles; you push, push, push; it's a travesty.

"What we'd like to do is, we're going to re-walk that and go through this thing again," McGowan told the miner, "and there's no rush now. We don't want to peter you out there or anything like that. But we would just like to get that out of the way. . . . It'll do nothing but make the picture all the clearer for anybody, you know, down the road that has to make any decisions in respect to any difference in things, make things really clear in the eyes of the court. In this respect we want you to look at us as a vehicle to bring out everything to your advantage. We are the collection agency or the collection vehicle, and then we put it into the court process. And then the more enlightened we can make them, the better."

Warren said he had no problem with the plan. White asked him if he was hungry. Warren asked for a beef sandwich with mayo and mustard. White left to get some food.

"Is there anybody notifying my wife what's happening?" Warren asked.

"What would you like as far as that goes?" McGowan said. "What would be best for you?"

"Maybe if you had Nancy or somebody was available to go tell her that I did it, but I didn't fuckin' mean to do that."

"Okay. What I'll do is, I'll ask her."

McGowan left. Warren sat alone. Twice, he sighed heavily.

McGowan came back after talking to Defer, who had said she'd go see Helen. White came back with the sandwiches. The men made small talk as they ate, talking about the poor quality of the food. Warren said the sandwiches were probably full of sodium nitrate: "Guaranteed to give you intestinal cancer, that stuff."

Trying to lighten the mood, McGowan told a story about a summer job he'd had at a meat packing plant: "Along comes this head of this cow, and I said, 'This is trimmed up pretty good. Where are you gonna get meat off of that?' And this old, little guy next to me, he pulled everything off. He had half the beak taken off. Great big gobs of hunks of meat coming off the side. Little things in the eyes and around the eyes, he had a mound of meat like that, I couldn't believe it. Then he said, 'That's great wieners,' and he just throws in the lips and eyelids. I couldn't believe it."

The three men laughed. Warren turned the subject back to the crime, again saying that he had no idea the bomb would kill anyone. "It's amazing how convinced you are with something like that till you fuckin' start coming to daylight, and, you know, at six o'clock in the morning I was coming down the road, and that fuckin' guy come along by me. I was thinking, 'Holy fuck! How about some son of a bitch is walking back there [on 750] and just happens to stick his hand out or something?' And that's what started it. After that I was a nervous fuckin' wreck."

McGowan told Warren that his wife must have suspected he had done it.

"She had a clue, probably, anyways," Warren said. "She was always of the opinion that it was someone inside. I used to tell her that I fuckin' doubt it. I know corporations aren't that moral, but not many of them go around fuckin' deliberately trying to do stuff to their people. And you know that Sunday, when they had the big interview after that Friday," Warren said, referring to the press conference after the blast where Terry Legge lost his temper. "And all of these fuckin' guys, like Harry and them, they get me as a tech rep. Well, I really felt smart sitting around that table with Jim Evoy and all them guys. . . . You know, I'm there trying to keep these guys from coming out with outrageous fuckin' statements, eh, 'cause, fuck, I know what happened. You know, I tried to tell them, 'Nooo, you know, guys now, come on. They wouldn't fuckin' do that. Jesus.' But the guys hate that woman so fuckin' much."

Warren said he was so frazzled the morning of the blast that he told fellow striker Terry Coe about seeing the two shadowy men. "There were guys," Warren said. "I seen guys go by like that. Couple of times before, the exact same scenario, and it could have been one of them guys. But it was fuckin' security."

"But you didn't see anybody that time?" White asked.

"Not that night, no. I wasn't even up there. But I had seen before. This same thing had happened before."

"So you never, never asked anybody to give you a hand or keep an eye out for you or nothing?" White asked.

"No. Fuck," Warren chuckled. "If you're gonna do something like that, do it by yourself. You guys would have known about it a week later if anybody would have been with me or helped me or any fuckin' thing. I'm sure there's guys that had suspicions of me."

After the bomb went off, Warren said he went back to Yellowknife to the Polar Bowl for lunch. He heard on the TV that the men were dead. One striker's wife took off screaming. "I was racking my fuckin' brain. Like, how in the fuck? . . . Must be hauling guys in a fuckin' ore car. . . . I just felt horrible about it. Jeez, you'd never think of hurting a guy underground. Last thing in your head."

"It's that old-time miner's credo," McGowan said.

"Just fuckin' horrible," Warren said. "And then six guys that you know. There was a couple of them I knew pretty good. Fuckin' Vern

Fullowka, I was gonna lend him money for fuck sakes. . . . The rest of them guys—I didn't really know them too good. But just the same, fuck. If those nine volts wouldn't have worked I would have just did that shaft trick, and away I would have went."

Warren started thinking back to his interview with McMartin. He couldn't remember the officer's name, but said, "He was trying to tell me, he said, 'Well, that took a lot of balls.' What the fuck, balls? It was a lack of fuckin' brains. If it woulda worked out, nobody would have gotten fuckin' hurt. Or at least not killed. Would have been something you could think about in a few years without getting too shaky. But I know I started shaking at six in the morning, and I didn't fuckin' stop all day. I went and laid down in bed. I couldn't even sleep."

Warren recalled meeting another CASAW man on the day of the blast. "He says, 'What the fuck was Joe Pandev doing in there?' He said, 'I can't believe that guy was in there and crossed the line.' I said, 'Well, you do what you gotta do, I guess.' He says, 'You know, the way you gotta look at this, Roger, if they weren't there, they couldn't get hurt.' And I was thinking to myself, 'That's fuckin' easy for you to say, partner.' Jesus fuck."

Warren spoke with such conviction about his regret that White and McGowan were starting to feel sorry for him. Maybe he was telling the truth. Maybe he hadn't meant to kill. McGowan kept thinking about all the jerks he'd interviewed in his career, how he would give them their Charter warning, and they'd take a hike and there was nothing he could do. But here was Warren confessing to mass murder, a fellow who seemed to have a good moral fabric, but he was spilling, just babbling away.

Just shut up, Roger, McGowan thought to himself. You have said enough.

White left to go to his house to pick up sweats and sweatshirts for himself and McGowan and a sweater for Warren for the reenactment trip into the mine. Warren asked for a newspaper. He got an *Edmonton Journal*. McGowan left him; at once, he went to work on the crossword puzzle. Alone in the room, Warren sighed. "Fuck," he said. He dug into the puzzle, finishing it in fifteen minutes.

McGowan decided to make a quick call to his wife. Sheila was still up watching TV in Hay River.

"We got him," McGowan said.

"What?"

"We got the confession. I can't talk very much now. We're going to go down in the mine."

Sheila asked who it was.

"Roger Warren."

She had never heard the name before, but it didn't matter. She was elated. It's fate, she thought. It's fate that Dale is there in the end, after all the sacrifice.

Just before 1:00 A.M., Saturday, October 16, Warren and the RCMP officers left to head out to Giant Mine. In the women's change room at the C-dry, the men changed into underground coveralls, steel-reinforced mining boots, hard-hats with mining lamps and belts with generators. Warren's movements were carefully controlled, and McGowan could see something click in him just then. He became more downcast. It was as if he realized that the rest of his life would be like this. He couldn't go home. He couldn't stop at a store. He had to do exactly what he was told. He was a prisoner.

The group drove out to Akaitcho, parked, then walked up to the black headframe. Welders had removed the steel mesh over the shaft.

"This will be the last time I'll be going underground," Warren told McGowan. "The next time I'll be six feet under."

The plan for the reenactment was for Warren to lead the way. Vern White would ask him the questions, forcing Warren to again explain himself fully to someone who hadn't heard the story.

The group was accompanied by two RCMP Ident officers with a still camera and video camera, and by Rob Moore, a Royal Oak manager. Moore was told he should say nothing to Warren, even if Warren spoke to him. At the top of the shaft, it crossed Moore's mind to push Warren down. He might have done it, but for all he knew Warren still might implicate others in a murder conspiracy.

White used a hand-held microphone to interview Warren. The old-time miner looked down, his eyes rarely meeting the camera, his most noticeable feature his thick, dark eyebrows. Compared with White and McGowan, he looked ragged, the strain of thirteen months of deception showing.

White read Warren his rights, then asked, "Okay, Roger, I'd like you to explain to us now where we're standing."

"We're at the Akaitcho headframe."

"Okay, I'd like you to explain to us the last time you were at this location."

"It was September 18, 1992, probably around 2:00 A.M."

Warren described how he got in by standing on the barrel. Then White asked, "Was anyone with you at that time?"

"No, I was alone."

The men started down the ladders at 1:30 A.M.—White, Warren, McGowan, then explosives expert Gary Christison, then Ident men Wayne Locke and Scott McKenzie, then Moore. As they started their descent, a rock fell—boom, boom, boom, boom, boom—crashing into the darkness. A moment later another rock fell, landing square on McGowan's helmet. The blow hurt like hell. McGowan figured if the rock had hit his shoulder, it would have broken it for sure.

Both White and McGowan were nervous, wondering if the old wood planks would hold their bulk. McGowan tried not to look down, just stare at the rung in front of his face. He could hear Warren giving advice on where to walk and what to hold. The officers were thankful they were with the miner, although they were worried Warren might try to jump. McGowan knew they would be in big-time trouble if he did, but how could they get around it? They could harness Warren, but then if he jumped he'd take two lives instead of just one.

The group made it to the bottom of the shaft.

"What's your condition now, Roger? You okay to continue on?" McGowan asked.

"Oh yeah."

"Not tired or anything?"

"No."

Though McGowan knew the videotape would bring the mine and the crime to life for the judge and jury, he worried about how he and White would be perceived. He feared the whole thing might look oppressive, with little old Warren crunched into an eight-foot by eight-foot shaft, smack between two big, burly cops. To make up for that, McGowan decided to continually ask Warren how he was feeling.

The group set off behind Warren, making the one-mile trek toward the blast site. Warren set a fast pace. He hunched over, his head forward so it wouldn't hit anything. He walked down the middle of the tracks, pounding over holes, rocks and ditches, clunk, clunk, clunk, clunk. He never hesitated. He knew exactly where he was going.

As they neared the 712-scoop shop, they heard the popping of distant explosions. McGowan thought it was the central blast, but it was just some minor blasting. It occurred to him how strange this night was; it was a little more than a year to the day after the blast, and now they were again walking through the mine to the scene of the crime. We're doing it again, McGowan thought. You're doing it again, Roger.

Warren took the team to all the main spots, the 712-scoop shop, the 907-powder magazine and 712-cap magazine. They had a coffee in the scoop shop.

"This is exactly the way I felt on that night because it's sure tuckering me out," Warren said.

Along with the recorder on the camera, McGowan taped Warren on his microcassette. It was damp and cold in the mine and McGowan thought it wouldn't hurt to double up; this turned out to be wise because the microphone on the camera started to malfunction, missing large chunks of the conversation.

Warren told his story in great detail. He spoke easily now that he didn't have to rack his brains for what he had said before. The story came right from his memory, right down to the fact that when he picked up the scoop that night, the engine was still warm, the night shift having left just a few minutes earlier.

The group headed toward the blast site. Warren told them to stop at the exact location. Though he was the primary investigator, White had never been to the site. For the first time, the reality of the crime hit him. He looked around at the pipes, dirt floor, train tracks, the shallow remnant of the crater.

Jesus, White thought, nine people got the shit blown out of them right here.

McGowan felt dread. It still seemed like a mass grave to him. The last time he was here, human remains were everywhere. Now, nine white crosses were painted on the walls.

Warren started talking about what he had done, but McGowan was dissatisfied. "Can you just maybe kneel down and show us exactly the angle you might have put it and describe in a little more detail as to what you did and how the setup was?"

Warren stooped and went to work, pantomiming the assembly of his bomb, anchoring the drill steel, rigging the trip wire, hooking up the B-line to enable the device. McGowan knew the jury would have to

330 The Third Suspect

be convinced by this. The detail was so precise, Warren saying he had to try three times to properly anchor the drill steel, that he tested the trip wire, found it was tight, loosened it so no vibration would set it off and covered the bomb with a cardboard box so no one would see it.

McGowan now believed that he had everything he needed. He decided to push Warren about his intent. If Warren stopped talking now, nothing much would be lost.

"You've worked in the mines before," he said. "What did you think was gonna happen with that explosion?"

"Well, I worked in the mines for a long time, but I never once in my life ever put a bag of powder somewhere beside a drift and let it go, so I wasn't that sure. . . . It probably would have been better off if I would have blew myself up. But it didn't happen, and what else can I say?"

"Just one more thing, and I'd like your honest opinion here," McGowan said. "The last time you were here, since that time there's been nine people who died in this very area as a result of actions that you took. Do you have any thoughts about that right now?"

"Well, I've been dreadfully sorry about it for over a year now. And what else can you say? I mean, there's nothing's ever gonna repay that."

All the men were tired now. It would have been ideal to retrace Warren's route out of the mine, but it was approaching 6:00 A.M. The men decided to take the C-shaft elevator up and finish shooting their video at the B-138 portal.

When they got there and turned on the camera, White asked Warren if he was okay with what had happened or if he had thought he needed a lawyer.

"No, I was okay. Nobody coerced me into anything. It was my own decision."

Warren agreed to one final task. The group headed out of town to find the pond where he said he had chucked his bag full of supplies. They found the small slough, surrounded by pines, poplars and the hardrock of the Canadian Shield. It was only a few yards off the highway. Warren pointed out where he had tossed the bag. The group headed back to town. Light snow drifted down from the dark sky. After turning Warren over to the guards at the RCMP detachment's jail, White drove McGowan down the street to the Explorer. It was now after 8:00 A.M. They had been up for twenty-four hours.

All the way back from the pond, White had been in a contemplative mood. More than anything, he felt sad for Warren. He believed Warren's story. He could see in Warren his own father, Hector, and the other old-time miners of Cape Breton, not necessarily in the killer, but in the man who had helped him and McGowan navigate the Akaitcho mine shaft. The Cape Breton miners lived for the mine just like Warren, and being down in Giant had reminded White of just what an awful job it was. These guys deserved sainthood, he thought. What a way to make a living, to live in a hole in the ground all your life, and then to have a strike and the company bring in scabs. It would have killed his dad and his union mates.

In Cape Breton they had never made much money either. Vern remembered how his dad had to borrow money to buy him a saxophone in grade nine. Jesus, Vern could spend $200 and think nothing of it.

He could see his dad, four months off work, his job going down the tubes, broke, unable to provide for his family, and there were the scabs taking his check. Hector White would have been right up there fighting. He was a believer. He preached the union. He lived it. If anyone had tried anything like this in Cape Breton, it would have been worse than in Yellowknife, and they wouldn't have had to wait for months to pass. There would have been deaths on the picket line. For sure one of those men could have gone in the mine to set a bomb, not thinking he was going to kill, then realizing it too late, just like Roger Warren said he had. That didn't excuse what Warren did. But his story was nonetheless tragic.

Just before dropping off McGowan at the Explorer, White turned to him. "You know, I could see someone like my father doing that," he said.

"Is that right?"

"Yeah. He wouldn't even think about it until it was too late. I can see him saying, 'I can't do anything about it. God, if I go back down I'll get caught. I just hope it doesn't work.'"

McGowan got out of the vehicle.

"We're getting the Stockholm syndrome," White smiled, referring to a victim's willingness over time to empathize with the hostage taker. Then White drove away through the whispery snow.

Chapter 21

THE
CELL
JOB

A T NOON ON SATURDAY, OCTOBER 16, 1993, Dale McGowan reported to the task force office. He'd had only three hours sleep. At once he was swarmed by officers wanting to shake his hand. Both Inspector Al McIntyre, who had flown in from Ottawa on the RCMP jet, and Superintendent Brian Watt congratulated him and Sergeant Vern White for their work in the reenactment.

The investigators felt they had enough to convict Warren of murder, but any good investigator knew there was never enough damning evidence, not when things could go haywire in a second during a trial. Reporters outside the task force office clamored for interviews, but the Mounties' first task was to get Warren to take them out to Cameron Falls for another videotaped reenactment, this time showing how he had burned his boots. In the slough outside town, divers had already found Warren's satchel of items left over from building the bomb. The police hoped to locate fragments of the burned boots as well.

The day was clear and just above freezing, about average for Yellowknife in mid-October. At 3:00 P.M., McGowan and White met Warren in his cell and asked if he would be willing to do the reenactment. Warren had no problem with the plan, though he felt as down as he'd been since he started confessing. Sitting in a twelve-foot by twelve-foot cell had made him realize the enormity of what had happened. He had slept fitfully on his narrow bunk, his rest interrupted every fifteen minutes by a guard checking on him. The guards had been instructed to say nothing to Warren, just to make sure he wasn't trying to hurt himself.

Warren knew he had ruined his and Helen's life. He feared she would abandon him if she hadn't already. Why hadn't she come to see him yet? And what about the union guys? Warren wanted to see some of them. He was tired of seeing only cops.

Before heading out from the detachment, McGowan and White asked Warren if he wanted to see a lawyer. "Well, I should get one, one of these times," he said.

Warren was taken to a private room. He tried to call the union's lawyer for criminal matters, Austin Marshall. He couldn't get through. White showed Warren a list of lawyers, but the miner said he didn't need one after all, that all he really wanted to do was contact Helen. McGowan asked Warren if he was still willing to go to Cameron Falls. Warren said he would go, that he could talk to Helen later.

The three men pulled out in an unmarked police car, White driving, McGowan in the back seat with Warren. Just then, Warren broke down sobbing. He told White and McGowan that he had never lied so much in his life, that lying was almost as bad as killing the nine guys.

"It's okay, buddy," McGowan said, putting his hand on Warren's shoulder. "There was a lot of weight on your shoulders. There's no doubt about it. . . . We understand that sometimes good people make mistakes, and there's definitely no question as to the amount of pressure you guys were under. You know, it can drive a guy to do some strange things at times. So we understood that."

"You okay now, Roger?" White asked.

"Yeah."

"Like coffee?"

"Yeah, that'd be a good idea."

McGowan didn't want Warren blubbering. An emotional man was more likely to feel self-conscious, then shut up and stop cooperating. White drove to the McDonald's drive-thru, then the men headed out on the Ingraham Trail toward the mine site on their way to Cameron Falls. Before they passed the picket gates, McGowan told Warren he could duck his head. McGowan didn't like to parade any prisoner around. There was no need for that, not if society was supposed to be civilized. Parading prisoners was like public hangings or the pillory. Warren slumped a bit when they passed the other strikers.

As they drove, McGowan thought about this new story from Warren about burning the boots and throwing them in the water. The Ident guys were sure the footprints through the mine were made by size eleven Kamik boots, not the size ten boots that Warren was now saying he had destroyed at the falls. Warren had no reason to lie now about his boots, but he was only human, McGowan thought. He could make a mistake. Maybe he was wrong about what boots he wore into the mine. Maybe he had two pairs of boots at the time of the blast, and he had on the size eleven Kamiks but didn't realize it. Maybe he burned the wrong boots.

Just as the men parked, Constable Randy McBride caught up to them. McBride had a message from McIntyre asking White to make sure they asked Warren more about his intent between 6:00 and 9:00 A.M. on the morning of the explosion. Warren had had at least two hours to call in a bomb threat, but he hadn't done it.

The men started walking toward the falls. They were guarded by two members of the ERT team, armed with semiautomatic pistols and submachine guns. At the top of the first rocky precipice, the rush of the water could be heard more than half a mile away. The trail descended into the valley, weaving its way through trees, marsh and rock. The hike took half an hour. Warren took them to the edge of the river, where a video was shot of him describing to White how he had destroyed the size ten Kamik boots. Warren said he had walked in with a plastic milk jug full of gasoline, then cut up the boots, soaked them with gas and set them on fire. He threw the scraps in the water.

Warren himself found the fire pit where he had burned the boots. Under a rock, Locke found a large chunk of melted rubber. Divers found the charred remnants of the boots in the river the next day.

On their way back to Yellowknife, McGowan drove while White sat in the back with Warren. White focused on McIntyre's directive regarding Warren's intent. White asked what Warren had thought would happen to the loki driver, even if there were seven cars in the ore train.

"In retrospect, he'd probably be either seriously injured—or maybe even dead," Warren said.

McGowan asked if Warren understood at the time that someone might get hurt by his bomb.

"Of course I did," Warren said. "Anytime you're using explosives there's always the possibility. If you say something else, it's just a lie."

When he realized he might kill someone, Warren said he should have called the mine. "I was going to and I just didn't. Like, I've kicked myself a thousand times since. But I didn't. It was a combination of indecision and basically cowardice. I'll admit it."

The convoy drove past the mine site again, then into town, traveling below the rocky hill where the Explorer was perched.

"Dale?" Warren said.

"Yes, Roger?"

"What's gonna happen to me now?"

McGowan told Warren that Crown prosecutor Peter Martin would come up and lay charges and that a defense lawyer would meet with him, maybe in his cell.

As they pulled in front of the detachment they saw a press scrum at the front door, but none of the media saw them drive into the garage. McGowan took Warren to his cell. Before dropping him off, he again told Warren he could have a lawyer.

"I have no fuckin' time for lawyers," Warren said.

McGowan left Warren then. He met White in the hallway and found out that two more RCMP officers, Dean Ravelli and Mike Brandford, were preparing for another interview with Warren. McIntyre wanted a fresh team to go in, a set of fresh ears to listen to the story, but also new officers whom Warren had never met; he would feel no need to talk to them, which again drove home the point that everything he was saying was being given freely and voluntarily.

McGowan told White that Warren had to talk to a lawyer now, that he had asked for one before going out to Cameron Falls, and if they didn't get him one it might become an issue.

McGowan was ready to go home to Hay River. It would have churned in him forever if he had walked away with no answers, but now he could leave knowing he had done his job.

While Warren was at Cameron Falls, his family and the union had been trying to reach him. Helen Warren had contacted Harry Seeton. Austin Marshall had visited the RCMP detachment and had also left messages.

After hearing about the contents of White's interview with Warren on the intent issue, Peter Martin told McIntyre to write up an information sheet charging Warren with nine counts of murder.

At 6:37 P.M. Warren was introduced to Ravelli and Brandford. Warren answered their questions about the blast. After forty-five minutes, RCMP bomb expert Jean-Yves Vermette came in to get still more details. Warren drew another picture of the device. The interview was interrupted repeatedly, three times so Warren could talk to various defense lawyers, and once so a Justice of the Peace could read Warren the nine formal charges of first degree murder.

Next, Warren went with the police as they searched his apartment. Nobody was home. Warren led the investigators to his hard-hat in the closet. He showed them coveralls, a knife and a belt he had used in the mine. The police also seized fishing line, plastic tubing and a copy of "Footsteps of the Murderer."

Just before 10:00 P.M., Warren was taken back to his cell, only to discover another prisoner there. The new prisoner sat on the bottom bunk, a middle-aged fellow, slightly bigger than Warren, with longish, silvery white hair. He wore a striped white and green shirt, blue jeans and white runners.

The prisoner looked up at the guards. "It's cold in here. When do I get some smokes?"

He then turned to Warren. "Whatever you do don't wake up the guy next door. I don't think he's all there."

"Hey, no," Warren said.

The cell had a double bunk bed with a metal frame. The mattress was a thin, rolled piece of foam covered with gray plastic. There were no pillows, except for the books the guards had left in the cell, which the prisoners slipped under the mattress. Each bed had a thin blanket. A stainless steel toilet and sink sat in one corner of the mustard yellow, cinder block cell.

The stranger sat on the lower bunk. "Is this your bed?" he asked Warren. "'Cause I'll take the top bed. You want to lay down?"

"No, I'll sit here," Warren said, then sat down beside the stranger. The two started to talk. To get comfortable, both men put blankets behind their backs so they could lean against the cold cement wall without feeling the chill.

"Do you smoke?" the stranger asked.

"Yeah, yeah," Warren said. "I ran out, too. . . . It's a rule here that you can't smoke."

"Like, they won't give you one? 'Cause I got some in there in my stuff."

"I can't believe I'm in fuckin' jail," Warren said.

"Yeah," the stranger agreed.

Just then Corporal Brandford came into the cell area. "You want some smokes, I'll only give you one."

Brandford handed over the cigarette, then left.

"Those guys must be the plainclothes guys or something," the stranger said.

"They're Homicide."

"That's all they do?"

"Right at the moment that's all they do. I've been charged."

The stranger introduced himself as Harry. He asked Warren how long he had lived in Yellowknife, which led Warren to mention Giant Mine and the labor dispute. "We been on strike here now since fuckin' May 22 last year."

"Yeah, I heard something about that there. Still no hope, eh?"

"No."

A moment later, Harry asked Warren if he knew who had won that night's opening game of the 1993 World Series between the Toronto Blue Jays and the Philadelphia Phillies.

"No," Warren said. "Fuckin', we were just over at my house, and I was hopin' my daughter would be home. She always watches it."

Harry mentioned that he was up in the Territories looking for work when he got picked up by the cops. "I'm a butcher. I've done some bartending, too, but what happened is, I got to bartend now because, well, the reason I'm in here is fuckin' support."

"Oh yeah.'"

"The old lady. And if I make any money, they'll come after me. . . . The thing is, last time I was in court, like, I said to the judge, like, 'Putting me in jail doesn't help me pay the money.' They give me so long to pay, but I've been trying. Fuck, you can't get work. It's tough, and if you make too much money then they just want you to pay fuckin' more."

"Fuckin' cocksuckers," Warren said.

"Well, it's getting to be bullshit."

"If it was reasonable, I could see it," Warren said, "But fuck, the worst thing about it, the guy pays support usually because he's got kids and God knows how much of that's getting to the kids."

Just then the guard brought in their supper trays.

"You know who won the ball game?" Harry asked him.

"Last I heard it was 4–4."

The two men started into their meal of roast beef.

"It's not what I would call totally fuckin' delectable," Warren said. "Not even a fuckin' serviette."

"No eh," Harry said.

"Jesus Christ. My wife ain't the best cook in town, but it makes this stuff taste good."

"How long have you been married now?"

"Since April of 1970."

"Holy fuck!"

"Yeah, probably the fuckin' smartest thing I did."

The two men began to chat casually, complaining about high prices, low corporate taxes, Canada's national debt and the coming federal election, then returning to the World Series.

"Be nice to see the Blue Jays win it again," Harry said.

"Yeah, just to piss off the Americans," Warren said. "So goddamn arrogant."

Warren stopped eating for a moment. "Most of this fuckin' shit would gag a fuckin' maggot."

"The union pretty strong out here?" Harry asked a moment later.

"No, not really. But this was not much to do with the union, really. Just that this place is the first place that in fuckin' near fifty years that anybody ever used a replacement worker in the fuckin' mine."

"Is that right?"

"They just never did that."

"How long they keeping you in here now?"

"Oh, if they got their way it would be about fuckin' thirty years."

"Thirty years is a long time."

"Oh, I'm gonna be here forever."

"Let me put this together now. You said these guys are Homicide?"

"Yeah, that's what it is."

"Oh, is that right? Am I okay to go to sleep tonight?"

"Oh yeah, that could be the only fuckin' thing that will save me from life is I never did nothing before or since."

"What's the charges?"

"Well, last year I think there was fuckin' seven guys coming down the fuckin' track."

"Right."

"Seven or nine guys that got fuckin' killed."

"Oh yeah."

"Well, I'm the fuckin' guy who was responsible for that."

"Is that right?"

"I was not directly responsible. I had this thing set up so that type of fuckin' vehicle wouldn't hit, but it did. Somehow some vibration or whatever the fuck. I had it set up so that only one type of thing could hit it was the fuckin' cars that carried ore."

"Uh."

"But whatever happened it didn't fuckin' work that way."

"So that's what they got you charged with. It's all over the mine strike."

"I don't think any of them believe that I actually meant to do that because I mean, fuckin', I played hockey with those guys and everything for years and years. But they knew I went there deliberately and fuckin' did something. And, of course, they're gonna charge me with the highest fuckin' count, eh. First degree. Then it's up to a lawyer to try to get that reduced to fuckin' whatever, manslaughter, criminal negligence causing death, whatever. If they even can, I don't know. I told 'em, I showed them everything I did."

Harry listened intently. It was his job. He was RCMP Corporal Harry Ingram, and as Warren got into the details of the blast, he knew he was going to succeed, that Warren was ripe to tell him everything. That didn't surprise Ingram. He was an expert at undercover work.

The plan to put an agent in with the arrested murderer had been in place for six months, though Ingram didn't know he would be the one and only got the call to come up to Yellowknife after Warren had started confessing on Friday night.

That evening, Ingram had been in Rocky Mountain House, in central Alberta, keeping tabs on a drug pusher from a surveillance van. He got a call telling him he was needed at Edmonton's Municipal Airport by midnight.

"I'll stop in at home to get a change of clothes," Ingram said.

"Where you're going, you won't need a change of clothes," his boss said, and Ingram realized he was going to jail.

He had less than two hours to get to Edmonton, a trip that usually took three. He jumped in an unmarked police car, a 1993 black Grand Prix. He couldn't find the switch for the siren, but roared ahead anyway at 110 miles an hour. He pulled into the RCMP hangar in Edmonton with ten minutes to spare. The flight was packed with investigators from Edmonton, an RCMP handler and his dog, and Crown prosecutor Ron Reimer, who had worked with Bill Farrell on the wiretaps. The other investigators talked about the files they had worked on for more than a year, none of it making much sense to Ingram. He felt like the kid coming in from the sticks. He did gather, however, that everyone was surprised that Roger Warren was the man, instead of two other suspects. Ingram was content in his ignorance. The easiest way for him to be a stranger to Warren was to know nothing or only what he had read in the newspapers.

While Ingram hadn't heard much about the murder investigation, the officers on the airplane had all heard of him. His name was synonymous with undercover work. He'd been involved in more than sixty clandestine operations and had brought down hundreds of bad guys, most of them drug dealers. In a pulp fiction novel, Ingram would be the lead detective. He grew up in a strict religious family, no drinking, smoking, gambling or television allowed, but he grew up to be a smoker, a drinker, a lady's man and an obsessive worker. He was thirty-eight and had been divorced twice.

Ingram relished his work. He bent the rules as far as they could go. He had faced dozens of internal investigations, but none had stuck. His bosses worried that he drank too much and once stipulated that he could stay undercover only as long as he stayed dry. He was as comfortable sitting at a bar talking to cops as he was shooting pool with bikers, pimps, addicts and dealers. He never worried too much about playing roles. He told the cons his name was Harry. He just tried to be himself. He usually fit in so well that people never asked him for his story, but if they did, he stuck close to his own life, maybe saying he worked in a grocery store—he'd actually been an assistant produce and meat manager before he got on with the RCMP. Ingram was so believable that when it was time to bust one drug dealer, the fearsome leader of a bike gang named the Bounty Hunters, the biker laughed and wouldn't believe that Ingram was a cop. But when Ingram walked into the cell the next day, the biker said, "I'm going to kill you."

He had done undercover work for fifteen years, first in Calgary, then Victoria, British Columbia. His hair had gone from brown to silvery gray. He wore it long at times, other times in an Afro. At six feet and two hundred pounds, he had a cop's build. He used to envy the guys who were ethnic or skinny or just 5'7". He did what he could to fit in, dressing like a normal Joe, which was actually how most criminals dressed. He tried to avoid looking too rough, like a biker or a thug. He wanted trust, not fear.

He had done a few cell jobs earlier in his career. He had the perfect qualifications in those days: he was single, available and he looked like a shithead. But he hadn't gone into any prison cells in recent years, not since the new Charter of Rights. No longer could the police throw an agent in with a bad guy who had refused to talk to them. Even if the criminal told his story to an agent, not for a second thinking he was talking to someone in authority, the courts would throw out the confession. The bad guy had a right to silence and a right to a lawyer, and if he had refused to talk to officers in uniform, he didn't have to talk to one in a T-shirt and jeans.

The RCMP suspended cell jobs for a time until the rules were worked out in the courts. In the end the police decided to use the tactic only to bolster an already strong case, such as when a man had confessed. He might tell the agent something more than he would tell a cop. In Warren's case the hope was that he might be more willing to admit to a cell mate that someone else was involved in the crime. There was also one other prime consideration: if Warren's other confessions were thrown out of court because a judge ruled that Warren had been intimidated by people in authority, there would be a chance a confession to an agent might still stand. If Warren didn't know Ingram was a cop, Warren's lawyer couldn't argue that he had talked because he felt threatened or had been offered something.

Ingram thought he would be heading immediately into the cell when he arrived in Yellowknife, but he was put on standby because of Warren's all-night reenactment in the mine. The following day Constable Charlie Chetwynd came to his room in the Explorer to brief him. Ingram thought the investigators would present a cover story to him, but Chetwynd told him to say whatever he felt comfortable with.

Ingram and Chetwynd planned to go watch the World Series, but on their way to a restaurant they were paged and told to get to the office. Ingram was going to jail.

The guards hadn't been told that Harry was a police officer. He was stripped, ordered to face the wall, hands over his head and feet apart. The guards checked every part of his body, including his anus. His clothes were handed back to him, and he was taken to Warren's cell.

As he and Warren started talking, Ingram tried to take a passive role. He wasn't there to interrogate the miner; he was there to be an everyday guy with everyday concerns and average curiosity. Once Warren got talking about the crime, Ingram played dumb, saying he had no idea how to set up a dynamite charge, in order to get Warren to describe his act in layman's terms.

Ingram only had to nod and make a few comments for Warren to keep talking. Warren appeared seized by a need to confess and keep confessing. He was going on only a few hours sleep and had been talking almost nonstop for two days. He worked his way to the issues of the strike, how Peggy Witte brought in scabs and the riot at the mine that led to riot cops coming in and a bunch of strikers getting charged. "Like, this fuckin' shit should never have happened," Warren said. "Like, as soon as there was that violence I knew that place should have been shut the fuck down. . . . That woman should have fucked off. She's just a fuckin' American hooker."

Warren's thoughts jumped all over, but always returned to his own predicament and how it would play out in court. "I know I could have stayed out of jail for years," he said. "They never would have caught me. They had some fuckin' circumstantial shit. I doubt if they ever would have gone to court ever."

"Must be a relief though?" Ingram asked.

"In a way. It's like this is what it's got to be now. I've taken the guilt off me. I'm fucking up not only nine guys, but the fuckin' one hundred people that are left in the fuckin' union. But now I gotta balance that against my wife and two kids. Apparently my wife is real fucked up."

"So you been in here for a year and a half now?" Ingram asked.

"In here?"

"Yeah."

"Oh fuck no. Yesterday at 5:30, 6:00—that's the first fuckin' time I was ever in custody. . . . Well, go get a university degree, I guess. Fuck it."

"Is there anything I can do for you, Roger?"

"Not much," Warren chuckled. "Not unless you got a .22 there that won't hurt much."

"A guy never wants to do that."

"No, fuck. I thought about it last year, and then I said, 'I can't do that. Fuckin' get on with it.'"

Ingram asked Warren if the union would stand behind him.

"Well, according to the lawyer, they're doing everything that I told them because they are just so fuckin' happy that I didn't implicate them, none of them. I mean, I'd never try to blame them or fuck all. It had nothing to do with those guys. You just decide it's on your own shoulders. Nobody helped me. Nobody fuckin' covered for me."

"What do you want to learn in prison?" Ingram asked.

"A brain surgeon, fuck it," Warren said and both men laughed.

"Yeah," Ingram said. "I thought you were gonna say a gynecologist."

The two men had connected. One was in for murder, one supposedly for nonpayment of support, but Ingram worked hard to put himself on the same level as Warren. The system had screwed them over, and now they were stuck in the same crappy cell with no coffee and no smokes.

Warren told Ingram about his attempt to convince his wife to put all their assets under her name. "But I couldn't tell her why. I couldn't. She kept saying, 'What are you, crazy? What if something happens to me?' Because fuckin' people will fuckin' try to sue you! You know, we got this bullshit victims of crime shit, eh."

"Yeah."

"Oh yeah. It's not bad enough you're fuckin' tied up for life, but they still want to take every fuckin' cent you got. . . . They'll want to see my mother, my fuckin' wife, my kids fucked up."

When a guard walked by, the two men learned that the score in the World Series game was 8–4 for Toronto. The conversation eventually trailed off. Through the night, Warren snored loudly, keeping Ingram awake. Both men were up and talking again by 5:00 A.M. on Sunday, October 17.

Warren was happy to have finally slept well, but now that he felt stronger and rested he was less inclined to kick himself for what had happened and more inclined to focus on Peggy Witte and the federal government. He loved the idea that his confession might force an end to the strike, even if Witte didn't want it to end. "Makes me fuckin' mad just wondering what kind of excuse she's gonna come up with now," he said. "It would be a dandy, I can fuckin' tell you. But I think now if you come up with an excuse now, I think you'll be fuckin' toast."

"Yeah," Ingram said.

"Tell her to get the fuck out of the country probably or something. People are fed up with her fuckin' shit you know. None of this stuff would have ever happened. Some stupid fuckin' Yankee cocksucker. And then you got a fucker like Mulroney there, fuckin' suckin' American cock all his life, that faggot. I mean, if I was really gonna fuckin' try to kill somebody, the cocksucker, he'd make a prime candidate, fuck."

"What is she using for an excuse for not settling now?" Ingram asked.

"Oh, she said she can't settle till there's charges brought on this murder case, eh."

"Oh, is that right?"

"Well, now there's fuckin' charges. Now what's your excuse, you fuckin' fat cunt? I'd like to see that, that's what I'd like to see. Well, it's the only fuckin' reason that'd ever make me fuckin' tell 'em. Who cares? Fuck it. . . . But I couldn't live any longer with thinking, 'Jesus, if we had somebody arrested, is this the only thing that's really keeping these fuckin' guys from getting the fuckin' strike settled?' I doubt it, but let's fuckin' see. It's twenty years for me, maybe, to find out, but it might be worth it, you know. That's the way I was thinking. It's like you're thinking rationally, but I'll tell you there'll be some fuckin' fury if that woman puts a straw in front of fuckin' settling that thing now. And now the guys are probably demanding all the replacement workers to get the fuck out of there."

The two moved on to talk about other matters, including Warren's various back and hand problems, his baseball ability, his mining technique, then back to Peggy Witte, but this time Warren praised her for being a strong entrepreneur, especially when it came to raising money. "Like, she's not fuckin' stupid, no question about it. I admire her actually, and she's good at that stuff. But she's one of these people, she's got her ideas. Like, she thinks she's in 1925 fuckin' Alabama or some place. Even the Americans don't do that shit now."

Warren told Ingram that during the strike it seemed like everyone was against the union, Witte and Royal Oak, Mulroney and the government, the courts, the RCMP. "Nobody's helping you. That's why those other guys did stupid fuckin' shit."

"Just kinda builds and builds."

"Yeah. What happens is, it gets into a fuckin' war."

Warren rambled on hour after hour through the morning and afternoon. Ingram was certain Warren had no idea he was a cop. He certainly didn't feel like a cop. He was so close to Warren now that there wasn't much room for lies. Ingram wasn't necessarily on Warren's side, but he understood the miner's frustration. He could see how things would get ugly with replacement workers. He wasn't offended by the intensity of Warren's hatred. His job was to soak it up until all of it was gone, until Warren had nothing new to say.

"Fuck, it was madness is what it was," Warren continued. "And I just couldn't believe I did it. Went around for fuckin' weeks there in a fuckin' daze. Like fuck, even if the fuckin' car did hit it, you'd kill the guy on the fuckin' motor. I didn't even fuckin' regret it. That's the kind of mind-set you needed."

"Yeah," Ingram said.

"You got guys in there and you fuckin' despise the cocksuckers. You can say, 'Well, I don't hate 'em bad enough to kill 'em,' but it gives you a way different outlook. . . . You kind of disregard the other guy's safety. Well, he gets a little fucked up, it won't bother the fuck-up. But, you know, you'd feel terrible about it, but at the same time when you're doing something, you say, 'Ah, fuck this, who gives a shit?' Like, it's a weird fuckin' way to be. Well, it's like a fuckin' war. Look what people do to each other in war. That's fuckin' hate."

If someone else had ever been charged for the mass murder, Warren said he would have gone in and confessed. "Them guys didn't do it, but they tried to let on they did it. I knew that. 'Cause I talked to those guys, I told 'em that I wouldn't believe it, that's just bullshit."

"Weren't they worried?"

"A little bit, yeah. Well, you can fuckin' imagine."

"Yeah."

"But I told 'em, 'You're just lucky that's the RCMP and not a fuckin' provincial police force 'cause you guys would've been locked up a long time ago. The RCMP, they're pretty fuckin' careful. Even when they're positive themselves, they don't ever do nothing until they're fuckin' absolutely sure beyond any doubt that they can get a conviction."

Ingram arranged to leave the cell for the moment on the pretext of making a phone call. Outside, he talked to his handler, Charlie

Chetwynd, asking if he could turn it into a more aggressive interview, asking more pointed questions. Chetwynd told Ingram he'd have to talk to the bosses first. If they decided to go ahead with the plan, Ingram would hear a horn tooting in the parking lot.

Ingram returned to the cell. The longer he was with Warren, the more Warren minimized the enormity of his act. Each time Warren ran through his story, he presented himself as less and less responsible for what had happened. He seemed shallow and noncommittal when he talked about the bomb, as if he had no deep feelings about killing the men. But he was angry that he'd been charged with first degree murder. "I can say this at most is total criminal negligence," he told Ingram. "But if somebody just tries to prove that's fuckin' deliberate, they're gonna have to have one fuck of a smart lawyer. I can't believe it."

"Well, I wonder how that works," Ingram said. "Murderer, eh?"

"'Cause the only thing that is to decide in court now is, like, what is the ultimate fuckin' charge on the thing. It's not a case of see who did it, or prove that somebody did it. It's, like, what was in his head when he did it? And all they got to go by is past fuckin' behavior, really. And very little else."

The next time a guard came by, Ingram spoke up, asking if he could ask his superior officer if it would be all right for them to have a cup of coffee.

"I'll try," the guard said.

"Be real nice to him," Ingram said. "Call him 'Sir.'"

"I'll give it a try, anyway, okay."

"Tell him we're elite fuckin' prisoners," Warren said.

"That's right. We're special," Ingram said.

"Yeah, stressed out," Warren said. "Fuck it."

Warren asked Ingram how he got picked up. Ingram went into a story about how he was traveling to Yellowknife with a friend when their car broke down. An RCMP car pulled up and offered him a ride. He told the cop his name, and the cop must have checked it because he told him he was under arrest and would be sent back to Alberta.

"I knew they were getting serious about that nowadays," Warren said.

"Fuck. They get so fuckin' stupid, this fuckin' government because, like, it's not gonna do my old lady good, me sittin' in here."

"Well, I'd pay big money to be charged with that," Warren said.

"Yeah, fuck."

"I'll give you thirty grand," he joked.

"Uhmm, well, Jesus," Ingram said, pretending to mull over Warren's offer to change places with him. "I'd get her off my back for that, but I don't know how much I'd enjoy myself. Not much."

Warren laughed. "Not much for a while."

"Yeah, she'd have a heyday with that, but I think I might still be here."

Warren kept laughing, almost giddy now. "Keep the cocksucker in!" he said, mimicking the outraged protest to keep in jail the man who was convicted of the mass murder. "Make sure he doesn't do it again!"

A moment later Warren told Ingram about his visit to the mine with the RCMP to walk through the crime scene. "They wanna make sure you're not bullshitting, eh. Like, basically, a guy could bullshit. There was enough stuff in the paper and that—a smart guy could convince 'em that you did that shit."

"Is that right?"

"And then a little later pop up with something to show that he completely didn't do it. 'Cause there's nothing, like, they can say, 'Well, this is the only guy that could've known this.'"

"It would be interesting to see what those guys who were doing that other blasting are saying now, eh?" Ingram said a moment later, referring to Shearing and Bettger.

"Yeah, I wonder," Warren said. "Well, half our guys are such a bunch of dumb fucks, they'll all be sittin', I can just hear 'em, 'Oh yeah, well I knew there was something wrong the other day.' Boy, I'll tell ya, everybody'd know what happened."

Ingram listened for the horn that would signal that he could take a new approach, but he never heard it.

Warren kept talking, telling Ingram how on the morning of the blast he had thought of asking striker Kelly Rhodes for a ride back to town so he could warn someone about the bomb, but Rhodes wanted to stand at the main gate and yell at the guys coming on the morning shift. "It was stupid, you know. All I had to say was, 'Jesus, I hope you can give me a ride because I gotta shit bad.' You know, something like that. I couldn't think of it, eh. The fuckin' panic."

Warren was called out to talk to his lawyer, Glen Orris of Vancouver, whom Warren had contacted on the recommendation of the union. While Ingram waited for Warren to return, he thought that might be bad news for him. "Heads up here, guys," he said aloud, knowing that the cell was bugged and an RCMP monitor was listening in. "It could get awful cold in the cell because good chance his lawyer's going to tell him 'If you're in a cell with anybody, make sure you don't talk to him.'"

But when Warren came back, he continued to talk, completely unsuspecting. Ingram told Warren he had gotten a message from his mom, that she was going to try to bail him out. The two kept talking, first about hunting, then about the situation at the mine, but Warren was only going over the same material. At 5:30 P.M. Ingram was allowed out to make a phone call. He told his handler that it was over, that Warren had said all he was going to say. Ingram felt confident that no one else was involved. He came back to the cell for a moment to tell Warren he was being escorted to Red Deer, Alberta. They said their good-byes.

Ingram hadn't felt particularly stressed in the cell, but he noticed that he smelled awful, as bad as he had ever smelled in his life. He must have sweated gallons. He had to hold his black leather jacket at arm's length because it smelled so foul. He tried to find a store to buy some fresh clothes, but it was Sunday and they were all closed. Chetwynd ended up giving Ingram some of his clothes. Back at the Explorer, Ingram jumped into the shower. Afterward, he headed over to the task force office, right away filling out a form to collect forty hours of overtime.

Ingram found a strange, almost depressed mood at the office. For one thing, everyone had worked crazy hours since the confession on Friday night, and there was a ton of work still ahead. Even so, Ingram thought things were a bit too gloomy. He understood how keyed up the investigators had been about Shearing and Bettger, how they were so sure they were just about to make an arrest, then suddenly the case took a sharp turn. Many of the officers seemed to be second-guessing themselves. How did we miss this? How could we not see? The team did save face, however; it wasn't as if Warren had ever been dropped as a suspect.

The investigators arrested Shearing and Bettger and charged them for the other strike-related explosions at the ventilation shaft and the satellite dish. Both men were also charged with break and enter for the June 29 graffiti mission. Bettger was also charged with possession of explosives dangerous to public peace and with the intent to endanger life, charges relating to the bomb found in Rob Wells' trailer.

The RCMP also reinterviewed the men Warren had seen on the morning of September 18 after he came out of the mine. The police wanted to see if their stories would change now that Warren had been arrested. The charred remains of two boots that divers found in Cameron Falls carried the strong smell of gasoline. When Sergeant Wayne Locke studied them, he found they were size ten Kamik boots. Since they were the wrong size, he dismissed them as being the boots that Warren had worn in the mine.

On Sunday evening Warren finally talked to his wife, Helen, on the phone for fifty minutes. He told her he had confessed. Later that night Glen Orris's assistant, Gillian Boothroyd, who had caught a flight from Vancouver, talked to Warren for about an hour.

Warren met with Boothroyd again at 9:35 A.M. the next morning, Monday, October 19, the day Warren was to make his first public appearance in court.

At the appearance, prosecutor Peter Martin told Justice Michel Bourassa that the Crown would be ready to proceed with a preliminary hearing on the matter in three months, as early as January 1994.

Afterward, Ravelli and Brandford asked Warren if he would grant another interview. Though he had met with Boothroyd twice already, Warren agreed to it. The officers asked a number of questions about the contents of the bag from the pond and about the items found in the search on Warren's apartment. Warren answered, then unloaded what he considered to be a bombshell—that Royal Oak had ignored obvious signs that the mine was broken into on the morning of September 18, 1992, and had allowed the nine men to go to their deaths. Warren said he was sure he had been spotted by a security guard coming out of the B-138 portal. He also said that he left the scoop on the B-ramp, when the log-in records would have said it had been left at the 712-scoop shop. Also, he left a loki plugged in at the scoop shop, when it should have been charging at the charging station. Finally he said he left all kinds of good footprints around the 712-scoop shop. "You know there's three or four large signals right there. And yet nine guys go down the fucking drift and get killed. It was a fucking shock to me. I can tell you that, and I'm being totally candid now. . . . I was never gonna reveal that to you guys. I was just gonna give that to my defense attorney."

Warren continued to spout. "Why the fuck didn't somebody walk down the drift? Fucking Byberg or somebody would've went. A dunce would see that fucking thing, a dunce, anybody."

Warren said he had thought the bomb might be found, which is why he had brought rags with him. He tried to clean off any fingerprints. "It was Giant supervision that killed the guys, I'm telling you. The strike caused it. I mean, I did it, I'm directly responsible for killing those guys. I know that. I put the device there and everything, but then there was lots of warning, lots."

Warren said there were more warning signs than had been left by Shearing, Bettger and St. Ammand on the June 29 graffiti mission. The difference then was that the replacement workers coming to work that day had actually seen the graffiti and had refused to work until the place was checked out, Warren said. "Peggy probably phoned up and said, 'Why did you guys lose a day's production?' And they didn't want that to happen again. I'm telling you, it's gonna make an awful fucking impact in that courtroom. And unless somebody shoots me it's gonna come out."

Warren kept rambling, pushing the crime as far away from himself as he could, sounding as if his story was so strong that only an idiot would be unable to see the truth of the matter. He was starting to run from his confession. In the following year, in the months leading up to his murder trial, the running would get more swift and more desperate.

Chapter 22

TIRED OF HATE

Rumors of Roger Warren's innocence spread as fast as news of his arrest. One story picked up and reported by the local media had the RCMP banging around Warren's apartment on the night of his arrest, perhaps seizing him at gun point or roughing him up. The story came from Warren's neighbors. There *had* been bumping and banging at Warren's apartment, only it didn't happen on the night he confessed; it came the following night when Warren guided the police on the search of his home.

Others gossiped that the Mounties had taken a man in a black hood over to Akaitcho and down the shaft, but the man in the hood wasn't Warren; it was someone else. It was all part of a clever game the police were playing to make everyone think Warren was guilty in the hope of getting more information on him.

CASAW's belief in a conspiracy was so strong that when a union lawyer, Leo McGrady, visited Warren in prison, McGrady asked Warren if Royal Oak had paid him to set the bomb. Warren told McGrady no one had paid him anything, that he had set the blast on his own, but hadn't meant to kill. He told the same to his wife, Helen, and to his own lawyers, Glen Orris and his assistant, Gillian Boothroyd.

Warren's admissions had little effect on the CASAW hardcore. They still believed that the blast was an accident or that someone from Royal Oak had set the bomb. The rumor with the most currency among the hardcore was that Warren was dying of cancer and had decided to make the sacrifice to end the strike for his union brothers.

The RCMP paid little heed to the stories of Warren's innocence. The investigators worked to pull together the case as quickly as possible to show the defense they were confident. White went to work preparing the court brief. It took him seven days to make the changes from the anticipated arrest of Shearing and Bettger to the arrest of Warren. Within five weeks, he was able to send Warren's lawyers the full fourteen binders of information. With such a quick turnover, the defense wouldn't be able to later complain that the Crown put them at a disadvantage by failing to disclose their case promptly. There was also some hope that once the defense had studied the evidence, it would try to plea bargain, perhaps accepting a second-degree murder conviction without a trial.

Warren's preliminary hearing was set for February 1994. While a cell was prepared for him at the Yellowknife Correctional Centre, he was taken to the maximum security prison in Edmonton, a jail known as the Max. Dale McGowan, back from his home in Hay River, volunteered to escort him. McGowan met Warren at his cell in the detachment. "Roger," he said, "I want to tell you, don't talk to me about the mine stuff because it's just more evidence that I'd have to give down the road."

"Yeah, no problem."

At the RCMP hangar at Edmonton's Municipal Airport, the two were met by Dean Ravelli, who drove them to the Max. McGowan had never before been to the prison. They drove up to the main gate, the only way in through the barbed-wire fence. They were told to stay in their car and to drive over a grate, where the vehicle was checked from below. They were then asked to drive forward through the gate. When they were in, the electric gate screeched closed behind them, the razor wire screaming *ZHEE! ZHEE! ZHEE!* The gate boomed as it locked shut.

A grim-faced guard approached. "Okay, bring this guy out."

McGowan got Warren out of the car and took off the pair of handcuffs he had earlier put on Warren.

"Okay," the guard told Warren, "keep your hands pointed forward, keep looking directly ahead, don't move until I tell you to move."

Warren stuck his hands out. Massive, steel handcuffs were clamped on.

"Roger, you will not move unless I direct you to move," the guard repeated. "You will not do anything unless I tell you to do that. Do I make myself clear?"

"Yes."

The place gave McGowan the creeps. It was the real business. He felt sorry for Warren. You're just a withered, fifty-year-old man, meek and mild, he thought. You're going into a place full of pumped-up guys, covered in tattoos, all macho, who don't give a shit about nothing. I don't care how tough a miner you are, you're in a different game now. You're not going to last here.

Warren was only at the Max for a few weeks before being sent to the Yellowknife Correctional Centre. Al Shearing and Tim Bettger were jailed in a different wing of the center. In early November 1993, all three got bad news from the union: they would have to get their own lawyers and pay for their own defense. "The union never condoned any sort of premeditated violent acts," Harry Seeton was quoted in the *yellowknifer*. "Therefore we can in no way be involved in the defense of our members who are accused of it."

The union was wise to distance itself from Warren. An end to the strike depended on outsiders believing that CASAW wasn't a terrorist organization and that its men had suffered long enough. Immediately after Warren's arrest, the union executive put forward the notion that Peggy Witte now had nothing more to worry about, and bargaining should start at once.

Royal Oak's emphasis was the opposite. The mine management stressed that not only had Warren, Shearing and Bettger been charged for acts of terrorism, but that the RCMP's investigation was continuing and more arrests could be made. Until all the charges against union members had been laid, management held that it wouldn't be appropriate to discuss the labor dispute. Royal Oak was also asking the Minister of Labour, Bernard Valcourt, to investigate CASAW for its illegal activities during the strike. In its press release, Royal Oak offered condolences to the families of the dead men, then aimed a cheap shot at CASAW: "Royal Oak wishes to express its sympathy towards other members of the Canadian labor movement who have stood squarely behind CASAW during this dispute."

It appeared that Witte wanted to use the arrests as a sledgehammer to crush the strikers, whether they had set a bomb, thrown a rock or stood silently on the picket line from day one. But Witte's most compelling argument for refusing to settle was now gone. With Warren's arrest she would no longer be forced to take a murderer back into her mine.

From November 3–10, the Canada Labour Relations Board held hearings in Yellowknife into CASAW's complaint about Royal Oak's negotiating tactics. The board listened to testimony from both sides, then came out with an overnight decision—Royal Oak had indeed failed to bargain in good faith.

In their report board members J.F.W. Weatherill, Michael Eayers and Mary Rozenberg gave as fair an accounting of the strike as had yet been written. Both sides were thrashed.

Royal Oak took a significant risk in taking over Giant Mine because of the difficult labor relations and the deteriorating quality of the ore, the board said. When the contract came up in the spring of 1992, both sides initially bargained in good faith. Royal Oak was not out to break the union. Indeed, both sides reached a tentative agreement, a deal that saw the union make concessions that were essential for the mine to keep operating, the board said. Even so, a few union miners who were not on the bargaining committee pushed the union membership to reject the agreement. To prevent a strike, Royal Oak opened its books to union accountants, but it had no effect. The union wanted more money and other concessions. "It appears from the evidence that the union simply did not accept the economics of the situation," the board said.

Of course, the CASAW men were entitled to reject the tentative agreement and go on strike. Likewise, Royal Oak was entitled to bring in replacement workers. If Royal Oak hadn't brought them in, the probability was high that the mine would have shut down and never reopened, the board said. With the replacement workers, Royal Oak surpassed previous production levels. The strike was a failure. Nevertheless, both sides were still obliged to bargain in good faith. By standing firm on the forty-three fired men, by saying there would be no new negotiations until CASAW had accepted their termination, Royal Oak failed to demonstrate good faith. But the board added: "We must note that the union, too, has on a number of occasions failed to bargain in good faith, although it would appear by now to have retreated from what can only be called the irrationally optimistic—and obviously unacceptable—positions it put forward from time to time."

The board said that it was usually careful to limit its intervention, but anything but direct action in this dispute would be a cruel waste of time. "These parties, both of them, have repeatedly demonstrated the degrees of obtuse intransigence which led the very experienced special mediators, Ready and Munroe, to state that this has been the most difficult labor dispute either of them had witnessed. The pathetic history of the parties' negotiations, and the tragic events which have attended the failure of those negotiations, lead us to share the pessimism which the mediators and others have expressed."

The board ruled that the union and the company must follow Ready and Munroe's plan to end the strike. Aside from a few issues, the initial tentative agreement would be the basis of the new three-year contract. The company had thirty-five days to bring back the first of the CASAW workers. The fate of the forty-three fired men would be decided in binding arbitration by Ready and Munroe. All workers at the mine were cautioned to behave. Two words were banned on company property: *scab* and *murderer*. Using either word was a firing offense.

After eighteen months, hundreds of arrests, mass defections, a riot, a mass murder, broken marriages, financial ruin and an ugly, corrosive battle with the RCMP, ninety-six percent of the CASAW men voted to accept the same deal they had rejected in April 1992. In the end, they lost one day of holidays and their free airfares, picked up a few days on the safety tours of the mines and had their salaries tied to the price of gold. Still, for the CASAW men, the board decision was a relief. They had hungered to destroy Peggy Witte, but the strike had been a series of disasters for them, one spirit-crushing incident after another, a time of humiliation, regret, frustration and unholy hatred.

Royal Oak management was upset by the board's decision and vowed to fight it in a higher court. Management also fired six more strikers, including Harry Seeton, who resigned as union leader. Nevertheless, Royal Oak was compelled to send out back-to-work letters to 130 CASAW strikers and lay-off notices to fifty of its replacement workers.

The placards on the Road of Shame came down. On December 1, 1993, six weeks after Roger Warren's arrest, the surface workers went back to work. Two weeks later, the underground miners went down the C-shaft. They all had to take a two-hour safety reorientation from manager Don Moroz, who was now in charge of mine safety.

Moroz spoke to group after group, looking out at surly, bitter faces.

"Listen, it's been a long, tough road for everybody here. Let's put it behind us," Moroz told the men and tried to sound like he believed it himself. "There is a mine to work here. I can't tell you how to act downtown, but when you're inside, act accordingly."

To some strikers, Moroz and his fellow middle managers were as bad as Peggy Witte herself. But just as many of the strikers were humbled. Jim O'Neil had feared that the mine would be like a time bomb, that he and the other line crossers in particular would be singled out for retribution. But O'Neil was astonished at how well things went. The groups rarely talked, but they didn't openly clash either. The miners were sick of the rancor, tired of waking up in the middle of the night, their heads swimming with the poison of the situation. When they got back to work they were instinctively quiet, stoic and accepting. They knew the poison well by now, knew its ways and its symptoms, and they did what they could to prevent a new flare-up. When the line crossers, replacement workers and strikers were together in the lunchroom or in the man-cage or a man-car, the strike was never mentioned. It was finished. But the fate of Roger Warren was still in doubt and consequently less easy to set aside. The mass murder continued to pollute the mine. A new bout of hatred came whenever there was a new development in the case.

In February 1994, four months after the arrest, Warren's preliminary hearing was held. It was moved out of the regular courthouse into a large meeting room at the Yellowknife Inn, increasing the seating capacity from one hundred to three hundred. People had to pass through a metal detector gate to get into the court. Security guards also used hand-held metal detectors.

The first three rows of the court were reserved for the families of the victims and the accused. At least one member of each of the nine families attended the hearing. Along with several dozen supporters, they formed an angry wave that threatened to wash up over Warren at any moment. Warren rarely looked at them.

The widows talked at length for the first time at the preliminary hearing. The conversation eventually got around to what had happened to the men during the blast. It occurred to Carol Riggs that the men were so tangled up that some piece of each man was mixed in with the remains of her son, Shane, that had been returned to her. That didn't bother Carol. She felt good that she had a little bit of everybody in the urn of Shane's ashes.

A few union men showed up throughout the hearing, including new union president Rick Cassidy. Helen Warren came every day, a petite, tense woman with short brown hair, glasses, hand on her chin, face creased with anxiety.

At the preliminary, the Crown had to establish that there was enough evidence to proceed with a trial. It did so, calling the police and mine witnesses who would later testify at the trial, including mine foreman Noel O'Sullivan.

O'Sullivan's job was to explain various aspects of the mine to the judge, then lay out how he himself had pieced together his theory that Warren was the murderer. O'Sullivan spoke with as much conviction and authority as prosecutor Peter Martin had ever seen in a Crown witness.

Martin arranged to take the defense lawyers Glen Orris and Gillian Boothroyd down the C-shaft to the blast site. If they were to understand the case, such a visit was essential. It was difficult to imagine the blast site on 750 without seeing it. The mandatory guide from Royal Oak accompanied the lawyers. At the site, Orris asked the guide on which side of the tracks the bomb had been placed.

"Go ask your fuckin' client," he shot back.

One of the widows, Doreen Hourie, also visited the blast site in her own quest to understand and accept what had happened. Hourie saw the nine crosses painted on the wall and the fragments of wood blasted into the rock. From what she knew of mining it was now clear to her that Warren had meant to kill Norm when he planted the bomb. She wept at the site, the spot where Norm had last breathed.

After coming up the C-shaft man-cage, Doreen picked up her mail at the mine. Dozens of sympathy cards had come, including one from Norm's old hockey team. She read the names. One of them was Roger Warren, Norm's old teammate. It troubled Doreen that Warren knew Norm. She wanted to believe that if someone actually knew him, there was no way that person could kill him. Doreen's fever for vengeance raged now, but she was angriest at Harry Seeton, not Roger

Warren. She believed Seeton had engineered the strike. "They made a big mistake," she told the other widows. "They should never have left me behind. If CASAW think they had a real fight because they didn't want their job, they better look out! They think that I'm not angry now? They think that they can take my husband's life, and I'm going to be understanding? I'm going to go on with life?"

Seeton showed up at the preliminary hearing one day. Outside the courtroom, someone pointed him out to Doreen. Immediately she went up to him.

"Are you Harry Seeton?" she asked.

Seeton smiled and put out his hand. "Yeah," he said.

Doreen punched him in the face. Seeton backed away as the small woman continued to attack, shoving, punching, clawing. Seeton got free and hustled off.

"I'll make sure you stay the hell out of here," Doreen howled. "We'll see what you have to say when you're dead."

The other widows applauded.

"He is lucky I met him in the hallway when I didn't have nothing in my hand," she said. "If I was driving a car, if I had a knife or a gun, I would have killed him."

Seeton complained to the RCMP. He wanted them to charge Doreen with assault and with uttering threats. When the Mounties refused, Seeton hired his own lawyer to prosecute the case. In the end, however, the Crown decided it wasn't in the public interest to lay charges against Hourie. The union men and their supporters were outraged. Columnist Lee Selleck wrote in the *yellowknifer:* "The decision, like others before it, calls into question the objectivity of officials in the justice system."

By the time of the preliminary hearing, the mine was almost completely reintegrated, with twenty-five line crossers, a hundred and twenty replacement workers and eighty-five CASAW members working together. The operation produced its quota, but there was no spirit. Many men put in their hours and hustled home. They no longer lived for their work; they worked for their paycheck. A few dozen miners and managers decided to leave. The union, too, lost its direction. At the national level, the two thousand CASAW members voted to join the 170,000 members of the Canadian Auto Workers. The days of the purist, Canada-only CASAW chauvinism were gone.

Union dues went from $80 to $200 a month. The non-CASAW men

had to pay, but they were considered union members in poor standing and had few rights. They especially hated the high dues because they knew the money would help pay for the coming arbitration hearings of the forty-nine fired CASAW men. None of the line crossers or replacement workers went to the union hall, where a painting of a giant pink pig still hung on the wall.

The forty-nine fired men called themselves the CASAW 49ers. Among them were sixteen men charged with rioting at the mine on June 14, 1992. At the same time as Warren's preliminary hearing, they went to trial and were acquitted. Terry Legge was one of men who got off, but Legge still worried about his chances for getting back on at Giant. He knew he had to testify at Tim Bettger and Al Shearing's preliminary hearing. On the stand he'd have to bring up his role in the vent shaft bombing, which would likely be a firing offense.

Claudia pushed her husband to forget Royal Oak. Terry did apply for work elsewhere, but he never got hired. He feared he had been blackballed within the mining industry. He told Claudia that he had to go through with his arbitration because he didn't want to lose all he had put into Giant Mine. He had fifteen years seniority.

"Who cares about that?" she said. "There is lots of jobs. We'll find something. Hell, if we got to go on welfare for a while, we'll do that."

Legge shook his head. "I want to be there," he said.

At the arbitration hearing, Royal Oak tried to nail him for his participation in the riot, but arbitrator Vince Ready ruled that Legge would get his job back. Legge was happy to have won against Royal Oak, and his return to work was less difficult than he had feared. He hated seeing the men who had crossed the picket line, especially the ones like Jim O'Neil who had betrayed CASAW. But Legge soon fell back into his old habit of going to work a half hour early to meet with the other men in the shop and have coffee and talk. He got to know a few of the replacement workers, and he realized most of them were okay. They all had a story, some unemployed for years, some on welfare, some about to lose everything. Legge could have been friends with some of them, but he always held back in the end. "You're a nice guy," he said to one man, "but there is only one thing wrong with you, and we both know what that is."

One of the first men to make Legge feel back at home was Noel O'Sullivan.

"Good to see you!" O'Sullivan said when they met. "Hey Legge, how's she goin'?"

Legge would chat with his old boss, even if some of his union brothers tapped him on the shoulder and told him not to get chummy with a Royal Oak manager.

"Go fuck yourself," Legge would shoot back. "I'll speak to who I want to. I knew him long before I knew you."

Still, Legge no longer cared for his job the way he had before. He used to think he made a difference, but now he realized he was completely replaceable. In a way it made the job easier for him. He no longer had to pressure himself to get the job done quickly just because the boss wanted it done fast. He went to work, put in his time, fixed everything that was handed to him and fixed it well, but if there was no work he didn't go looking for it. He got his $23.90 an hour and was satisfied.

Like everyone else, Legge learned never to say "scab" at work. He even tried to stop saying it at home and the union hall to try to break the habit. One day he was coming out of the hardware store when he found himself facing his old friend Keith Murray. They hadn't said a word since Murray had crossed the line, but now Murray asked, "So have you been hunting yet?"

"No, I haven't been," Legge said. "Well, that's not true. I have been, but I haven't scored."

The two chatted for another minute, then went on their way. Legge couldn't figure it. He knew he should never have talked to Murray, that he had sworn up and down he would never socialize again with a line crosser. Yet having talked he didn't feel so bad. He was getting tired of the hatred, too.

He wished all the criminal matters would go away. He had felt betrayed by Vern White after Warren's arrest. Legge had believed he wouldn't have to testify because Bettger and Shearing weren't going to be charged with murder. But White told him he'd still have to testify against the two men on the vent shaft blast. White also told him that their initial interviews had been secretly taped, a fact that enraged Legge. "Vern, I can't fuckin' believe you guys! I'm being straight with you, and as I was talking to you, you're buggin' me anyway."

"I understand you being frustrated," White said, but still he insisted Legge would have to testify.

"Yeah, but you told me Tim Bettger did the murder," Legge shot back.

"Terry, I believed it," White said. "I was wrong."

White explained that this had been an unusual investigation. Normally the police wouldn't tap telephones or secretly tape conversations, but this was mass murder. It was too big to fool around. It had to be done this way.

White didn't feel guilty about his actions during the investigation. He didn't feel that he had tricked Terry Legge or anyone else. The RCMP had wiretapped people because they thought they were linked to acts of terrorism, and in the end many of them had been, Legge included. Yes, he had been wrong about Bettger, but how could the investigation not focus on the Bear with all he had done and with all the trash he was spewing about committing more crimes? It would have been wrongheaded to go any other way.

Legge went on a rant against White to his wife. "Vern is off of my good books," he told Claudia. "He's not to be trusted. Come on! Where's that Royal Canadian Mounted Police honor? They're the biggest crooks that walk out on the street."

Legge started to go over the consequences of not testifying at Shearing and Bettger's preliminary hearing, which was slated for the end of June 1994. Legge knew he might go to jail, but he wouldn't have to speak against his two union brothers, and he might not lose his job in the end.

Legge never visited Bettger or Shearing in jail, but he kept up on them through the union newsletter, which published letters from them and from Roger Warren.

Bettger and Shearing wrote:

"To our brothers and sisters greetings.

"For some time we have been trying to get a letter out to you, but till now the time hasn't been right. We were pleased beyond telling when we heard that the [so-called] riot charges were thrown out by the jury. We all know how corruptly the RCMP have performed their duty. When Harry Seeton was assaulted recently is only one more example, but it is heartening to know that the fruits of their labors are not all bearing fruit in the courtrooms.

"We wish we could say that the justice department is impartial but sadly that cannot be done. We all know that this lockout was all about standing up for our rights.

"We believe that now more than ever the RCMP will be working hard to destroy our solidarity. . . . They will be working diligently to perpetuate the lies they have told concerning Roger and concerning us. They are lying to the world by perpetuating our incarceration. They know that many people will be swayed in their beliefs because: they're in jail, ergo, they must be guilty.

"Don't you believe it.

"Being in this hateful place has revealed to us some deeper truths—prison is a place where you learn that nobody really needs you, that the real world beyond those bars, guards and fences does go on without you. Every day is the same and without a calendar the days and weeks just kind of blur together, just like a fuzzy nightmare.

"Prison lets you discover your genuine brothers and sisters while the phony ones and the snitches slither away like the snakes they are. Prison is designed to swallow up a man's spirit by locking him up in a cage. But the true man will not allow his spirit to be consumed. As long as he still believes.

"In the face of whatever the RCMP and government does, we intend to continue to stand because we still believe. Tim and Al."

And Roger Warren wrote: "Hello out there. I would like to take this opportunity to thank you all for the support that you showed me and my family throughout this dilemma and especially at the preliminary hearing. I would of wanted to give my thanks personally to all of you but there are men here with guns who insist that I stay at least for now. I am mad because Royal Oak still hasn't sent my recall letter. Oh well, I still may get it in today's mail. Brother Roger W."

A few days before Bettger and Shearing's preliminary hearing, White visited Legge again to talk about his testimony. White had a stack of transcripts, some of them from interviews, some of them from taped telephone conversations. Legge was astounded. He had received notice that some of his telephone conversations had been tapped, but he didn't expect to see such records were kept. There was no privacy, he thought.

Legge was particularly upset when he found out that White had secretly taped the very meeting during which White told him many of their other conversations had been secretly taped. When he found out he'd been had again, Legge had to look at himself in the mirror. "How stupid are you, guy?" he said aloud. "All these guys have been telling you how fuckin' rotten these guys are, how dirty they are, you know."

Before the preliminary hearing, however, the Crown worked out a deal with Legge, Luc Normandin, Conrad Lisoway, Art St. Ammand and Rob Wells, the other men who would testify about the September 1 vent shaft blast, the June 29 graffiti mission and the bomb found in the trailer. They would take the stand, but the courtroom would be closed. If Royal Oak wanted to fire any of them based on their testimony, the company would have to wait until Shearing and Bettger's trial itself. All the union men agreed to testify.

At the task force office, the investigators showed Legge some of the evidence for Warren's murder trial, including dozens of photographs of Warren walking through the mine with White and McGowan. The pictures astonished Legge. Though Warren had been arrested and Helen Warren had been told he confessed, Legge still hadn't believed Warren was the killer. He thought it was just a rumor, something the Mounties had told Helen to get her to break down and give them some information. After seeing the photographs, however, and hearing the gist of Warren's confession, Legge changed his mind.

Warren had to have known he was going to hurt someone bad by putting the bomb beside the tracks, Legge thought. Maybe a guy might live if he was on the loki pushing in six or seven or eight ore cars. Still, it was hard to believe that Warren was just trying to blow a car off the tracks, not with that much explosives. "I can't believe it," Terry told Claudia when he got home. "This was murder. He really knew what he was doing. It had to be murder."

Legge wasn't one to keep his beliefs to himself, but a large group at the union hall had no time for what he was now saying about Warren.

"We still abide by it was an accident," the union's vice-president, Marvin Tremblett, told the *Edmonton Journal*. "I'm going to tell you something: You guys are going to get the shock of your life when it's all over. You and this town and everybody else are going to get the shock of their life when it all comes out. That's all I'll say."

The belief that Warren was innocent had only grown stronger since his arrest. And now many union men believed they had some evidence to prove it.

Chapter 23

STONES

ROGER WARREN felt glorious when the Canada Labour Relations Board ended the strike. His confession had accomplished one of the things he had hoped it would. Now, Warren reasoned, if only he could get out of jail, things would be perfect.

Even as he was confessing, Warren had started to back away from his responsibility for the crime. Now he concluded that it was wrong for him to take any of the blame. He decided to get word out to his union brothers that he was not the murderer, that he had falsely confessed to the crime.

Warren was still upset with the union executive for refusing to pay for his lawyers. His bill was running into the tens of thousands. If he wanted to keep his lawyers, Glen Orris and Gillian Boothroyd, he'd have to apply for Legal Aid money. Warren knew that Shearing and Bettger had the same problem. Though the three men were separated, they felt a bond. They all considered themselves to be martyrs. Shearing requested a meeting with Warren, but was turned down. Soon, however, the three men were smuggling notes back and forth. In mid-December, two months after the confession and just as the first CASAW miners headed back to work underground, Shearing sent Warren a list of questions asking what he had told the RCMP. One day before

Christmas 1993 Warren sent a note in reply. The contents of the note were soon the talk of the union hall.

"Dear Tim and Al.

"All I can say guys is that I've tried to see you guys since your first message. I put in requests too and was flatly denied.

"I feel responsible in part for your predicament as well as mine. I don't know how much I can say as Glen is still studying everything. I will say this much. I think we would still be on strike if I hadn't 'confessed.' I'm not the man in the black hood. I could have walked away anytime. I felt like it, and did on 3:30 P.M. on October 15, because like you guys, they wouldn't arrest me.

"I went back at 5:30 P.M. fully intending to get the joke over with, but the thought of another winter of this bullshit was just too overwhelming. I won't say any more, except to say that most if not all the 'evidence' I gave them is bullshit and based on stuff I'd learned over the past thirteen months, including the *Journal* story. I just hope I haven't buried myself by being too convincing. If I'd have known the union wasn't going to help with costs I'd be home with my family now. I never thought this shit through, which was stupid. The RCMP was pretty suspicious at some things a few days later, but I wouldn't say any more to them. I don't think they really care. They just wanted somebody on the 'guided tour.' I had to look around for a man-way and went the wrong way, but it didn't seem to bother them. Also we never traveled up and out B-138 because I would have been lost as well as dead climbing, despite listening to people talk about it for a year. Anyway, bye for now. Hope to see you soon. Roger."

The note made its way from Shearing to the union hall to Warren's lawyers, Orris and Boothroyd. The defense lawyers went to work. They knew they were up against an overwhelming bundle of evidence proving Warren's guilt, most of it coming from Warren's own mouth. The net effect of the taped and videotaped confessions was that the Crown no longer had to prove beyond a reasonable doubt that Warren was guilty. Instead, the defense had to give the jury a reasonable doubt that the confessions were false. Only then could the jury begin to consider Warren's claim that he hadn't committed the murders.

From the start it was clear to the defense that Warren would have to take the stand, an unusual and risky move, as it allowed the Crown a chance to attack the defendant in front of the jury. But Warren could not sit mutely, allowing the judge and jury to hear only the Roger Warren who rambled on about setting the blast. He had much explaining to do, starting with the most basic question: Why would anyone confess to the mass murder of nine men if he wasn't guilty?

The answer Warren came up with was that he wasn't in his right mind. When he owned up to Gregg McMartin, he was so distraught—clinically depressed, in fact—and thinking so darkly about himself and his future that he was ready to take the fall for mass murder in order to prove his worth as a man and end the strike. The main cause of this extraordinarily black mood, Warren decided, wasn't that he had killed nine men and was destroyed by guilt. It wasn't that he knew his bloody act had sickened everyone including all but a few of his own union brothers. Nor was it because he at last realized that the blast he had set to end the strike had instead prolonged it. No, Warren decided his dark feelings grew out of many smaller but enormously debilitating problems, chief among them the loss of the job that gave him his identity. Almost as bad, the medication he took for his heart condition had taken away his sex drive. Finally, Warren feared he had testicular cancer.

Whatever the true cause of Warren's depression, it's clear that when he confessed he was in the grasp of something much bigger than himself. He was as astonished as anyone that he had been so weak as to break down and tell the police he had committed mass murder. It took him almost a year to understand why he told his story to McMartin and the other RCMP officers. Warren put together the full story of his depression and his confession with the help of two Vancouver psychological experts brought in by the defense team. They were forensic psychiatrist Dr. Shabehram Lohrasbe and forensic psychologist Dr. Robert Ley.

Doctors Lohrasbe and Ley first met with Warren in September 1994, just as the trial was beginning. Dr. Lohrasbe had supplied expert evidence in more than three hundred trials, most of them on behalf of the Crown. This gave him added credibility in the Warren case. He would more likely be seen by the judge and jury as impartial rather than as a hired opinion who was used again and again by defense lawyers.

Dr. Ley was brought in to do a psychological assessment of Warren to see if he was vulnerable to interpersonal pressure, and if the confession might be unreliable. In his career Ley had assessed more than two hundred people charged with murder. He had examined for false confessions in eight prior cases. He was an expert in child abuse and false memory syndrome.

When Glen Orris contacted Dr. Lohrasbe, he told him the defense would argue that Warren was not guilty, that he had confessed falsely. "This guy must either be the most cool, cold-blooded psychopath I've ever seen, or there is something wrong with this," Orris told the doctor.

To prepare for their interviews with Warren, the two doctors read all the information on false confessions. There wasn't much, except for some work done by forensic psychologist Gisli Gudjonsson in England. It was no secret that people sometimes confessed to crimes they didn't commit. Gudjonsson found false confessions came from people in four groups: the mentally ill, who actually believed their confessions were true; fame seekers, who wanted the notoriety of the crime; people trying to protect someone else; and people trying to escape an intolerable situation. At times the police put pressure on an individual who was malleable, adding an element of coercion to some false confessions.

Dr. Lohrasbe met with Warren for an all-day session at the Yellowknife Correctional Centre in early September. The next day the doctor met briefly with Warren's wife, Helen, and daughter Ann. Dr. Ley spent twenty-five hours interviewing and testing Warren in two sessions in mid-October. Dr. Ley also interviewed Ann Warren briefly. Both doctors reviewed Warren's confession to McMartin and the videotaped reenactment. In the end they both leaned toward believing that Warren's confession was indeed false.

In Dr. Lohrasbe's opinion, Warren had no history of an anti-social personality and no history of violence. He had a good vocabulary but was inarticulate. Dr. Ley found Warren to be intelligent, with an IQ of 108, and quite humble, not like violent people who tended to be aggressive and narcissistic. Warren did very well on a general knowledge test. In his vocabulary test, he scored 99.9 percent. His reading and spelling were at a university level.

Dr. Ley gave Warren a test designed by Gudjonsson. The test showed Warren had the type of compliant personality susceptible to giving false confessions. The only problem with the test was that it had not yet been validated by other researchers, so it lacked a firm scientific foundation.

The psychological experts delved into Warren's childhood. Warren told Dr. Ley that he was a bright, athletic child, with no behavioral problems in school. He was not aggressive or combative. To the psychologist, this information was telling in Warren's favor. It was rare to find an aggressive, violent adult who was not the same during adolescence.

When Warren talked to Dr. Ley about his father, he became teary-eyed. His father was a hunting guide who worked hard, but he was a weak, insecure man. Warren judged him harshly and didn't want to be such a wimp himself. His parents split up when he was in his twenties and Warren became estranged from his dad.

Dr. Ley found the seeds of the false confession to McMartin in two minor criminal matters from Warren's youth. When he was seventeen, he got picked up for shoplifting, Warren said. He claimed he had only done it on a dare from two older boys. When he agreed to plead guilty to minor theft, he was given probation. From this, Warren first learned the benefit of cooperating with the police, Dr. Ley concluded. The next incident came when Warren was nineteen. He had been drinking and barhopping. He and a buddy stole a car to joyride. The car crashed. Although Warren wasn't clear on the story—he said he was intoxicated at the time of the crash—it seems he was pressured by a social worker and his father to take the rap for the stolen car and drunk driving, even though he wasn't sure he was the driver. Warren decided to go along with it. Again he pleaded guilty, but got only four weeks in jail. This, too, he considered to be a positive contact with the police.

The doctors focused on the explosion in 1987 that killed Vince Corcoran and blinded Danny Mino. Doctors Ley and Lohrasbe concluded that Warren lost his love for mining following the blast. He was anxious and depressed, the classic symptoms of post-traumatic stress disorder. One side effect of this disorder was that Warren would try to avoid all reminders of the event, which the psychiatric experts believed made him an unlikely candidate to recreate such an event himself by setting the murderous bomb.

Warren told the doctors his real troubles started after the blast of September 18, 1992. Warren said he was terrified of being a suspect. The investigation quickly became a nightmare for him. After he successfully got through his first meetings with Defer, McGowan and the two polygraph operators, Dauk and Keane, he had felt strong, but he saw that the police weren't going to drop the matter. If they weren't hammering at Shearing and Bettger, they were seizing his boots and calling him in again for accusatory interviews. He couldn't seem to shake the RCMP.

He spent months listening to other strikers talk about what had happened that night on the picket line, but he couldn't find a way to close the lengthy gap in his own alibi. He worried about what other strikers had told the police about him. He knew he was wet that morning, but he wondered if fellow strikers noticed it and told the police. He also knew he had mentioned to other strikers like Terry Coe that he had seen the two shadowy men. Had Coe passed the information on to the police?

In his interviews with the investigators, Warren struggled to match his story to what he thought everyone else was saying, but still the police kept after him. He hated the attention. What were they getting at? Why did they harp about him being stressed out at Nettie's coffee shop? Why did they keep asking him about his reasons for going back to the picket line that morning? What did they know?

Despite the strain, Warren agreed to come into the task force office on October 15, 1993, and not just because he thought the lab test on his boots would exonerate him. From the start, Warren had surmised that the person who had committed the crime would most likely tell the RCMP to screw off. So his plan was to cooperate, just as an innocent man would. Warren was also won over by Dale McGowan's approach. McGowan was smart, not like the other cops, who in Warren's estimation were so stupid they would study for a hearing test. McGowan also seemed fair. He had empathy. He certainly wasn't like some of them, like Bill Farrell, whom Warren and the other strikers regarded as a devil because of his accusatory interviewing style.

Warren told the doctors that his first major scare was the suspected heart attack after his interview with Dauk one month after the blast. He was given a beta blocker that lowered his blood pressure, but the medication had the side effect of decreasing his sex drive. He and his wife used to have sexual intercourse four to six times a week, but in the months after the blast, they rarely had intercourse. Even when Warren could perform, he felt no pleasure. He felt like half a man. It even seemed to him like his genitals were shrinking. He wished he could take intravenous testosterone.

One day in March 1993, six months after the blast, he felt a terrible pain in his groin while playing hockey. In the bathtub he discovered what looked to be a third testicle. He feared it might be malignant, but didn't get it checked out by a doctor until after his arrest when he pointed it out to Nurse Cynthia Stokes in the prison hospital. He told Stokes that the lump in his scrotum was causing him pain. One day later, Dr. Andrew Gee examined the lump. He found it to be a globule of hardened fluid known as a spermasticile. It was neither cancerous nor malignant.

Warren told the psychiatric experts that during the winter of 1993 he had felt all the worse because he was no longer the breadwinner of the household. He believed his career as a miner was over. He had been fired for his participation in the June 14 riot. He feared he would be blackballed in the industry. Even if he somehow got back on at Giant or at another mine, his heart and physical ailments were so debilitating that he worried he would fail to cut it as a hardrock miner. He was flabby and his hands and back were bad. He'd never again be the Ace, never again take home $50,000 for four months' work as he had in the four months leading up to the strike. All he was good for was driving his wife and daughter around when they needed a lift. He felt like a shell compared to his former self—lethargic, weary, worried.

The RCMP's pursuit of Shearing and Bettger enraged him. It was hard to believe that even the dumdum police gnomes could be so stupid. Warren knew Shearing and Bettger were innocent. He felt guilty and responsible for their situation. The search on Bettger's house was bad enough, but the ultimate indignity came when other CASAW strikers joined in the campaign, with Rob Wells turning in the bomb he had found in his trailer. Warren couldn't figure it out. It was like waving a red flag in front of a bull. Why not give the bomb to one of the old-time miners? They would know how to get rid of it. Giving it to the cops meant that all the strikers became that much more paranoid. The suspicion of everyone in the union became more intense. That was the last thing he needed.

Warren said he had started to feel melancholy by the first anniversary of the strike. He couldn't shake the sadness. He didn't understand what was happening to him, but he felt like he had no presence, like he was invisible, transparent. He knew he was starting to lose it. He saw other people talking at the union hall or in the picket shack, he saw their lips moving, but he couldn't make out what they were saying because there was too much noise in his head from his own raging inner conflict. He felt split. One side of him was straightforward, diligent, humble and obedient, but too weak, almost like his father had been, never standing up for himself, which Warren hated. The other side of him—proud, selfish, aggressive, sinister even—judged his weak side harshly. Again and again Warren caught one side of himself talking to the other. He was surprised that none of the other strikers mentioned it to him.

Before the strike Warren had been hyper. He had needed only four hours sleep. He could work hard in the day, then go out at night and pitch, mixing fastballs and junk pitches masterfully to defeat batter after batter. But during the strike, he sat around doing nothing all day, and when he was on the mound he had no energy. He didn't care if he won or lost. He felt no competitive flame, just a tiny spark. He felt diminished in spirit. Things didn't seem to bother him anymore. Some dummy would make a harebrained comment about politics, and where once Warren would have crushed him with rhetoric or hyperbole, he let it go. He suffered fools.

To get away from the turmoil, he and his wife left on vacation on June 1, 1993. They visited their daughter Pat in northern Alberta, then drove through Jasper, Banff, Radium Hot Springs, Glacier, Yellowstone and Wyoming. Next, they visited relatives in New York state, Ontario and Manitoba. But no matter how far they went, Warren couldn't escape his despair. He tried to be pleasant around Helen, tried to be his old energetic, upbeat self, but he could only fake it. He started to hallucinate about gas station attendants, believing they were having strange thoughts about him, that they wondered what this loser was doing with that lady.

In Winnipeg, Warren heard that the Attorney General was using a rarely used legal tool known as a direct indictment to charge him and other strikers for the riot, even though his charges had been dropped at a preliminary hearing. It was one more indication to Warren that the Crown and the police would never give up. They were a relentless force, trying to crush him.

When he got home in the first week of July 1993, he went right over to the union hall to hear the latest news. The Blitz package was the hot topic. Even before McGowan told him what was in it, Warren had learned from other strikers about the Progression Theory, the trip wire found at Bettger's house, the explosives in Wells' trailer, the murderer breaking into the Akaitcho shaft and escaping out the B-3 area of the mine. Warren wondered where the cops got all this information, which of the strikers had blabbed.

His daughter Ann told him that McGowan had said he could call if he wanted to find out more about the seizure of his boots, but Warren decided not to phone. Sooner or later McGowan and the Mounties would be back. They were as inevitable as the rain. Why hurry the process if you could avoid it, Warren thought, even if it was just for a few days?

The debate in Warren's head was constant by the first anniversary of the blast. He told Doctors Lohrasbe and Ley that his sane, straightforward voice continued to tell him to resist the police, but the aggressive side of him got louder all the time. It was a sinister, raucous voice. It put down his sane side, referring to it as Meat, a piece of useless meat. The sinister voice detested Meat for not bearing up under the pressure. Every morning when Warren awoke, the sinister voice chirped sarcastically: Well, Meat, what world-shaking events are you going to shape today?

On the picket line Warren couldn't believe that his fellow strikers treated him the same as before. Couldn't they see the difference? Couldn't they see what had happened to him?

One of the strikers went so far as to tell Warren that he was looking forward to going back to work so the old Ace could train him. Warren was astounded. This fellow was so close to him, yet he couldn't see.

Warren now saw himself as horrible and evil. Food tasted like sawdust to him. He slept poorly. He was drinking more and more, mixing alcohol with his tea or coffee. When he saw young miners with their young wives, he got all choked up, knowing how hard the strike was for them.

The *Edmonton Journal*'s anniversary story, "Footsteps of the Murderer," pushed the debate inside Warren to another level. He saved his copy of the story by the couch in front of the television. He constantly scanned it. Warren told Doctors Lohrasbe and Ley that it was as if this article had a strange hold on him, a magic spell. It became like a forbidden thing; he knew he shouldn't look at it—it made him feel like going to talk to the police—but he was drawn to it nonetheless. The words had power over him. He believed that if he ever spoke them aloud they would make him do something he didn't want to do, and bad things would happen.

At the same time, the article angered him, just as it angered many at the union hall. The animosity around town had died down, but here the newspaper was dredging up all the old poison. What purpose could it serve? It would only make everyone in Yellowknife look at one another again and think suspicious thoughts. Warren believed the cops had to be behind it. He found it remarkable that the story so closely mirrored what he had heard in his interview about the Blitz package. He was furious at the Mounties for not letting up on the union or him. Why didn't they just believe his story?

The night before his interview with McMartin, the argument within him reached a new intensity. Warren had to leave the picket shack a few times because he was so worried that the other guys would notice him talking to himself. He now felt utterly worthless, but one thought kept occurring: If he was falling into hell because of his own psychological troubles anyway, why not make his fall count? Why not confess? All the strikers knew how devastating another winter on the line was going to be. Why not stop it from happening? It would be one hell of a good way to get at Peggy Witte. A solution to the murder meant that the government might at last be forced to step in. It wouldn't bother him to be arrested, Warren reasoned. What was worse: sitting in a picket shack or sitting in jail?

Warren came home from the night shift on October 15, 1993, and tried to watch a movie, *At Play in the Fields of the Lord,* but couldn't follow it. He had a coffee and again scanned the *Journal* article. Warren told Doctors Lohrasbe and Ley that the sinister voice was starting to prevail, spouting: Go for it, Meat. You've got the stones. Your cojones might be gone, your hands might be gone, but you have the stones to confess. You know you have. Only a few people have, and you're one of them.

Don't be retarded, Warren's rational voice had replied. Are you crazy? What about your wife and family?

But the sinister voice shot back: Yeah, what do they need you for? What are you good for, Meat? You are a glorified chauffeur.

The debate continued as Warren dozed on the couch through the morning. He slept only fitfully, and Dr. Ley concluded that Warren was sleep deprived when he went to see McMartin. He was less resistant, more compliant to the wishes of other people, more likely to make a bad decision.

At noon Warren got up to go have lunch at the Polar Bowl across the street. He had never felt so distressed. All he had ever wanted in life was to do his work and come back home to his family, but that seemed gone forever.

Warren told the doctors that in the interview with McMartin he was overwhelmed. He had never met a cop who was so adamant. He had never heard one go on and on and on about him being guilty. At times Warren said he tuned out McMartin's patter to focus on the debate in his own head. The sinister voice kept pushing him to go for it. He felt like he stood on the edge of an abyss. He was tempted to step off. Warren said he was greatly impressed by McMartin's connection to Crown prosecutor Peter Martin and the Attorney General's Department. McMartin clearly had special powers.

When Warren managed to get out of the interview room to take his daughter Ann to her physical therapy session, he was glad, but he didn't feel overwhelming relief like he thought he might. At the hospital, the sinister voice berated him for not being a man and confessing: You blew it! You had your chance!

Warren then drove his daughter home. Ann mentioned the number of police cars around. She reminded him that later that night they would be celebrating Helen's birthday at the Monkey Tree.

At home Warren sat down on the couch. Again he felt drawn to the "Footsteps of the Murderer" article. He picked it up, scanned it, studying the information in it. It was such a load of bullshit, he thought, but still he wondered if he should go in and confess.

Forget it, the sane voice told him.

Get with the program, the sinister voice shot back. What good are you? You might as well do something good. You are going down anyways. You might as well make it count.

But by the time Warren had left to pick up Helen from work, his rational side had won out. This is bullshit, he thought. We are not going to do this kind of stuff. When I get home, I'll phone them up and tell them, "Sorry, I won't be seeing you anymore."

Still, he was curious to see what else McMartin had to say about the investigation. He decided to go back to the interview room. He continued to listen to bits of McMartin's seemingly endless rap, but he told Doctors Lohrasbe and Ley he was in such a state of crisis that he couldn't really concentrate. At one point he felt as if he were standing outside his body. He stood against the wall, looking at McMartin and himself, seeing through his own coat, seeing the wrinkles in his shirt. He said he couldn't bear to look into McMartin's eyes. They seemed like black holes. It felt like McMartin had grown to a gigantic size. Meanwhile he was shrinking, fading. Still, he resisted the urge to confess. He thought about how it would destroy him. He knew how much his fellow strikers would hate the man who had set that bomb and ruined everything. And what about Helen and their daughters? But when he thought of Helen, the sinister voice snarled at him: She is better off without you. You know the only thing you're good for. Go for it.

At one point Warren had a vision. He felt like he was standing on top of a valley, looking down at two armies, one of them huge, the other very small. He knew he could stop his army from being wiped out, even if it meant he got wiped out doing it. Again the sinister voice whispered: Get some stones. You have got the stones. What are you scared of, Meat? Go for it. Warren was terrified at the thought, but the sinister voice said: If it's not terrifying, it's not worth doing.

McMartin kept telling Warren to act like a man, to be a man, do the right thing and confess, and both the psychiatric experts concluded that the phrase shook Warren to the core. It pushed the right button for a man who was feeling like half a man. Warren didn't care about the consequences for himself and his family, the experts concluded, he cared only about solving the crisis brought on by McMartin's pressure. He was so depressed, his thinking processes so mangled, that he had no thoughts for the future. He only wanted to do this one thing to prove his manhood, and this explained why he made sure his confession was so detailed and believable. It became a challenge for him to make the RCMP believe his story.

Warren told the doctors that he got the details for his confession from the "Footsteps of the Murderer" article and from information he had picked up talking to other strikers.

In the end Dr. Lohrasbe came up with three possible diagnoses for what Warren had told him. It was possible that Warren was making up his symptoms, that he had never talked to himself, never feared he had cancer, never was depressed, never had problems with his sex life. It could all be a ruse to help him beat the charge.

It was also possible that everything Warren said was true, but the cause of his problems was a complete mental breakdown brought on by his murder of the nine men.

Lohrasbe tended to discount these first two options. He didn't think Warren was lying to him. He dealt with criminals all the time and was used to people trying to get away with lies. Warren didn't strike him as a very good liar. He also thought Warren was telling the truth about the root cause of his depression—that it wasn't caused by a guilty conscience, but was rooted in the other problems in his life. Dr. Lohrasbe could not make his diagnosis with certainty, but he did conclude that Warren's confessions were likely false. His diagnosis was that Warren was clinically depressed at the time of his interview with McMartin and that this depression had had drastic implications for Warren, who was likely an innocent man.

Dr. Ley was even stronger in his conviction that Warren had made a false confession. Throughout the investigation, Warren had been compliant with the police, the psychologist concluded. Warren found them to be nice and helpful though he was also angry with them because they kept focusing on him and other union men. He was clinically depressed when he met McMartin, which made him apathetic, pessimistic and malleable. He considered himself a useless person. His mental processes had slowed down. He was impulsive and self-destructive, but here he faced the biggest psychological crisis of his life. When he at last confessed, he wasn't only doing something positive for the strikers, Dr. Ley concluded, he was lashing back at McMartin and the police. It was as if Warren was saying, "I might not have a dick, but I can fuck you guys."

Chapter 24

FREELY
AND
VOLUNTARILY

HE YELLOWKNIFE COURTHOUSE stood on what the union men
called Fascist Square. The courthouse was kitty-corner to the
RCMP detachment and across the street from the Department of
National Defense. Built to withstand the Arctic winter with windows
that were little more than peepholes, the courthouse was a stark struc-
ture. It had the bunkerlike quality of most Yellowknife office buildings.

The Territorial Supreme Court was on the second floor. The court
had a high-tech feel—the desks for the lawyers and the judge, along
with the boxes for the jury and the prisoner, were finished with chrome.

Warren's trial started at 10:00 A.M., September 6, 1994. Security
was tight. Guards and metal detectors were stationed at the courtroom
door. Before Warren arrived at the building in the morning, court officers had swept the parking lot, using mirrors attached to the ends of
long sticks to look under cars and inside vents. They found no bombs.

The court clerk announced, "All rise," and then Justice Mark de
Weerdt briskly entered the room. The court officers bowed to de
Weerdt, who sat down. "Please be seated," the clerk announced.

Justice Mark de Weerdt sat elevated on a seeming pedestal of
chrome, illuminated by a large, inset ceiling light. Below the judge sat
the court reporter and the court clerk, who was surrounded by boxes of

evidence. Televisions were positioned around the front of the court-room so the judge, the jury, the lawyers and all in the public gallery could watch the various videotapes to be played.

De Weerdt was sixty-six, tall, with silver hair and a kindly face. He was near the end of a career that had included five years as a Crown prosecutor, five years as a defense lawyer, three years trying appeals and two years as a juvenile court judge. He had started his career as an RCMP officer. He'd been a soldier and a tour guide. For a time, he was the house counsel of a British Columbia insurance company. He had directed fifty-five other lawyers in the federal Department of Justice in Vancouver. He had been a Supreme Court judge in Yellowknife for twelve years.

Through the trial de Weerdt was to be repeatedly tested by both lawyers. Both Martin and Orris were hugely competitive. De Weerdt invariably disregarded their bluster while allowing both as much time as they wanted to make their arguments. He didn't use his authority to bully, nor did he take a point made in argument personally. His style was to push the lawyers to work through and examine the legal issues, then to make his own ruling, but only after giving the party that was going to lose one final chance. If he felt it necessary to chastise either Martin or Orris, he did so gently, always with a smile.

While the look and the technology of the courtroom were modern, the lawyers addressed the judge as "My Lord" and called each other "My friend" and "My learned colleague." They all wore the flowing black cloaks of the British system of justice. Their dress and demeanor lent credence to the idea that this wasn't a normal civilian inquiry; it was the highest, most authoritative and dispassionate tribunal in the land, steeped in traditions that assured fairness. The appearance that justice was going to be done was essential in this most political of murder trials, where the participants on either side were unlikely to accept a verdict that contradicted their prejudices.

The courtroom was as divided as the town itself. The defense lawyers, Orris and Boothroyd, sat on one side, Roger Warren right behind them in the prisoner's dock. He was protected from the crowd by a short metal fence and Plexiglas.

Warren's family sat behind him in the public gallery. Helen and her sister Cathy usually attended. Sometimes Warren's daughters, Ann and Pat, came as well. They were surrounded by union people. Some of the union men attended frequently, such as Jack McPhee from Con Mine and Joe Ranger and Sam Pollock from Giant. The only man from the union executive who came to court with any regularity was Bob Kosta. Harry Seeton didn't attend once.

Peter Martin and his assistant, David Guenter, sat at a desk beside the defense table. Behind Martin and Guenter were the widows. Only a few of them sat through the whole case—Judit Pandev and Doreen Hourie—along with Shane Riggs' mom, Carol.

The two factions often glared at each other, but rarely talked. Five court sheriffs provided security. Two RCMP officers in their traditional red serge uniforms, service revolvers in holsters, guarded Warren. Orris asked de Weerdt that the Mounties who took the stand during the trial not be allowed to wear the red serge. Orris said he was already fighting the RCMP's unofficial motto that the Mounties always got their man, and the uniforms only reinforced the idea. De Weerdt ruled against Orris, saying it was traditional in the Northwest Territories for the RCMP to appear in the Supreme Court in red serge. However, de Weerdt did grant Orris one concession: that Warren's RCMP guards not sit right next to him, but at either side of the courtroom.

The security was extreme for Yellowknife, but a few days into the trial the need was made clear when taxi drivers outside the Explorer reported to court sheriff Don Smith that they were picking up the proceedings on their two-way radios. Smith told de Weerdt, who instructed the sheriff to announce this to the court. Court adjourned so the RCMP could investigate. Peter Martin returned to say that the police believed the transmissions were not accidental, but had been done by someone who had brought a transmitter into the courtroom. There were no further reports of any transmissions, and no transmitter was ever found.

The first two months of the trial were taken up with a voir dire, a trial within a trial, during which the jury is out of the courtroom and lawyers argue over legal issues in their absence. The purpose of this first voir dire was to see whether the material in Warren's confessions would even be put to the jury.

De Weerdt had to decide if Warren's confessions were made freely and voluntarily. If they weren't, he would rule them inadmissible. The Crown's case would be over before it started. On the other hand, if de Weerdt said the jury could see the confessions, Martin expected that Orris and Boothroyd might try to make a deal on Warren's sentence before the jury portion of the trial commenced.

The defense's major thrust was to attack Sergeant Gregg McMartin's tactics. If that first part of the confession fell, Orris would then argue that all the other confessions should be thrown out as well because if Warren had never confessed to McMartin, he would never have confessed to McGowan, White, Ravelli, Brandford and Ingram, the cell plant.

The onus was on the Crown to prove beyond a reasonable doubt that the statements were made freely and voluntarily. The reason for the law was straightforward. If the police were allowed to force confessions by using threats, bribes or torture, neither society nor the truth would be served. Coerced statements would be common and many would be false.

Martin argued that Warren was well aware of his legal rights, and that even though Sergeant McMartin may have offered Warren an inducement by mentioning the possibility of a light sentence, the inducement had no real impact. Martin held that Warren confessed for his own reasons. He realized that it was best for everyone if he ended the agony of the strike and the murder investigation. He also felt remorse and was tired of lying. Martin argued that Warren was thinking about confessing even before he saw McMartin. Indeed, Warren himself had told this to Harry Ingram in the jail cell.

Orris argued that Warren would never have falsely confessed if Sergeant McMartin hadn't made threats and offered inducements. McMartin told Warren he was directly connected to Peter Martin and the Attorney General's Department, which was not only a lie, it intimidated Warren, who for seventeen months had been feeling the force of the government crushing him and his union. Orris said McMartin also had disregarded Warren's right to remain silent, and he hadn't listened when Warren talked about getting a lawyer.

One by one, the various Mounties who had dealt with Warren took the stand. The tapes of the confessions were played. Most ran for hours. The voir dire dragged into October. If Orris had any hope of winning, he had to call Warren. Even if they lost the voir dire, taking the stand would give Warren a chance to face Peter Martin and prepare for the bigger test yet ahead at the jury trial.

In the second week of October, a month into the voir dire, Warren took the stand. He spoke hesitantly at first, his voice a monotone, but soon he was making eye contact with his lawyer and gesturing freely. As was his custom, Orris stood across the courtroom, forcing Warren to speak loudly so everyone in court could hear.

Orris helped Warren by starting out with the easy subject of his personal history before moving on to the strike and his first interviews with Constable Nancy Defer immediately after the blast. Warren told Orris that he was surprised when he found out he was a suspect, and he wasn't enthused about the RCMP's attention on the union. "If it was warranted I didn't mind it, but I wasn't sure if it was warranted," he said.

Orris realized it was time to let everyone in on the defense's secret. "Now, Mr. Warren," he said. "Let's deal with this for a moment. As far as the blast on September 18 was concerned, the one that killed the nine miners, did you have anything to do with that?"

"No."

"Do you know who did?"

"No."

Warren's answer astonished many in court, at least those on the Crown's side of the courtroom. They had just sat through four weeks of Roger Warren's confessions, hearing again and again that Warren set the bomb but hadn't meant to kill, hearing it so often that they were certain this would be the line of defense, with Orris fighting to get the charges dropped to mere criminal negligence.

During the following adjournment, de Weerdt asked for a transcript of Orris's questions and Warren's answers. When court was recalled, de Weerdt asked Orris if this line of questioning was relevant to the voir dire. After all, the purpose of the voir dire wasn't to establish if Warren had committed the crime.

"I am not going to go further with that question," Orris replied. "The purpose of the question, my Lord, was simply this: It's anticipated in the course of the evidence that Mr. Warren will give and is giving that he will give certain reasons as to why he was emotionally upset and under pressure and things of that kind when dealing with the police. I anticipate that my friend's cross-examination will say that the reason he was under or felt under that pressure, or felt the oppression, was really not because of the police, but because of a guilty conscience, or a guilty mind, in that regard. And in order to counter that inference, or counter that line of cross-examination, was the only reason I asked those questions."

Orris moved on, asking Warren about his continued dealings with the police through 1992 and 1993. At one point he asked Warren why he kept dealing with the RCMP, McGowan in particular. Warren said he wanted to clear himself. He realized what was at stake for him and the union. "This was something that was a lot more than just a crime. It had come down to: Solve the crime or you're never going to work again. I mean, we were told that."

In his testimony Warren detailed some of what he had told Doctors Ley and Lohrasbe about his reasons for falsely confessing, though he did not mention that he had met with either psychological expert. He told the court that he was profoundly depressed because he had lost his job and his identity as a hardrock miner, but he didn't bring up the violent arguments raging inside his head. He never mentioned his sexual dysfunction or his fear that he had cancer or his hallucinations as he sat listening to Sergeant McMartin. When McMartin confronted him, he said he decided to remain calm, to exercise his right to remain silent. At last he left to take his daughter to therapy. While he feared McMartin, he later returned to the interview room because a few things McMartin had said piqued his curiosity. He wondered if McMartin wanted him to finger Bettger and Shearing, as McGowan had pushed him to do in their August 6, 1993, interview. He also wondered what McMartin was getting at when he suggested that the bomb might have been set to damage equipment, not to kill the nine men.

"What was it that he was saying that made you fearful?" Orris asked.

"It was just his manner. Like, it was just like a waste of time to even raise the slightest objection to anything he was saying. . . . I'd say I was basically browbeaten."

"When you felt that way, Sir, why didn't you simply leave?"

"I think I wanted to leave a couple of times, but I got the impression that I couldn't. . . . When I'd try to leave or make a motion or a suggestion that I was going out to see my wife or this or that, he would get right on me. He'd just overwhelm me, in other words. And if it would have been an ordinary officer, I probably would have said, 'Well, shove it. See you later.' But this guy had already impressed me with his importance, and definitely there is no question about that. Because he mentions the Attorney General and, I mean, you're talking about the full power of the state."

Orris asked Warren if he had wanted a lawyer.

"The guy had no intention of getting me any kind of lawyer, and I didn't want him to get me a lawyer because the minute you mentioned lawyers to the guy, he went ballistic. My personality wasn't in the greatest shape and his was. He was just dominating me. I'm usually not like that, but in this particular situation I was."

"Now, you eventually tell him how this explosion was set up. You remember that, do you not?"

"Yeah, I think I started out to tell him how it could be set up and then it ended up that's what it was."

"Now, Mr. Warren, when you admitted it, could you tell us what was in your mind? Why you did that?"

"At first I figured I'd get another response from him. Like he'd say, 'Now, tell us the truth now. Now, we know you didn't do it, but we know you know who did.' I really thought that's what they were going to do, but as it kept going on—no, this guy, he's buying this. And so I just kept on with it to see how far I can go with this and these guys. Like, I got to trip up sometime. There has gotta be things that they haven't told the public that's going to trip me up, and they're going to say 'Okay, why would you do this? What are you, obstructing justice or something?' But as I was talking they just kept accepting it."

Warren testified that he confessed, hoping he could get a lesser sentence. "I'm doomed anyways, but with a little help from these guys, according to McMartin, I could get as little as two years, eh, so this was quite a thing to work for as far as I was concerned. The best thing I could do was to help these guys. Definitely don't object to anything they want to do."

Warren told Orris that when he met Corporal Ingram, he first thought Ingram was some kind of counselor or police officer put in his cell to keep him from hurting himself.

Orris ended his questioning with only a few minutes left in the day. De Weerdt suggested the court should adjourn over the Thanksgiving long weekend, but Martin asked if he could commence with his cross-examination, knowing that once he had started his questioning, Warren would be bound by his oath not to talk to anyone about his testimony over the weekend, including his lawyers. Martin jumped in where Orris left off, asking Warren if he had read the transcript of the cell conversation between himself and Corporal Ingram.

"Yes, I have."

"All right. I missed the part where you asked him whether he was a police officer or there to guard you?"

"Oh, I never asked him that."

"Why not?"

"Why would I? It was just obvious to me. . . . I got guys out with rifles when I'm out in the bush there with them. People are guarding my family. And they're going to throw me in a cell with a stranger? . . . I was pretty sure he was a police officer. I'm not saying I was positive, but I thought of it, definitely. And especially when he wants to talk about mining. He wants to talk about stuff that no layman or anybody on the street will ever ask a guy."

When court reconvened on Tuesday, October 11, Martin was able to get Warren to agree with him on a number of key points: that Corporal McGowan had always treated him with respect, dignity and professionalism; that during accusatory interviews with Dauk, Keane and McGowan, he knew he was free to leave the room, but stayed anyway; that he had been read his rights numerous times and fully understood them; that he understood he had the right to a lawyer, and in fact knew he could get free legal advice from the union's lawyer, Austin Marshall, who was only a telephone call away.

"So you were never intimidated by the police or fearful of them?" Martin asked Warren.

"No, I wasn't."

"And certainly you were not either intimidated or fearful of McGowan?"

"No, other than the fact that he was a police officer. They were figures of authority. They had a lot of power."

"Let's not talk foolishness here," Martin said. "If you were fearful and intimidated of them, Mr. Warren, you are not going to keep coming back to meet with them. Obviously, when McGowan calls you for a meeting, you are going because you see him as quite harmless, someone you can easily handle and don't mind giving a hand."

Martin next turned to Warren's suggestion that he was intimidated by McMartin's link to the Crown and the Attorney General's Department. Martin reminded Warren that just before he left to pick up his daughter, McMartin had again spelled out this connection. "So at this point you clearly know, as you put it, that this man is a special policeman, that he is associated with the Attorney General's Department. Is that correct?"

"Yes."

"And your answer to this is to stand up and say you have to pick up your daughter and take her for her therapy appointment and you leave."

"Yes."

"You don't ask permission. You leave?"

"Yes, I did."

Martin suggested that after Warren came back at 5:30 P.M., he also knew he could leave at any time and could contact a lawyer whenever he wanted, but he didn't do it.

"I didn't think I needed him," Warren said.

"You didn't want a lawyer? You could handle this problem yourself?"

"Yes, I didn't think it was that big of a problem."

Warren's posture was now closed, his arms close to his body, his hands clasped, head down, his eyes almost never making contact with Martin.

Martin wondered if the defense would use psychiatric experts, so he asked Warren if he had been examined by a psychiatrist after his arrest.

"I don't remember," Warren said.

Martin then turned to the confession itself, asking Warren to explain again how he came up with the details of his story.

"All the part about setting the blast, all that stuff, the technical stuff about it—I made that up," Warren said.

"So, actually as we watched the video, we see you lying?"

"Yes."

"And convincingly lying."

"I put some details in. It is very convincing."

Martin only had to deal with whether Warren had confessed voluntarily, but he realized this might be his only chance to get some answers from Warren. Martin believed that Warren was lying about almost everything now, but over the weekend he and his assistant, Guenter, had been able to pinpoint what they considered to be the biggest lies. To start, there was the satchel of items found in the pond and the burned boots found in Cameron Falls. If Warren had only decided to confess when Sergeant McMartin hit him hard in the interview, when did he get a chance to plant the satchel and burn the boots? And why did he do either act?

Martin first asked about the satchel. In May 1993, Warren explained, he was afraid Tim Bettger and Al Shearing would be charged with the murders. He decided to gather things that might be used in a bomb, put them in the satchel and throw them in the pond. If Bettger and Shearing were ever arrested, he would either make an anonymous call to the RCMP or to a newspaper, maybe sending them a map as well. He would claim that the wrong men had been arrested and that the real murderer had left this satchel in the pond.

To Martin, this story sounded like the whopper of all whoppers. Until this point, he had leaned forward on his lectern, his forehead creased and eyes boring in. He had peppered Warren with questions, never letting up. But now Martin relaxed. He stepped back from the podium and slouched. He put his hands in his pockets. A quizzical look on his face, the hint of a grin on his lips, he said to Warren, "Actually, I am sorry for being so thick about this. I don't see the point of your explanation of putting that stuff in the pond. Why did you do that?"

Again Warren tried to explain, saying he did this covertly to help free someone if he were wrongly arrested and charged.

"How could it help?"

"It would have been quite a question. You have got these guys, but they don't know anything about this stuff."

Martin asked Warren if he had done anything else to obstruct justice, and Warren moved right away to the burning of the boots, claiming that in early September 1993, about a month before he confessed, he took a pair of old green boots out to Cameron Falls. They weren't Kamik boots, they didn't have the draw string at the top, but they were similar. He cut them up, doused them with gas, burned them and threw them in the river.

"What was the purpose for doing that?" Martin asked.

"Same thing. To reinforce this."

"I gather the idea, as I understand it then, Mr. Warren, that depending on how the police investigation went, and on what you heard, you would play God?"

"Well, I suppose I never got a chance to, but I might have. That probably was my mind-set at the time."

As Martin pushed, Warren seemed to shrink in his chair. He slouched more and more until all Martin could see was an unhappy face peeping out from the witness box. Warren got so low in his seat that Martin fleetingly considered walking over and saying, "Are you still there, Roger?" Martin could see that Warren was failing, and before he finished his questioning he wanted to take one run at breaking him completely, catching him up in his lies so that Warren had no choice but to tell the truth and again admit he had set the blast.

Martin started by going over Warren's state of mind in October 1993, how Warren was convinced the strike wasn't going to end, how he worried about the effect it was having on the families of the strikers, how he feared Shearing and Bettger might be arrested, so much so that he apparently had planted the bag and burned the boots in order to free them. "Mr. Warren," Martin said, "I suggest to you that the reason you confessed to this crime, the reasons were these reasons that I have just outlined to you, and your own personal overwhelming sense of remorse, Mr. Warren."

"That's not true," Warren said, his body tight and closed, his eyes down.

"Mr. Warren, you have a sense of remorse about what happened here?"

"Of course I did, the same day it happened."

"And that's because you did it."

"No, it is because I hate seeing anybody getting hurt or killed underground."

Warren's answers now came hesitantly. Martin was ready to spring his final trap.

"I wonder if you would just listen to this tape here," he said to Warren. "And just so you understand it before it has started, this is the conversation between you and White and McGowan on the afternoon of October the 16, 1993, shortly after three o'clock, just minutes after you had been taken from cells."

The court clerk located the tape and handed it to Constable Ken Morrison, who placed it in the stereo. The most heartfelt, painful moment of Warren's confession filled the silence of the courtroom, Warren breaking down and sobbing as he sat in the police car with White and McGowan on their way to Cameron Falls:

Warren: Yesterday, when I was sitting having a coffee with my wife, she didn't know nothing about it, but I decided, fuck, I'm sick of it.

White: You're sick of what?

Warren: Sick of this lying bullshit.

White: So you just felt it was time to get it out in the open?

McGowan: Take a weight off your shoulders.

Warren started to weep then.

White: You okay, Rog?

Warren: *(sobbing now, his voice cracking with pain)* I just never did that before in my life, that lying like that. I hate lying. Did it for a year now.

McGowan: It's okay, buddy.

Warren: Almost as bad as doing that, killing those guys.

The tape ended.

"That was the truth?" Martin asked.

Warren paused, his eyes down, his body tense and closed, as if a rifle shot had just whizzed by his head. It seemed like he was no longer thinking of his answer, but his mind was somewhere else. "The emotional part was mainly because at this time I figured my wife had disowned me for confessing," he said at last. "She didn't seem to want to get in touch with me. I couldn't get a hold of her. That was the main thing that was concerning me."

"I couldn't hear that among the tears—you mentioning your wife," Martin shot back.

"Pardon?" Warren said, wearing the look of a man headed for a collision with a freight train.

"I couldn't hear any comment about your wife among the tears," Martin repeated.

Again Warren hesitated, then said, "No."

"I just heard these—" But Martin was interrupted by Orris, who shot to his feet. "Excuse me, excuse me," the defense lawyer said. "I am sorry. I wonder if he would let Mr. Warren finish the answer, please."

"I obviously struck a nerve here," Martin said. "Would you finish your answer?"

Orris remained standing. "It struck a nerve because my friend has done that on a number of occasions, and I just wish him to stop. That's all."

Now when Warren spoke he had regained his nerve. The moment had passed. Orris's timely interruption had worked.

"The reason I broke down was concern for my wife, what this was going to do to my wife and child, the one that was at home immediately," Warren said. "And when I broke down, I just let it go on as if it was because of lying or killing the guys, whatever. I just kept playing along with it. And that's the only way I can explain it. It was a false thing, really. The only thing true about it was the emotion. But at the time I had an overwhelming sense of abandonment."

"But even at that dark, emotional moment, as you would have us say, you were able to lie, as you tell us now, and lie convincingly?" Martin asked.

"Yeah, I would say so."

"Thank you," Martin said, then sat down, his questions completed.

Warren was the last witness of the voir dire. The court adjourned for one week as Justice de Weerdt worked on his decision. On Friday, October 21, he released his findings to the public. On the key issue, de Weerdt ruled that Sergeant McMartin had indeed offered Warren inducements to confess by spelling out the benefits of confessing to manslaughter. Yet, de Weerdt said, Warren hadn't confessed because of McMartin's inducements. He confessed freely and voluntarily for his own reasons: "The evidence shows that the accused was for some time carefully weighing the pros and cons of making his confession well before he in fact finally made it. He may indeed have been tired of lying when he finally decided to confess to McMartin; but I am satisfied that this alone was not the true reason for his decision to do so. His conscience was clearly troubling him deeply. The relief which he admittedly experienced following his confession is altogether inconsistent, it seems to me, with the emotional stress which he would instead have felt if he had only then begun to embark on a complex series of deliberate and detailed falsehoods designed to masquerade as the truth."

De Weerdt was most impressed by the reenactment video from the mine. "There is no indication whatsoever that he may have been actually inventing details of the tale, which had already unfolded in his interviews with Sergeant McMartin and the other officers on the previous day. On the contrary, the accused's tone and demeanor, as shown and heard on videotape, is very convincing as to the truthful intent of his statements and as to his utter sincerity during the entire reenactment."

De Weerdt concluded his judgment saying that Warren was an enormously controlled and self-confident man. He fully understood his Charter rights. He told the RCMP what he wanted to say, nothing more. His rights had not been violated in any way. The confessions were admissible evidence. "I am completely satisfied that if the administration of justice were to be brought into disrepute, it would only be as the result of the exclusion, not the admission, of the impugned evidence at trial."

With de Weerdt's decision, the Crown prosecutors and the RCMP officers celebrated. At last Vern White felt some relief, far more than he had felt on the night of the confession. White was proud that de Weerdt had said that he and the other investigators didn't go too far, that they had done their job. At last, White believed, justice had been done.

The real trial was to start on Monday, October 24. Over the weekend, White and the other investigators waited for the call from Orris to Martin offering a deal. The call never came. Warren and his lawyers were going for all or nothing. The trial would now almost certainly end with an outright acquittal or a murder conviction.

Chapter 25

HIS OWN WORDS

THE FIVE MEN and seven women of the jury must have realized that their task in deciding Roger Warren's fate would be difficult. No matter what they decided, one side was going to be bitter. But the jurors had some protection. By law, no one could pester them through the trial. And by law, they could not talk about what had gone on in the jury room after the trial ended.

In the jury selection, Justice de Weerdt asked persons with a close connection to the company, the union, the investigators or Warren to eliminate themselves. Martin and Orris then scrutinized each candidate and eliminated those they found lacking. They selected a group of men and women who generally remained keen and attentive through the long run of the trial. They were aged thirty to forty-five and looked to be people who had made a commitment to Yellowknife, not twenty-somethings passing through or packsack workers up on the latest contract. From their neat, trendy and casual dress—only one man ever wore a tie and he wore one every day—the jurors looked to be engineers, government workers and small business owners more than gold miners, mechanics or mill workers.

On October 24, 1994, the jury got its first good look at Roger Wallace Warren. The jurors sat along the right wall of the courtroom, looking out at the public gallery on their left. De Weerdt presided on the jury's right, and ahead of them were the tables where the Crown and the defense sat. Behind Orris and Boothroyd was Warren. He looked more like a crumpled, tired old salesman than a man who had recently been known as the Ace, arguably the best hardrock miner at Giant, a gruff, kick-ass expert of the drill-and-blast game. Warren was far from a malignant presence. Indeed, he had little presence at all. If he hadn't been sitting in the prisoner's dock, he would have been nearly invisible. Though he had been imprisoned for more than a year, his skin was brownish. He was fifty, but he looked ten years older. His graying black hair was combed back on the sides, the court's dim light reflecting off the top of his balding head. He had a beak of a nose and dark eyebrows. He wore conservative, aviator-style glasses, the rests wearing red imprints on the bridge of his nose. The blue blazers and gray double-breasted suits he wore were spiffy, new and set off nicely by floral ties, but they were overshadowed by the slouched shoulders, the dead, close-set eyes. If he was moved by the proceedings, he did not show it. He rarely made eye contact with anyone. He slumped in the prisoner's dock. He stared forward, focusing on nothing in particular. Even as the charges against him and the names of the nine men were read out, he was completely still.

The effect of reading the names on the crowd in the courtroom, however, was electric. It might have been easy to think of the nine men as faceless, anonymous pawns. For a few the victims were nothing more than nine dead scabs. But when their names were read out, everything changed. The court clerk spoke each name in a normal voice, but each resounded like the beat of a drum, one name, one beat, the seemingly endless list, Joe Pandev, Vern Fullowka, Shane Riggs—the realization that each of these men represented an individual, a life, a family— Norm Hourie, Arnold Russell, Malcolm Sawler—the quick, flickering image of how so many men had died at once, obliterated—Chris Neill, Robert Rowsell, David Vodnoski—the shocking reminder of the scope of the crime, the wrongness of it, the grief. It touched anyone who could be touched. Most affected were the two relatives of victims on hand the first day—widow Judit Pandev and Carol Riggs, mother of Shane Riggs. As the names were read they held the strange hope that this time their Joe or their Shane would not be on that list. It was so strange to be sitting here at a murder trial, they thought, so unreal, and if only that name wasn't read out, they could get up, walk out of court and head back to their old lives. But then came the name. Again they were shattered. Carol hunched over and wept. Judit clamped her hand over her mouth, tears streaming down.

Justice de Weerdt commenced to explain to the jury the law of Canada regarding homicide. A homicide, he said, could be either first or second degree murder or manslaughter. First degree murder was not only intentional, but planned and deliberate. Second degree was neither planned nor deliberate, but the killer nevertheless had the intent to kill or cause reckless bodily harm when he acted. In manslaughter, the accused killed while committing another crime, but had no intention of killing.

Justice de Weerdt told the jurors that he would be the judge of the law while they alone would judge the facts. He asked them to consider all evidence before they made any decisions. "Please be sure to keep an open mind," he concluded.

The trial was slated to run for six to eight weeks, ending sometime in December, but before Christmas. First up, Peter Martin would make his case; then Glen Orris and Gillian Boothroyd would have their turn before de Weerdt again talked to the jury and it retreated to make its decision.

In his opening address, Martin leaned forward slightly, arms resting on his lectern. He made clear the point that he most wanted the jury to remember—that Roger Warren had confessed to this crime, that Warren's own words would be the most damning evidence.

Martin didn't need much else. The jury would hear more than a dozen hours of Warren confessing. They'd see him in Giant Mine retracing his route and his actions. The confession was confirmed by physical evidence, such as the murderer's footprints through the mine. It was confirmed by Warren's lack of an alibi and his odd behavior around Robert Carroll on the morning of the blast. It was as long and coherent and detailed a confession as Martin had ever taken to trial.

Martin looked directly at the jury as he spoke. His voice was strange to the ear at first. His sentences were blunt, his rhythm staccato, his enunciation deliberate. He rarely wasted a sentence. His voice was loud, commanding and to the point, and though it was exaggerated, it was an effective tool. Over the course of the long trial, both his clarity and brevity would serve him well. There was rarely a moment when it felt like he was wasting time or confusing the issue.

Martin gave the jurors a brief history of the strike, then told them that Warren broke into the mine and set up his bomb. As he was leaving the scene, Warren realized that his bomb would kill, but he did nothing about it.

"For the next two and a half hours no one knew there was a bomb in that mine except Roger Warren," Martin said, stressing this point, for if the jury accepted it, Warren would be convicted of murder and not manslaughter. The law said that Warren's realization that his bomb would kill was the same as his having the intent to kill. Even if he wasn't thinking of killing when he rigged the bomb, he could have stopped the mass murder with one telephone call. But he did nothing.

In his initial dealings with the police, Warren tried to deflect suspicion onto other men, Martin said, but at last he confessed. The jury would hear Warren describe his crime in his own words. As for Warren's story that he only wanted to blast an ore car and not kill anyone, Martin told the jurors to ask themselves one question: "Are these the rationalizations of a man hoping to minimize his involvement in this most horrible crime?"

Martin decided against showing the jury photographs of the charred, dismembered corpses. He felt he didn't need to rely on such a disturbing display to sway them. Nevertheless, the jurors had to get an idea of what the underground and the blast site looked like, and the first video that Martin played for the jury was of the carnage. The camera traveled down the dark tunnel, zeroing in on the twisted steel, broken pipes, chunks of wood blasted into the hardrock and, somewhere in the wreckage, the bodies of the nine miners. The bodies had been edited out, except for one largely intact body on the tracks, Arnold Russell. When they saw Russell's corpse, Judit Pandev and Carol Riggs fled the courtroom. Carol headed right for the washroom, followed by victim relief worker Diane Barr.

"If Mrs. Warren comes in, I'll shove the door right in her face," Carol seethed.

The Riggs were a hot-blooded clan, and Carol had barely been able to reign in her rage during the pre-trial voir dire. Sitting so close to the enemy infuriated her. She couldn't get at Warren so she focused on Helen and her sister Cathy. Carol controlled herself only because she knew an outburst could get her banned from court. But after the verdict came in, she told Judit that she wanted to get her hands on Helen.

Tracey Neill had been in Yellowknife for parts of the initial six-week voir dire, but after she got the gist of the Crown's case, she left, planning to return when Warren's defense started up and she could find out something new. Doreen Hourie had also been at the voir dire, sitting with Judit and Carol. Doreen had to leave for a family funeral, but she returned a few days into the Crown's case. Sheila Fullowka and Bonnie Sawler were the only other widows to attend any part of the trial, each coming up during the Crown's case for a few weeks.

Doreen, Judit and Carol accepted the decision of the other widows not to attend, but the acceptance came hard for Doreen. Back at the preliminary hearing in February, she had heard some of the other widows talking about getting on, starting a new career, even meeting a new man. The talk had angered her. Where was their loyalty? How could they be so cold? Over the summer, though, Doreen started to understand. The other women had loved their men, but many had children to support. They had to get on with it. For her and Judit and Carol, though, there was no moving forward. They had lost everything, including much of their peace of mind. The only way to get it back was to attend court every single day. Norm and Joe were the eldest of the nine dead men, the closest to retirement. Both Doreen and Judit had been ready for the next stage, the happy years of their retirement in the sunny lake country of south central British Columbia. When it was taken away, they were destroyed.

Judit was upset that so few people from town ever sat with them in court. She had lived in Yellowknife all her adult life, and now she wondered where all those friends were. The Warrens were surrounded by supporters almost every day, but Judit thought no one gave a damn about the three women. It was as if the three of them had some disease. It was a cruel town, Judit decided, quick to wash its hands of her and anything else to do with the murder.

Judit stayed in a room with a hot plate and fridge at the YWCA. One day the girl at the front desk asked her, "Why did you come back to this torture?"

"I don't want them to forget there was a man, nine of them," Judit said. "They are not here anymore and somebody has to represent them. Otherwise they will be forgotten. How would it be if the front row was totally empty, and the jury looks over and sees that?"

Every day the three sat in the same seats in the first row, directly behind Peter Martin and David Guenter, Judit on the aisle seat so she could stretch her arthritic leg, Carol next to her, then Doreen, then someone from victim support services, usually Diane Barr. The women came to court together, went through the metal detector gate one after the other and left for lunch together. At night they often met or talked on the telephone. If a reporter asked for an interview with one, all three showed up to share their stories. "Our three heads—we got a perfect vegetable garden," Judit joked with her friends.

Doreen still thought about suicide. Her prayer every night was that she would not wake up in the morning. If she downed all her pills at once, she thought that might do the trick. But she knew Norm would have wanted her in court. She also feared that if she killed herself she would end up in a different place in the afterlife than Norm. They would never again meet.

Doreen made sure to get to court each morning and afternoon with time to spare. She felt sick with apprehension when the proceedings started without her. It seemed as if all the people in court watched her as she walked to her seat in the front row. She could hardly breathe. To make sure this didn't happen, she stopped leaving the courtroom on the regular morning and afternoon breaks. She stayed in her seat and stared at Warren or Orris. When the judge and jury returned to the court, and all in court were ordered to stand, Doreen had to pull herself up, grabbing the railing in front of her. She could not bear to look at the jury. She feared they would see how desperate she was for them to convict Warren.

It deeply hurt Doreen to go to court every day, but it kept her alive. Some days she heard things that made her want to cry, but she kept it in, not wanting to give the CASAW faction the satisfaction of seeing her tears. She didn't want them to know how beat she really was. She fixed a smile on her face. The turmoil inside made her hot and itchy. She tried not to scratch too much, but she couldn't control it. Some days her arms bled from her nails digging in.

She stayed with friends out at the Giant Mine townsite. She looked in the mirror and could not believe what had become of her. She was sad, rapidly aging and drug-addicted. At night she walked around and everything reminded her of Norm. The mine whistle blew to end the shift and she was right back in July and August 1992, Norm working underground, CASAW men shouting threats over the line at him.

It hurt Doreen to see Warren still breathing. His testimony in the voir dire and the confession tapes enraged her, all the talk about how Warren just had to travel for a few more minutes past the spot where he set the bomb and he could have blown up the shaft and shut the place down. Or he could have blown up a few scoop trucks in the 712-scoop shop. That would hurt Royal Oak far more than killing men, Doreen thought. Men lined up for jobs, but machinery would cost Witte money. Even as he set the bomb, Warren could have used just a few sticks of powder, instead of thirty sticks and the full bag of AMEX. Norm might have come home mangled, but at least he would have come home.

The worst moments came when Warren talked about his second thoughts after setting the bomb, about maybe calling in a bomb scare, but not doing it because he was wet or he didn't have to take a shit so he had no excuse to ask for a ride. *My life is over because Roger Warren didn't have to take a shit!* In moments of rage, her voice cracking and rising high, Doreen swore to Judit and Carol that she was capable of anything, that if Roger Warren got off, she would gun him down and not feel a moment's remorse. The thought helped her cope with any fears that Warren might go free. She would take the $50,000 in blood money and use it to hunt him down. And if she ever did knock off Warren, no one would have to go through the charade of giving her a high-priced lawyer, a judge and a jury, she told her friends. She would stand up and say she did it, and that would be the end of it. Wherever she would go, it could be no worse than the place she was living now.

Sometimes Doreen looked at Warren's slender hands. It was hard to accept that these were the hands that had killed Norm and the hands that had had the power to change things by making one phone call. If Warren ever looked over, she stared until he turned away. Sometimes she had to bite her finger to keep herself from standing and shrieking at him: "That's enough, you son of a bitch! Just get this over with! Quit pissin' around!"

Couldn't he see the pain he was causing by dragging this out? God, it had to be just as tortuous for him and his family to keep playing this game. Doreen wasn't so blinded by hate that she didn't notice the suffering of Helen Warren and her daughters. Doreen saw herself in Helen's pinched, agony-scarred face. Helen was going through the same thing, and Doreen felt for this woman who loved a man who would do such a thing. Roger had ruined her life, too. Doreen hoped that the Warrens felt the same way about her, that they accepted that she had a right to her suffering. She knew this wasn't likely, though, not with the way she stared down Roger, aggravating the Warrens and their supporters. "I don't know why she doesn't quit staring at him," she overheard them say.

Peter Martin planned to tell the story of the crime in chronological order. First to testify were the RCMP officers who found the footprints at Akaitcho and in the mine; then came the Royal Oak miners such as Don Moroz, Keith Murray and Noel O'Sullivan, who found the bodies on the 750-drift; then came striker Max Dillman, who could place Warren on the picket line that night; then Nancy Defer, who first dealt with Warren; then McMartin, McGowan and White, who got the confessions; then the bomb experts; and finally Brandford, Ravelli and Ingram, the last officers to hear Warren confessing.

Martin saw the evidence taking no more than four weeks to present, but Orris had his own plan. Where the Crown wanted things to be smooth and seamless, he wanted them ragged and torn. He not only had to attack each piece of the Crown's evidence, but he had to put forward the defense's platform that the confessions were false. Otherwise the jury might wonder why he was even bothering. After all, Warren had admitted doing it, hadn't he?

Orris pounced as quickly as he could, ambushing the Crown's case on the second day when Sergeant Wayne Locke was on the stand. Locke told the jury about tracking and photographing the footprints in the B-3 area of the mine. Locke said he measured the prints and made casts of them. He found them to be the length and proportion of a pair of new size eleven Kamik boots.

Locke had also been the videotape cameraman on the October 16, 1993, reenactment. Martin didn't want to talk about the reenactment until later in his case and planned to recall Locke to the stand at that point. Orris, however, used Locke's participation to the defense's advantage. Orris questioned Locke about Warren's demeanor on the night of the confession, then asked: "Are you aware, Sir, that the defense thinks that these confessions are false, are untrue?"

Locke stumbled. Martin jumped up to object, saying Locke could not possibly know what the defense was thinking, which is what Locke eventually answered.

Orris, of course, didn't care what Locke said. He had planted the idea that maybe the case against Warren wasn't so perfect as the Crown was suggesting.

Orris and Martin both wore the black robes of the court, both resided in Yellowknife at the Executive House apartments, both worked out every day after court at the Bodyworks gym and both presented much more warm and friendly demeanors outside the courtroom. In court, however, they were all argument and fight, though their methods had little in common. They were physical and stylistic opposites. Orris had the look of a heavyweight boxer, Martin a long distance runner. Orris was tall, Martin was short. Orris was thick, Martin was thin. Orris was bald, Martin had a full head of hair. Orris had a mustache, Martin was clean shaven. Orris roamed the courtroom, sometimes standing at his desk, sometimes beside the jury, sometimes right next to the witness. Martin invariably rattled off his questions from his lectern. While Orris sometimes rambled, Martin was invariably direct. Orris exuded confidence and made a better first impression, but Martin's efficiency played better over the trial's long haul.

Doreen Hourie, Judit Pandev and Carol Riggs all harbored mild crushes on Martin. He had become their anchor. Every day when he and David Guenter strode into court in their dark robes, the three women sat taller in their chairs. Yes, they thought, maybe today will be fine. Maybe we can survive today. The three couldn't see Martin's face as he asked his questions, but they studied him nonetheless. If he scratched his head, they worried, wondering what was troubling him. If they saw his jaw clenched, they feared something had gone very wrong. When Martin and Orris argued over a legal point in a voir dire, Doreen kissed her ring and prayed that Norm and the spirits of the other men would work on de Weerdt so he would rule in favor of the Crown.

"We're hanging on every impression on your face, every smile you make, every move you make, or you bite your lip," Judit said to Martin one day.

"Okay, I promise, from now on I'm gonna smile," Martin said.

Helen Warren hated Peter Martin. She called him a little fucker. Carol Riggs had the same contempt for Orris. She had only disgust for a man who would defend the person who had killed her son. Doreen Hourie realized Orris had a job to do, but if he was going to play his games trying to free Warren, she decided never to speak to him. If Doreen couldn't catch Warren's eye, she looked over at Orris and Boothroyd. Sometimes Orris looked back; Doreen glared at him until he looked away. She wanted Orris to know he didn't intimidate her.

Judit Pandev saw in Orris a man determined to free his client, but she thought he was a gentleman nonetheless. Early in the trial, he had introduced himself and shook her hand.

"I know how you feel because I have lost a member of my family through accident," he had said.

Judit had just nodded, afraid that if she spoke she would weep.

"I know you don't like me very much right now," Orris said.

"Uh, no, not really," Judit laughed. "My problem with you is you're too damn good."

Orris also laughed. "I understand. I understand."

Martin and Orris almost never conceded a point, but only rarely were their clashes angry. Most often they were characterized by dogged, learned, if somewhat hyperbolic rhetoric and extreme self-interest. On any given issue it was common for both Orris and Martin to claim their respective positions were backed by the relevant laws and to strongly suggest to Justice de Weerdt that if he didn't agree with them, he would not only be making a grievous error in this trial, he would be defying the entire history of Canadian jurisprudence. On at least one occasion, both Orris and Martin raised the specter of a mistrial if they should be ruled against. As was pointed out by one trial observer, CBC radio reporter Joclyn Cozac, with Orris and Martin battling there was never any shortage of testosterone in the courtroom.

In the second week of the Crown's case, the first week of November 1994, Martin asked shift bosses Don Moroz and Keith Murray to rate the chances of someone surviving a blast of one bag of AMEX and between twenty-five to thirty sticks of powder (a smaller number than the thirty sticks he actually believed were used) if he stood eighty feet down the train tracks and a number of ore cars were in the way.

"Extremely slim," Moroz said. "The concussion would kill him. . . . Anybody who has worked around powder knows there is a concussion effect, and you do everything you can to get out of the way."

"Zero," Murray said. "The concussion would beat you up pretty bad."

Both Moroz and Murray had dreaded showing up in court, knowing how Warren and his CASAW supporters would view them. Yet both were determined to testify. For the memory of the nine men, Moroz was prepared to run a gauntlet of union men to get into that courtroom.

Murray sat in court only a few feet from his old best friend in the prisoner's box, but for the forty-five minutes he testified, he didn't look at Warren once. The hardest part for Murray was seeing Warren's daughter Ann in the courtroom. He had coached her in baseball. She looked at him as if he were betraying her dad.

Up next was former mine manager Terry Byberg, who talked about seeing Warren parked on the Ingraham Trail on mine property at about 9:30 A.M. on September 18. In his cross-examination, Orris asked what would happen to a striker if he was found walking on Royal Oak property. Byberg said the Pinkerton guards would arrest him and hand him over to the RCMP. The man would then be fired. Orris was laying the foundation for what Warren would later say on the stand.

Before Noel O'Sullivan's testimony, Martin asked Judit Pandev, Doreen Hourie and Carol Riggs to leave the room. O'Sullivan would be the only man to talk about the gruesome scene, giving details that the three women still did not know.

After describing the carnage to the jury, O'Sullivan talked about tracking the footprints through the mine. He testified about the key discovery at the 425- and 575-levels of the Akaitcho shaft, where it was clear from the footprints that the murderer got lost trying to find the ladders to the next levels down.

Like Murray and Moroz, O'Sullivan told the jury about the lethal nature of that many explosives in a drift. In his own mind, O'Sullivan had no doubt that Warren meant to kill. With Warren's experience, he had to know. No matter how rushed he was, he still had to haul eighty pounds of explosives off the loki and put it beside the track, and eighty pounds was no small load. He still had to hook up the B-line to the DCD cap, knowing full well that if the bomb went off then, he would be vaporized.

O'Sullivan ended his direct evidence by describing how in May 1994, he and Sergeant Gary Christison had walked the route described by Warren. Even with a hip that was increasingly sore and was soon to require surgery, O'Sullivan had made the trip in three hours.

O'Sullivan expected Orris to be antagonistic, but the cross-examination was uneventful. Afterward, Martin thanked him. O'Sullivan was glad that he had played the role he did and glad that the matter of Warren getting lost in Akaitcho was proving to be a key piece of evidence for the Crown, just as it had been key to his own deliberations.

Since the arrest, O'Sullivan had been reconsidering his opinion of Warren. At first he felt somewhat sad that his theory had been proved true, that such a respected, hardworking man as Warren was facing a mass murder charge. Slowly, though, any regret was replaced by contempt. He bristled when he heard that many of the CASAW men still thought of Warren as a friend, a hero, even an innocent man. O'Sullivan suspected that the union hardcore resented him for helping the RCMP. If the murder had remained unsolved, they could always have said it was an accident, an inside job, with a cover-up by the RCMP and Peggy Witte.

At one point in his testimony, O'Sullivan was asked by Martin to identify Warren for the jury. It was the only time the two made eye contact, Warren glaring back from the prisoner's box. He had looked like an angry man to O'Sullivan. But he thought Warren also looked like a coward.

O'Sullivan had come to believe that only a coward would blow up men in the dark, then deflect blame on his union brothers. Only a coward would confess, then recant. A coward was capable of anything, O'Sullivan thought. A coward would blow the world apart if he could rather than face the facts.

Nancy Defer, now a corporal and stationed in Iqaluit on Baffin Island, was the first of the Homicide Task Force investigators to take the stand. Defer introduced Warren's first interview with the RCMP, which she had conducted on September 25, 1992, one week after the blast. The tape was played, Warren laying out his alibi.

Gillian Boothroyd cross-examined Defer. Defer admitted that she thought Warren was telling her the truth when he described his alibi of walking up and down the picket line. But Defer said her suspicions were raised one month later when she asked Warren to show her his clothing from that night, and he presented the size eleven Kamik boots with the defaced soles.

Boothroyd was an odd match with Orris. While his game was self-assurance, she presented herself as compassionate and empathetic. Of the four lawyers, she was most likely to give up a point of argument. In court Warren sometimes turned and waved at Helen, but the person he spoke to most often was Boothroyd. He considered her to be a real fighter. She believed strongly in his innocence. Some days, to the disgust of the widows, Boothroyd fawned over him, smiling, bringing him packages of Cameo cigarettes.

"Coffin nails, Mr. Warren," she said as she handed the packs to him.

"They make me want to live," Warren said.

The assistant Crown prosecutor, David Guenter, meanwhile, was a distilled version of Martin. Martin often relied on Guenter to make legal arguments. Guenter's manner was even more matter-of-fact and concise than Martin's, a tendency much appreciated by de Weerdt.

Martin decided against playing tapes of the various interviews between Warren and the RCMP from November 1992 to August 1993, both to save time and to spare the jury from hearing the police's same old questions followed by Warren's same old denials. The interviews were also speckled with references to crimes committed by Al Shearing and Tim Bettger, and Martin wanted the jury to hear as little as possible about those.

Martin jumped from the Defer interview to Warren's showdown one year later with Sergeant Gregg McMartin. Orris had gone after McMartin in the pre-trial voir dire and McMartin expected the same during the trial, but he had no huge worries. He believed he had done nothing wrong when he interviewed Warren. There had been no yelling, screaming or knocking over tables and chairs. He believed there were no outright threats or promises though de Weerdt had seen a few inducements.

McMartin had thought about that interview a lot in the following year. He'd left Yellowknife the day after the interview and felt like he could have floated home to Calgary on the adrenaline high from the biggest coup of his career. On the plane he'd had a few celebratory drinks and wore a smile that wouldn't leave his face. He kept thinking back to a phone call he got from Peter Martin in the early morning, how Martin had congratulated him and said, "Gregg, you have absolutely no idea what you have just done."

But when McMartin had at last got home to his wife in Airdrie, a bedroom community outside of Calgary, he'd crashed. He came down with the most throbbing, debilitating migraine headache of his life. For two days, he lay in the dark on the couch, unmoving, wet towels on his face, trying not to think, unable to shut off the verbal battle between himself and Warren.

He started to dream about Warren—fuzzy, tension-filled dreams, where the only thing McMartin saw clearly was Warren's face. It was not the face of an innocent man, someone who set a bomb and didn't mean to kill anyone. McMartin kept thinking back to the interview. Warren had been so cold, so unemotional. It was strange. Even the worst murderers McMartin had run across usually choked up a bit about their crimes. The only real emotion Warren ever showed was excitement about making the bomb. McMartin didn't think Warren's remorse about the nine men was heartfelt. McMartin had no sympathy or compassion for the man. He was a liar and a murderer, nothing less.

Getting him to confess had been the highlight of McMartin's career. He thought it was a hell of a way for him to cap off things, and a hell of a kick start for his planned private practice in polygraph, statement analysis and detective work. His testimony at the trial was his last big job before he handed in his gun and his badge. On the stand, he briefly set the scene of the interview, describing the task force office, the interview room, his own dress and Warren's dress and demeanor. The tape was then played, hour after hour of McMartin droning on, getting louder and more insistent, then the angry back-and-forth sparring, then Warren's capitulation.

McMartin worried about how the relatives of the dead men would take the part of the interview where he mimicked Warren's antiscab rhetoric and praised Warren for being man enough to kill scabs. Before this section was played, McMartin asked Martin to tell Doreen, Judit and Carol that he had only said these things because Warren wanted to hear them.

Despite this precaution, McMartin still felt near tears when he heard himself spewing this hatred about the nine dead men. But afterward, Judit met him outside court and gave him a hug. She told him he did a great job. She didn't care about his talk and neither did Carol or Doreen. McMartin could have kissed Warren's ass if it got him to confess, Doreen thought. Without McMartin's work, Warren might still be a free man.

In his cross-examination of McMartin, Orris had to start changing the jury's perception of Warren's confession. He wanted to make the jurors see the interrogation as a sleazy, rough and manipulative con job where McMartin had used blatant threats and promises to get an innocent, depressed man to confess. Orris had to show moral outrage at McMartin's interviewing style. If he didn't, the jurors certainly wouldn't.

By his size alone, Orris was an intimidating man, but in his cross-examination of McMartin he raised his voice a notch until it had the quality of a wrecking ball. McMartin's response was to freely admit his lies to the jury, then attempt to justify them. Yes, he was lying when he told Warren he had been working closely with Peter Martin and the Attorney General's Department. But he only said this to explain why an unknown officer had come all the way from Calgary to talk to him. Yes, he was lying when he told Warren he was absolutely convinced he hadn't set the blast to kill anyone. Indeed, McMartin said he didn't know if the blast was deliberately set to kill or not. He was just trying to show himself as an understanding man. "The effect I wanted to leave on Mr. Warren was: You can talk to me; you can tell me what happened; I'm not going to think it's such a heinous crime."

Orris accused McMartin of using the fact that there would be no end to the strike without an arrest to put Warren in a certain state of mind. McMartin turned around Orris's attack. He told the jury he did the things he did because he was sure of one thing: "I was convinced Mr. Warren set that bomb, and I wanted to know what the truth was."

Any time Orris pushed him, McMartin came back with this point: "I believed in my mind that Mr. Warren had knowledge," he said. "He knew something about it. Otherwise he wouldn't be lying."

In a break in the trial, Orris complained to de Weerdt about McMartin repeatedly saying that Warren wasn't telling the truth. De Weerdt decided he should talk to the jury about the issue. When the jurors returned to court after the recess, de Weerdt reminded them that while Constable Defer had said she thought Warren was telling the truth in his first interview, it was just her opinion, just as Sergeant McMartin's assertion that Warren was a liar was only his opinion. "One way you could put it—these opinions are irrelevant," de Weerdt said. "They are not evidence on which you can reach a conclusion on whether Mr. Warren is truthful or not truthful."

Orris next looked at the threats McMartin leveled at Warren, how McMartin kept telling Warren that if he didn't quit lying it would show he was a cold, callous Clifford Olson-type murderer. When Warren still didn't budge, Orris said McMartin threatened to go back to Calgary and report to the Crown prosecutor. "What you were saying to Mr. Warren was, 'I don't believe you. I work very closely with Peter Martin. I am convinced you set the blast. If you don't confess to me, I'm going back to tell Peter Martin that you don't give a shit, so do what you have to do because he doesn't give a shit.'"

"Yes," McMartin said.

"'Unless you say you're sorry, I'm threatening you with a first degree murder charge.'"

"Mr. Warren may have taken it that way."

Orris next attempted to question McMartin about Al Shearing and Tim Bettger. It was a tactic Orris would try to employ again and again during the testimony of the RCMP officers, and one that Martin strenuously battled.

The issue was whether the illegal activities of Shearing and Bettger had anything to do with the charges against Warren. Orris argued that Shearing and Bettger's cases were relevant. He said the RCMP's pursuit of these two men affected Warren's state of mind on the night he confessed. Warren was worried that the police were not only going to arrest innocent men, but men who had been on the CASAW executive. If Shearing and Bettger went down, Warren feared the union would go down as well.

Again and again the jury had to leave the courtroom so Orris and Martin could argue this matter in voir dires. Orris claimed he should be allowed to bring up the fact that Tim Bettger had a bomb on the picket line at the time of the blast, the bomb later found in Rob Wells' trailer. Orris said he merely wanted to show that other CASAW strikers had been engaged in this type of activity during the strike.

Martin suspected that Orris's goal was far more ambitious. He feared that Orris brought up Shearing and Bettger to try to create a reasonable doubt about Warren's guilt. It was an obvious move. If most of the RCMP investigators had been all but convinced that Shearing and Bettger were the culprits, couldn't a jury be sold the same idea? At least it could create a reasonable doubt for them about Warren's guilt.

But Orris insisted this wasn't his intent at all. He knew the rules of the court prevented him from accusing Shearing or Bettger. In order to blame either man, Orris first had to show that they had been on the picket line after midnight on September 18, that they were at the scene of the crime. Orris knew both men had solid alibis for the night, which was why the RCMP never charged them.

With McMartin on the stand, the Shearing and Bettger issue came up as Orris tried to enter into evidence the *Journal*'s "Footsteps of the Murderer" article. Orris pointed out that McMartin had used a map from the story to help Warren describe his route through the mine. Orris also said that the *Journal* story had affected Warren's state of mind at the time of the confession so it should be admissible in court.

Martin's opposition to the *Journal* article was vehement. He knew the article not only spelled out the Progression Theory, but it clearly stated that the police believed in it. Martin told de Weerdt that the article could only cloud the issue for the jury. "The article is a work of fiction," he said.

"It makes good reading though," de Weerdt smiled.

"It is most misleading," Martin continued. "It is a work of fiction anchored by only a few facts."

At best, Martin said an edited version of the article should be entered, containing only those facts that dealt with the blast, not with the evidence linking Suspect 1 and Suspect 2, Bettger and Shearing, to the murder. Justice de Weerdt didn't allow the jury to see the article, but said he might later reconsider his decision if it became apparent that it had affected Warren's state of mind.

Orris's questioning of McMartin finished on that note. The cross-examination's effect on the jury was impossible to tell, but Roger Warren at least wasn't impressed with McMartin. Afterward, Warren boasted to Sergeant Jim Barr, his escort to and from jail, that he could learn to do McMartin's job in a couple of hours, but McMartin could never make it as a miner because he was fucking lazy.

The Crown's case lasted five weeks, but all it really needed was fifty-five minutes, the length of time it took to play the video reenactment of Roger Warren in Giant Mine. The video came in the middle of the Crown's case.

On most days every second chair in the courtroom was empty, but the place filled when word got out that the reenactment video was coming. Four television sets were positioned, one for the witness, one for the judge, one for the jury and one for Warren, the lawyers and the gallery. No one looked away from the screen as the video played.

In full color, Roger Warren led Vern White and Dale McGowan

into Akaitcho, showed them where he got his explosives, then, at the blast site, kneeled and mimicked the construction of the bomb. Doubt, like fear and anxiety, is not just a state of mind, but a physical state. As the reenactment video played, doubt evaporated from the core of many people in the courtroom, including some people in the CASAW gang, who had held out until then that Warren was innocent. The video changed the trial. From that point on many of the jurors looked as if the rest of the case was a formality. They sat back, their eyes glazed, whenever Orris tried to make a point.

The video also acted as a balm on Judit Pandev, Carol Riggs and Doreen Hourie. From then on it was much easier for them to walk into court. Doreen started to feel so strong that she decided she would try to quit taking her pills. She was drained at the end of each day, and it occurred to her that if she didn't quit the tranquilizers when she was exhausted it wouldn't be any easier after the trial. She barely made it through court on her first drug-free days, but she felt better about herself. More and more she was becoming the leader of her little group. Every day she told Carol and Judit a few jokes to keep them loose. She tried to set aside her anxieties about the trial. She convinced herself there would be justice. All she wanted to hear was the word *guilty*. She didn't care if it was for first, second or manslaughter. Guilty was enough. On the day of the verdict she planned to wear a T-shirt that she'd had made up with Norm's face on the front and the caption: "CASAW '92 Never Told Norm It Was A Live Or Die Vote."

But after she dropped the medication, Doreen started to dream again. In her sleep she saw Roger Warren down at the 750-drift, working quickly to rig his bomb, just as he had done in the video reenactment. She couldn't stop him. Nor could she stop the man-car as it came down the tracks and triggered the device. Bodies were blown everywhere. She checked them, but they had no faces. She never saw Norm's face. She wondered if he had suffered. She knew he had died instantly, but still there had to have been that moment of pain when Norm was ripped from this life to whatever came next.

Doreen believed that Norm's spirit was with her in court, and Judit and Carol believed the same about Joe and Shane. One day Judit turned to Carol and asked, "Did you say something?"

"No," Carol said.

Judit was sure she had heard a whisper. Another day she felt a cold hand touch her cheek, just the way Joe would touch her. She knew he was around her. She came to court not just to represent him, but to be with him.

Behind Roger Warren was a row of empty seats. The prisoner's box blocked the view so no one ever sat in the chairs, but Doreen, Carol and Judit believed that the ghosts of the nine men sat there.

Peter Martin was leery to call union strikers, believing they would likely be hostile witnesses. With striker Alex Mikus, however, Martin decided to take the risk. Mikus didn't want to testify, but he told Martin he would only tell the truth, which was all Martin wanted to hear.

Martin wanted to show the jury how Roger Warren went about putting together his alibi. Even before he met with Defer one week after the blast, Warren had talked to some strikers who had been on the line, but he didn't get to them all. Warren had told Defer that he had slept on the bus at gate three from 3:00 to 5:00 A.M. where he saw Leo Lachowski and Kelly Rhodes. But after going over all the alibi stories and cross-referencing, the RCMP had found that Mikus had visited the bus at 4:00 A.M. and hadn't seen Warren. When Warren found this out, he changed his story to say he must have left before Mikus came by. Martin wanted the jury to understand Warren's machinations, and calling Mikus was the best way to do it.

Mikus was a clean-cut man, middle-aged, plainspoken, with a strong Eastern European accent. He told the jury that in the days after the deadly blast, he had seen Warren around the union hall saying he was afraid the police would nail him. "He was kind of upset because he didn't have an alibi for a couple of hours."

Mikus next described his visit to the strikers' bus at gate three. He told the jury he didn't see Warren inside or outside the bus. Mikus said he had talked about his visit to the bus around the union hall.

Next, Martin called Giant Mine supervisor Brian Broda, who said he had seen a man who looked similar to Warren on the Ingraham Trail at 6:00 A.M. on September 18, 1992. This evidence meshed with Warren's various stories and put the miner right near the B-138 portal, the killer's exit from the mine.

To round out the Crown's case, Martin called explosives expert Jean-Yves Vermette. Vermette showed the jury an important piece of hold-back evidence, the remains of two detonated blasting caps found at the blast site, one located near ground zero, the other one up the drift, near the same spot where Warren had confessed that he tested his nine-volt battery to make sure it would detonate the cap.

Many of the items that Warren had confessed to using in the bomb were not found at the blast site, including the nine-volt battery, the toggle switch and the fishing line trip wire, Vermette told the jury. But he said this didn't surprise him. The bomb's fireball was two thousand degrees Fahrenheit, hot enough to vaporize many metals. Parts of bombs were usually lost in explosions, Vermette testified.

Vermette said that even if Warren's plan had worked and he blew up an ore train, not a man-car, he would have killed someone. At the site of the deadly blast, the explosive pressure was ten times the lethal limit. Vermette said the pressure on the ore train's driver, seventy-seven feet from the blast, would be ninety-six pounds per square inch, well above the lethal limit of twenty-nine pounds per square inch. The pressure on the ore train's driver could collapse his lungs and break up his liver and other vital organs. His body could be picked up and hurled against the hardrock wall.

In his cross-examination of Vermette, Orris again tried to get at Shearing and Bettger. He asked Vermette about the items he had found in the search of Tim Bettger's house on March 30, 1993. When Martin objected, the jury went out so the lawyers could argue whether the issue was relevant to the trial.

"There were some very significant items found at Mr. Bettger's residence," Orris said, referring in particular to the clothes peg activation device. "It sets out someone else in Yellowknife who obviously was involved or may very well have been involved in the building of an explosive consistent with the blast of September 18, 1992."

Justice de Weerdt ruled that Orris could establish through Vermette that the house had been searched. The RCMP's investigation of Bettger might have played on Warren's state of mind when he confessed. But de Weerdt said that Orris could not ask about any of the items found in the search, that this information was an irrelevant side issue.

To put all the Crown's hold-back evidence in a neat package, Martin called on Vern White, who had been promoted to Sergeant. During Warren's preliminary hearing, White had been nervous and drank water compulsively, believing it helped him control both his nerves and the pace of the questioning; if he was stumbling he could always pause to have a sip. But now White was strong on the stand, sure of Warren's guilt and bothered that the miner was trying to slither out from under the weight of the evidence.

White testified that Warren knew things that only the RCMP and the murderer could know: The killer getting momentarily lost in the Akaitcho shaft's 425- and 575-levels, as the footprints showed; Warren showing the police how he parked the scoop at the 907-powder magazine, which matched up with the tire tracks and footprints left behind; the DCD test blast caps, entered into evidence by Vermette; the bag of material for the bomb dumped in the pond outside Yellowknife; the drill steel rod, which Warren said he had used to anchor the blast. "It meant nothing to the investigators until pointed out by Mr. Warren," White testified.

One piece of evidence that didn't quite fit was Roger Warren's boots. The trial didn't hinge on the boots, but Martin couldn't overlook them. The police believed that the murderer had on size eleven Kamik boots and that these were the ones with the defaced soles they had seized from Warren's house. But when Warren confessed, he was adamant that he wore size ten Kamik boots, the boots he burned and threw in Cameron Falls. Either Warren was mistaken about which boots he had worn that night, the police were mistaken in their measurements or a manufacturing error in the size ten Kamik boots gave them soles a quarter of an inch too large, making them leave behind footprints for size eleven Kamiks. Martin and the RCMP favored the first option—that in his haste Warren thought he wore the size ten Kamiks, but actually wore the size elevens.

After Warren's arrest, the RCMP had followed up on Warren's claim that he bought items for the bomb at Canadian Tire. Martin recalled Corporal Defer to show the jury a receipt for the purchase of snowmobile hose, fishing line and electrician's tape from the store on September 17, 1992.

One other piece of evidence entered was the contents of the satchel found in the pond where Warren said he disposed of items he'd used in the blast. The items included batteries, plastic tubing and fishing line. They were found in a Canadian Tire bag inside the satchel.

The final week of the Crown's case was taken up by Robert Carroll's testimony about Warren's unusual behavior at Nettie's coffee shop, the discussion between Warren and Harry Ingram in the cell and Warren's final interviews with Mike Brandford and Dean Ravelli. Through it all, the jury was subjected to hours and hours of Roger Warren weeping, cursing, babbling, laughing, all the time confessing his guts out, adding new details, building on old themes, sounding as if he were telling the truth, the whole profane and ugly truth. The jurors heard a Warren who was a different man at different times, rude with McMartin, friendly and contrite with McGowan, foul and arrogant and open and real with Harry Ingram. In the cell he swore like a miner, the old Ace of Giant, suffering no fools, heaping abuse on Peggy Witte, Brian Mulroney and the RCMP, cutting down his union brothers, calling them dummies and, most damning of all, making clear his hatred for scabs and his malevolent desire to get them out of the mine.

The RCMP investigators were generally pleased with how they had done on the stand, though they would have been more pleased if they were now battling a murder versus manslaughter defense, instead of one that attempted to proclaim Warren's innocence and tried to sully the RCMP's tactics. The investigators thought it ridiculous that anyone would say they had latched onto the first man who wanted to confess. After all the stress, the restless nights, the hardship and the fear, the Mounties had become obsessed with getting it right.

Even if Warren had walked out of his interview with McMartin at 3:45 P.M. on October 15, 1993, and had never come back again, the focus of the investigation would have shifted from Shearing and Bettger to him. His silence and his fear that he was going to be arrested would have been enough. The unrelenting, intrusive techniques that society permits the RCMP to use in order to hunt down murderers and other criminals would have been used on Warren. His phone would have been tapped again. He would have been followed. The police would have tried to get Marvin Farris or some other informant or undercover agent close to him. If Warren was shattered before the McMartin interview, he would have disintegrated completely in the following months. He would have told someone about his crime, if not an RCMP officer then an informant, if not an informant then a close friend. The secret would eventually have made its way into open court.

The investigators worried that Warren would somehow convince the jury to let him go free, but they knew one thing: If Warren did walk, there would be no renewed investigation. No new list of suspects would be drawn up. The investigators did not have a reasonable doubt about Warren's guilt. They had no doubt he was the one.

Chapter 26

THE FRAUD

THE COURTHOUSE was full on November 29, the first day of Roger Warren's defense. All the seats were taken except for the row behind Warren. Union supporters made up most of the crowd. They had suffered through five weeks of the local newspapers and radio stations reporting the damning evidence of the Crown's case, but almost all were certain Warren would now set things straight. Since Warren's testimony at the pre-trial voir dire, the union strikers could talk openly about Warren's false confession, and even men like Terry Legge, who had previously been convinced of Warren's guilt, were starting to have doubts.

While the strikers knew many of the details of Warren's new story, the Crown, the investigators, the media, the widows and ordinary townspeople could not guess what was coming. There was speculation that Warren would change his story once again. Perhaps he had decided after hearing the Crown's substantial case that it would be best to return to his original confession. If he was lucky he could still get manslaughter with parole in ten years.

The first surprise of the day was that Gillian Boothroyd, not Glen Orris, gave the defense's opening remarks to the jury. Orris said they had flipped a coin and Boothroyd had won. In any case it would not hurt to have Boothroyd speak. The defense could not dictate to the jury. It had to get them to empathize and sympathize, and Boothroyd was the one to get them in that mood. She sincerely believed in Warren's innocence. She was soft-spoken and earnest. She stood before the jurors and spoke clearly and plainly: "Ladies and gentlemen, for the last five weeks now we've heard the Crown's case against Roger Warren. In thinking about this last night, I thought that I would like to compare it, if I can, to a theatrical play where the central character against Mr. Warren is essentially the confessions, the alleged confessions, that he's made, that you've heard over a number of days at this trial. Now, if that's the central actor in the play, it's probably obvious to you that without that actor, the whole story falls apart."

To make its case, Boothroyd said the defense would first call on Warren, who would say right off that he had nothing to do with setting the blast. "He wasn't underground," Boothroyd assured the jury. "He doesn't know who was underground. He knows nothing about it."

After the blast, when the police started investigating, Roger Warren felt panic because he was on the picket line that night, but he realized few people had seen him there, Boothroyd said. She admitted that Warren also told two significant untruths in his first interview with the police. He did see two people on mine property that night, but he saw them at a different place and at a different time, not walking on a road at 2:00 A.M., but actually in the B-138 portal at 6:00 A.M., and one of the men had a gun. Warren could not tell the police the truth about this sighting because he was snooping on mine property, which was a firing offense.

Five witnesses would be called to confirm Warren's alibi, Boothroyd said, and the three-hour gap in Warren's unaccounted time would be cut to only ninety minutes. One witness, a woman named Pamela MacQuarrie-Higden, would tell the jury that she also saw two suspicious men on mine property at 6:00 A.M.

The strikers and the members of Warren's family who saw Roger Warren on the morning of the blast would say he wasn't wet and he was acting normal. Witnesses, including Warren's own wife, Helen, would say Warren's demeanor didn't change much in the thirteen months after the blast. "Ask yourself whether that supports the suggestion that someone who committed this horrendous crime could hide it from his own family members," Boothroyd said.

She then moved to the focus of the defense: "We're still left with a tremendous hurdle of understanding why a person like Mr. Warren would go and confess to a crime, particularly a horrendous one that he didn't commit. In order to understand that, you have to get in Mr. Warren's head."

Boothroyd then summarized Warren's psychological problems: his failing health, his depression about being off work, his belief that he had cancer, his impotence and the post-traumatic stress that had result-ed from the accident in 1987 when his friend Danny Mino had been blinded. She told the jury that two psychiatric experts, Dr. Shabehram Lohrasbe and Dr. Robert Ley, would testify about Warren's impaired mind-set at the time of his confession. The defense would also call evi-dence to show how Warren put together the details of his false confes-sion, the two main sources being the unending picket-line speculation about the blast and an *Edmonton Journal* article published on the anniversary of the blast.

One other person would testify, Boothroyd said, Danny Mino him-self, flying in from Eastern Canada. "Mr. Mino will tell you that he has come to Yellowknife to testify because he owes his life to Roger War-ren."

Boothroyd concluded by promising that the alleged confession would be bathed in light. "And with the benefit of that light, we will be able to see every single crack, every single fissure, every single flaw in that confession. And you'll be able to see it for what it really is, and that is, that it's nothing but a fraud."

Warren then took the stand. He swore the customary oath to tell the truth. Orris took his position beside the jury box, making sure that Warren would have to speak up.

"Roger, the blast of September 18 of 1992 in the Giant Mine, the one we've been talking about, did you have anything at all to do with that?" Orris asked.

"No, I did not," Warren answered, projecting his voice.

"I want to deal, Roger, with why on October the 15 of '93 you told the police that you did. In order to do that, I want to take you back, and I want to start in Ontario."

Orris then went into a series of questions that allowed Warren to detail his background and his mining experience. The main point was to bring up how when he was nineteen, Warren had confessed to drunk driving and stealing a car, even though he didn't really know if he had in fact stolen the vehicle. He only did it, he said, because his dad and his parole officer told him that the four week sentence wouldn't be so bad.

In a brief voir dire to establish the admissibility of Warren's car theft tale, Martin turned back to Boothroyd's opening address, telling de Weerdt he was still reeling from her remarks. He said he had not guessed that Warren would talk about depression and impotence, and he knew that without his own psychiatric experts to debunk the claim, he could be at an unfair disadvantage.

Orris was not compelled to disclose any speck of Warren's defense to Martin, but Martin had never dealt with a defense lawyer who had not disclosed such a matter early in a trial, and he felt there had been no hint of such a defense in Orris's cross-examination of the police witnesses. He accused Orris of defense by ambush. "I am most uneasy as we proceed here," he said. "I would have hoped that some form of notice might have been given and it wasn't so."

When the jury returned, Orris delved into the strike at Giant Mine. Warren said that before the strike he had been a passive union member. He voted to go out because he didn't like a clause that allowed the company to move workers around arbitrarily, taking someone from the underground, for instance, and putting him in the mill. "As far as I could see, it was so they could punish somebody. . . . If you said the wrong thing to the wrong guy, I guess somebody could get on you."

Orris then engaged Warren in a technical discussion of what he actually did as a miner each day. The conversation was mundane. The two had been talking now for more than an hour, but after Warren's initial statement of innocence, nothing had been said about the murders. The gallery watchers knew more had to be coming, but Warren and Orris kept on talking in painstaking detail about seemingly inconsequential matters, such as how Warren had drilled a rock face.

Just then, an unidentified woman stood up in the back of the courtroom.

"Excuse me!" she shouted out, glaring at Warren. "I hope the fuck you die a slow death!"

It was as if an apparition of one of the nine dead men had shouted it out himself. All the onlookers trembled, momentarily shattered, shocked back to the reality of the hatred of this case, of the mass murder at the 750-drift and its consequences.

"Yes!" Judit Pandev said, and she, Carol Riggs and Doreen Hourie pumped their fists.

The woman walked out of the court, courtroom guards in quick pursuit.

"It's okay, Roger," Orris said, then resumed his questioning, and it did seem as if it had been okay for Warren. Perhaps with his hearing aid, he had not heard the outburst. He continued droning on, but for the next few weeks, Orris, who had always seemed the epitome of cool, kept looking over the his shoulder, scanning the courtroom, as if he feared that another ghost would suddenly appear and banish Warren to burning hell.

Before the court broke for lunch, Peter Martin pointed out that Helen Warren was in the courtroom, which violated the order excluding witnesses from the proceedings. Now that it was clear she was going to testify, Martin said she had to leave. Orris asked that she be allowed to stay since the matter was obviously of such importance to her, but de Weerdt refused his request. In the end Orris and the Warrens decided that Helen would stay, but that she would not testify after all.

After lunch Orris and Warren covered Warren's participation in the June 14 riot and how he had been fired by Royal Oak for going onto mine property. Despite his termination, Warren said he was hopeful he would get his job back after the strike ended.

Warren then told the jury how, two months later in August 1992, he went on holidays. He stayed away from the picket line when he came back, but then union leader Bill Schram called him. Warren agreed to do picket duty again. He started to spend his time on the picket line, walking up and down the Ingraham Trail. It killed time and was also good exercise. On September 18, Warren said he worked the midnight to 8:00 A.M. shift. That night he dressed in an old parka and green rubber boots. He brought a can of Pepsi and an Eatmore chocolate bar, and got a ride to the line with striker Max Dillman. Dillman dropped him off at gate six, where he saw a number of strikers, including Brian Drover, Frank Woods and Tom Krahn. They talked for about an hour, then Warren said he and Tom Krahn headed out on the Ingraham Trail. Krahn said he was going to walk toward the bus at the main gate. Warren said he went to take a pee. Warren said he followed Krahn a few minutes later, but not taking the public highway. Instead, he walked on a road on Giant Mine property. He did this, he explained, to avoid being seen by Pinkerton security guards, who had been known to harass strikers.

When he got to the bus at the main gate, it was about 2:30 A.M. and Krahn had already left. Striker Leo Lachowski was asleep, Warren told the jury, but he talked for a bit with striker Kelly Rhodes. Warren said he dozed off on the bus. He left between 3:30 and 4:00 A.M. As he headed out, he saw a number of vehicles drive off the mine property. Warren said he walked toward gate two, and was standing in a ditch when he heard a little sports car drive by, a Firenza. He thought it had a familiar sound and that it belonged to a young striker named Kelly Schneider.

Warren told the jury that he then retraced his steps back to gate six. He walked right past the strikers' tent at the gate. He felt like snooping so he walked down a road onto mine property. If he had been caught he would be charged with trespassing, but he said it was a macho thing to do. He was also curious to take a look down in the B-138 pit.

The time was about 5:30 A.M., Warren said, when he saw someone climbing up out of the pit, moving laboriously up the rock bank.

"I could see it was a human being anyways, walking up the bank, just a black shape," Warren testified. "I couldn't see good."

After the black shape left, Warren said he went closer to the portal entrance and ducked behind some oil drums. He wanted to see if anything was happening. In a moment, he heard swearing or yelling, then saw movement in the portal. A man appeared. He took off his jacket and shook it. He had on a hard-hat and light. He had a bony face and was clean shaven. He looked tall and slim and had a sharp-boned build. He took off his helmet and washed his face with a black cloth. His jacket had a checker lining, Warren said. He appeared to be carrying an assault rifle. It was thin and had a clip on it. "I was positive that's what it was. It had a pistol grip handle and it looked like a gun. There is no question about it."

The second man also went up the bank. As soon as he was gone, Warren went in the opposite direction. Just then, a truck tore out of the pit; Warren was sure it was a security vehicle. He feared he had been spotted. He said he went up toward the highway, then crouched to see what he could. About two hundred to three hundred feet north on the

Ingraham Trail, he thought he saw a man walking. Just then, a truck came along, traveling very slowly. Warren said the man appeared to make a hand signal to the truck, which then kept going. The man jumped in the bush and was gone. Warren guessed the man might have been the first shadowy man he had seen coming out of the mine because he appeared to move in the same laborious manner, a jerk in his stride.

After seeing this Warren returned to gate six, where he met up with Drover and Woods. He asked a few leading questions, he said, to try to ferret out if they knew anything about the man with the gun. He came up with nothing. He was concerned that union men were up to something, and he wanted to put a stop to it. Even so, he didn't want to say much because he didn't want to be seen as a guy who yapped too much about this kind of stuff. Warren told the jury there was a hear-no-evil-see-no-evil attitude on the picket line. You quietly checked out things; you didn't shout it from the rooftops.

With Warren's new alibi out, Orris asked for a short voir dire so they could again discuss the alleged crimes committed by Bettger and Shearing. Before the jury left, however, Martin stood up to blast a lightning strike on the defense, telling de Weerdt and the jury this was the first time he had heard this new alibi and it was the first time he'd heard about the psychiatric defense. Martin said he no longer believed the trial would be done before Christmas, as had been planned, and the jurors should be asked about their availability in the New Year.

Martin's quick strike had two effects: if anyone on the jury believed Boothroyd's opening statement and Warren's story, it might help to break the spell, clearly showing how little the Crown thought of the new alibi and the psychiatric defense; it also alerted the jury to the fact that if they were going to be forced to sit through many more weeks of a trial that already seemed endless, it was Glen Orris's fault. The jurors looked fed up as they headed back to their waiting room.

With the jury out, Orris told de Weerdt that in the future Martin should keep such comments to the end of the trial. Martin was unabashed and again stressed how troubled he was by Warren's seemingly brand new defense. He said a significant adjournment of one or two weeks would be needed for the Crown to find its own expert in psychiatry and for that person to review the case. "For me to muddle along blindly here, unknowingly, as to what's important and what's not important when it comes time to meet these experts or present my own, that would be irresponsible."

Orris then moved on to the purpose of the voir dire, telling de Weerdt that he wanted to question Warren about his knowledge of the June 29 graffiti expedition, the July 22 satellite dish explosion and the September 2 vent shaft blast. Orris said he didn't necessarily want to say that Shearing and Bettger were involved in these crimes, just that Warren knew CASAW members were involved. The evidence would show that there was an escalation of violence on the picket line, which would explain why Warren would withhold the information about the man with the rifle in the B-138 pit from the RCMP; he was concerned that CASAW members were involved in the September 18 blast, but he didn't want to put any more pressure on the union until he had checked things out himself.

De Weerdt ruled that Warren could talk about his knowledge of various acts of vandalism committed by CASAW members in the summer of 1992 as long as he didn't mention any names.

Warren was exasperated by the wrangling. Martin and Orris were like two kids fighting over candy, he told Sergeant Jim Barr that night after court had ended, the two men driving down the icy streets through the dark winter to Warren's cell in the Yellowknife jail.

Warren had done well on his first day on the stand, but he was even more relaxed and forthright on his second day. He sat back in the witness box, his arms resting on the chair rests. He spoke easily and at length. He looked Orris in the eye. The day started with Warren telling the jury that some of the earlier bomb blasts at the mine were generally supported in the union, but not by him. "I thought it was making the strikers look bad in the eyes of the public."

Warren didn't think such acts would end the strike. Only the government could end the ludicrous situation by forcing Witte to take out the replacement workers and negotiate, he said.

Orris asked Warren what he thought of the replacement workers. Warren said he had no personal animosity toward them. He resigned himself to their decision to cross the line. "It's just like a guy going into a voting booth. Just because he's going to vote for some moron like Mulroney or one of his ministers, I can't do anything about it."

"All right."

"I mean, I even sat and discussed a guy going in to be a scab. I advised him I wouldn't do it. The next day he did it. What could I do about it? Punch the guy out or yell at him or scream? That was his decision and he made it."

Warren told the jury that he didn't like the way the mine opened again so quickly after the men had died. He also didn't like the replacement workers coming into town on the night of the blast to brawl in the bars with CASAW members. Still, Warren said it occurred to him that someone in the union had flipped out and set the bomb. He decided to keep an eye out himself, but not help the RCMP too much in their investigation. He knew he might have been recognized by the person driving the truck in the B-138 portal at 6:00 A.M. on September 18. He feared that would haunt him, putting him in the wrong place at the wrong time. In his first interview with the RCMP, Warren said he was going to tell his bare bones story about what he had done that night on the picket line, then go his merry way.

"Okay, what happened in the interview?" Orris asked.

"Just one thing: I was being interviewed by a woman, instead of a man, and that made it bad."

"Why?"

"It's just I have more empathy with women than I do with most men. It's disarming. And the lady was very disarming. She mentioned that as far as she was concerned the Pinkertons were the prime suspects. I took that with a grain of salt, but it was basically my idea at the time, too. And during the course of describing where I had went, I got a little ways through it and I just had this urge. I said, 'I've got to tell this woman something. I can't just totally ignore this stuff, you know.'"

This is when he told Defer about seeing the two shadowy men on the mine road at 2:00 A.M., Warren said, something he actually had seen a few nights before the blast. However, he described the face of one of the two men as the face of the man with the rifle he had seen in the B-138 pit at 6:00 A.M. on September 18.

Orris went over one more time Warren's reason for refusing to tell Defer that he himself had been in the B-138 pit that morning.

"I just wasn't going to admit being on the property," Warren said. "You know, why ask for trouble?"

In his efforts to show that he wasn't in the pit, Warren said he also told Defer that he was the guy on the Ingraham Trail who had been spotted by mine supervisor Brian Broda. "That was my reasoning; flawed as it was, that's what it was. At the time it seemed a good idea."

"So, the person that Mr. Broda said he saw on the road, was that you or not?"

"No, that was not me."

On his way home from his interview with Defer, Warren testified that he cursed himself, seeing how fishy his story must have sounded; in the pitch dark of 2:00 A.M. it would be hard to see anyone's face, even a few feet away. "I realized it was pretty stupid to tell about guys at the wrong time in the wrong place."

Next, Orris tackled the boots with Warren, and now the issue became even more confused. Warren said he had on green rubber boots that night, but they weren't the size eleven Kamik boots that he showed to Defer and McGowan one month later on October 16, 1992; nor were they the boots he burned and threw in Cameron Falls. Instead, they were boots he had purchased many years earlier in Snow Lake, Manitoba. When Defer and McGowan asked him to show them what he wore that night, however, he no longer had the Snow Lake boots or his parka. The boots had a hole in them and he had spilled diesel fuel on his parka. He had tossed both of them in the garbage. Warren said he had bought the new pair of size eleven Kamik boots in early October. He just showed McGowan and Defer the new Kamiks instead.

"Did you tell the police that they were not the boots that you were wearing that night?"

"I didn't see any significance to it. I figured I told them I wore green boots. Who cares, you know? Why make an issue out of it? It will just draw suspicion."

Orris asked Warren why he had cut and burned the soles of the green boots he showed the police. Warren said the new pair of size eleven Kamiks had been uncomfortable so he had cut off a piece of the sole, then a few days later he was out hunting and he burned them in a fire. He even put black soot around the trim. He said he did that because, in his first interview with Defer, he had told her he had burned the Snow Lake boots by standing too close to a bonfire. He wanted to make sure his new boots and his initial story were consistent.

"In any event, did you know at that point those were the kind of boots the police were looking for?"

"I doubt I would have had them sitting there in plain sight for them to look at if I had any inkling that they were that important. It would be like putting a vanity plate on your getaway car."

Warren's supporters in the gallery let loose with laughter.

Orris next led Warren through his dealings with McGowan, Dauk and Keane in the months after the blast. Warren testified that some union men told the RCMP to shove it, but he gave repeated interviews, partly to try to clear himself, partly because he felt guilty for having lied to the police about the location of the two shadowy men. He considered admitting that he had made a misleading statement, but he was still afraid of placing himself in the B-138 portal and implicating himself in the crime. When Dauk first pressured him about the two shadowy men during their meeting on October 19, 1992, one month after the blast, Warren said he felt both faint and angry.

"All right," Orris said. "What was making you angry?"

"Just that guy was touching me."

"How close was he to you?"

"Touching my knee. He kept coming closer and getting in your face. It's a technique they use, I understood that, but he was a lucky little boy it wasn't about twenty years before that. He probably would have figured he was in a car accident on the seventh floor [of the Explorer]. I don't like people touching me."

"All right," Orris nodded.

"It's the one thing that will make me quite violent."

When he talked to the RCMP's composite artist, Warren said he merely described the face of the man with the assault rifle he had seen in the B-138 portal.

Warren said he agreed to take the polygraph tests so he could be rid of the RCMP. He was sick of them. In the February 14, 1993, interview with Dauk, Warren said that he learned for the first time about the significance of his size eleven Kamik boots, that they matched footprints found at the Akaitcho shaft. "I didn't really believe him. I thought maybe a different size or something because why wouldn't they arrest a guy if they had that much: the time missing on his evening and the guy has got the same kind of boots?"

After the February polygraph test, Warren said he thought that he had at last cleared things up because the police didn't contact him for many months, not until August 6, 1993. But that summer, Warren told the jury, he found out that the riot charges, which had been dropped at the preliminary hearing, were on again. The Crown was using a direct indictment to push the charges ahead.

"Excuse me," Peter Martin stood up. "Where is this going to, is what I would like to know. What is the point of this?"

"I anticipate," Orris said, "that Mr. Warren will tell us that he understood the direct indictment was a result of instruction from the Attorney General or the Attorney General's Department in that regard. He was upset about that. It obviously caused him concern. . . . Obviously that will connect up with October 15."

"All right," de Weerdt said to Orris. "I am sure you, as very experienced counsel will appreciate, that the jury, like the judge, may have difficulty sifting the wheat from the chaff."

"Certainly," Orris said.

"If we can stick with the wheat."

"That's exactly what I'm trying to do," Orris said, then asked Warren what effect the direct indictment had on him. "It was just like these guys were never going to stop. They are this relentless force trying to crush you."

Warren said that the October 15, 1993, interview impressed him because McMartin said he was with the Attorney General's Department, again reminding Warren of the power of the state.

Orris knew that if the jurors were going to side with Warren, they had to completely understand and agree with his motivation for lying to the police about the two shadowy men, then not correcting the lie in the next thirteen months. Before delving further into the McMartin interview, Orris returned to the point, again asking Warren why he didn't clear up the matter.

"After the investigation was progressing, there was so many people terrified," Warren explained. "I was terrified, too. I just didn't want to be even thought of as a suspect. And I figured if I told them I am in such proximity to these people they would just say, 'Forget those people. We have got you in that place at that time.' And forget it. It was a nightmare."

"Okay, you were lying to them and felt that you were obliged to continue. What effect was that having on you?"

"I couldn't get away from it. It just kept coming at me. I just figured I had to keep cooperating to try to get them to realize that it is a waste of time wasting time on me. But it didn't really happen."

Orris now felt ready to plunge into the trickiest aspect of the defense: Warren's psychological problems. He led Warren through a discussion of his mental anguish, talking about his diminution in spirit, his raging inner conflict, his fears about cancer, his impotence, which was possibly related to his heart medication, and his feelings of inadequacy arising from losing the job that had given him his identity.

Warren's description of his symptoms was riveting. The jurors who had lost interest during Orris's cross-examinations of Crown witnesses now sat forward intently watching and listening. Warren talked about his belief that the strike would never end and that the idea of falsely confessing came to him after he read the *Journal* article "Footsteps of the Murderer." With the information in the article and what he heard in the Blitz package, Warren told the jury he thought he could pull it off.

Warren said he kept the *Journal* article beside his couch and constantly scanned it, even though he knew he shouldn't. "It was almost like they were words of a spell. You couldn't say them, but you could look at them. Like, there is certain words that if you utter those words, bad things happen. I don't know. You have to get the place exorcised or something."

"A magical spell is what you were talking about?" de Weerdt asked.

"Yes," Warren said. "I was drawn to it. It was like a forbidden thing. I shouldn't look at it, but I was, all the time."

When Orris asked Warren to identify who Suspect 1 and Suspect 2 were in the *Journal* article, Martin jumped up to object. De Weerdt sent out the jury so he could hold yet another voir dire.

"My Lord, with respect, we have gone too far with this," Martin said. "This article contains information which has the potential to be extremely prejudicial and may well be completely false, and for us to say, 'Well, it may have played on his mind, let it in, I say that's wrong.'"

"It wouldn't be the first time that members of the public thought that the press haven't quite got the story right," de Weerdt said, smiling.

Martin proposed that the article be cut in half, leaving in points about the blast, but nothing else.

Orris disagreed. "Mr. Warren has told us that he has read it on many occasions, that in fact he studied it. It was sort of like a spell that he was drawn toward. This article in its entirety should go to the jury."

De Weerdt sided with Orris, saying that the article was relevant to Warren's state of mind when he confessed. However, Warren was not allowed to identify Suspect 1 and Suspect 2 as Tim Bettger and Al

Shearing. Martin wasn't appeased; he spelled out his concern in the clearest terms yet: "The concern of the Crown was that the jury not be distracted by these other crimes and what else happened. That's the concern. And that the intermixing of the suggestions that those who are responsible for other crimes are responsible for this crime. That's what this story says."

But Orris was allowed to proceed, entering the article as a court exhibit and questioning Warren on it. "As far as you were reading it on the eighteenth of September, what effect did it have on you?" he asked when the jury returned.

"Just, I was surprised at the amount of information in it. And I wondered where they got it. I figured some of it had to come from the investigators. . . . With the amount of information in it, I kept dwelling on the idea that somebody with knowledge of this type of thing could actually confess to this and get away with it. You could make it stick. I just kept having this conversation in my mind over it."

Warren next attempted to explain the satchel in the pond and the burned boots in Cameron Falls, the two items he had shown the RCMP after his arrest. He said he filled the satchel with things someone might use in an explosion, then threw the bag in the pond in May 1993. At about the same time, he found boots similar to the ones he'd heard were used in the mine, he said. They weren't Kamik boots, but he thought they were close enough. He burned the boots and chucked them in the river in September 1993 only a month before he was arrested. Warren told the jury he did both acts for the same reason. He said he was sure Al Shearing and Tim Bettger were innocent; they both had alibis and were acting like innocent men. Even so, he was worried that both men would be wrongly arrested. If that ever happened, he would anonymously contact the RCMP and tell them about the bag in the pond and the boots at Cameron Falls, saying that they had arrested the wrong men and that the real murderer had disposed of these items.

The night before his interview with McMartin, Warren testified that he wrestled with giving a false confession. In the end he decided a confession was the only thing that would end the strike, that the strikers couldn't count on the government. "I figured I knew enough that I could probably swing it. There were things that I didn't have too well in my head that I couldn't possibly know about. I would just fake it, be vague."

Warren next described the turmoil in his head as McMartin hammered at him and why he ultimately decided to confess. "I figured I might go down. I might end up with twenty-five years in jail, but in the end I would win because I did it for a principle. The system is not for a certain group of people. It is for everybody. If it doesn't work for everybody, then you have to do something to wreck the system. As far as I am concerned, I wrecked the system."

"Tell us what you mean by that," Orris said.

"Well, I can guarantee you the strike would still be going on unless there was intervention. . . . They would have just kept on using that excuse. It is charges before talks. And in my state of mind, I said, 'No, that's it.' I read that *yellowknifer* article there, especially that 'Charges Before Talks,' and I said, 'Lady, the last thing you want is charges, but that might be the first thing you are going to get, and you stretch that elastic too far and I am going to be the little razor that's going to cut that sucker.' . . . There was anger and frustration and probably not being in the best mental health, but if you are wrecked, who cares? Go for it."

"What do mean if you were 'wrecked, who cares? Go for it'?"

"Well, I just felt like I wasn't my same self, and I didn't want to be around too much anyways if I wasn't. So it wasn't any great loss to anybody. I figured my wife could adjust quite easily. That will tell you how irrational I was. Concern about her didn't bother me until the next day. And it was sort of, like, at quarter to eight at night, or whenever this [confession] happened, I looked into the abyss, to use a phrase from Nietzsche. And the next day at around 3:00 in the afternoon, the abyss was looking at me. And it was pretty horrible. It was like being in a horror movie."

On Friday, December 2, Warren's fourth day on the stand, Orris finished his direct examination by dealing with some of the Crown's hold-back evidence. Warren said he came up with his description of the triggering mechanism for the bomb by thinking back to the items in the satchel bag in the pond and how they would be assembled into such a device. In the endless speculation at the union hall after the blast, he had heard that a DCD cap could be detonated with a nine-volt battery so he used that information as well. He told the police about the satchel in the pond and the burned boots because he had taken the time to plant the items so he thought he might as well use them. Warren testified that he learned about the path down the Akaitcho shaft from his talk with Al Shearing a few nights before the confession.

Warren also attempted to explain why in his confession he had said he tested a DCD cap up the tracks from the blast site in about the same spot as the post-blast team had later found a spent cap. First of all, Warren said, if he had set the bomb he never would have waited until he was underground to test the caps. He would have done it before he went down. Secondly he said, "I just used that as part of the story just to make it fit."

Warren also said he told the police he refueled the scoop because it would make the story sound more authentic. He wanted to convince them, he said, and he also wanted to leave himself with no outs. He knew he might later want to retract his confession in order to get out of jail, but that wouldn't be good because it wouldn't end the strike. He made sure he did the job. "I wasn't playing to lose. I may have been playing to lose personally, but I wasn't playing to lose in the bigger scheme of things."

The key moment of the day came when Warren talked about how he had manipulated his confession in order to avoid a first degree murder conviction. "The best-case scenario would be to get charged maybe with manslaughter or something, so I was trying to convince them of this," Warren said. "I mean, McMartin kind of laid it out for me, you know, and I sort of tailored my admission to within the parameters that he laid out." Warren said he had to think hard about McMartin's suggestion before he hit upon the ore train scenario and then went with that idea. Nevertheless, Warren testified, that amount of explosives would surely kill.

On the face of it, Warren had just made a mistake. If the jury decided that he had set the bomb, he had just told them that he knew the explosion would have been lethal. He had given them a reason to convict him of first degree murder. But Warren had no choice in this matter. It would be foolish to suggest that the bomb wouldn't kill anyone, and such a suggestion might also turn the jurors against him. They might think he was trying to have it both ways—claiming he was innocent, but trying to get a manslaughter conviction in case he was found guilty. If he was an innocent man, he had to act like one and admit what any experienced miner would surely know.

Chapter 27

WEB OF LIES

GLEN ORRIS had done his best to show Roger Warren as a hard-working, loving family man who had only made the mistake of confessing because the police took advantage of his depression. Orris played on Warren's past record in the mine and his demeanor, which suggested every aging, blue collar worker in Canada, maybe a juror's father or uncle, a crumpled, gruff, but likable fellow.

In his cross-examination, Peter Martin had to fight this portrayal of Warren. To show that Warren was a liar and a murderer, Martin had to treat him with the contempt such an individual deserved. If Warren truly was a demon who would set such a bomb, he had to be unmasked or the jury might be emotionally unprepared to convict him.

Before attacking head-on, however, Martin went back to the subject of the murderer's intent, focusing again on Warren's knowledge that the bomb he had described would surely kill.

"You understand how lethal that would be to a person standing eighty feet away straight down the drift?" Martin asked.

"Yes, certainly."

"Is that person dead?"

"Yes, I would say."

"Okay. And I understand that you have the same opinion if there is an ore car standing between that person and the bomb, the bomb of this nature?"

"Yes, he would be, even if he didn't get hit with anything, the atmospheric pressure would seriously injure him or kill him."

Martin went on to show that Warren knew how to set such a bomb. He questioned Warren in his usual style, putting specific questions to him that required only yes or no answers. Martin quickly established that Warren could set up the bomb he had described in about ten to fifteen minutes, that he could drive a scoop and a loki, and that he knew where the explosives and powder were kept near the 712-scoop shop. Martin then went through the confession, not asking Warren if the things he had told the police were true, just asking him to confirm what he had said. Warren had confessed over four days, often rambling, repeating himself and adding details. Martin wanted to put all that information in a neat package so the jury could easily understand how Warren said he planned the bomb, broke into the mine, set the device and escaped, only to realize after he was spotted by Brian Broda that his bomb might kill someone. Warren had no choice but to agree with Martin on every point. As he spoke, Warren sat upright and still, his arms next to his body, rarely looking Martin in the eye.

"Mr. Warren," Martin said, "for a man of your intelligence, if it was unclear to some of your fellow strikers, it was certainly clear to you that Peggy Witte would not settle this strike so long as she had replacement workers and union people who had crossed the line to work the mine?"

"Yeah, it wouldn't take a Rhodes Scholar to figure it out, I think."

"And I didn't suggest you were a Rhodes Scholar, but you have told us that you clearly saw the plan as being that?"

"Yeah, it was plain."

Martin had asked Orris if there were any reports he could study from Doctors Lohrasbe and Ley, outlining Warren's supposed condition at the time of his confession in October 1993. Orris said he had nothing, so Martin decided to skewer Warren on the subject, starting with one of the same questions he had asked Warren in the pre-trial voir dire: "When was the first time you saw a psychiatrist after your arrest?"

"I am not sure," Warren said, but after prodding from Martin, he recalled he had first seen Dr. Lohrasbe some time in the summer.

"And this man was here to help you? You realized that?"

"If he could. If he came up with a finding that was the wrong one he would have had to say so."

"But clearly the potential was that he would help you?"

"Yeah, I hoped so."

Martin asked Warren if he had ever read any material about this defense or discussed this defense with anyone. Warren said he hadn't. He said he realized the enormity of what he had done the day after he confessed to McMartin, but he didn't get help for his condition until Dr. Lohrasbe's visit at least ten months later. Nor did he tell his wife and family that he falsely confessed because of his psychiatric problems.

"Why wouldn't you?" Martin asked.

"I am just not one of these touchy feely guys, I guess."

"I am not talking about touchy feely. I am talking about a man who falsely confesses to murdering nine men. I would have thought you explained to your family that the confession was false. Why didn't you?"

"My family assumed it was false."

"So you didn't have to tell them that?"

"No."

Warren did say that when he was with Harry Ingram in the cell, he alluded to the confessions being false. "I made reference to a hoax a couple of times quite plainly, but for some reason I can't find them on the tapes, or the noise, or whatever was there was blanking it out, or something happened. I made reference to, 'We have a Royal Oak and now we have got a Royal Hoax,' at least twice, distinctly, but I can't find them anywhere."

"Did you hear your lawyer ask Corporal Ingram that question, whether the word *hoax* was mentioned?"

"I don't think so because it is not on the tapes."

"I don't think he did either. Are you making this up now?"

"No, I have said it before."

Martin confronted Warren deliberately. He knew Warren had been tough-minded enough to be able to deceive the police for thirteen months until McMartin's hardball approach got the confession. Martin intended to be just as hard and relentless now. "Okay, so we are clear then, you may have used the word *hoax* to Corporal Ingram. In any event, you didn't tell your family it was a false confession, and the next time you addressed the matter of a false confession was when you saw Dr. Lohrasbe, is that right?"

"No, the next time is when I sent the note to Tim and Al."

"And then Dr. Lohrasbe?"

"If I said that I wouldn't be answering truthfully."

"Well, let's start answering truthfully for a change, Mr. Warren."

"Excuse me, my Lord." Orris stood up. "I am sorry. My friend can leave his editorial comments and arguing to the jury."

"It is a fair comment," Martin shot back in his own defense.

"Well, this is cross-examination," de Weerdt said, allowing Martin to proceed.

Martin asked Warren if this new defense of his depended on him being an honest man.

"I think I have basically been an honest man all my life," Warren said.

After establishing that Warren had never told his own family physician, Dr. Andrew McMillan, about his mental problems through the winter and summer of 1993, Martin asked, "When did you first tell a psychiatrist or a psychologist about these alleged feelings of worthlessness?"

"When I met them."

"When did you realize that this defense that is now being put forward was available to you?"

"I never realized it."

"'*I* never realized it,'" Martin snapped, "but when did *you* realize it?"

"It just sort of evolved."

Martin asked if Warren was willing to undergo testing by a Crown-appointed psychologist and psychiatrist. On the advice of his lawyer, Warren said he wouldn't.

"Incidentally," Martin said, "do you realize that by refusing to be examined by a Crown psychiatrist and psychologist that certain conclusions follow from there? In other words, that the Crown would be at a disadvantage and not be able to verify the findings of your experts?"

"I guess it could happen, yes."

"But your answer is no."

"So far, yes. Until I have different advice, that's what I will stick to."

Martin prodded Warren about his new alibi, asking how the three- to four-hour gap would be reduced to ninety minutes. "Who will say that?"

"I am not sure."

"You have no idea?"

"I have an idea, but I am not sure."

"Okay, give us your idea, Mr. Warren, and stop playing games."

"There was somebody came to the picket at around 4:00 A.M. that I couldn't identify for a long time, but I think we have got it narrowed down to who it was."

"And?"

"That's the alibi."

"There comes a time with these secrets, you have to let go of them," Martin said, exasperated. "Who is it?"

"I can't think of the name."

"Mr. Warren, I suggest to you that what you told the police in October of 1993 was true, that between 1:00 and 1:30 on the eighteenth of September you went from gate six to Akaitcho, and you were in the mine from then until approximately 5:30 and 6:00 in the morning. And I am suggesting to you that this so-called alibi you are talking about now is a fabrication, as you indicated it was to Corporal Ingram in your undercover conversation. What do you say about that?"

"I deny it."

Martin went over how Warren had told Ingram that he realized it was safe to say he spent the night at gate three because he knew strikers Leo Lachowski, Kelly Rhodes and Dave Madsen had been drinking and wouldn't remember if he was there or not. Next, Martin asked Warren about his new story about seeing two men in the B-138 portal, one of them with an assault rifle. He asked Warren when he first came up with this story.

"The first time I revealed it to anybody I think was in February of '94."

"Okay, when was the first time that you came up with it, that you thought of this story?"

"I never thought of it. That was the original story. The original event."

Martin told Warren that it was so dark that night he could not possibly have seen the first man climbing up out of the B-138 portal. Warren disagreed, saying the portal had white rock that reflected light.

"What light is it going to reflect, the starlight?"

"I know if something moved there, a black shape, you could see it."

"A bear?" Martin asked.

"Who knows? At first I thought it was maybe a coyote or something that caught my attention, or a fox running around there."

"A fox?" Martin jumped on the bizarre comment. "So you may have seen a fox run over to the bush," and, a moment later, he added, "Okay, so we see this dark form—fox, coyote, bear, person—and your response is to go deeper into the pit. Is that right?"

No, Warren said, he crouched down, waited a few minutes, then went into the pit to see if anything was happening. It was then that he saw a second man standing about 150 feet away in the exit portal itself. The man walked forward until he was only eighty feet away.

"You got a look at the gun, is that right?"

"Yeah, when he gathered everything up and put his coat on and picked up, it appeared to me to be some type of assault rifle or a weapon of some kind anyways, unless he was using a cane."

"No, no," Martin protested. "Actually, you were much more precise than that last week. You knew it was an assault rifle because the barrel was too thin to be a shotgun, and you saw a clip that was six or seven inches long."

"It appeared to be, yes, it did."

Martin wondered why Warren had been able to see the lining of the man's coat, but still could not recognize the person. Was he sure that the man wasn't one of the CASAW boys?

"I wouldn't say I knew it for a fact," Warren said. "I had one guy did pop into my head," referring to but not naming Conrad Lisoway, "and it scared me quite a bit in succeeding days."

After watching the man with the rifle leave, Warren said he was sure he was spotted by a security guard in a truck. "I got out of there as quickly as possible."

"You were scared to death, right?"

"I wouldn't say I was scared. I have never been scared to death in my life, if you want to know the truth."

"You are a pretty cool customer no matter what happens."

"I wouldn't run away. If he said, 'Stop,' I would have had to stop. No one said it, so I got out of there."

Never before during the strike had Warren seen anyone carrying an assault rifle, but when he got back to gate six and saw his fellow strikers Brian Drover and Frank Woods, he didn't mention the incident. "It was tempting but I didn't," Warren said. "I didn't think we were under attack or anything."

"Should you have not at least alerted your friends to the danger which lurked in the darkness only a short distance away?"

"I don't think anybody else would have either. That's the way it was. It was like you didn't go around saying, 'I just seen this over there.' How about if it was one of our guys doing something and there was trouble over it? Somebody else would know."

"If this story were true, Mr. Warren, do you not think everyone else would have said to these guys, 'Listen, fellows, this is what I just saw?'"

"No, I don't think they would."

In his direct testimony, Warren said he'd made leading comments to Drover and Tom Krahn to try to find out what was happening in the B-138 portal. Martin knew from an interview the RCMP had done with Drover after Warren was arrested that Warren had actually mentioned something about going into the mine to blow up a powder magazine by wiring it to the ignition of a scoop. Now Martin asked Warren directly if he'd said anything to Drover or Krahn about a scoop or a powder keg. Warren said he might have mentioned a scoop, but couldn't be sure.

"What did you tell Terry Coe that morning when you went back to the line after breakfast at Nettie's?"

"I don't remember."

"You don't recall what you told him?"

"I don't recall telling him anything."

"Did you tell him about seeing two men?"

"Yeah, I mentioned something about men. That's possible."

"What did you say? Where did you tell him you had seen these two men?"

"Well, on a mine road or something."

"Why would you tell him about the two men and not Drover or Wood?"

"I don't know."

"Can I make a suggestion? The reason you told Coe is because it was after the explosion and you already wanted to set up a diversion, to divert suspicion from yourself, to take suspicion away from yourself."

The questions and answers were taking a disturbing turn for the defense. Warren invariably started out denying Martin's suggestions;

then after Martin probed more deeply, Warren admitted certain points. To get the truth out of Roger Warren, it seemed, was no simple matter.

Martin turned to Warren's story about his boots and his parka, bringing up the strange coincidence that on the night of the blast Warren had on boots he had owned for fourteen years and a parka he had owned for four years, but then got rid of them both by the time the police asked to see them only one month later.

Martin explained to Warren and the jury the Crown's theory about the boots. Warren mistakenly thought he wore the size ten Kamik boots into the mine when actually he wore his other pair of Kamiks, the size elevens. Afterward, he burned the size tens and threw them in Cameron Falls. He knew everyone on the line was being asked to describe the clothing of everyone else on the line. He didn't know if other strikers like Max Dillman, Frank Woods and Brian Drover had reported to the RCMP that he had on green Kamik boots, so he had no choice but to show the police a pair of green boots. He didn't have the size ten Kamiks, so he showed them his size elevens. "If they [the other strikers] said you were wearing green boots, and you said you were wearing something else, that would attract suspicion to you," Martin suggested to Warren.

"Yes, so when the police came I had green boots," Warren admitted.

"Right, and that's the reason you told Corporal Defer you were wet because you *were* wet. And the reason you have made that acknowledgment is you thought the other people on the line would probably have seen that you were wet and reported that."

"Yeah, but I don't think anybody reported that I was wet, like, as if I had been crawling around down in the mine."

"You know that now, but at the time you didn't, so you said you were wet because you jumped in a ditch."

Warren was becoming less resistant to Martin's attacks. The prosecutor leaned over his lectern, his brow creased with concentration, his eyes bearing in on Warren. Martin next pursued a massive problem with Warren's defense—his behavior at his first interview with Nancy Defer one week after the blast. Through rapid-fire questions, Martin established that Defer gave Warren a day's notice for the interview, that he understood he wasn't a suspect at the time, that he knew it would be a routine interview about his actions on the picket line and that Defer treated him with respect and kindness.

"And you were upset about this crime—nine men being murdered?" Martin asked.

"Yes, I was."

"Right, and priority or not, you were anxious that it be solved."

"Yes, I was."

"Right. And it was clear, Mr. Warren, at that time, and I think you told us last week, that if you did make observations at the B-138 portal that the police would be very interested in that, that would be important information to them?"

"Yes, it would be."

"Right. So now with twenty-four hours to prepare, you go on the twenty-fifth of September, and you plan to lie to Constable Defer. Is that right?"

"Yeah, I wasn't going to actively lie, but I wasn't going to say anything about the 138."

"No, no. You planned to tell a lie. That was your plan," Martin scolded. "Let's do this. I just want to have it clear here that the first time you were asked by the police to help them in this, to help them try to solve the crime, the first words from your lips are a series of lies. Is that a fair description?"

"I wouldn't say the first words, but during the course of my description, I did lie."

"Yes, and lie and lie. Let us take a moment to count the lies, Mr. Warren."

Martin went through the statement, pointing out the lies, giving Warren no choice but to admit the truth: When Defer asked him where he had worked, he named a number of areas in Giant, but didn't say he had worked at the 750; when Warren said he saw the two shadowy men at gate five after 1:30 A.M., that was a lie; when he said the two men wore dark jackets, pants or coveralls, and caps with no peaks, that was a lie; when he said they walked quickly, that was a lie; when he said he went to gate five, that was a lie; when he said he saw union leader Bill Schram reading or sleeping, that was a lie (Schram hadn't been out there that night); when Warren said he saw a Pinkerton guard asleep in his truck at gate five, that was a lie; when he said he left the bus at gate three to go back to gate six, that was a lie (Warren was now saying he had gone in the other direction); when he said he walked past gate six because he saw the flashing lights of a vehicle, that was a lie (he now said he was actually talking about the vehicle he later saw in the B-138 pit).

To end that first interview, Warren had told Defer that nothing unusual happened. It was just a quiet night. Now, of course, Warren was saying he had seen the man with the assault rifle.

"Which do you want to say is a lie?" Martin asked. "Your evidence here last week or what you told her then?"

"What I told her then."

"So let's say that conservatively what we have here is eight to ten lies in your first meeting with the police. Would that be right?"

"That would be pretty close."

"And this is how you plan to help the police?"

"I didn't plan on helping. I figured the police would do their job themselves."

"But you are telling them these lies?"

"Well, I shouldn't have told them."

After going through how Warren had changed his alibi only after talking to striker Alex Mikus, Martin asked, "Mr. Warren, do you consider lying to the police in a homicide investigation a serious matter?"

"Normally, yeah, it would be pretty serious."

"Well, if we were talking about the murder of nine men, do you not think that your lies that you told them and the misinformation you gave them was a serious matter?"

"Yes, it was."

"These weren't white lies. These were big lies, Mr. Warren. In all of the other statements to the police, you told these lies, did you not?"

"Basically, yeah."

Martin then read Warren some material from his August 6, 1993, interview with McGowan, during which McGowan hit him with the evidence against him, and Warren replied: "I don't know what I can do to clear this up. It doesn't seem to do me much good to try to cooperate."

"Do you remember you said that?" Martin asked.

"Yes."

Martin read another line from the transcript, where Warren said: "What do you want me to say? Like, I have told you, it is nothing to do with me. This is where I was. This is what I did. The best I could corroborate it. That's it."

"That's what you said?"

"Yes."

And again Martin went to the transcript for another quote from Warren: "As far as I am concerned, I can't do anything else. What else can I do?"

"I ask you this question," Martin said. "Did telling the truth ever cross your mind?"

"Yeah. At that time it was crossing it quite strongly."

"Why didn't you do it then?"

"I was just feeling I told such a tangled web of lies that it is hard to get them back now."

"But, now, here you are again telling us more, Mr. Warren," Martin said, then pointed out that in his direct testimony just last week, Warren had told the jury that by the time he talked to McGowan in August 1993 he was convinced he had done all he could to help the police. Warren admitted that he had lied on the stand, but claimed it was inadvertent. "It wasn't a deliberate lie. I was describing to Mr. Orris what the effect of the various interviews were."

"That's exactly my point though," Martin said. "You had not been doing everything you could to resolve it. Indeed, you were still actively lying to them."

"Yes, that's true."

"All right, so by suggesting to us that you had done everything you could to resolve it, you were lying to us?"

"Strictly speaking, yes, you are right."

To end his first day of cross-examination, Martin turned to the matter that worried him most, the *Edmonton Journal* article. Martin handed Warren a copy of the article and challenged him to find any facts he had used from the story in his confession. Warren said he learned about the route out of the mine from the article's map. He also learned that the killer took a scoop down to the powder magazine.

Martin then asked Warren what part of the *Journal* story he rejected, giving the RCMP a different version during his confession. While the story said the murderer broke the window to get into the shack over the Akaitcho shaft, Warren said he'd heard from other strikers there was no window, so he told the police that. The article said the trip wire was strung across the tracks, which was more information Warren said he rejected.

Martin read to Warren the portion of the story detailing the murderer's climb down the Akaitcho shaft. Nowhere did it mention the killer getting lost at 425- and 575-levels, a key bit of hold-back evidence.

Warren said he himself would never get lost in the mine. He only told the police he got lost in order to make his story more realistic.

The *Journal* story also said Suspect 1 picked up two twenty-two kilogram bags of AMEX to use in his bomb. "Did you tell the police you used two bags of AMEX, Mr. Warren?"

"No, because I didn't believe it. I thought it was something they had put out."

"But this is the police theory here."

"Well, it is a different theory than what they come out with shortly after the blast."

"Excuse me. You say that this article was the one that convinced you that you could confess to this, even though you didn't do it. . . ."

"But if I would have memorized it and ran in there with it, they would have suspected," Warren interrupted. "One of them probably would have noticed that it was exactly word for word what they had down there, so it wouldn't have been very convincing."

"Let's do this," Martin said. "Let me finish my question, and I will let you finish your answer."

"Okay."

"You thought it was the police theory. You thought it irresponsible for them to put out such details. You said that with this information you could falsely confess. This information is that two forty-nine-pound bags of AMEX were used in the explosion. And I am asking you, did you repeat that to the police?"

"No, I didn't."

Martin also pointed out that the article said the murderers used batteries for their bomb, not just one nine-volt battery, as Warren had said in his confession. Martin summed up by again going over the many things Warren had rejected and the few things he had taken from the article. He then asked, "Could you tell us then that if you believe this to be the police theory, what better source could you have to convince them that you did it?"

"Things I heard. Things I figured out myself."

"Would you not agree that departing from this script, the official police theory as you understood it, would be very risky for you in trying to convince them you did this?"

"No, I thought it would be safest to do that."

Martin then pointed out all the information Warren had said in his confession that wasn't in the article, such as a description of the device itself, where he bought things, how he tested two DCD caps and used one for the bomb, how he used a drill steel to anchor the bomb, how he refueled the scoop on the way out. Again Warren said he made these things up to make his story sound convincing. "I think I did a fairly good job."

Martin returned to Warren's weakest claim: why he told the RCMP he got lost at the 425- and 575-levels in Akaitcho when no one knew that but the police because they had tracked the murderer's footprints.

"I figured it would be more realistic."

"Why did you tell them that you got lost coming down Akaitcho?" Martin asked again.

This time Warren said he told the police he got lost to make the time sequence work out in his confession. If he went down Akaitcho at about 1:30 A.M. it didn't make sense that he would take so long to get to the 712-scoop shop; he had to say he got lost to make up for the extra time.

"Can I ask you one question that's been driving me crazy?" Martin said. "If this confession is false, in addition to all the other anomalies I have just pointed out, could you tell us why you insisted that the boots they had were not the boots you used in the mine?"

"I don't know. From what I heard I didn't think they were."

"Stronger than that," Martin scolded. "You used the word, and I am quoting you, 'Guaran-fucking-teed those are not the boots I used in the mine.'"

"One reason would be that I bought them later, after the blast," Warren said of the size eleven Kamiks.

"But why didn't you just capitulate?" Martin asked, half exasperated, half bemused. "This is a false confession. The police believe those are the boots. They have told you that. Why don't you just say those are the boots? Why don't you say that?"

"Just to make it more convincing, I guess."

"But actually to make it less convincing. Right? The police believe those are the boots and you are guaranteeing them they are not. Would you like until tomorrow morning to think about that?"

"No."

"I guess there is no real answer to that then?"

"It was sort of like, I had done this stuff, threw this stuff out," Warren said, referring to the burned size ten boots at Cameron Falls, "and I wanted to use it, so I did. I thought it would be a convincing detail."

Martin was still dissatisfied. Again he asked why Warren didn't just stick to the police theory that he had on his size eleven Kamiks.

"I figured that they knew they weren't the boots. I didn't know they knew, but I thought they did, and they had always been saying that before, but it wasn't really true."

"Is that really what you figured?" Martin said, disbelieving.

"Yeah, I did."

Martin ended on this note. The first day of cross-examination went as well as the Crown could have hoped, save for Warren making an outright confession on the stand. Just as he had done in the pre-trial voir dire, Martin tore apart the logic of Warren's stories, but still the prosecutor wanted more. He believed that Warren's biggest lie was his psychiatric defense, and he thought one way he might be able to attack it was through Warren's testimony in the voir dire: how he had shaped his answers at that time to make it seem like he talked involuntarily to the police, how he cleverly revealed few of his symptoms so the Crown would be unprepared for the psychiatric defense. Martin believed that if he could prove Warren had lied under oath during the pre-trial voir dire, he would not only destroy Warren's credibility, but he might even force him to come clean.

The second day, Martin began by clearing up a few matters from the previous day. He knew the issue of the boots would likely be confusing to the jury, so he again asked Warren why he didn't just tell the police that he had worn the size eleven Kamik boots instead of taking them out to Cameron Falls to show them where he had burned the size ten boots. "Why didn't you say, 'Listen, forget Cameron River. There is nothing there. These elevens are the ones I wore?'"

"I thought of that, but I didn't do it."

"Does this make sense to you, what you are telling us now?"

"Not too much."

"No. Would this make more sense to you: that you burned these boots at Cameron Falls shortly after the murder because, as you remembered it, you wore those size ten Kamiks into the mine on September the eighteenth? And the reason you thought you wore those size ten Kamiks is because the difference for you between wearing size ten Kamiks and wearing size eleven Kamiks is one pair of socks. You wear one pair of socks with tens and two pairs of socks with elevens. So that was the one difference—and the fact that the boys at the union hall are saying the police are looking for size tens. That's a long question. Do you understand it?"

"Yeah, I understand it, but those boots weren't burned until over a year later."

If that was so, Martin asked, why had Warren told the police that the remnants of the boots had likely been taken away by the ice of the previous winter? Warren went to what was now his standby answer: He did it to make his story sound more realistic.

"And I gather these lies are coming very easily to you," Martin said.

"Yeah, at this time here."

"Right. Well, not just at this time. I think we are already at least settled on this. When it comes to lying, you are a convincing liar."

"I guess so. When I have proper motivation."

"Right, and there is no question that this week and last week you have got proper motivation to lie."

"Yeah, the last couple years, I suppose."

"Right," Martin said, then turned to the items from the satchel in the pond. He pointed out that they were in a Canadian Tire bag and that Warren told the police he bought the tubing and fish line at Canadian Tire. This story matched up with the receipt the police got from Canadian Tire for a purchase at 6:00 P.M. on September 17, 1992.

Warren testified that he didn't get the tubing from Canadian Tire as he had told the police in his confession. He actually had it already. It was off a carburetor.

"Would it not have been easier to say to them, 'Listen, instead of buying this thing, I already had a piece of tubing'?" Martin asked.

"I figured it would be more convincing to say you went to a store and bought it," Warren replied.

Warren described how he put the odds and ends together for the satchel, but Martin shook his head and said, "Mr. Warren, I tell you where I am leading you to, in case it is not clear to you. I am suggesting to you that what you are saying to us is utter nonsense, and that the reason you put this bag in the pond was simply the same reason you told the police on October the fifteenth. These were items you wanted to get rid of."

"All I had to do was throw them in the garbage."

"But you were concerned about the police investigation finding them there, and the pond was a safer place."

Next, Martin had Warren examine a court exhibit, the charred remains of the boots from Cameron Falls. In his voir dire testimony, Warren had said the boots weren't Kamik boots at all; they were old boots he found in a junkyard. He had testified they didn't have the laces on the top like Kamik boots did.

Martin asked Warren to tell the jury what he saw on the sole of one of the boots.

"It could be a piece of lace," Warren admitted. "It looks like maybe a piece of lace."

"Would that be the same kind of lace found in your size eleven Kamik boots to tie up the top?"

"It looks similar."

Martin then reminded Warren that he had earlier testified about the boots at the pre-trial voir dire. "You were under oath at that time?" Martin asked.

"Yes."

"Your oath said that you would tell the truth, the whole truth and nothing but the truth?"

"Yes."

Martin then read out Warren's voir dire testimony, complete with the assertion that the Cameron Falls boots weren't Kamik boots and they didn't have laces on top. "Are you telling us now that they didn't have a top with laces on them?"

"If they did, I never seen it," Warren said. "I didn't handle them too much. I just handled them with my glove and cut them up and burned them."

The final item carried over from the previous day was Warren's alibi. Martin asked again for the identity of the man who had seen him at 4:00 A.M. on September 18 and what this person would say.

At first Warren said he didn't know what the man would say. After Martin prodded some more, Warren said he knew who the guy was. After more prodding, he said the man's name might be Gino.

"Where did this man, Gino—where is he alleged to have seen you?"

"I don't think he saw me. It was that I seen this little car go by, and it always stuck in my mind because of the sound of the engine."

"So that's the alibi?" Martin scoffed. "Is that what you're telling us?"

"Yeah, I saw this car and later connected it to him."

"I thought we were talking about alibi. What you are talking about is that after the strike when you had talked to everybody else on the picket about what they had done, where they were and what they had seen, from that point you understood there was a car that drove by and that's what we are talking about now. Is that it?"

"No, I mentioned that a lot of times before that," Warren said, in reference to his November 6, 1992, interview with McGowan where he had mentioned hearing the sports car go by.

Martin now focused on Warren's testimony about his mental state in his pre-trial voir dire testimony. Martin started out asking why Warren had told him he could not recall having seen a psychiatrist or psychologist after his arrest. Warren said the question wasn't clear.

"That was my mistake?" Martin asked.

"Yeah, it was."

"You were on your oath at that time to tell us the truth, the whole truth and nothing but the truth, and when you were asked this question: 'Were you examined psychologically or by a psychiatrist after your arrest in these matters?' you say that the whole truth and nothing but the truth is: 'I don't remember.'"

"Yeah, I was thinking in the context of a week or two weeks, something like that, not eight months or something."

"We are going to come back to this, Mr. Warren," Martin said, "because I am suggesting to you that this answer was consciously given. You knew exactly what the question was, and your answer was intended to deceive us."

Martin asked Warren why he had not mentioned in the pre-trial voir dire anything about hearing voices, about his raging inner conflict, about McMartin having eyes like black holes and about his own prior planning to confess. His own lawyer had asked him again and again about how he was feeling during the McMartin interview, Martin said, but none of his psychological problems had been mentioned in his testimony. He challenged Warren to find any of these symptoms of psychological distress in the transcript from the voir dire. "I am going to suggest to you firstly that at no time when you were under oath in the voir dire did you give a hint of this sworn evidence you have given here last week about your mental condition. At no time. Do you agree with me or not?"

"Yes, I agree with you."

"Right, and the reason you did that, Mr. Warren, was to deceive us."

"I wouldn't say that."

"What was your reason?"

"I just didn't want to admit to being so screwed up at that time."

"But, Mr. Warren, you were in a court of law, not a union hall. You were under oath. You weren't telling fish stories. So why didn't you tell us the truth, if this is the truth?"

"False pride, I guess. I just couldn't bring myself to bare my soul that much. . . . I actually hadn't articulated it in my head really. . . . I hadn't written any of this stuff down, but subsequently I did. But I hadn't up until then. I am sure that's what my counsel wanted me to do, but I wouldn't do it."

"Your counsel asked you at least four times what was in your mind and what you were feeling."

"Yes, and I resisted him every time and didn't tell him exactly what it was. I hadn't really articulated it. You feel stupid talking about stuff like that."

"I am going to suggest to you the reason you didn't say that or drop any hint of what you are telling us now is the same reason why you lied when you were asked if you had been examined by a psychologist or a psychiatrist after your arrest. You intended to deceive us."

"Well, I am telling you you are wrong."

"But you had no difficulty last week going on and on about your third testicle, about the sex life with your wife, about the—"

"No difficulties?" Warren scoffed and shook his head, looking as if Martin had truly insulted him on this point, that there was no doubt he was telling the truth now.

While the jury was out on a break, Orris rose to say that Martin's methods weren't fair, that when Warren testified in the October voir dire he was only answering his questions within the context of whether or not his confessions to the police were given voluntarily. Warren had been talking about the effect the police had on him and nothing more, just as he was instructed to do.

In response, Martin told de Weerdt: "The question of the voir dire was whether or not these statements were voluntary. Mr. Warren want-ed to impress you that they were not voluntary. You found otherwise. Mr. Warren now tells a different story. He says, in effect, the statements were completely voluntary in keeping with a pre-arranged plan of his. . . . There is absolutely no merit, none, in what my friend has just said."

Nevertheless, when the jury returned, de Weerdt acted on Orris's concerns. He told the jurors they had to remember that the issues of the trial were more general than the issues of the pre-trial voir dire.

Martin resumed his questioning, but the Roger Warren he now faced had suddenly found new confidence. Warren refused to be hurried or led by Martin. He swatted Martin's questions away as if they were bothersome mosquitoes, not deadly daggers. Martin didn't back down and the cross-examination became as bitter and heated as a picket-line squabble.

As he had done in the pre-trial voir dire, Martin played the tape of Warren's weeping breakdown in the car on the trip to Cameron Falls with McGowan and White. "So even in that very emotional moment for you, you were able to lie very fluently and apparently convincingly, is what you tell us now?"

"Yeah," Warren said, ready this time to fire back his answer, "and you notice just before that I was talking about sitting with my wife for coffee?"

"That's right."

"And this here just goes with it, too. Sure I was lying. I was lying right then. I had been lying all night. I had been lying all year. As far as killing the guys, no, and that's your problem, you see. A guy lived forty-nine years and never even slapped anybody, and all of a sudden you have to convince people he killed people. It's a toughie."

"It is not a toughie at all," Martin shot back. "And I am suggesting to you that what you are doing now, Mr. Warren, is lying. The only part of what you have said in this case that is true is the confession from October the fifteenth to eighteenth. Everything else is a lie. You lied to the police for a year before that. You lied at the voir dire. And you are lying to us now. Do you agree with that?"

"You can say whatever you like," Warren scoffed. "I am denying it."

Warren battled Martin on every point, refusing to even admit that he hated Peggy Witte. "Actually I admire the woman," Warren said, "but the way she was operating the labor relations, I didn't care for it. It is a step back in time."

"The way you described her to Corporal Ingram and again—"

"I am ashamed of that, actually," Warren cut in.

"Well, those are your true feelings about her, aren't they?"

"I am ashamed of referring to her that way. It was a derogatory thing to do. Just because she is female has nothing to do with it."

Martin could not build up any momentum. Warren's will was now as strong as his.

"I suggest to you, Mr. Warren, that on September the eighteenth, 1992, you went into the mine, and you set up this device to kill some workers and to change these laws, and, more importantly, to stop the operation of the mine and force management back to the negotiating table."

"You are suggesting that?" Warren snapped back.

"I am suggesting that."

"I am denying it."

"I am going to tell you something else, Mr. Warren. The reason that you are here admitting to us that you lied, and the reason that you committed perjury, was to hide from us the fact that you are also a murderer."

"You can suggest whatever you like. I am just denying it."

Martin was done, his final effort to break Warren unsuccessful. The Crown prosecutor was surprised by Warren's new face. He had not seen it before, though the men at Giant Mine knew it well. Martin had run up against the old Ace, a tough, chippy, hugely confident man.

Warren had to be happy that he had stood up to Martin, yet he had just made his biggest miscalculation of the trial. In revealing his strength Warren had done himself as much harm as he would have had he broken down sobbing and then confessed. Until now the jury had only seen a Warren who was sympathetic, a tired, sad uncle or father figure who had been harassed by the police into confessing. Now another man sat in the witness box, a man with the will to face down a dogged, incisive Crown prosecutor on his own turf. It was hard to imagine the weak, humble Roger Warren climbing down into the dark of Akaitcho to set a bomb to murder nine men. This new Roger Warren, however, looked like he had the nerve. The Ace could pull it off.

Chapter 28

LAST CHANCE TO FIGHT

PROSECUTOR PETER MARTIN had shown that Roger Warren's recantation of his confession was farfetched. Warren himself showed his abrasive, bitter core. But Warren was also entirely convincing when he talked about his mental torment. That testimony had to raise some speck of doubt. It was up to the rest of the defense witnesses to confirm Warren's testimony, proving that Warren's mental breakdown was real and that a false confession was within his realm of possibilities. It wasn't enough for a self-admitted liar like Warren to make these claims. Others had to verify them. But almost without exception, the defense witnesses failed to live up to their billing in Boothroyd's opening address. And in cross-examination Martin invariably got something that harmed Warren out of each witness.

First came Warren's daughter Ann, a government secretary. Ann, twenty-three, seemed a sweet young woman, soft-spoken, smiling shyly. She clearly adored her father, but her testimony didn't help him much. As expected, she said she had seen him on the morning of September 18 when he came home from the picket line. He was no different than usual, she said. In the summer of '93, however, he became more distracted and would sometimes come home drunk. He would forget to pick up her or her mom from work because he was drinking at the Polar Bowl. Still, Ann didn't mention the one thing Boothroyd had promised she would talk about in her opening address—that in October 1993 before the McMartin interview, Ann had heard her father talk about falsely confessing.

Orris next called Dr. Andrew McMillan, Warren's family physician, and Cynthia Stokes, the nurse at the Yellowknife Correctional Centre. McMillan confirmed that Warren had a bad heart and was put on medication, with possible side effects including depression and impotency. In cross-examination Martin established that McMillan had seen Warren a number of times in the winter of 1992–93, but not once did Warren complain of impotency or depression, nor did he ever mention any lump in his testicles. Nurse Stokes confirmed that she had examined him for such a lump in January 1994, and a nonmalignant one had been found. But Stokes had also examined Warren every week in jail after his arrest, and not once did he show any signs of depression. Warren had told her that he was okay. Stokes said he appeared to be eating and sleeping normally.

Ex-miner Danny Mino followed. Mino came into the courtroom wearing dark glasses and led by his German Shepherd Seeing Eye dog. Mino had decided to come to Yellowknife because he couldn't believe that his old partner had set the blast, not after Warren had seen what explosives had done to him and Vince Corcoran. Yet Mino's testimony also fell short. Boothroyd had said in her opening address that Warren saved Mino's life, but Mino only said that Warren was first on the scene, nothing more. He clearly respected Warren, but he also said that Warren was a hard man to work with. "He had a grumpy attitude. Like, he was an old coot. He cursed everything in general. That is the way he was. I think that is when he was at his happiest."

A Wal-Mart clerk, Pia Williams, came to court with a receipt showing that on October 9, 1992, a pair of Kamik boots had been purchased at the store, which was consistent with Warren's claim that he had purchased the size eleven Kamik boots after the blast. Still, it proved nothing. The boots were paid for in cash, not by a credit card, which would have identified the buyer. No one from the store testified that the buyer was Warren.

Orris next called a number of men who had been on the night shift at the picket line on September 18, 1992: Brian Drover, Tom Krahn, Leo Lachowski, Kelly Rhodes. Only Rhodes claimed to have seen

Warren during the hours in question, 1:00 A.M. to 6:00 A.M. The rest said they hadn't seen him. When they admitted this, they invariably looked over at Warren with apologetic faces. But they could not lie even if they had wanted to; in their initial statements to the RCMP, none had mentioned seeing Warren. They were caught.

Drover, who spent the entire shift at gate six, told the jury that if a striker was caught on mine property, the Pinkertons would hold him until the RCMP arrived to arrest him. Drover also said that it was best to stay away from the Pinkertons. They would verbally harass a striker, especially if a man was on his own. Drover said he would jump off the road to avoid the Pinkertons, just as Warren said he did in his various alibis.

On the night in question, Drover said he saw Warren at gate six until 1:00 A.M.; then Warren disappeared. "I don't know if he went to gate five or what," Drover said, the sorry look flashing on his face. He said he didn't see Warren again until 6:00 A.M., when Warren came walking down the Ingraham Trail. He was neither muddy nor wet nor fatigued, Drover said, as a man would be if he climbed through the mine.

When Martin questioned him, Drover admitted that Warren was sweating a little bit when he first saw him at 6:00 A.M. Drover said this was normal for a man who had been out walking. Martin also got from Drover that Warren hadn't mentioned anything about seeing a man with a gun. Despite his reluctance to go along with anything Martin suggested, Drover did admit that if he had seen a man with a gun he would have told his fellow strikers about it. He also would have told the murder investigators.

Striker Kelly Rhodes testified that he saw Warren at the bus at gate three sometime before 2:10 A.M. when *Star Trek* went off the air that night. The story matched what Rhodes had told the RCMP when they first interviewed him shortly after the blast. Martin didn't try to prove Rhodes was necessarily lying about seeing Warren, but he did try to show that his memory could be faulty. Rhodes worked hard not to give Martin the answers he wanted, but still Martin established that Rhodes was under a lot of stress in September 1992, not only because of the strike, but because his girlfriend's father had crossed the picket line. The nights blurred into one another on the line, Martin suggested to Rhodes, and on the night in question, he had been drinking. Martin then brought out his hammer. He reminded Rhodes about a statement he had made to the RCMP after Warren's arrest, in which he had again described that night on the picket line, but changed his story. He no longer said Warren had ever been at the bus. Rhodes said the RCMP threatened him, and he was still drunk from the night before when he gave the interview. He insisted that Warren was in the bus that night.

Following Rhodes was Gino Orsi, whom Warren had billed in his testimony as the man who would close the gap in his alibi to ninety minutes. Orsi was a mechanic at Con Mine. He told the jury he was a CASAW supporter and often dropped in at the picket line. On September 18, he said he was driving home in his Pontiac Fiero after his shift. He decided to drop in at gate three. Leo Lachowski let him into the strikers' bus. Orsi said he stayed for about an hour. He never claimed to have seen Warren, but the defense's proposition was that Orsi's sports car was the one that Warren had seen and heard, but had mistakenly identified it as the Firenza owned by striker Kelly Schneider.

Gillian Boothroyd made note of the fact that Orsi had once been a police officer in his native Sicily, presumably because that would imply he was an honest man. In his cross-examination, Martin wondered why Orsi was only coming forward with information now, that if he were a police officer he must have realized such information would be crucial to the murder investigation. Martin also wondered why Orsi had refused to speak with Sergeant Vern White, who had tracked Orsi down after Warren revealed his name on the stand. Martin suggested to Orsi that he had his nights mixed up, that he had stopped in at the bus at gate three one or two nights earlier.

Striker Leo Lachowski, the next defense witness, proceeded to contradict both Rhodes and Orsi. Lachowski said he was at the bus at gate three the entire night. He said he went to sleep around 2:00 A.M., after Rhodes had already gone to bed. Lachowski said he didn't see Warren, nor did he recall seeing Orsi at any time that night.

The most important new evidence came from striker Tom Krahn. Krahn started the night shift at gate six with Warren, Drover and the others. Krahn then went walking on the Ingraham Trail, but he never saw Warren until the following morning at gate six at about 7:00 A.M. At that time Krahn said he gave Warren a ride to gate three.

"Roger mentioned he had almost been seen on the property," Krahn told the jury. "He said he'd been down in the B-138 portal area. He said he'd seen several people."

Krahn had been interviewed by the RCMP half a dozen times, but this was the first time Martin or the investigators had heard this story. It appeared to confirm Warren's latest alibi about seeing two men in the B-138 portal. In cross-examination Krahn told Martin that he didn't tell the police about this conversation with Warren because he didn't want Warren to get in trouble for walking around on mine property. Krahn admitted that he had deliberately lied. "I wasn't under oath when I was interviewed by the RCMP," he said. "I didn't feel obligated to tell them. I felt Roger was in enough trouble. He may have been in the wrong place at the wrong time."

Martin reminded Krahn that he also had been under oath at Warren's preliminary hearing, but he didn't bring up this story then. Martin also established that Krahn was Warren's friend and Krahn now wanted to help Warren.

Next came the testimony of Pamela Ann MacQuarrie-Higden, who had been promoted by Boothroyd as someone who would corroborate Warren's story about seeing the two shadowy men at 6:00 A.M. MacQuarrie-Higden was a nurse at Con Mine. She had an odd obsession with the strike at Giant. She told the jury that she kept a journal about the strike and listened to a scanner. On the night in question, she was driving by Giant Mine at about 5:50 A.M. on her way to work when she noticed more smoke than usual was coming out of Giant Mine's roaster stack. Such was MacQuarrie-Higden's interest in the minutiae of the dispute that she reached down for her notebook as she was driving; she wanted to add this information to her other jottings. Just then MacQuarrie-Higden said she momentarily saw two men on mine property. She saw them from the back, but she noted one of them was 6'1", the other 5'6", both of them in camouflage gear, the tall one with a beard, the short one skinny, the tall one looking like an outdoorsman with the high cheek bones of a third-generation native. MacQuarrie-Higden's story had been interesting enough to the RCMP that they interviewed her nine times in the months after the blast. The RCMP had stopped dealing with her in December after psychologist Allan Hayduk interviewed her and decided that her story was unreliable, that she was likely mixing up this sighting with a sighting of two men one week earlier.

In his cross-examination Martin wondered how MacQuarrie-Higden could have noticed such details as the high cheekbones if she had only glanced at the men in the dark from behind as she was driving past them. He pointed out that MacQuarrie-Higden was on medication at the time. She also believed she was being followed in the supermarket. About a month after the blast, she was hospitalized for stress.

Throughout the defense's alibi evidence, Vern White had been supplying Martin with background information on each new witness. After Warren's testimony White had worried about the case, fearing a hung jury. He believed there was no chance that Warren's new story would convince eleven townspeople (one juror had dropped out because of an illness in her family) of his innocence. But Orris had only to find one sympathetic juror, perhaps one who had gone in with an anti-Royal Oak, anti-RCMP mind-set. All Orris needed was that person to think, Jesus, do I want to be the one to put this old man in jail for the rest of his life? Yet after watching the mix of contradiction and hostility that was supposed to confirm Warren's story, White was much more sure that the jury would convict. He thought it was the Crown's best week of the trial, the defense not presenting anything solid, just throwing dust into the air, hoping some of it would get in the eyes of the jury.

In this last week of the defense before Christmas, the gossip around the courthouse wasn't about Krahn or MacQuarrie-Higden, but about the naming of Peggy Witte as Canada's Woman of the Year by *Chatelaine,* a Canadian women's magazine. The decision was based on Witte's clever but ultimately unsuccessful bid to take over Lac Minerals, a company four times larger than Royal Oak. "Although she lost the battle, Witte won respect—and our nod as Woman of the Year—for her boldness and tenacity," the editor wrote.

Chatelaine's headline read: "What it takes to be Peggy Witte . . . and what it costs. To play with the big boys in the molto macho mining industry, you need guts, smarts and comeback-kid tenacity. The controversial boss of Royal Oak Mines has learned to recover fast from betrayal at work and heartbreak at home."

The profile was less gushing than the headlines, but it was as much as anything a justification for Witte's use of strikebreakers and her recent decision to move her head office from Vancouver to Seattle. The magazine's selection of Witte had a unifying effect in the divided Yellowknife courtroom. The widows, the Warrens, the lawyers, the security guards, the court staff, the RCMP investigators, the journalists, the CASAW supporters and the townspeople in the gallery joined in disbelief and disgust. A group of Yellowknife women announced a boycott of the magazine. One of them, Lynn Fogwill, told Canadian Press: "It's her leadership of her company I hold responsible for tearing this community apart."

On January 3, 1995, the court reconvened after a two-week Christmas vacation. Glen Orris called Al Shearing, who proceeded to confirm Warren's story that as they read the *Journal* article "Footsteps of the Murderer," they had joked that someone should go in and confess to the murder in order to end the strike. In the same conversation, Shearing said he had admitted to Warren that he was involved in the June 29 graffiti mission along with two other miners. The trip down and back took six hours, the point being that if the Crown was saying Warren made the trip in four hours, he wouldn't have had enough time to pull off the crime.

The final element of the defense was the psychiatric evidence from Doctors Shabehram Lohrasbe and Robert Ley. Both men first had to tell their evidence to de Weerdt when the jury was out so de Weerdt could rule on its admissibility. Neither man convinced the judge he was expert in the field of false confessions. In fact, the evidence showed that there really was no field of false confession research, only the unverified work done by Gisli Gudjonsson in Britain. However, both doctors were allowed to give their diagnosis that Warren was clinically depressed at the time of his confession, which might have made him more susceptible to falsely confessing.

Doctors Lohrasbe and Ley proved to be formidable opponents for Peter Martin. Their imperial demeanor on the stand defied anyone to disagree with their insights into human nature. While other witnesses crumpled under Martin's barrage, they listened intently, chewed on his questions and assertions, played with them, then shaped an answer that gave up as little as possible. The doctors cloaked themselves in a self-assuredness as daunting as the red serge of the RCMP officers.

In his testimony Dr. Lohrasbe listed Warren's symptoms: his impotency, his sleeplessness, his inner turmoil. During the McMartin interview, when the police interrogator kept telling Warren to be a man, it struck a chord in Warren, who felt he was failing as a man, Dr. Lohrasbe said. "If you're going to go down in a blaze of glory, they hit just the right note."

Sergeant McMartin put great pressure on Warren, and Dr. Lohrasbe

said depressed people tend to go along with the flow. McMartin limited Warren's choices: Either he had to confess or he would be lumped in
with people like convicted child killer Clifford Olson. (Dr. Lohrasbe
didn't mention that when Orris had called him up to examine Warren,
the lawyer had limited Dr. Lohrasbe's potential diagnosis in a similar
way, saying Warren was either truthful or the most cool, cold-blooded
psychopath he'd ever seen.)

Dr. Lohrasbe told the jury that if he had seen Warren in October
1993 and Warren had described his symptoms, he might have tried to
get him hospitalized. At least he would have put him on anti-depressants.

Martin's goal was to show that Warren was making up the symptoms. Martin called Dr. Lohrasbe's diagnosis incomplete and one-
sided. He said the doctor had spent only eleven hours with Warren and
talked only to Warren's wife and daughter to confirm his findings. Dr.
Lohrasbe said he wished he had spent more time with Warren, but he
believed he got a complete picture of his patient's makeup. "There's
always the possibility that someone else can provide you with relevant
information, but it would be a never-ending list."

Martin argued that outside confirmation of Warren's symptoms
was crucial because the miner had admitted lying again and again to
the RCMP. "You don't have to rely on the word of a man who tells you
he is a liar," the prosecutor told the doctor.

Dr. Lohrasbe's first contact with Warren had been eleven months
after the confession. The doctor agreed with Martin that it was difficult
to assess a patient's mental condition so long after the fact. He also
agreed with Martin that if Warren had lied to him during the assessment, his evaluation would be useless. The doctor stressed, however,
that he was not naive when it came to spotting liars. Some of the information Warren gave him was remarkable, but it was still believable.
People trying to con a psychiatrist are frequently forthright, but Warren was reluctant. Dr. Lohrasbe doubted that he was being deceived.
"He would have to be Machiavelli to pull it off that way," the doctor
testified.

Martin referred to a letter Warren had written to his two psychiatric experts to explain himself. In the letter, Warren wrote that he had
threatened to call a lawyer in his interview with McMartin, "just to
watch the pismire go wild." (A pismire is the equivalent of ant urine.)

Warren wrote that McMartin was a dupe whom he had planned to mislead: "Every time in my life when I'm attacked or frightened, I attack. Never given an inch."

Martin asked if this combative attitude didn't contradict Dr. Lohrasbe's idea that Warren was so depressed that he would just go with the flow. Dr. Lohrasbe said the letter didn't change his diagnosis.

At last Martin asked Dr. Lohrasbe if Warren could have been depressed, not because he was out of work and feeling inadequate sexually, but because he had killed nine men and had lengthened the strike for his union brothers. The doctor said this was a possibility, but he stood by his diagnosis. "The origins of Mr. Warren's depression can never be nailed down," he claimed.

Dr. Robert Ley described Warren's depression in the same terms as Dr. Lohrasbe, but he was less willing to consider the possibility that Warren had fooled him. Dr. Ley said he couldn't guarantee he was right, but he stuck to his diagnosis of depression. He appeared to have supreme self-confidence in his ability to divine the truth and was quite certain that Roger Warren had not lied to him.

Martin did have one rude surprise for the defense during Dr. Ley's testimony. In the psychologist's two hundred pages of notes from his interview with Warren, Martin and Guenter had found a portion where Dr. Ley asked Warren if he had confessed to various people, including his wife and his lawyer. Dr. Ley wanted to find out how far Warren had gone with his so-called false confession. Warren told Dr. Ley that he had confessed to his wife, his lawyer and also to the union's lawyer, Leo McGrady. Dr. Ley's notes were open to cross-examination, allowing Martin to get at areas that otherwise would be closed off because of solicitor–client privilege.

But Dr. Ley wasn't fazed by this line of questioning. He merely told Martin that false confessors sometimes don't recant for a long time. Warren refused to take back his confession because he wanted his union brothers to get a settlement in the strike.

After Dr. Ley, Orris closed his case. Martin asked if he could call a number of rebuttal witnesses to refute matters that had only been sprung upon the Crown during the defense's case. De Weerdt allowed Martin to call two more witnesses, Calgary psychiatrist Dr. Julio Arboleda-Florez, who testified about how difficult it would be for anyone to hide the symptoms of depression, and Yellowknife Correctional

Centre psychologist, Eldon Bossin. Bossin told the jury that he interviewed Warren for about forty-five minutes on October 30, 1993, only
two weeks after Warren's arrest. It was part of the normal assessment of
a new prisoner, Warren having just returned from the federal penitentiary in Edmonton. Bossin was looking for any signs of suicidal behavior and depression, but said he saw none. Nor did Warren say he was
depressed. "I think he was handling the situation very well," Bossin
testified. "There were no clinical indicators to indicate anything to get
in the way of him being able to cope."

The trial was now the longest in the history of the Northwest Territories. It had started on September 6 when the sun was still high in the
sky. Now it was January 13 and the sun was a pea on the horizon. Both
teams of lawyers had been traveling to and from their homes in Calgary
and Vancouver for four and a half months now, only seeing their families every second weekend. In town they had worked endless hours, but
now the work was almost done, only one last job remaining, their closing arguments. Since the defense had called witnesses, tradition dictat-
ed that Orris speak to the jury first, Martin second. However, Orris
requested that he get to go last, and for once Martin conceded the
point. Martin didn't want to give the defense any grounds for appeal.
He didn't believe going last made much difference to a jury and certainly not in a case like this. The men and women of the jury had invested
three months in the case. They were going to make up their own minds,
not be swayed by something a lawyer said in a one-hour speech.

The courthouse was full for the closing arguments. The various
factions were well represented. On one side sat Helen Warren, the couple's daughters, Pat and Ann, CASAW's defense lawyer Austin Marshall, strikers Bill Schram, Luc Normandin and Sam Pollock. On the
other were widows Doreen Hourie, Tracey Neill and Judit Pandev,
bereaved mother Carol Riggs, RCMP officers Myles Mascotto, Ken
Morrison, Al McIntyre and Mike Brandford. Both Helen and Roger
Warren leaned forward in their seats, their hands on their chins. The
courthouse was never so quiet as the moment before Martin commenced his address. The poisonous years of fighting and suffering had
come to this, two black-robed lawyers, one judge, one jury, one
accused, one last chance to fight. The arguments that had filled the
restaurants, the mines, the union halls, the homes and the courtroom of

Yellowknife since September 18, 1992, were now to be distilled into two speeches by two outsiders. The factions both dreaded and looked forward to what was to come.

Martin turned his lectern toward the jury. He started out by addressing the acrimony of the dispute, impressing upon the jurors they could not let the poison infect their present considerations. They had to base their discussions only on what had been said in the courtroom. "We all know that this case is the subject of a lot of rumor and gossip. It seems almost everyone in Yellowknife has some opinion on this case. . . It is necessary for you to rid from your mind all these rumors and gossip."

Martin told the jury that Roger Warren was a good worker who believed replacement workers should be outlawed and forced from the mine. He set the bomb to kill at least one person, scare other workers and force the company back to the bargaining table. Martin reviewed Warren's initial alibi, focusing on how in his first interview with the police he had lied repeatedly, though he wasn't yet a suspect.

As for the boots, Martin said all that was known for sure was that the killer used reasonably new Kamik boots without marks on the soles. The size eleven Kamik boots that Warren gave to the police had defaced soles. "Why is this man defacing his boots? There is no good answer to this question other than he has something serious to hide. . . . This is the work of a guilty mind. This is the work of a man who is trying to avoid detection."

Martin told the jury that the case against Warren wasn't just strong, it was overwhelming. "You have strong, clear, incriminating evidence of guilt." That evidence included the items in the satchel that Warren threw in the pond. Martin asked the jurors if they believed Warren's account that he had planted the satchel to obstruct justice if the RCMP arrested another union man. If jurors thought Warren was lying about this, Martin said they should remember that Warren had said it under oath. The truth, Martin said, was that Warren threw the items in the pond because he wanted to get rid of any evidence linking him to the blast.

Martin next asked the jury to study Warren's story about finding the boots, then planting them in Cameron Falls to obstruct justice. "Does this story have the ring of truth? Or do you find yourself saying, 'Come on. This is just not true. Like the rest of it, it is just not true.'"

The logical inference, Martin said, was that Warren was convinced that he wore the size ten Kamik boots into the mine so he burned them and threw them away. "Warren would have you believe it was just a matter of bad luck that he bought and defaced the exact boots the police were looking for in their investigation."

Martin also said there is only a quarter of an inch difference between size ten and eleven Kamik boots, and sometimes there were manufacturing errors, which could affect the size. Perhaps Warren did wear the size ten boots into the mine, but they had left size eleven footprints. "We may never know the truth. The one person who knows the truth is not telling it now."

Next, Martin dealt with the ethics of the McMartin interview. He asked the jury if they felt that Sergeant McMartin had been too direct with Warren, then answered the question: "Ladies and gentleman, we weren't dealing with a fourteen-year-old boy who threw a brick through a window. This is a murder. It was time for the accused to come clean and stop lying to the police."

It was right for McMartin to confront Warren, Martin said, and the end result was the confession, which didn't only consist of Warren admitting that he did it, but was complete with illustrations, demonstrations and reenactments. Warren provided information that the police didn't know, as well as the hold-back evidence, such as getting lost in the 425- and 575-levels of Akaitcho. Warren described how he thought and felt that night when he set the bomb. His story was full of emotion and told in minute detail. He spoke with spontaneity, detailing how he used a knife to close the hatch on the Akaitcho shaft behind him, how the string on the trip wire was too tight so he loosened it, how he was terrified when he enabled the bomb.

Martin turned to the moment when Warren broke down and started to cry the next day as he rode in the car with McGowan and White to Cameron Falls. "What is he saying at his darkest moment, his weakest moment? He is saying he regrets killing those men. He is saying he's tired of lying."

Warren was now claiming he was depressed and confused, but Martin said the footprints in Akaitcho confirmed the confession. It was evidence only the murderer and the police knew. "On reflection you must agree this is a most compelling case. It is hard to imagine a clearer or more compelling case."

Warren was a problem solver and what he was doing now was trying to find a way out from this overwhelming case, Martin said. The
entire defense was based on Warren's credibility, but in the voir dire
when he talked about why he had confessed to McMartin, he made no
mention of hearing voices or his inner torment or McMartin's black-
hole eyes. "He is not a fourteen-year-old boy who is confused. He knew
he was talking on the stand. He's lying under oath. It's that simple."

Warren was claiming that the *Journal* article gave him the details to
confess, but it was clear from Warren's own testimony that he ignored
the information from the article, that nothing in his confession had
come from there, except maybe the route. As for Warren's psychiatric
defense, Martin asked the jurors to look again at the video reenactment
in the mine. "Did anyone think that he was depressed when they first
saw him on the videotape?"

If Warren was so compliant, respectful and willing to go along with
the police, why did he lie to Defer from the start? "This man is not
compliant. These doctors are simply wrong. They've been fooled."

Warren was supposed to have had a serious bout of depression,
Martin said, but neither Stokes, the prison nurse, nor Bossin, the
prison psychologist, had noticed anything wrong with Warren, nor did
Warren mention his problems to his family physician, Dr. McMillan.
Even if Warren was depressed, Martin argued, it meant nothing. It cer-
tainly didn't mean that the confession was false.

"The accused in this case has one hope: that you will misunderstand what is meant by a reasonable doubt," Martin concluded. "There
is nothing about this defense that comes close to raising a reasonable
doubt. What would happen to our system if this was all that was
required to raise reasonable doubt, a few lies and help from a few
friends? The evidence says this man committed murder. He has, he did
so, and now this professed problem solver has done his best to dance
around the Crown's case. And he sits here now wondering if he has
been able to fool you, and if you will let him get away with murder."

Martin sat down. He had done an able job, though many in the
gallery noticed that he hadn't once mentioned Warren's testimony that
a bomb such as he had described would surely kill, evidence that could
lead to a first degree murder conviction. Instead, Martin had stressed
Warren's story from his confession, and how, if it was believed, it would
result in a second degree murder conviction.

The omission was planned. Martin knew that if he pressured the jury to go for first degree murder, if he claimed Warren had lied about his intent when he set the bomb, if he argued that it was in fact a planned and deliberate murder, Martin would dilute Warren's confession, the strongest piece of evidence. He would do the defense's job of casting doubt. It would be a dangerous proposition, especially with Orris about to try to convince the jury that the entire confession was a lie.

Martin's speech shook the relatives of the dead men. Doreen Hourie had bent over and prayed as he talked, asking God that his words get through to the jury. Doreen felt she was regressing now, that she was weak again, out of control. Over the Christmas vacation she had gone home to Vernon, British Columbia, for twelve days, but she had found no respite. She was low with grief one moment, then high with hope the next, talking about how poorly Warren had done on the stand. Her stepdaughter Darla had told her, "You know, Doreen, I know you have to go there for yourself, but it's not going to change the outcome no matter what happens. Dad is still not going to come home. You have to be prepared for that."

Doreen had managed to stay off the sleeping pills, though nightmares plagued her. She awoke in fearful sweats, afraid that she was going to miss the verdict. She worried about getting back on time for the resumption of the case. She dreamed she arrived late, only to be confronted by Peter Martin. "You're late," he raged at her in her nightmares. "How could you do this? How could you let us down? You were the only one we were counting on to be here and you missed."

Doreen felt intimidated by Martin, not by anything he did, but by what she had given him. She had never asked any man to carry her except Norm, but for the past four and a half months she had asked this of Martin. She had put her faith in him, and now, in her mind, Martin's closing address was a symbolic passing of that trust and that faith to the eleven jurors.

Doreen had had to fight to keep from weeping as Martin spoke. She tried to reassure herself that the jury would come through, but she was finding it increasingly hard to deal with the fact that they might not. It was getting to be too much for her, this entrusting of her life to strangers. After Martin was done she was exhausted and elated and agitated all at once. She and Judit went to the public washroom in the hallway to gather themselves. Judit was still flying from Martin's words, believing that the case was won, that it was almost time to celebrate. In the washroom, the two widows came upon Warren's daughter Pat. Judit went into a stall, shut the door and sat down. "Don't you feel like dancing?" she said aloud, knowing full well that the comment would stab the Warren girl. "I feel like dancing."

"Yeah, I guess so," Doreen said.

Upset at Judit's glee, Pat Warren hurried out of the washroom, only to return a moment later. She glared at Doreen.

"You couldn't handle the truth, could you?" she snapped.

"If you want to know the truth," Doreen shot back, "that fucker is dead one way or the other!"

The threat sent the Warren girl hurrying out again. It was no idle threat. Doreen still held to her vow that if Warren got off, she would hunt him down. And if the Warren women caused her any trouble after the verdict, she would be happy to get into a scrap. Judit told Doreen that she'd like to help out if it came to a fight, but she knew she would back away. Part of her wanted to bash them, but she recalled how Joe had always told her to turn away from violence. She decided she would try to honor him and walk away with dignity.

The widows, the Warrens and the rest of the crowd gathered again in court after lunch to hear Glen Orris. Orris moved from his lectern to stand directly before the jury. Whereas Martin spoke from his notes, Orris had a general plan, but shaped his message as he went. He started out by admitting to the jurors that it was a difficult matter to defend a man like Roger Warren. "What we have to deal with is my own client Mr. Warren's attempt at self-destruction."

Orris proceeded to detail evidence that cast doubt on the Crown's theory. It didn't make sense that the Crown believed only one person set this blast, he said, when clearly it would take more than that. Also, if the man who set the blast traveled down Akaitcho and left such obvious footprints, wouldn't he take care to cover them up?

At the very least, Orris said, Warren had been seen on the picket line between 2:00 and 6:00 P.M. This didn't give him enough time to set this bomb. As for Leo Lachowski, Orris said it was no wonder he hadn't seen Warren because Lachowski was asleep. Jurors also had to remember that Orsi had said he was there and Warren had said he saw Orsi's car. "Roger Warren can tell us what he saw, and we can prove that that happened."

Warren's bad back, his bad hands and bad heart meant he could not have climbed into the mine to commit the crime. Yet the Crown said he did this, then came out and the other strikers saw no sign that he had been on this arduous mission. No one said he was dirty, as he would be if he had gone into the mine. Warren told the police that he had gone in to blow up the C-shaft, yet he had a toggle switch, batteries and tape, items that wouldn't be needed to blow up the shaft. "The police didn't push Mr. Warren on any of these inconsistencies at all. They had somebody who was prepared to tell them he had done it, and that's all they wanted."

A safety-conscious miner would never set up such a bomb, Orris said. "This device is very, very dangerous. Mr. Warren would not be doing this. It is completely against his personality. It is completely against his previous experience."

Orris then described Warren's mind-set after the blast, explaining again why Warren had lied to the police about seeing the two shadowy men on the mine property at 2:00 A.M., instead of in the B-138 portal at 6:00 A.M. So why did he lie to Defer?

"Because he couldn't hold back what is important," Orris said.

Orris admitted that it was stupid for Warren to deface the size eleven Kamik boots, but if Warren had really worn these boots in the mine, why didn't he just get rid of them?

In the year following the blast, the pressure on the union increased with the search on Tim Bettger's home, then the Blitz package aimed against Shearing and Bettger. Orris again explained why Warren had planted the satchel in the pond and the boots in Cameron Falls. Then Orris said these, too, were stupid acts. However, they only made it clear that Warren was not thinking rationally in the spring, summer and fall of 1993.

Orris went on to detail the psychological ills that pushed Warren to falsely confess: his unemployment, his failing health, his impotency, his depression, his desire to end the strike. Doctors Ley and Lohrasbe did many tests on Warren and interviewed him for many hours, Orris said. They were experienced investigators who had their own ways of assessing truth. They believed his story.

McMartin didn't care about Warren as a man. McMartin didn't know about the effects of the strike. All he knew was what he had read in the *Edmonton Journal* article, Orris said. Dr. Lohrasbe had said that all Warren's options were taken away by McMartin's approach. This angered Warren, who decided he could screw the RCMP for their pressure tactics by falsely confessing. "At least if no one can save me, if I have to be the scapegoat, at least I'll get this strike settled—that was his main thought pattern, as irrational as it may be," Orris said.

Only when the strike was over did Warren write his letter to Bettger and Shearing in jail. "Once the strike was settled, you would expect a recantation and that is what happened."

Orris pointed out that Warren himself had said that if the bomb had been set up the way he described it, it would certainly kill. "Does that sound like someone who was trying to protect himself?"

Orris concluded by reminding the jury that reasonable doubt was there to protect everybody, including people who were self-destructive and very, very stupid. The evidence, he said, didn't prove Warren's guilt; it proved his innocence.

"If you convict Roger Warren, the people who did this terrible crime would have gotten away with murder."

Chapter 29

THE RECKONING

ON MONDAY, JANUARY 16, 1995, Justice Mark de Weerdt turned in his chair, looking away from Roger Warren, the defense lawyers, the prosecutors and the gallery, to directly face the jurors. They were all that mattered now. It was time for them to decide.

"Your sense of duty has been noted and greatly appreciated," de Weerdt said to begin his charge, his summation of the facts and the law. Just as he had said to start the jury portion of the trial, de Weerdt stressed the jury's dominant role. "At the end of the day it will be you, the jury, and you alone who will judge what the facts mean. Weigh them without sympathy or prejudice."

De Weerdt didn't attempt to go over all the evidence or even to focus on the highlights, as Orris and Martin had done in their closing remarks. Instead, he gave his impressions of both the Crown and the defense cases. His thrust concerned two points: Roger Warren's credibility and the testimony of psychiatric experts Ley and Lohrasbe, and prison psychologist Bossin.

On the first matter, de Weerdt dwelled on the discrepancies between Warren's testimony in the pre-trial voir dire and the trial. The judge read passages from the voir dire concerning Warren's motivation for confessing and reminded the jurors about Warren's testimony on the same subject during the trial. It was a hint that Warren had changed his story under oath, a hint de Weerdt was allowed to give at this point in the trial, but only if he did it with care.

Likewise de Weerdt hinted at problems with the testimony of the psychiatric experts. If the jurors saw fit, they did not have to accept any expert opinion as conclusive, especially where the experts disagreed, de Weerdt said. For example, Doctors Ley and Lohrasbe gave their opinions, but they didn't consult with Dr. McMillan, Nurse Stokes or Bossin, who had examined Warren only a few weeks after he had confessed. Doctors Ley and Lohrasbe made the diagnosis of depression after the fact, but the three medical experts who saw Warren at the time, when he was actually supposed to have been depressed, did not notice any such symptoms, nor did Warren mention them.

To help the jury sort through the months of testimony, de Weerdt suggested a plan. First the jurors had to determine if Warren was the killer. If they had no reasonable doubt that Warren had set the bomb, the next important step was to decide his intent. Was the act planned and deliberate? Had Warren thought about the consequences of killing nine men? Did he slowly put together his plan and carefully enact it to kill or badly injure even one man? If the jury had no reasonable doubt he did these things, de Weerdt said the verdict would be first degree murder. De Weerdt reminded the jury that Warren himself had testified that this bomb would kill.

If the jury did have a reasonable doubt about first degree murder, de Weerdt told them they could convict Warren of second degree murder. To come to that verdict the jury had to be convinced beyond a reasonable doubt that Warren intended his bomb to kill, but that the act was committed in a rush with none of the forethought and planning of first degree murder. De Weerdt alerted the jury to a point Peter Martin had made in his closing address: Even if Warren realized he would kill only as he escaped from the mine, that knowledge was the same as having the intent to kill, and the verdict would be second degree murder.

The final verdict for homicide was manslaughter. If the jurors believed Warren set the bomb, but only intended to damage some machinery and never realized that he would kill anyone, then that was the proper decision.

No sooner had de Weerdt finished and the jury had left to start its deliberations, than Orris and Martin were on their feet, both upset at various aspects of the charge. Martin wished de Weerdt had done a better job of summing up the Crown's evidence, wedding the acts of Warren's alleged offense to the laws of homicide. Orris was upset about de Weerdt's handling of Warren's credibility and Dr. Ley's and Dr. Lohrasbe's testimony. He also thought de Weerdt's description of the law regarding homicide wasn't clear enough. In the end Orris wrote a few brief paragraphs, again explaining the laws. Martin agreed to what Orris had written, and the jury was quickly recalled to hear this addition to the charge.

That day the jury established a pattern that would continue until it reached a decision. The jurors met through the afternoon, then sent a message out just before the supper hour saying that they would not be deciding anything that night. Everyone in court was free to go home.

Outside the courtroom more than thirty members of the Canadian news media gathered each morning. They sat and waited, reading, playing cards and Scrabble, ordering in pizza, going over the myriad theories about the case and purchasing $2 guesses in the pool on when the verdict would come. The out-of-town reporters and producers were anxious to leave frozen Yellowknife (though the weather was comparatively mild through the week, a daytime high of about five degrees Fahrenheit). The out-of-towners guessed that the jury would be out no later than Tuesday night. But the local reporters knew full well how townspeople had agonized over this dispute. The jurors wouldn't come back too quickly, the locals reasoned, even if they had a verdict. They couldn't appear to be too hasty. The verdict would come in on Wednesday or Thursday, the locals guessed. One matter that the out-of-towners and locals almost unanimously agreed upon, however, was the jury's verdict. The consensus was second degree murder.

Tracey Neill and her mother, Roseanne Quintal, also waited with the reporters. Tracey was cordial, but she asked that she not be quoted in any stories. She'd had her share of attention. She was aware that Doreen Hourie, Judit Pandev and Carol Riggs had attended the entire trial. She didn't want to come in at the last moment and take any attention away from them.

Doreen, Judit and Carol waited out the jury at the chapel in the Salvation Army building. They held hands, sang songs and prayed. Doreen asked God to work on the jurors so they would give Warren at least a second degree murder conviction and twenty years without parole. Carol and Judit wished the death penalty was still in place. They hated the idea that their tax dollars would help feed Warren. Judit pictured Warren on death row, not knowing when he might die, living with the anxiety.

Doreen tried to put aside her hunger for vengeance. She told Judit and Carol that she didn't give a shit what happened to Warren in jail, even if he was put up in a penthouse cell and got cheesecake and thirty channels. As long as he was found guilty, that would be good enough. It had to be good enough, Doreen told herself. She had to accept it. More than she needed vengeance, she now understood that she had to accept and move on. Her malevolence toward Warren and CASAW was destroying her.

Doreen thought the jury would come back with a verdict by Wednesday, the third day of deliberations. On Tuesday, however, a note came that made this seem unlikely. The jurors asked to see a transcript of Warren's entire six hundred pages of testimony from the trial. A dozen theories quickly circulated among the reporters. The consensus was that the jury was being methodical, wanting to go over this key document page by page. Unlike the widows, the RCMP, the media and all the interested townspeople, the jurors had not hashed out each day's evidence as it came up. Indeed, de Weerdt had instructed them not to do this, but to wait to hear all the evidence. They had a lot to talk about.

On Wednesday the jury made a second request, this time asking for the testimony of striker Alex Mikus. Mikus had been to the bus at gate three at 4:00 A.M. on September 18, 1992, but he hadn't seen Warren, though Warren had initially claimed he was there. While Mikus's testimony had been damaging to the defense, Orris, Boothroyd and the few pro-Warren members of the media saw the request as a positive sign. If the jurors were still dealing with Warren's alibi, they apparently had not yet decided that Warren was the man who had set the bomb.

On Thursday morning a doctor was requested for one of the jurors. The juror was rushed to hospital in an ambulance. The court officers came back to report that it seemed the juror had been momentarily paralyzed with exhaustion but was now all right and ready to resume his duties. De Weerdt allowed him to rejoin the other jurors. All the jurors looked tired and frayed, as if they weren't sleeping well. That afternoon they sent word that they had yet another message for the court. Again the courtroom filled, Tracey Neill, Roseanne Quintal,

Carol Riggs, Doreen Hourie and Judit Pandev moving in behind Martin and Guenter, the media in behind them. But no one sat in the section behind Roger Warren. The CASAW section had been empty since de Weerdt's charge on Monday. Neither his family nor his union supporters were with him through that final time of waiting. Without them Warren seemed to be fading from the courtroom. He was a forgotten man. The stressful, foreboding hours wore on him. He looked as if he had ingested some strange toxin, his skin growing darker by the day, his body shrinking, crumbling in on it itself. He looked as if knew he was going to go to jail.

The issues raised in Warren's defense seemed puny now, old fishing tales half-remembered. Without his supporters, there was nothing to give them life. Surely Helen Warren and the couple's daughters hadn't abandoned him; they were waiting at home in their apartment, in agony and in prayer, believing he was innocent and that the justice system would likely fail him. Just as surely, however, if the CASAW faction held their convictions as strongly as the widows did, if they were convinced Warren was innocent and a guilty verdict would be a miscarriage of justice, many would have waited out the verdict alongside Warren. But no one showed.

The jury's latest request was for a copy of de Weerdt's charge. After getting advice from Orris and Martin, de Weerdt decided to ask the jury to be more specific about the part of the charge it wanted. The jurors came back to ask if they could have only the section of the charge dealing with the laws of homicide.

The case, it seemed, was over.

Unless something entirely unexpected was going on, the jury had made up its mind that Warren had set the bomb and was only deciding what to convict him with. Afterward, Boothroyd and Orris followed Warren out of the courtroom. Their job now was to help him deal with the latest turn.

At 3:30 P.M. the following day, Friday, January 20, 1995, word came that the jury had its verdict. The lineup in front of the metal detector door formed at once, twenty-five people deep, then fifty, then one hundred, then two hundred. Many who came late didn't get in at all.

In the courtroom Tracey Neill's mom, Roseanne Quintal, turned to Doreen Hourie, who sat in the next seat.

"What do you think?"

"He'll get second degree," Doreen said, then held out her hand. "Pray."

Roseanne grasped it and the two shut their eyes.

De Weerdt called the court to order. "I'm informed that the jury has a verdict," he said. "Please bring in the jury."

The jurors filed in, none of them looking at Warren. Each of the jurors looked more pale, more fatigued, less composed, as if the nature of their talks had taken something away from each man and woman. Several female jurors had red eyes from crying. As soon as Doreen saw that she knew they had made their painful decision, but it was the one she wanted.

The jury foreperson, a distinguished, middle-aged woman, stood up. In a clear voice she said, "We find the defendant not guilty of first degree murder, but guilty of second degree murder."

One of the jurors, a young blond woman, started to weep. Doreen put her hands over her face and bawled as well. She and Judit hugged.

"We did it," Doreen whispered.

"We did it," Judit echoed.

There was little joy at that moment, only relief and a terrible sense of completion, a door slamming shut. Roger Warren was a liar and a murderer, but it was nonetheless hard to see him stand alone, a withered old man, stripped of his comforting stories and facing his punishment. Only one other CASAW man was in the room, Robin Janz, but he was quick to leave after the verdict. Peggy Witte was out of the country.

In the strict terms of the criminal law there was no collective responsibility for the mass murder. But if there had been no Roger Warren, someone else would have stood in his place in the prisoner's dock. The dispute at Giant Mine was headed for a homicide one way or another. Chris Neill and so many others in Yellowknife had been right. Someone had to die.

Both factions had wanted war more than peace. They wanted to dominate, not share, to destroy, not build. Witte had worked out a tentative agreement with the union moderates, but it was bound to be voted down. She had treated so many of her employees with contempt that most wanted to lash back. The strikers believed that by withdrawing their labor they could beat her into acceptance and ruin. It only increased their horror and malice when Witte refused to take their abuse.

Peggy Witte saw herself as a bold capitalist, a creative super-woman, a brilliant individualist. If no one else had used strikebreakers in a Canadian mine in fifty years, it was high time someone did. She would ignore the strike, brush off the gun held to her head as if it did not exist. Bring on the helicopters!

Ultimately the line crossers and replacement workers were little more than pawns in the bigger game of getting Giant Mine to produce gold at a profit. After the nine men were murdered, Witte showed the steel in her will, strong-arming the mine back into production. But she also showed the steel in her soul when she gave her epitaph for the murdered men: "Nine men have lost their lives to keep the Giant Mine open."

The nine men had crossed the picket line to make money and escape unemployment, not to engage in a crusade on behalf of Royal Oak. They lost their lives because one man had snapped, not so they could become martyrs for Royal Oak's shareholders.

Although Witte's actions were incendiary, the union could have turned Yellowknife against Royal Oak through clever and more passive resistance. Instead, a small element within the union devolved into thugs. They gloried in their rage. They appalled many townspeople as well as many of the more sensible strikers, who either got other jobs, stewed silently on the line or stayed home.

The union leadership failed to control the violent clique. The executive condemned the line crossers, but never lashed out at members for downing power poles, breaking into the mine to paint sinister graffiti or setting off bombs at the satellite dish and the vent shaft. Whenever blame was thrust on CASAW, the executive wallowed in the union's victim status. It tried to put the blame on Royal Oak and the government for not enacting antiscab legislation.

Would antiscab laws have been any kind of answer? Not likely, not with a union determined to punish its employer. If Witte hadn't brought in strikebreakers, the mine may well have never opened again. But some form of binding arbitration could have stopped the strike before it started. The majority would have been happy to be back at work. Roger Warren never would have felt compelled to impose his own deadly solution.

Without a strike Warren would have lived out his quiet life. His temper would have erupted when a mechanic or a trammer was too slow doing his job or when his shift boss gave a better-paying heading to some ass kisser or when he thought about the stupid politicians wasting his taxes. He would have cursed loudly, but as he told his friend Danny Mino, his bark was worse than his bite. He would never beat up anyone, except with his acid tongue. He was sure of his intellectual superiority over other men and other miners. As long as he could hold onto that belief, he would be content.

Witte's use of strikebreakers twisted Warren. He had been the best miner, but the mine didn't want him. He had been an outstanding employee, but the company now cherished the scabs, whom he saw as the ultimate ass kissers. It didn't make sense. It was illogical. It offended his intelligence and his sense of superiority. A dark, profane anger built within him.

"Does somebody have to die before we get rid of these fucking scabs?" a striker had yelled out on the picket line two weeks into the strike.

"They do, they do," Warren had threatened. "And we'd better soon get it done."

It will never be known if Warren's bomb was set to take out the man-car, but it's clear that Warren didn't care about the consequences. He thought the strike had created a new morality. As he explained to Corporal Ingram, it was war, it was hate. Indeed, if he was back in wartime and he had snuck across enemy lines and pulled off such a plan, the Queen herself would have pinned a medal to his chest. If the government was too corrupt to chase out the scabs, then the union would have to do it. If mechanics like Shearing and Bettger were too tame and inept to get the job done, it was up to a hardrock miner. Leave it to the best man in the mine. Leave it to the Ace. Only he had the audacity and nerve to pull it off.

Warren thought he'd be a hero. He had no idea that as much as anyone else he would be sickened by his act. He thought it wouldn't upset him. He thought he could take eighty to eighty-five pounds of poison, load it in a scoop, set it beside a drift, rig it to a firing mechanism, kill who knows how many men and remained untouched. Warren was as confident and hard-headed as they came, but in the end it meant only that he was all the more shattered when he found himself crumbling. His heart went bad. His mood deteriorated. His spirit faded. He felt like nothing more than a stinking piece of meat. He despised himself for not having the willpower to fight off the rot. But he had touched the poison with his own hand. It had infected him, just as it would infect any sane man.

In the end Warren realized that the bomb had failed on all counts. His confession redeemed him, but he failed yet again when he recanted during the trial. Not only did he fail to convince the jury, he debased himself. His old nemesis, Corporal Dale McGowan, for one, could not understand why Warren recanted. When Warren had finally confessed to the police, he had broken down, babbling, weeping. He said he was sick of lying, yet he had lied repeatedly on the witness stand. It didn't make sense to McGowan, especially because he thought of Warren as basically a decent man. Indeed, telling lie after lie was much less than the proud old Ace would have done. By the time of the trial, however, Roger Warren was no longer that man. He was ruined.

When he heard the verdict, Warren stared ahead, focusing on nothing, a bland look on his face, unmoving. De Weerdt asked the jurors to retreat once more and come up with a recommendation on the length of time that Warren should serve before he was eligible for parole. The jurors filed out. Members of the media gathered around the relatives of the dead men.

"I feel relieved now, I really do," Carol Riggs said. "Now everyone will know the truth."

"All these people who beat their breasts for two years, they can eat it!" Judit Pandev said. "That's my satisfaction. I heard it—he's guilty. I'm grinning like a monkey from ear to ear."

"I feel good," Doreen Hourie said. "I feel thankful. All I wanted was to hear *guilty*. Now the nine men can rest. Now the nine miners can rest."

Only Tracey Neill was somewhat disappointed. She still believed the act was first degree murder. You couldn't find a more experienced man in the mine who knew what explosives would do to the victims, she said.

The jurors soon came back. They filed in, again not one of them looking at Warren. The jury foreperson stood. De Weerdt asked her for the recommendation.

"We, the jury, recommend the defendant not be eligible for parole for twenty years," she said.

Judit, Doreen and Carol let out a quick clap and whooped, "Yes!"

De Weerdt told the court that he would hold over sentencing until the following Thursday. Sergeant Jim Barr took Warren out of the courtroom to the holding room. Alone now, the convicted murderer shook his head.

"Ah fuck it," he said.

For the first time, Barr clamped handcuffs on Warren, then led him to the RCMP car. As they headed outside, TV lights flashed on. A television reporter intercepted Warren. "How do you feel now, Roger? What do you have to say to the families of the dead men now?"

Warren turned his head and let Sergeant Barr direct him to the car.

The press scrum outside the front of the courthouse surrounded the main players of the case. Inspector Al MacIntyre told the reporters that people in the community could now get on with their lives. "It was an extremely difficult investigation. It was the most difficult investigation I've been involved in over the years."

Jim O'Neil left with tears in his eyes, unable to speak. "I'm a mess," he said.

"I feel for everybody, even Roger," said Roger Carroll, the man who had first told the police about Warren's odd behavior on the morning of the blast. "I figure he was a victim himself of mass cultlike thinking."

Glen Orris refused to say anything to the reporters, though by the next day word had gotten out that he planned to appeal the conviction, claiming that Warren did not get a fair trial.

Peter Martin's jaw was set, his face aged with fatigue. There was no sign of joy or relief. "I think you can't lose sight of the fact nine men were killed here and nine families are grieving," he said.

Martin praised the jurors, saying it was obvious from the questions they asked and the time they took that they were serious about their duty. The verdict of second degree murder was the right one.

In the end only a small group of hardcore CASAW men believed in Warren's innocence. The rest of the miners followed the lead of their new president, Rick Cassidy. He was a decent man, and his public statement regarding Warren's conviction appeared to show that he was ready to accept and move on. "I imagine it was a tough decision," he said of the verdict. "The decision today in the Warren trial brings to an end years of tension, both for the workers at Royal Oak Mines and the community of Yellowknife."

In the days following the verdict, Doreen, Carol and Judit walked around town, saying hello to people, not caring where the others had stood in the strike or how they felt about the verdict. The three women felt emboldened. Many people came up to them to say, "Thank God," and "Good luck." They shook hands and hugged. Judit and Doreen heard stories that in some offices people had stood up and cheered when they heard the verdict.

Judit no longer felt she had to mope around with her head down. She felt welcome in her old town. She felt like her old self. "This is me," she told Doreen and Carol. "I found *me.*"

On January 26, 1995, the day of sentencing, a few reporters converged on Warren as he walked from the RCMP car to the courthouse. One asked Warren how he felt. Warren kept walking, then muttered as he entered the courthouse, not loudly enough for the reporters, but loudly enough for Sergeant Barr to hear him say, "Like I'm going before Judge Roy Bean."

The courthouse was again full, but now more union supporters showed up, including Al Shearing and Tim Bettger. Justice de Weerdt asked both Martin and Orris for their sentencing submissions on Warren. Martin called for twenty-five years without parole, asking de Weerdt to consider the eight widows and the many children without fathers. Orris made no submission as to the length of parole. "Roger Warren maintained and still maintains he is not responsible for this blast," he said.

De Weerdt proceeded to explain his reasons for the sentence he was about to give. The judge said that on the whole Warren didn't fit the pattern of a violent offender, although he did give the impression of having long-bottled-up feelings. He had a well-concealed but potentially violent aggressive streak that came across in Martin's cross-examination. This crime was no bungling attempt by an amateur, de Weerdt said. The bomb was set to destroy the morale of those working in the mine, to create havoc, and at least to cause injury and likely death to the ore-train operator. "It was nothing less than an act of terrorism," de Weerdt said. "Unless a higher court otherwise decides, Roger Warren will carry the guilt of his stupid and despicable crime with him for the rest of his days. Yes, but the pain which he has inflicted will be borne mostly by others: the families of the immediate victims, his own family and all who have been touched by the events of September 18, 1992, at Giant Mine.

"This is a case in which the circumstances call out for a stern denunciation which will leave no mistaken impressions in the public mind."

De Weerdt asked Warren to stand. Warren rose, his lawyers Glen Orris and Gillian Boothroyd standing with him.

"Have you anything to say before the Court pronounces sentence upon you?" de Weerdt asked.

"No, I have nothing to say," Warren said.

De Weerdt sentenced Warren to life in jail with no parole for twenty years. Before Warren left the court, Sergeant Barr told him, "Because of the need for security on you and that you're a convicted murderer, I have to handcuff you."

Barr handcuffed Warren in full view of the gallery. Judit Pandev was ecstatic to see Warren in chains. This was the exclamation mark on the verdict, what she had been waiting to see for more than two years, the public humiliation of the murderer.

The widows and members of the Riggs family went to their old hangout, Ryan's, for coffee with Peter Martin. "You put up a fantastic fight, and I will not forget what you did here," Judit told the prosecutor. "As long as I live, as long as I can remember, I will remember."

Doreen Hourie also thanked Martin. On behalf of the widows and other family members, she gave him a present, a commemorative print showing a grieving miner kneeling before the C-shaft. She had written on it: "Peter, from you we drew our strength."

Right up to the end, Doreen had struggled with her urge for revenge. Now that urge had been tamed. The verdict had been better than revenge. It was justice. Revenge was seeing Warren in handcuffs. Justice was the certainty that he belonged in them. Revenge would have taken one second and one bullet. Justice took two and a half years, the self-sacrifice of dozens of men and women and many millions of dollars. Justice was painstaking, but had the power to purge the poison. The trial was a reckoning for Roger Warren, but also for Doreen. She had given her life to the RCMP, then to Peter Martin, then to the jury. Now they gave it back to her. Norm could rest. She was free.

EPILOGUE: JULY 1, 1995

THE WIDOWS AND RELATIVES of the nine murdered men, along with the Worker's Compensation Board, have filed a $34 million lawsuit against Peggy Witte, Royal Oak, Pinkerton Security, the Northwest Territories government, CASAW, Roger Warren and others for combined negligence. Each relative has a different claim, ranging from $1.22 million for Carol Riggs to $5.66 million for Tracey Neill.

Judit Pandev is living with her family in Waterdown, Ontario. Doreen Hourie is living in Vernon, British Columbia. Both Judit and Doreen spend much of their time caring for their granddaughters. Carol Riggs lives in Lake Cowichan, British Columbia, where she continues her work selling Spanky Wear, the casual and children's clothing line produced in honor of her son. Tracey Neill is working for the federal Justice Department in Calgary, Alberta.

Jim and Jane O'Neil, and Terry and Claudia Legge, continue to live in Yellowknife. Both Terry and Jim are still employed at Giant Mine.

Harry Seeton works at the mine, but is no longer on the union executive.

Keith Murray has gone to work at a gold mine in Snow Lake, Manitoba.

Don Moroz lives in Saskatoon and works in a mine in northern Saskatchewan.

Noel O'Sullivan is recovering from hip replacement surgery and plans to go back to work at Giant Mine.

Peggy Witte has set up her head office in Seattle, Washington, where she is engineering the continued expansion of Royal Oak.

Gregg McMartin retired from the RCMP shortly after the trial ended. He now runs a private polygraph and investigative firm out of his home in Airdrie, Alberta.

Corporal Dale McGowan continues his plainclothes duties in Hay River, Northwest Territories.

Inspector Al MacIntyre is head of administration and personnel for G-division, the RCMP's designation for the Northwest Territories.

Vern White is the sergeant in charge of the community policing section for G-division.

Constable Bill Farrell is working on patrol in St. Albert, Alberta.

Randy McBride has been promoted to corporal and has moved to Coppermine, Northwest Territories.

Corporal Harry Ingram is a shift supervisor in Red Deer, Alberta.

Corporal Al McCambridge continues his work in the General Investigations Section for G-division.

Ken Morrison was recently promoted to the rank of corporal and will be sent to work in the Déné settlement of Lutsel Ke' on Great Slave Lake.

Nancy Defer is a corporal at the RCMP detachment in Iqaluit, Baffin Island.

Peter Martin resigned from the Crown Prosecutors' Office. He is now the president of the Alberta Law Society.

Marvin Farris is in the Witness Protection Program.

In a plea bargain, Al Shearing and Tim Bettger were sentenced to two and a half years in jail for setting off the vent shaft bomb and for breaking into the mine on the graffiti mission.

Bettger received an additional six months for the satellite dish bombing.

Charges were dropped against Shearing for the satellite dish blast and against Bettger for the bomb discovered in Rob Wells' trailer and for the Flying Truck Scenario.

Justice John Vertes of the Northwest Territories Supreme Court said Shearing and Bettger were cunning and deliberate in their actions, but Vertes added that he did not believe they pose any future risk.

At the hearing, Bettger said he and Shearing were provoked by Royal Oak, the Pinkertons and the RCMP. "But I make no excuses for what I did," Bettger said. "The media attention has been most damaging to my family. It was difficult, especially during the investigation. I apologize to my family for the trouble I put them through."

Helen Warren is still working and living in Yellowknife. She is receiving excellent support from her friends. Roger Warren is serving his sentence at Stoney Mountain federal penitentiary near Winnipeg, Manitoba. His appeal will likely proceed sometime in 1996. There is still some question about whether Glen Orris will handle the appeal. Legal Aid in the Northwest Territories may decide that a local lawyer should handle the matter. In the motion for appeal, Orris claimed Justice de Weerdt erred on at least twelve points of law relating to the trial and six points in his instructions to the jury.

To help Warren fight his sentence, three CASAW men—Blaine Lisoway, Bill Schram and Harold David—started the Warren Fund, which quickly raised $25,000. In a letter to fellow trade unionists, the three men claimed Warren was falsely convicted and could well die in jail if nothing is done:

"Roger was viciously prosecuted by the Crown, who received a great deal of help from the media, the judge, the police and inevitably, the jury. The entire case could be characterized as 'prosecution by character assassination,' said one observer. The trial was remarkable for the incredible number of errors and omissions that were perpetrated on Roger.

"Since the trial it has come to light that the jury was likely infiltrated and pushed into a guilty verdict. We are still waiting for details on this.

"Roger and his family and friends thank all of you who have supported the legal defense and sent letters of solidarity. In this bleak situation, as the orgy of self-congratulation continues in the media, these communications are one of the few things that give us hope and sanity.

"This was a sick, gross and unjust verdict. Roger is innocent. Please help."

David Staples (left) and Greg Owens.

About the Authors

David Staples and Greg Owens won the 1992 National Newspaper Award in Spot News Reporting for their coverage of the Yellowknife murders. The judges praised their work as a "vivid, detailed and compassionate account of a northern tragedy obtained and written beautifully under tough circumstances."

After graduating from the Carleton School of Journalism in 1984, David Staples became a feature writer and city reporter at the *Edmonton Journal*. In 1990, he received a National Newspaper Award Citation of Merit. Staples is now the *Edmonton Journal*'s City Columnist.

Greg Owens is a graduate of Algonquin College's journalism program. He has spent the past nine years as an *Edmonton Journal* crime writer and during that time has covered every major disaster in Alberta.